Yankees in Paradise

Yankees in Paradise

The Pacific Basin Frontier

Arrell Morgan Gibson
Completed with the assistance of
John S. Whitehead

Histories of the American Frontier
Ray Allen Billington, General Editor

Howard R. Lamar, Coeditor
Martin Ridge, Coeditor
David J. Weber, Coeditor

University of New Mexico Press
Albuquerque

Library of Congress Cataloging-in-Publication Data

Gibson, Arrell Morgan.
    Yankees in paradise: the Pacific Basin frontier / Arrell Morgan Gibson;
completed with the assistance of John S. Whitehead.—1st ed.
        p.   cm.—(Histories of the American frontier)
    Includes bibliographical references and index.
    ISBN 0-8263-1442-2 (cl)—ISBN 0-8263-1443-0 (pa).
    1. Pacific Area—Relations—United States. 2. United States—Relations—
Pacific Area. 3. Oceania—Relations—United States. 4. United States—Relations—Oceania. 5. Pacific Area—History. 6. Oceania—History.
I. Whitehead, John S. II. Title. III. Series.
DU30.G53   1993
303.48′27309—dc20   93-12957
                                                                                      CIP

To my youngest grandchildren—
Derek Morgan Ash
Camille Alexandra Ash
Grace Sara Gibson
Morgan Emily Gibson

CONTENTS

Maps

Illustrations

Foreword

The late Arrell Gibson was a true pioneer in the literature of western history. He constantly strove to expand the definition of the West by devoting attention to the environment, native peoples, and ethnicity long before it became an accepted practice by other authors. He also sought to expand the boundaries of the West beyond the limits of the contiguous, continental western states. His textbook *The West in the Life of the Nation*, published in 1976, included Alaska and Hawai'i for the first time within the limits and concept of the American West. That simple inclusion was not enough for Luke Gibson (as his family and friends called him). He saw far beyond Alaska and Hawai'i and worked to understand the entire Pacific Basin frontier as a region undergoing the same expansionary process that took place in continental North America. The Pacific Basin Frontier was the focus of a special edition of the *Journal of the West* that he edited in April 1976. The posthumous manuscript he left upon his death in 1987 was his penultimate effort to understand American expansion into that region.

In his final book many aspects of the continental West gain a new meaning in the Pacific Basin context. The eastern shore of the Pacific—California to Puget Sound—is no longer the far boundary of continental expansion but part of a Pacific expansionary process ranging from California to China, from Alaska to Antarctica. The California Gold Rush is not merely the precursor of succeeding rushes in Nevada, British Columbia, and the Klondike, but also the precursor of the Australian Gold Rush. The missionary journey of Marcus and Narcissa Whitman to Oregon in 1835 becomes the successor to the missionary journey of Hiram and Sybil Bingham to Hawai'i in 1820, both couples being sponsored by the American Board of Commissioners for Foreign Missions. Once again Arrell Gibson has expanded our concept of the American West.

As will be obvious throughout *Yankees in Paradise: The Pacific Basin Frontier,* Gibson was always keenly interested in distinctive frontier stages as well as the process or means by which a region became Americanized. In this study, for example, he sees maritime and whaling frontiers that were followed by mining, missionary, agrarian, and military frontiers. However, Gibson was also fascinated by what he called a "hedonist frontier" in the Pacific Basin—that is, the discovery by American writers of the attractive qualities of both the peoples and their island worlds in the Pacific. That discovery, ranging from Herman Melville to James Michener, created an image of a tropical paradise in the American mind.

Gibson stood in the threshold between two waves of western writing. While he included so much that was original for his era, he died just at the moment that the "new" western history gained force. In the six years since his death a literal deluge of writing has appeared on many of those aspects of western history that Luke helped develop—particularly the environment and native peoples.

When the series editors asked John Whitehead of the University of Alaska to edit the manuscript for publication, they faced a difficult question. Should Gibson's manuscript be rewritten to reflect the literature since his death or should it be left as he wrote it in the period 1976–87? After much thought, it was decided that the manuscript should be left as Gibson's work. While standard copyediting has been done on the first fifteen chapters, neither the text nor the footnotes have been changed. Because the footnotes to Chapter 15 were incomplete, the editors decided to remove them altogether as no notes to Gibson's precise sources could be found. Maps and illustrations were added since these were clearly intended to accompany the book.

Readers should understand that Gibson's work is one completed in 1987. The last two chapters of the book were unwritten, though Gibson left extensive notes on what he intended to do.

John Whitehead completed those chapters and included in them material published since 1987. There is one editing change, however, that was made consistent throughout the manuscript. Since 1987 there has been an orthographic change in publications using Hawaiian words. Thus Hawaii becomes Hawai'i; Oahu becomes O'ahu. This is now a part of the standard style sheet of Pacific publishers and of the University of New Mexico Press. This orthographic change reflects a heightened awareness of native Hawaiian culture over the last half-decade. Luke Gibson would have adopted it himself.

When Ray Allen Billington, distinguished historian of the American West, founded the Histories of the American Frontier series in 1957, he envisaged the completion of a set of volumes devoted to the regional and topical histories of the frontier experience. In the early years of the series, such fine volumes as W. J. Eccles's *The Canadian Frontier* and Rodman Paul's *The Mining Frontiers of the Far West* amply fulfilled Billington's hopes for scholarly but highly readable narrative syntheses about the frontier experience.

Since 1973, however, Billington expanded the definition of his series to embrace new topics and new approaches that would reflect interest in social, ethnic, and environmental history. Recent volumes such as David J. Weber's *The Mexican Frontier, 1821–1846: The American Southwest under Mexico*, Sandra L. Myres's *Westering Women and the Frontier Experience*, Elliott West's *Growing Up with the Country: Childhood on the Far Western Frontier*, and Donald J. Pisani's *To Reclaim a Divided West: Water, Law, and Public Policy, 1848–1902* have been fine examples of these new approaches.

However, in the most recent volume in the series, Terry G. Jordan's *North American Cattle-Ranching Frontiers: Origins, Diffusion, and Differentiation* (1993), and now in Arrell Gibson's *Yankees in Paradise* the series has begun to reflect an international and comparative approach, but always in the context of the American frontier experience.

The editors of the series wish to express their special thanks to John S. Whitehead for his careful editing and completion of the Gibson text. Both John Whitehead and the editors hope that their efforts honor in full Arrell Gibson's final distinguished contribution to the history of American frontiers.

Howard R. Lamar
Yale University

Martin Ridge
The Huntington Library

David J. Weber
Southern Methodist University

Yankees in Paradise

CHAPTER ONE

America's Last Frontier
The Pacific Basin

Frontier, the dominating word in the American nationhood epic, has compound meanings—a geographic situation, an expansion entity, a state of mind—and is inextricably associated with the so-called westward movement. To Americans frontier as a geographic area has meant a territory situated beyond the line of settlement, awaiting the altering application of pioneer initiative and ingenuity to exploit its resources.

The metaphysical impact of frontier on national culture and the American mind has been immense and sustained. The daring participated directly in the frontier experience; the timid and those with personal limitation or responsibility shared vicariously in the drama and adventure of the movement. Frontier as a state of mind has traditionally conjured up for Americans a place of opportunity, the promise of a fresh start, or the prospect of one's fortune, and has perhaps provided the means to escape the constraints of an increasingly complex eastern life-style.

Frontier in the national-legacy sense is also process—the means by which a region became Americanized. The saga of American nationhood recounts the heroic, near awesome thrust of its people across the continent in less than a century. Restless, expansive frontiersmen occupied successive portions of the forward territory, each called the frontier, and Americanized it; that is, they transformed it from wilderness to a functioning component in the nation's economic, social, and political life.

In 1893 Frederick Jackson Turner introduced the "frontier thesis." It deflected attention from the European origins of Anglo-American civilization to America's interior, the West. The Turner thesis, a multifaceted analytical scheme for interpreting the Amer-

3

ican heritage, cast the nation's history in a western context and designated frontier as a process for Americanizing a region. Much of Turner's thesis is instructive and useful for explaining the phenomenon of American continental integration, particularly his cyclical-frontiers concept for tracing the occupation and absorption of successive segments of western territory.

In the progression of American dominion from the Appalachians to the Pacific shore, Turner identified what he called the fur frontier, mining frontier, stock-raising frontier, and agrarian frontier as vanguard groups or expansion entities that Americanized the West. Turner's list should be amended to include in the process of continental occupation the military frontier, the overland-trader frontier, the missionary frontier, and the civilized Indian frontier. This last group, made up of Native Americans from the eastern United States, particularly southern tribesmen, was forcibly colonized in the West by the federal government. These Indian pioneers—Choctaws, Cherokees, Seminoles, Creeks, and Chickasaws—planted constitutional government, slaveholding, public schools, and other items of civilization in Indian Territory, just as their Anglo-American counterparts did in Arkansas, Missouri, and Texas. Each successive group created an identifiable frontier or community in which its members established and progressively enlarged the American presence.

Fur hunters moved well ahead of the line of agricultural settlement, taking animal pelts in which the wilderness abounded or trading with Indian hunters for them. Their enterprise was intensive, highly destructive, and restlessly mobile. As the harvest of pelts faded in a given hunting zone, the fur hunters moved on to virgin territory. Their migration opened new fur frontiers and marked paths in the wilderness that became highways for later-arriving groups.

Often pressing on the heels of the fur hunters were stockmen, who grazed their herds of cattle and horses on public lands. They, too, progressed ahead of the line of agricultural settlement. Their open-range enterprise required no investment of labor and capital in enclosures, and the natural mobility of their livestock made marketing simple. In the Far West, Anglo-Americans blended their stock-raising culture with the already well-established Spanish-American ranching industry.

The mining frontier coursed across the western wilderness, as prospectors restlessly searched for crude but essential minerals such as lead and the quick fortunes promised by gold and silver. Their discoveries led to stampedes or rushes, demographic bursts that created remote urban pockets and accelerated the new territory's progress toward integration into the national life.

The military frontier occupied another vanguard position in the American advance. Soldiers generally established an American presence ahead of the line of permanent agricultural settlement. They constructed forts at strategic locations in the forests, on the prairies and plains, and in the mountains. These tiny military enclaves often served as the first urban nuclei in the wilds of the West. Soldiers hewed roads across the frontier, established the first communication systems, fought Indians, and drove them from land coveted by settlers. They explored and mapped remote portions of western America and provided the first law and order for the region.

Another vanguard of American expansion was the missionary frontier. Missionaries worked among the Indian tribes, attempting to shape aboriginal communities to be receptive to the American advance. They also relocated tribes ahead of the Anglo-American settlement line, ostensibly to protect Indians from corrupting influences of the American settlements. Nonetheless they served the national purpose, removing Indians without the use of military force.

The mercantile frontier was yet another prime carrier of Anglo-American culture across the West. From depots at Westport and Fort Smith—the heads of navigation on the Missouri and Arkansas rivers, respectively, for most of the year—the wilderness merchants moved their goods in heavy-wheeled freight wagons drawn by great gangs of oxen and mules across the Southwest to the goods-starved Spanish-American settlements on the Rio Grande and into Chihuahua. The economic interests the overland traders built up in foreign territory were zealously protected by their national government. Whenever they were threatened by the host government, it became a matter of diplomatic concern and sometimes cause for military intervention by their government, corroborating the ancient maxim that "the flag follows the commerce."

The agrarian frontier has as its classic protagonists the hardy pioneers, usually the first Anglo-American agriculturalists. They eventually sold the clearings they opened in the forests and along alluvial bottoms to latecomers—the permanent farmers, planters, and town builders—and moved on to develop new speculative holdings.

The spectacle of the young American nation breaching the Appalachian barrier and surging in successive frontiers like a human flood tide with incredible velocity and irrepressible force westward across the continent has often been seen as one of the grandest epics of human history. However, interpreters of the American experience have allowed themselves to become so mesmerized by this rapid continental integration that they have overlooked the historical drama unfolding beyond the western land rim. There in the contiguous oceanic hemisphere—the Pacific Basin—was a frontier province in which the pageant of American expansion continued.

Again, so preoccupied were they with continental development, that they concluded, prematurely, that the frontier, the great energizing force in national development, had come to an end, that Americanization processes had terminated about 1890. This certainly is correct insofar as most of the contiguous national territory is concerned; it is not correct with respect to the Pacific Basin, because these processes continued to function there well into the twentieth century.

The purpose of this study is to illuminate the Pacific Basin as an environment that attracted Anglo-American attention, interest, and exploitation from the earliest days of national existence. It will demonstrate that the familiar expansion processes and agents at work on the continent were also present in this maritime realm; thus Americans reaching the Pacific shore, rather than marking the end of westward expansion, pressed into the adjacent water hemisphere, representing a continuum of this nation-building process.

The Pacific Basin's varied and opulent plant, animal, and marine life, as well as its mineral resources, were compelling lures for American frontiersmen, much as were the continental riches; thus those familiar expansion entities that transformed the North American heartland between Canada and Mexico also ventured into this vast oceanic territory. Some took on different names and altered functions due to differing resource quests, but the order of their progression into the Pacific Basin was similar to the pattern found on the continent.

The first of the Americanizing entities to appear in the Pacific Basin was the familiar fur frontier. Its highly exploitive character was matched shortly by the whaling industry, another nineteenth-century Pacific bonanza enterprise. In less than a century, whalers nearly annihilated the giant pelagic mammals for their oil and baleen, reminding one of their contemporary destroyers on the continent, the buffalo hunters whose mindless destruction of the western bison for their hides nearly exterminated these huge hairy beasts.

Other familiar mainland-fashioned frontiers continuing in the Pacific Basin were the mining frontier, missionary frontier, and military frontier. The military frontier, dominated by the navy, served much the same function in this water hemisphere as the army on the continent. The agrarian frontier appeared, although pioneer farmers, its primary protagonists, were absent. This Anglo-American expansion entity functioned from the beginning on a plantation-scale of operation, with large holdings as in the southern United States. In the Pacific Basin the mercantile frontier was represented by maritime vendors, the sea traders, carrying manufactured trade goods to island and mainland-rim markets aboard ships, rather than in freight wagons or by trains of pack mules.

A highly itinerant group of exploiters, which might be called gatherers, ranged over the Pacific Basin in small ships collecting its easily accessible bounty—*bêche de mer*, pearls, oyster and tortoise shell, bird nests, and woods (mahogany and sandalwood from the islands and construction lumber from the Northwest Coast)—all favored products in Canton, China—the Pacific's prime marketplace during the first half of the nineteenth century. Later Anglo-American gatherers added guano (bird, seal, and bat dung, rich in nitrogen) from the Pacific Islands and the South American coast and cattle hides from California and Hawaiian ranches to their car-

7

goes, the guano dispatched to world markets, the cattle hides largely consigned to New England boot and harness manufacturers.

The Pacific Basin's resource spectrum includes an environment perhaps closest to what Anglo-Americans conceive paradise to be—languid climate; mountains, forests, and beaches of striking beauty; easy access to exotic natural foods; a permissive native life-style; and amorous women. This was a lure for many Puritan-repressed Americans. Their covert wish during the nineteenth century to escape to paradise, fantasized by many, consummated by some, became a theme pursued by many writers. This hedonistic literary frontier has continued in the twentieth century to the present day.

This study will show how these frontiers or expansion entities, primarily committed to private interests, served civic purposes as well. In the unfolding order of imperial process, they fused with nationalizing currents to transform the Pacific into "Mar Columbiana." This combination of processes also bound the heartland of North America to the national territory. Nationalizing currents were an essential element fusing with the frontiers to form a symbiotic, mutually reciprocal relationship. The national government served as patron, the frontiersmen as agents who ventured into the wilderness, established American presence, and, having critical needs, petitioned their national government for succor and support. The government responded with supportive laws, favored treatment of their economic activities, subsidies, use of federal military forces to reduce the menace of native peoples and protect frontiersmen against the arbitrary actions of competing imperial nations. By diplomacy, purchase, and conquest, it obtained territory coveted by its vanguard citizens. These are nationalizing currents; their ultimate application occurred in two cases where, at the urging of its pioneers, the nation admitted the territory into the American Union as a coequal state.

Other nations made an imperial beginning in the Pacific Basin. The period from 1500 to 1700 was that of "Mar Iberica"; during the eighteenth century it was "Mar Britannica"; Imperial Russia held sway over the North Pacific for two centuries; France periodically attempted to establish some colonial strength there; and

Holland and Portugal were imperial pioneers on the western margins of the Pacific Basin. These nations exploited its resources and people, faltered, and eventually for the most part retired. As imperial competition in the Pacific Basin waned, the Anglo-American presence and dominion expanded, in some cases taking the form of territorial integration into the national life, in others maintaining a sustained and strong missionary, ideological-tutelage, military, and economic interest and presence.

Anglo-American imperial success in the Pacific Basin during the nineteenth century and for a considerable portion of the twentieth century is attributable largely to geographic propinquity; management of the territory based on equality between the national government and its frontiersmen; and an evolutionary expansion technique based on the aforesaid economic, military, and missionary frontiers fused with nationalizing currents, which functioned most efficiently, albeit inadvertently.

European nations claiming dominion over territory in the Pacific Basin were handicapped by the great distances that separated home governments from these lands. Slow communications, suffocating monopolies held by a favored corporate elite, and dependence on monolithic bureaucracies severely limited their ability to manage distant possessions. The United States government, on the other hand, as the constitutional agency for managing national interests and territories in the Pacific Basin was situated adjacent to its transcontinental estate. This simple yet strategic advantage permitted far more responsive oversight.

Early in the national life, American leaders eschewed the temptation to designate the West an unorganized imperial reserve, its people and resources to be managed and exploited by a colonial bureaucracy solely for the benefit of the thirteen proprietary states. Rather they made the very productive decision that the trans-Appalachian territory was to be settled, developed, and organized into states; and each state was to be admitted to the Union on an equal footing with the original states, the national government providing guidance and direction for the state-making process. This decision was first made in 1781, at the acceptance of the Articles of Confederation, was reaffirmed by the Northwest Ordinance of 1787, and in 1791 was embodied in Article IV, Section III, of the Constitution.

Leaders decisively and successfully applied this to the continental West, and its consummation provided the pattern and precedent for equality subsequently applied to large segments of American territory in the Pacific Basin. The results of this decision are immeasurable. One effect has been to endow the American frontier settlers, be they on the continent or in the Pacific Basin, with a sense of having a private and public stake in the future of the new territory; by the exercise of personal sovereignty through the ballot, they have been able to play a directive role in that process through the representatives they elected to Congress, and by petitions they addressed to the president and other public officials. Nationalizing currents coursed through every western settlement, combining with invasive eastern culture to expurgate wilderness ways, recasting the new territories into the familiar Yankee pattern. Eventually the Pacific Basin territories of California, Oregon, Washington, Alaska, and Hawai'i shared in this legacy of equality, largely due to the interaction of socioeconomic expansion entities (frontiers) with nationalizing currents (corroborative, support actions by the national government). The partisans of each frontier were carriers of Anglo-American culture, and each established a vital American presence in the western wilderness. Their enlarging population in each primal territory, be it continental or pelagic, set off what became virtually an inevitable process. This expansion technique evolved from private and public pragmatic adjustment to the milieu and crystallized into more or less established patterns of territorial integration applied by frontiersmen and their patrons in Washington, D.C., to the wilderness from the Appalachians into the Pacific Basin. From repeated applications, these currents were refined and regularized.

At the turn of the twentieth century, the statesman John Hay supplied an eloquently perceptive forecast on the Pacific Basin's prospects in the grand national design: "The Mediterranean is the ocean of the past, the Atlantic is the ocean of the present, and the Pacific is the ocean of the future." Certainly it is an intriguingly attractive area for study. Ernest S. Dodge, one of America's most prolific writers on the Pacific, concludes that

Since World War II the Pacific Basin has emerged as one of the most important and active areas of the world for historical research. . . . No other great inhabited area of the world has so much ocean in relation to the inhabitable land. Nowhere is the population spread so thinly. Nowhere else does it have such a remarkable homogeneity over so many thousands of square miles. This homogeneity is an indication of how, for seafaring cultures, an ocean can be a highway and not a barrier. For the right people it is easier to cross the sea than to cross the mountains. [It is a] region which will become ever more important to the world we live in.[1]

As a sort of American ethos laboratory, its synthesis begins to yield useful, instructive vistas on the true character of the westward movement of the American nation and the very certain work of its expansion processes. In addition it is the setting where presumptive, ethnocentric American goals for unlike peoples and cultures have been increasingly rejected and where national innocence has been dashed by recent ideological-military defeats in Korea and Vietnam.

CHAPTER TWO

The Natural Setting

The Pacific Basin is the earth's dominating geographic region, its character complex, its essence exotic. Only superlatives properly measure its mammoth grandeur, its gargantuan majesty. Its shape depends on the observer's imaginative propensity. Some have described it as a giant horseshoe, open at its southwest quadrant, or a wrinkled triangle, its apex at the Bering Strait, flaring to the south, its base flanking the northern margins of Antarctica. And the Pacific Basin is host for the world's most anomalous natural history and richest ethnicity.[1]

Polynesians called this water hemisphere *Kai*. Spaniards, pioneer European explorers of the Pacific Basin, gave it two names. Vasco Núñez de Balboa dubbed it "Mar del Sur," and among poets and romantics it is still the South Sea. Ferdinand Magellan, the first European to circumnavigate the earth, on seeking a passage from the Atlantic, and after tortured months of treading the roaring, deadly destructive waters of the strait that bears his name, when finally debouching onto (at the time at least) a quiet, peaceful water highway, named it "Pacific."

The Pacific Basin covers over one-third of the earth, an expanse of nearly 70 million square miles, and exceeds its combined land area. Its roughly triangular form extends nearly ten thousand land miles from the Bering Strait to the Antarctic Circle, and approximately the same distance along the equator from the Western Hemisphere to near the Asian mainland. Besides being the earth's largest body of water, it is also the deepest, ranging from an average depth of fourteen thousand feet to an extreme of over thirty-five thousand feet in the western Pacific, between Guam and Mindanao.[2]

This water hemisphere is outlined by a mountainous conti-

13

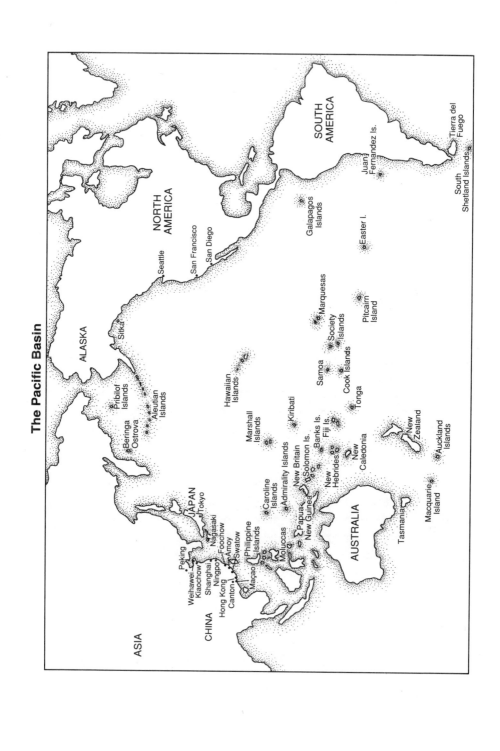

The Pacific Basin

nental rim described as the earth's great zone of "crustal instability," accommodating over four hundred active volcanoes. Protected inlets and estuaries providing harbor respite and access into the continental interior are abundant on its western margins but scarce on its eastern and northern periphery. Proceeding around the Pacific Basin counterclockwise, there is Valparaíso for Chile; Callao for Peru; Guayaquil for Ecuador; and Navidad, Acapulco, and Mazatlán for Mexico. San Diego and San Francisco are the principal natural harbors on the California coast. Business interests at Los Angeles and several other California coastal cities have altered the coastline and constructed harbor facilities.

Geographers claim that north of San Francisco Bay for nearly one thousand miles there is "hardly a cover to protect vessels" of any size. Much of the coast of northern California, Oregon, and Washington is a collage of offshore rocks, threatening shoals, and raging tides, obscured much of the time by thick fog. The mixing of turbulent tides and inland waters at the mouth of the Columbia river made it for centuries a hazardous passage for sailing vessels. Portland and Seattle have become great ports of the Pacific Northwest, followed by Victoria and Vancouver on coastal British Columbia. Geographers divide this portion of the basin shore into Pacific Mountains and Valleys and Arctic Plains and Highlands provinces; they are linked by a common cordillera—the Coast Range. It extends along the California coast, continues through Oregon and Washington, and bends into Alaska. Coast Range elevation varies from five thousand feet, with an occasional ten-thousand-foot summit in southern California, to nearly ten thousand feet in Washington and Oregon. The Coast Range is called the Cascades in Oregon and Washington, and its peaks include the spectacular Mount Ranier, over fourteen thousand feet, and Mount Hood, over eleven thousand feet. Along the interstitial western Canadian shore into Alaska, the Coast Range juts abruptly into the sea, its fjord-lining peaks often exceeding ten thousand feet. North of the Alaskan panhandle, glaciers descend to the Coast Range and extend into the ocean.

Like connective tissue, the Klamath Mountains of northern California and other intersecting highland systems fuse the Coast Range with inland ranges. Besides linking the Coastal Range and the Sierra Nevada, the Klamath Range marks the beginning of the Cascades cordillera and, like a giant highland dike, separates the Central Valley of California from the Willamette Valley of Oregon. In the southern interior is the high and rugged Sierra Nevada Range; one of its peaks, Mount Whitney, rises to nearly fifteen thousand feet. In California the Coast and Sierra Nevada ranges separate to form the Central Valley. This world-famous agricultural region, fifty miles wide and five hundred miles long, is drained by the Sacramento and San Joaquin rivers, which empty into San Francisco Bay.

Alaska shares the Arctic Plains and Highlands region with western Canada. The Coast Range, a strip often one hundred miles deep, rims the Alaskan littoral as far north as the Bering Strait; it includes Mount McKinley, North America's highest mountain at over twenty thousand feet. The Bering Strait area is a mix of mountains and glaciers, some of the glaciers exceeding in size the nation's smallest state.

The Alaskan-Aleutian coastline, extending over eighteen thousand miles and estimated to be nearly twice the combined length of the Atlantic and Pacific seaboards of the contiguous United States, marks the Pacific Basin's northern edge. Mariners have rated it the most difficult and dangerous in all the Pacific, exceeding in potential peril even Australia's Great Barrier Reef. Its "long stretches of rugged, shoal-studded coast," constant storms, heavy fog, and damaging ice in winter make approaches along much of its littoral hazardous if not impossible. The islands, peninsulas, and mainland contain few harbors, and even the river mouths' quiet anchorages are difficult to negotiate because of the height and speed of the tides. Offshore waters are a mix of crosscurrents; added to these are raging tides, "almost unpredictable in the maze of islands and passages," which combine to "make a labyrinth of eddies, cross currents, and tide rips." An added menace for deep-hulled vessels are the pinnacles of rock thrusting hundreds of feet from the ocean floor to within a few feet of the surface. Winds, fog, storms, contrary currents, and heavy tides have confused navigators for centuries. Often ships were dashed to pieces on the rocks. Hulls, ripped open by hidden reefs, sank. It was many years before navigators learned to sail these waters with any degree of success, develop craft that were seaworthy in this region, accumulate accurate maps and charts, and train pilots to navigate these treacherous waters.[3]

The Pacific Basin is conspicuous for its internal landforms. By contrast, the Atlantic Ocean is largely "clean," that is, for the most part unobstructed by archipelagoes (except for islands on its western periphery—Bermuda and the Caribbean group, and the South Atlantic Falkland and Orkney Islands—and the Azores, Canary, and Cape Verde Islands on the eastern perimeter). Islands break the monotony of the Pacific's vastness and often have yielded resources for trade, as well as fresh water, wood, provisions, and recreation for weary mariners. Even tiny coral atolls have become havens for shipwrecked seamen. And certainly its islands lend the Pacific Basin an exotic quality and increase its mystique.

The Pacific contains over twenty-five thousand islands, totaling more than a million square miles of land area. Aside from the large peripheral islands of Tasmania, New Zealand, and New Guinea, most Pacific islands are the product of volcanic and coral accumulation. Subterranean volcanoes build on platforms created by "outpourings of lava from rifts on the flat ocean floor" and eventually form a surface mass, at times of considerable extent. Hawai'i, the fiftieth American state, consists of an archipelago produced by subterranean volcanic action.[4]

Many islands and reefs situated in the vast tropical midsection of the Pacific Basin have been formed by coral accumulations. Coral is the product of a chemical interaction and fusion of colonies of fleshy marine polyps and algae. The polyps secrete lime from seawater; their skeletons and the associated algae convert to solid limestone, which forms atolls and coral islands. Some islands are created by accumulated coral forming caps upon the summits of submerged mountains that jut steeply from the ocean's floor.

Solitary islands such as Wake and Midway extrude above the ocean's surface at several points around the Pacific Basin. However, most islands form into clusters called archipelagoes and include the four so-called home islands and their small detached land associates that make up the nation of Japan. One island situated in the southeastern quadrant of the Pacific Basin—Australia—is classed by geographers as a continent, riding as it does its own tectonic plate. And sometimes they designate nearby New Zealand and New Guinea as minicontinents.

Western geographers have used several terms besides Pacific to identify regions in this vast water body. They often group all islands in the central and southern Pacific into a category called Oceania. They further divide Oceania into three classes: Melanesia, Micronesia, and Polynesia. Melanesia ("black islands") is named for the complexion of its natives, and includes islands south of the equator and north and northeast of Australia—New Guinea, the Bismark Archipelago, the Solomons, New Hebrides, the Admiralty, Loyalty, Santa Cruz, Fiji islands, and New Caledonia. Micronesia ("little islands") includes the Marianas and Carolines, Marshall and Gilbert islands, and Palau and Yap. Polynesia ("many islands") is a triangular-shaped area extending five thousand miles from north to south and four hundred miles from east to west, from Hawai'i on the north to New Zealand on the southwest, to Easter Island on the southeast. Polynesia embraces, among others, the Marquesan, Tuamotu, Society, Samoan, Tongan, and Cook islands. Tahiti, largest of the Society group, is the focus of Western man's quest for paradise. Far to the east of the Tuamotus lies Easter Island, or Rapa Nui, the outpost of Polynesia closest to the American littoral, and famous for huge and remarkable carved stone heads and other images.

American frontiersmen and their latter-day counterparts have shown sustained interest in exploiting the bounty of all productive Pacific islands, but their primary attention has been directed at the Hawaiian archipelago. Named the Sandwich Islands by their European discoverer, Captain James Cook, this cluster of over twenty islands situated twenty-five hundred miles west of San Francisco, owes its creation to volcanic activity, living organisms forming coral, the sedimentary process, and erosion. And vulcanism, the periodic lava flow from active volcanoes, adds to island size. The Hawaiian archipelago, totaling 6,500 square miles, stretches from Hawai'i on the east to Ni'ihau on the west. Its eight major islands are Hawai'i (4,021 square miles), Maui (728 square miles), O'ahu (604 square miles), Kaua'i (555 square miles), Moloka'i (260 square miles, Lāna'i (141 square miles), Ni'ihau (72 square miles), and Kaho'olawe (45 square miles). Hawaiian topography is largely rugged upland. Most of the islands support peaks from 3,000 to 5,000 feet. Snow-capped Mauna Kea on the island of Hawai'i rises to 13,684 feet. Slender valleys and narrow coastal plains make up the habitable areas of each island's landscape. The islands have been the scene of intensive agricultural exploitation in both pre- and postdiscovery times, although only about 5 percent of the land is arable.

The Pacific Basin is a vast territory; one finds both heterogeneity and homogeneity, diversity and unity, in its climate. Its ten-thousand-mile stretch from the Arctic Circle to Antarctica laps across two hemispheres, and thus its environment includes two contrasting sets of seasons; while it is winter, spring, summer, or autumn in the Northern Hemisphere, the opposite season occurs in each case in the Southern Hemisphere.[5]

Pacific Basin climate is the fascinating interaction of oceanic water, pelagic currents, varying temperatures, situation, the earth's rotation, the deflective force of contiguous bodies of land, the injection of contrasting and parallel wind belts, the collision of polar fronts (cold air masses from the Arctic and Antarctic regions moving to mingle with warm Pacific air masses), and the overpowering impact of the substratospheric jet stream. Pacific Basin climate ranges from intense and eternal winter cold in its north and south polar regions, to temperate marine conditions around its rim, to monotonous midtropical languor across its vast heartland.

Sebastián Vizcaíno, pioneer explorer in the service of Spain, called the heartland's weather a "benign climate." Its temperature uniformly ranges from 70° to a bit over 80°, with a daily range of between 9° and 16° and an annual range of up to 9°. Temperatures above 90° are rare. Oceanic influences temper the east and west littoral, giving these perimeters a mild climate with a small annual and diurnal temperature range. San Francisco has a 10° range between the coldest and warmest months.[6]

Pacific Basin climate—its meteorological elements a great body of water, currents, winds surface and aloft, the deflective force of continental rim, the generation of fronts, and its powerful jet stream—also creates weather far into the Asian and North and South American mainlands. Certainly daily, seasonal, and annual meteorological conditions for the United States are produced in the Pacific Basin and transported to the mainland by the westerlies and jet stream.

Rainfall is variable, daily, seasonally, and annually in Oceania. Fanning Island's annual rainfall has varied from 47.4 to 208.8 inches. In the calm doldrums there occurs a minimum of atmospheric expansion and rising air, which discourages rainfall; some islands in this portion of the basin, including Baker and Jarvis, receive only 20 to 30 inches of rainfall a year. Monsoon conditions on the western rim frequently soak and flood the continental interior with from 50 to 200 inches of precipitation each season.[7]

The presence of landforms also influences rainfall patterns. Some islands receive 250 to nearly 500 inches a year; others, generally on the leeward side of highlands, are virtual deserts. Typhoons, the Pacific Basin name for hurricanes, originate in the doldrums, the result of convectional heating. They produce wind velocities of from 75 to 150 miles per hour and heavy rains; this type of storm is called *baguio* in the Philippines. Other ocean-produced threats to life and property in the Pacific Basin are tsunamis, seismic tidal waves set off by earthquakes.[8]

Pacific winds and currents are vital for water circulation, climate creation, and sustaining marine life. On either side of the equator, belts of contrary winds parallel one another. Proceeding from the equator into both the Northern and Southern hemispheres, first is found the belt of equatorial calms (doldrums), two to three hundred miles wide, succeeded by the eastward-flowing trade winds, then the horse latitudes, then the opposite-moving westerlies.

The trade winds and westerlies add direction and drift to oceanic currents initiated by the earth's rotation and the eddying effect of water deflected by the Pacific Basin's continental rim. This drift is clockwise in the Northern Hemisphere, counterclockwise in the Southern Hemisphere. The upper stream, impelled by the trade winds, is identified as the Japan Current as it courses through the home islands of that archipelago. Proceeding into the north Pacific, it traces a passage south of the Aleutians and Alaska along the Northwest Coast. Its southern progression is frequently called the Black Current. The Southern Hemisphere companion current, flowing northward adjacent to the South American coast, is called the Humboldt Current.[9]

These Pacific currents are chilled and transport great amounts of enriched, mineral-laden water from the depths; this sustains prodigal quantities of plankton, which in turn support larger marine life. Thus the offshore currents in both hemispheres have become great food-harvesting grounds for early as well as contemporary peoples. The rich fish resource in Pacific waters also sustains millions of fish-eating birds—pelicans, gannets, and cormorants. Flocks often nest on islands in the doldrums, where rainfall is light. Their excrement, called guano, is washed away in areas of heavier rainfall; it accumulates on arid islands and in curing becomes a nitrate-rich fertilizer.

Other Pacific Basin features that embellish its ambience are its isolation and anomalous natural history, the one related to the other. Until the midnineteenth century, access to the Pacific Basin was difficult; its isolation was broken only at great risk for those who ventured through its eastern and western portals. In spite of three centuries of searching, Europeans found no water strait through the Western Hemisphere debouching into the Pacific. Its entryway from the west was at the southern tip of Africa, the Cape of Good Hope, often stormy and difficulty to negotiate, which opens onto the Indian Ocean, the mariners' highway eastward into the Pacific.

The most perilous entry into the Pacific Basin was via Tierra del Fuego, at the southern tip of South America. There mariners found "a treacherous labyrinth of narrow, cliff-bound channels churned by waves over forty feet high," yielding two openings, the Strait of Magellan and the Strait of Le Maire, via Cape Horn. Steam navigation after 1850 reduced the peril somewhat, because it permitted an indifference to contrary winds. And late nineteenth- and early twentieth-century excavation technology made possible first construction of the Suez Canal (which provided an alternative to the Cape of Good Hope passage) and, soon after 1900, completion of the Panama Canal (which allowed a detour of the dreaded Tierra del Fuego crossing).

Its vastness and the isolated situation of its landforms permitted the Pacific Basin to retain certain flora and fauna types long extinguished by evolutionary processes in other portions of the earth. Charles Darwin found what he regarded as confirming evidence for certain of his theories in the Galápagos and other Pacific archipelagoes, where distance and isolation had produced a sort of genetic explosion radiating from a few initial species of plants and animals.

Thus Pacific Basin flora and fauna represent intriguing responses to environmental determinants, particularly climate, situation, and degree of isolation (which has limited plant and animal genetic interaction). Between its polar antipodes, one finds a prodigious range of plants: succulent and chaparral growth on its arid southeastern rim; mixed conifers and increasingly lush and varied vegetative cover along the Northwest Coast, including one of the world's botanical wonders, the giant redwood forests; then vast shore-touching taiga stands of fir, cedar, spruce, and pine. The succeeding arctic coastal plain of tundra vegetation—mosses, lichens, sedges, hardy grasses, and low-growing shrubs—dominates the upper Alaskan, Aleutian, and Siberian coasts, blending into mixed forest growth in the more temperate south Asian rim.

Islands astride the trade winds receiving abundant rains throughout the year produce luxuriant flowering plants, shrubs, ferns, lichens, and dense tropical forests of sandalwood, mahogany, papaya, breadfruit, and macadamia, as well as the romantic banyan. Most beaches are lined with palms.

The Pacific Basin's rich and varied bounty has made it one of the most intensively exploited portions of the earth. Its exotic plants have yielded cherished spices and condiments. *'Iliahi,* the aromatic sandalwood, and mahogany are collected for conversion to perfume, ceremonial pieces, and furniture. Hardwoods are converted to timbers and planking for shipbuilding. Natives process the inner bark of the mulberry tree for tapa cloth, which they use for clothing and household coverings. Coconut palms produce coconuts for food and copra for industrial use; Pacific islanders fashion weapons from the bark and core, sails from leaves, and shelter from coconut wood. Soft woods from the Pacific Northwest are converted into huge seagoing canoes, houses, and tall totems.

Pacific Basin fauna is more dominant in the ocean than on land. Pacific waters sustain a rich pelagic life—mammals (whales, sea otters, sea lions, sea elephants, and seals) and fish, along with a wide range of birds. The sea otter, of the musteline family (related to land otters and minks), is distributed over a marine territory stretching from Kamchatka to Baja California. Its habitat is off-shore kelp beds, where it feeds on shellfish and seaweed. The sea otter, with a rich brown to black pelt averaging five feet long and prized for warmth and beauty, was the most valued of all wild fur-bearing creatures. Sea-otter hunters were among the pioneer exploiters in the Pacific Basin. Away from the basin's rim, land animals are relatively scarce; conspicuous exceptions are the exotic koalas and kangaroos of Australia and the surviving primordial lizard species and giant tortoises on the Galápagos.

The Pacific Basin environment is inordinately fragile. Arctic permafrost, which extends to the Alaskan and Siberian littorals, is frozen earth that is rock-hard, impervious, and in places a mile deep; it creates a precariously balanced ecological system that experience demonstrates can be thrown into chaos by careless treatment. Log buildings constructed by north-country pioneers less than half a century ago on the permafrost have sunk into the earth to a point where the windows are at ground level; the heat of the buildings melted the permafrost surface crust. Conserva-tionists urge "leave permafrost in peace . . . preserve its frozen state" by constructing buildings and pipelines on pilings, creating an air space so that heat does not reach the ground.[10]

Pacific Basin lands and waters yield many useful minerals and fossil fuels. Australian mines supply gold, copper, tin, lead, zinc, nickel, chrome, cobalt, manganese, antimony, coal, and iron ore. New Caledonia is a prime producer of copper, gold, lead, zinc, nickel, chrome, cobalt, manganese, antimony, coal, and iron ore. And the Philippine Islands are a source of gold, copper, iron ore, silver, chrome, manganese, and coal. The Pacific Basin's eastern continental rim, from Alaska to Baja California, is rich in several minerals and fuels including gold, silver, coal, and oil. The basin's offshore continental shelf is a source of petroleum, and prospectors search the ocean deep for mineral nodules.

Certainly one must include in the Pacific Basin's resource in-ventory the strategic situs of some of its islands. Richard A. Pierce says the Hawaiian archipelago "formed the hub" of a rich commercial traffic in the Pacific Basin between the Northwest Coast, Alaska, Canton, and the South Pacific. Guam and the Philippines provide their imperial tenants with a most favorable trade and military presence near the Asian mainland. Pacific waters make up a highway to the mythical riches of Cathay, Thomas Hart Benton's "Road to India." Its islands have been the focus of geographical fantasies—Isla Rica de Oro and Isla Rica de Plata. And its mystique generated the myth of paradise; the Pacific Basin's solitude and natural beauty have been a continuing source of creativity for writers and painters, and provide the basis for one of its leading twentieth-century industries—tourism. One of the principal resources of this local income-generating enterprise is the Pacific Basin's pluralistic and fascinating ethnicity.[11]

CHAPTER THREE

The Human Setting

The rimland and islands of the Pacific Basin have been the habitat of a mélange of peoples; no other environment on earth has accommodated such human diversity. This would have been the compelling conclusion of any pioneer explorer who might have undertaken a demographic reconnaissance of the Pacific Basin. Had he begun his survey on its southeastern extremity, at Tierra del Fuego, he would have found people whose ancestors in Pleistocene times had migrated from Asia to the Western Hemisphere. Then on the South American littoral he would have encountered the traditionally fierce Araucanians, who pressed the coastal tributary peoples of the Andes-dwelling Incas. Next were the affluent El Dorado communes on the upper edge of South America, succeeded by the Mayas and their tribute bearers of Central America; and aboriginal nations subject to the princely Aztecs occupied Mexico's Pacific shore. The observer would find that from coastal California into southern Alaska resided the North American aboriginal community, ranging from the culturally disparate and populous California tribes through the wealth-seeking, potlatch-practicing Northwest Coast nations to Alaska's unconquered Tlingits. Eskimos and Aleuts, dominant in the North Pacific, were succeeded by Siberian kinsmen on the Asian shore. They blended into the East Asian peoples of China, Korea, and the Japanese archipelago. Proceeding through Indochina, the Malay peninsula, and offshore islands, the explorer would have found a mix of Asian and Malay types. In Oceania the theme of diversity continues: blacks in Melanesia, Polynesian and Meso-Polynesian peoples in the central and southern Pacific and Micronesia, and contrasting peoples on the southwestern anchor of the Pacific Basin—aborigines in continental Australia, blacks in New Guinea, and Maori-Polynesians in New Zealand.

The pioneer observer would find that just as Pacific Basin people differed greatly physically, there was also considerable variance in their cultures, ranging from the most advanced and complex to the most primitive and relatively simple. On the eve of the sixteenth-century imperial intrusion into the Pacific Basin, there existed on its western rim in the kingdom of China a high civilization exceedingly rich, powerful, and supporting a scintillating culture that radiated its influence into the adjacent rimland areas of Japan, Korea, Indochina, the Malay Peninsula, and even to portions of the Philippines, Indonesia, and other more distant lands. Buddhist and Moslem cultures carried by missionaries and traders from Indian Ocean stations had penetrated the Pacific Basin's western rim and several adjacent islands, to increase the cultural complexity of that area. So-called native life-styles predominated in the remainder of the Pacific Basin, ranging from that of the Australian aborigines through more elaborate forms in New Guinea and Melanesia to increasingly complex systems in Polynesia and along the American littoral.

American frontiersmen, particularly those of the exploitive frontier, had contact with all of these peoples and cultures, but they were latecomers; by the time of the American advent, most Pacific Basin natives and their lands on the continental rim and islands had been absorbed into the Portuguese, Spanish, Dutch, Russian, and British (and to a limited extent, French) empires. American political dominion eventually was established over the peoples and their lands on the Pacific Basin littoral north of Mexico to the Aleutians (excluding the Candian Pacific face), the Hawaiian archipelago, and scattered islands in the western Pacific. A sketch of these peoples and their ways of life—Indians, Eskimos, Aleuts, and Polynesians—representing only a segment of a much larger geographical and demographic context but in itself replete in diversity, will suggest the magnitude of ethnic and cultural differences throughout the Pacific Basin.

Proceeding counterclockwise along the Pacific Basin's eastern littoral, over territory eventually appropriated by the United States, we first encounter the California tribes. This portion of the basin supported one of the most favorable of environments for aboriginal peoples. Its climate at lower elevations on the western slope of the Sierra Nevada and on the seacoast was mild throughout the year, making the problem of providing clothing and shelter rather simple. The area was rich in natural food resources: abundant wild plants; seashore foods, particularly shellfish; salmon in the rivers of northern California; deer in the upland country; and vast oak forests from which came the acorn, the staple food for most California tribes.[1]

The rich natural environment that made life easy supported a vast population, perhaps as many as three hundred thousand. It is puzzling that with abundant food resources and mild climate, no complex cultures developed there. This anomaly has been the subject of continuing speculation, some authorities believing that with mild climate, rich food resources, and an easy life, there was no challenge for the California Indians, no environmental goad to drive them to higher achievement. The rugged relief of this portion of the Pacific Basin littoral probably contributed to this "cultural inertia"; it also produced extreme cultural and political particularism.

Natives residing on the eastern rim of the Pacific Basin showed great diversity in physical type, language, and culture. One commentator has asserted that more different languages were spoken there than in any other single region of the world. Scores of dialects from dozens of parent languages were spoken by hundreds of different groups, which anthropologists call tribelets rather than tribes. Each tribelet consisted of from fifty to three hundred persons. The principal language families were Athapascan, Algonquian, Hokan, Uto-Aztecan, Shoshone, Penutian, and Yukian.

The material culture of the California Indians was simple. The tribelets practiced no agriculture, their people subsisting upon seashore gathering of marine life and shellfish, collecting upland plants, some hunting of deer and other animals on the Sierra slopes, catching salmon in season in the rivers of northern California, and taking trout and other freshwater fish in the Sierra lakes and rivers. Virtually all California natives depended upon the acorn as their staple food. Women and children gathered and shelled the acorns, crushed the nuts with stone pestles, and ground the coarse meal into fine flour. They spread the flour in large flat baskets and drenched the contents with water to leach out the bitter tannic acid. Generally the acorn flour was then eaten as mush, cooked in baskets filled with water and heated with hot stones, or as flat bread, baked on hot stones.

Native American dwellings in California ranged from temporary crude shelters in the south to the more elaborate plank houses in the north. These people had no pottery but excelled in making baskets, which they used for wearing apparel, hats, food containers, storage receptacles, and cooking vessels. Local crafts included skillful cedar wood carving. An extension of their material culture among most of the triblets was a strong wealth consciousness. They used many items to represent prosperity and personal wealth, including elaborately decorated skin and feather garments and strings of dentalium shells, which they used as money.

Social models of the California tribelet were simple. Several families made up a village, and from one to three villages made up a triblet. Each tribelet was an autonomous community with an established territory, a common estate that all members had the privilege of using. Tribelet government likewise was simple, managed by a community council of elders and a headman with limited authority. His primary duties were presiding over public matters and resolving internal disputes. Most tribelets lived at peace and had no military tradition of consequence.

In their religion the California Indians paid tribute to several deities, observed a number of religious festivals including a world renewal pageant and female puberty rites, and supported a clergy of shamans who presided over the religious establishment and served as healers. In their medical arts the California shamans applied magic, pantomimed conversion into animals, composed sand paintings, and used datura (jimsonweed). The individual's search for a spirit helper was an important religious duty, and datura was used to aid the worshipper in achieving this sublime state. The Hoopas, probably the most ostentatious of the California peoples, used religious festivals as times for displaying their wealth in the form of fine dress.

Neighbors of the California natives, the Northwest Coast tribes, occupied a territory extending along the Pacific Coast from northern California into Alaska. Its climate, tempered by the Japan

Current, produced rather stable, year-round pleasant temperatures. Abundant rainfall sustained dense forests of redwood, cedar, pine, and fir, all softwoods easily worked with primitive tools. The many different types of plants, shrubs, bushes, and trees yielded berries, nuts, fruits, and edible roots. The region's many streams debouching into the Pacific teemed with fish, particularly salmon. And food was readily harvested from the sea—halibut, cod, shellfish, and mammals including the sea otter and whale. The Northwest Coast competed with California as the richest natural-food-resource region on the Pacific Basin littoral; it supported a large native population with many tribes, representing three language stocks: the Na-Dene, Penutian, and Mosan.[2]

As among the California natives, making a living was easy for the Northwest Coast tribes. But while the California Indians languished in the mild climate where food was easily obtained, the Northwest Coast tribes developed a spectacular culture. Anthropologists regard their "highly distinctive," "unique" life-style as a separate development, an "isolate," because it evolved with little or no influence from Mexico or Asia.

The economic life of the Northwest Coast tribes was exceedingly complex, particularly in view of the fact that they were nonagricultural. They supported themselves by fishing, gathering, hunting, and trading; yet they were the wealthiest Indians of North America. The basis of their wealth was salmon. What corn was to the eastern tribes, rice to the Great Lakes tribes, buffalo to the Great Plains tribes, the acorn to the California tribes, salmon was to the Northwest Coast tribes. On a river stand in a few months an Indian family could easily catch, dry, and store enough fish for a year. Also from the ocean they took cod, halibut, and shellfish, and they hunted sea otter, seal, and whale from canoes. One of the most esteemed trade items in the Northwest Coast native economy was the eulachon, or candlefish. Indians netted candlefish and rendered them for oil used as food dressing or dried them for lighting their homes. Food was so easily obtained that a perpetual surplus was available. Thus they had time to devote to more elaborate economic as well as noneconomic aspects of life, as well as the inclination to do so.

Most of their travel was on rivers or along the seacoast from island to island in large dugout canoes made of red cedar logs, some of them seventy feet long, with elaborately carved bows. A single canoe could accommodate fifty oarsmen and three tons of cargo. There was much trading from island to island and at annual fairs at mainland settlements. Traders transported cargoes of foodstuffs, blankets, and wooden utensils from one market to another in the huge watercraft.

Tribal handicrafts centered on woodworking, largely with red cedar. Logs of this softwood were floated to the village beach, cured out, then split into planks with hard wooden wedges driven by large stone hammers. Workmen used the planks for many purposes, including construction of large, multifamily dwellings. Bowls, trenchers, tools, tall totems, and other decorative pieces were carved from this softwood. Woodworking tools included a stone adz and a beaver-tooth chisel. By steaming, bending, and sewing wooden pieces, craftsmen of some tribes fashioned wooden boxes of all sizes and shapes for many uses, including storing food and cooking by the water-and-hot-stone method. Most groups, however, made baskets for cooking. Women wove exquisite blankets on looms. Their fiber materials were mountain-goat hair, milkweed strands, and dog hair. Many tribes had large numbers of slaves who performed menial and routine tasks, freeing artisans for work on their special crafts.

Northwest Coast tribal social models were largely matrilineal and matrilocal. Several tribes practiced the moiety system for dividing the community to regulate marriage choice and select leaders. However there was very little sense of nationhood among these people; most associated through kinship, language, and culture rather than political commitment. Each community was largely autonomous. Local chiefs or leaders came from the highest-ranking clan or house in each moiety. Family association and identity were very important because of wealth distribution and social ranking through the family. The Northwest Coast tribes observed a social stratification nearly as rigid as the Natchez caste system. Below the chiefly families in each community were the nobles, followed by commoners, and below them were the slaves. Some social mobility was permitted, in that low commoners with skills for carving or some other valued talent could receive from the community chief a title and right to a crest with totem pole signifying noble status. Conflict among tribes of this region was frequent; the principal motives for aggression were vengeance satisfaction and taking captives who became slaves.

The religion of the Northwest Coast tribes required both individual and group attention. Each boy, as a part of his rites of passage to adult status, was expected to undergo fasting and purification rituals to make himself worthy of the vision from which he would receive his spirit helper or guardian. The public aspects of this religion centered on the clergy—the shamans—and their success in managing the supernatural world. Shamans were also healers. A major part of their religious activity was focused on placating animal spirits. Their way of life depended largely on fish and animals, and they believed that these creatures, existing for human benefit, had spirits that were released at death and would return repeatedly to serve people if not offended. Because material success was so important to the Northwest Coast tribes, and since this material success depended in large measure on the annual fish and animal harvest, placating the animal spirits received special attention.

Abundant natural resources made it relatively easy to accumulate a surplus of material goods, including blankets, baskets, skins, shells, curiously shaped copper plates, obsidian blades, albino deer skins, and strings of dentalium shells (Pacific Coast currency). The wealth of these tribes was a source of continuing public display. Besides individual prosperity displayed in lavish personal adornment, it provided the basis for one of the hallmarks of the Northwest Coast tribes and their most conspicuous custom—the potlatch. This public sharing of one's goods was generally preceded by a feast sponsored by the host. Modest potlatches could be held, even by a commoner, to commemorate the birth of a son, a marriage, or some other event of great moment in a family. The biggest potlatches were those held by rich, high-ranking nobles or the local chief himself, given to show his generosity and to shame his rivals by distributing in a single day huge quantities of goods—bales of blankets, great numbers of valued copper plates, and other items of value. Then the only way for others to gain greater status was to throw a bigger potlatch and give away even more goods.

The Northwest Coast Indian community included the Haidas and Tlingits who lived along the western Canadian and Alaskan littoral and offshore islands. Their lifeways included the advanced handicrafts, intense wealth commitment, and potlatches of their southern cultural kin.

In the far northern Pacific, along coastal Alaska and the Aleutian Island, were the Aleuts and Eskimos, similar physically, with characteristics of their Asian relatives, and speaking related languages. The Aleuts' homeland is the island chain extending southwest from the Alaskan mainland. Eskimos occupy the area around the Arctic Circle between sixty and seventy-two degrees north latitude. Most of these northern peoples live in a frigid desert, so cold that the atmosphere can hold only enough moisture to produce about four inches of precipitation annually. They must cope with the problem of brief summers and very long winters, a short time of barely warm light and a long period of cold darkness. This environment is one of the most discouraging in the world; yet through resourcefulness and great energy and inventiveness these peoples adapted and were able to cope and to work out a successful and satisfying life-style.[3]

Aleuts and Eskimos were primarily hunters and only minimally gatherers of plants and nonanimal foods, in part because the tundra, which made up most of their environment, with its permafrost and short growing season, sustains only limited plant life. They were primarily meat eaters, consuming great quantities of meat per person per day. During the winter an extended family averaging twelve persons consumed an estimated one hundred pounds of meat each day; a like amount was required for the household's pack of dogs. Game animals also provided skins and hides for clothing, footwear, shelter covers, hunting line, and other uses. Caribou hides and wolf and fox as well as grizzly, brown, and polar bear pelts were particularly valued for making clothing.

Most Eskimos lived in fixed villages near a beach or estuary. Their dwellings, framed of driftwood, bone, and antler pieces, were covered with sod and skins. They used temporary shelters during the summer, when away from their village.

These Arctic-dwelling natives spent most of their time collecting food, the period of most intensive activity occurring during the short summer. With the arrival of summer, as the frozen ground thawed a bit on the surface, vegetation grew, birds and animals moved north, and salmon began their search for river spawning grounds. Warmer temperatures caused breaks in the ocean's ice cover, forming expanses of open water where sea mammals could be found. Eskimo families moved from their villages; some traveled to the interior to hunt caribou and fish for salmon; others took to the sea in large skin-covered boats called *umiak*s to hunt whale and walrus. Every member of every family was engaged during the summer in gathering food for winter. Eskimo values stressed the duty of work and scorned indolence. With the approach of winter and shorter days, Eskimos returned to their villages with the food, skins, and hides they had collected. They stored their large boats on the beach and made any necessary repairs to their houses. When ice formed over the tundra, the men used dog-drawn sleds to carry them to hunting grounds near the villages, where they sought seals. Techniques for preserving food included caching meat packed in skin bags in the permafrost, and drying, smoking, or fermenting it and packing it in skin bags for winter use. Like bison-dependent Great Plains tribesmen who used virtually all parts of the buffalo in supply their food, clothing, shelter, and household needs, the hunters of the North Pacific used most parts of the whale. They ate the flesh and skin, the intestines they cleaned and converted to containers, sinew they fashioned into rope, baleen and bones were applied to several needs including framing for shelters, and blubber they ate or rendered into oil for cooking and heating.

Eskimo crafts included weaving useful and attractive baskets from sedges and shrub stems and carving figures from bone, soapstone, and sea-mammal ivory. Some Eskimo groups made crude pottery. Artisans carved colorful masks and other paraphernalia required in religious ceremonies.

In addition to the dogsled, these peoples used several types of skin-covered boats. The largest was the umiak, requiring a crew of eight to twelve oarsmen and used for hunting the whale and for moving goods in trade. The kayak was a widely used one- or two-passenger craft. The Aleuts, rated by some authorities the greatest hunters of the Pacific Basin, roamed the ocean waters in the *bidarka,* a highly maneuverable, swift, skin-covered boat with a cockpit for the oarsman in the stern and a forward cockpit for the harpooner.

Eskimo and Aleut social models were simple, consisting of the basic nuclear families that clustered into extended families in winter. During the summer food hunt, nuclear families—husbands, wives, and children—scattered into the interior. In prehistoric times little political organization was apparent or required. Eskimos and Aleuts associated in small subsistence units, and individual autonomy predominated. The only cooperative activity of consequence occurred during whale hunts, when the owner of an umiak formed an expedition.

During the winter men collected in the "men's house," a large community building. It served as a social, ceremonial, and recreational center. There they wrestled, performed feats of strength, or entertained with singing and dancing. Shamans held religious observances in this building to placate supernatural forces and to perform healing.

Eskimo polytheistic religion centered on a sea goddess and the raven, their creator, who served as the great manager of the universe. Annual festivals included dancing and singing, the participants wearing masks representing gods. Most religious attention was directed to placating the animal spirits, as was the case with the Northwest Coast tribes. Eskimo and Aleut hunters followed particular formulas and observed elaborate taboos in order not to offend these spirits, including opening the slain creature's skull to permit its spirit to move freely into the world, which they believed pleased the creature. They hoped that reports of their care and good treatment would reach other animals and that they would cooperate and permit themselves to be easily taken. Eskimo shamans were specialists in managing the supernatural, presenting the formulas for hunting success; and they were the community healers, using sorcery and magic in treating illness.

American political dominion was also extended (by annexation, conquest, and trustee assignment) to the island-dwelling peoples of the Pacific Basin, including the inhabitants of the Hawaiian archipelago, a portion of the Samoan group, Guam, the Micronesian cluster, and certain lesser islands. While these peoples differ in lifeways, Polynesian influences dominate, and a vignette of the Hawaiians will demonstrate the character of island life in this water hemisphere. It makes a striking contrast with the lives of Native Americans living on the eastern rim of the Pacific Basin.[4]

Hawaiians, or Sandwich Islanders, were largely concentrated in a land area of about sixty-five hundred square miles, on Kaua'i, O'ahu, Moloka'i, Maui, Lāna'i, and Hawai'i. Situated approximately twenty degrees north of the equator and twenty-one hundred miles west of San Francisco, in the trade-wind zone, the islands bask in a mild climate.

Native Hawaiians are bronze-skinned Polynesians. Their original home was perhaps southeast Asia, and it is speculated that they migrated from Indochina into the great Polynesian Triangle of the South Pacific, first settling in the Society Islands and eventually migrating to their present island home. By the time of their contact with Captain James Cook, in 1778, they were living an isolated oceanic existence.

These islanders fashioned an easy life based on horticulture. Native farmers intensively cultivated the narrow coastal strips of arable land on their volcanic islands through the construction of terraces and irrigation works, and produced abundant crops of bananas, breadfruit, yams, a starchy root called taro, and sugarcane. They also raised hogs and fowl, fished, and engaged in interisland trade.

Their island milieu encouraged the development of navigational skills. Polynesian sailors coursed over waters adjacent to their island homeland in large, twin-hulled outrigger sailing craft fitted with oars. Some native vessels, called "flying proas," were at least 75 feet long, double-hulled, and with crab-claw sails. Several Hawaiian double-hulled sailing craft were 108 feet in length, comparable to Captain Cook's *Endeavor*, which was 106 feet long. Guided by their mastery of celestial navigation and knowledge of prevailing winds and currents, Hawaiians traversed a circuit of perhaps a thousand miles.

Island artisans had no metals but creatively used local woods, fibers, shell, bone, and stone for utensils, buildings, art, and crafts. Religious images were shaped from stone, bone, and wood. Because of the mild climate, dwellings and most public buildings were simple wood-framed structures with thatched roofs and woven-mat walls. Stone was used to construct temples. A widely used cloth called tapa (or *kapa* in other parts of Polynesia) was made from the inner bark of the paper mulberry tree, but the most decorative garments were exquisite cloaks and headgear fashioned from bird feathers.

Polynesians generally followed the matrilineal mode of descent and had a hierarchical social organization. By the time of European contact, island clans had rigidified into castes, and tribal organization on each island approached a form of primitive monarchy, with tribal chiefs assuming the role of hereditary kings. In the precontact period, natives practiced plural marriage—both polygyny (more than one wife) and polyandry (more than one husband)—and among the *ali'i* (ruling caste), brother-sister marriage.

The basic unit of island society was the family, and several families in a clustered residence area made up a village. Each village was governed by male elders who served as lawgivers, enforcers, teachers of the young, and guardians of tradition. Polynesians had no system of writing, so instruction and tradition were transmitted orally by village elders to the young.

Government was an extension of the social caste system. Island chiefs became hereditary rulers, basing their right to rule on the claim of descent from the gods for themselves and their heirs. Island kings exercised total power over their subjects. As earthly agents of the gods, even the land belonged to them; the use of it was a privilege bestowed upon the people by the benevolent monarch.

Below the royal family in each island's social structure were the priests, or *kahuna*s, who presided over the religious system. The priests' principal functions were to placate island deities and foretell the future through divination. Placating the gods often included human sacrifice. The religious system was polytheistic and animistic; the principal deities were Kane, Ku, Lono, and Kanaloa. Kane was the greatest force in the Hawaiian cosmos, for he was the deity of light, in a sense the sun god. The Hawaiian myth of creation included the concept of Sky as father and Earth as mother. The religious system included the use of idols representing deities, which the Hawaiians placed in stone temples (*marae*) and households and used as fetishes to ward off evil spirits. Women were excluded from the primary rituals but had considerable status in civic affairs.

A class below the priests were the civil agents of the island kings, courtiers, and leaders of the warrior army. Next in the Hawaiian social hierarchy were commoners—farmers, fishermen, artisans, and traders.

Hawai'i, other islands of the Pacific, and the basin's waters and rimland, rich in material and human bounty, became the arena for a four-century-long empire-building contest soon after 1500 on the part of several European and Asian nations. The later years of this colony-forming epoch were marked by the advent of the United States; this vast water hemisphere became the last American frontier. By 1900 the United States had become the basin's dominant power, its supremacy due in large measure to the earnest application by its frontiersmen of those familiar expansion processes by which, in scarcely half a century, this aggressive young nation had absorbed much of the North American heartland. But as had been the case in its swift continental sweep, the United States had to contend with colonial nations already imbedded in the Pacific Basin—Spain, France, Russia, Holland, Portugal, and Great Britain—and eventually with Japan.

CHAPTER FOUR

Pioneer Explorers

European mariners probing the Pacific Ocean for the first time in the early sixteenth century faced uncommon challenges in their attempts to navigate this seemingly boundless water hemisphere. Certainly conditions of weather, tides, currents, and landfalls were quite unlike those they encountered coasting the familiar shores of northern Europe, the Mediterranean, and Africa. Spanish, Portuguese, Dutch, and English ship captains were entering waters for which they had no maps or charts. However, this lack could somewhat be offset by guidance from Polynesians and other native peoples. From the advantage of long residence, they had learned Pacific secrets, how best to cope with its hazards, and they had fashioned simple but functional marine technology including the outrigger sailing craft for their fishing, trading, and migration needs; and of great value to the newcomers, they had gained the crucial navigational experience and skills essential for sailing Pacific waters.[1]

The wind-powered sailing craft that carried the first European explorers into the Pacific were of the caravel and galleon classes: the caravel, about 100 tons, its length from bow to stern less than 100 feet, beam (width) less than 25 feet, and manned by a crew of forty; the galleon, up to 500 tons, 100 to 150 feet long, beam 32 feet, and with a crew of 150. Each type ordinarily was fitted with three masts. The flute, a Dutch-built anomalous galleon with a bulbous hull and flat bottom to avoid shallows off the Low Country coast, was called the "work horse" of Holland's trade fleet, and was well-adapted for sailing the treacherous Pacific shoals. Other ship types occasionally used for early Pacific exploration included the "snow" class, also called brig or brigantine, a two-masted, square-rigged craft 80 feet long with a 20-foot beam. Most European shipwrights preferred live oak or white oak for vessel frame, hull, and planking, and when it was available they selected straight white pine timbers for masts.

European ship captains cruising the Pacific were far removed—five to ten thousand miles and six months to a year—from home port and yards, docks, and repair facilities, and their wooden ships required frequent maintenance attention. Barnacles, crustaceans permanently attached to the ship's lower hull, caused drag, slowing the craft and fouling the rudder, making steering difficult. The teredo, a marine worm, burrowed into the hull and timbers much as termites infest wood on land, weakening the frame and creating hull leaks. Planking frequently pulled apart, opening leaks in the hold. And vessels often had their hulls gutted by hidden, barely submerged rocks and coral clusters. To clean and repair a ship's hull, the crew anchored close in to a sandy beach at high tide; at low tide the ship heeled over to expose one side of the hull. Crewmen scraped planks and resealed joints with tallow and oakum, strands of rope saturated with pitch. Rips in the hull they patched with burned lime made into a stiff mortar and mixed with tallow and oakum. At high tide the ship righted and the crew repeated the process on the opposite side, rendering the vessel seaworthy again.

Pioneer explorers ranged over these chartless waters aided by the astrolabe, a device that ascertained latitude by the position of the sun or stars, the compass that determined direction, the quadrant, an instrument that measured altitude, and native mariner guides. Crewmen determined their ship's speed by floating a chip of wood affixed to a line in the vessel's wake; the amount of line that had run out in the time measured by a minute glass yielded the speed in nautical miles or knots, so-called because of the knots worked into the measuring line. The chronometer, which determined longitude, was not available to mariners until the mid-eighteenth century, so that pioneer Pacific navigators had more or less to guess their longitudinal position.

Crews manning ships engaged in Pacific reconnaissance faced perennial danger from shipwreck due to contrary winds and violent storms, by pumps failing to drain leaky hulls so that seawater swamped the vessel, or by the hull being rammed and crushed by an angered whale, casting sailors into shark-infested waters, the survivors marooned on a lonely, treeless coral atoll or isolated island. And crewmen faced daily hazards aboard ship from insanitary conditions, rank bilge odors, holds infested with disease-bearing rats and vermin, exposure while sleeping on the deck between watches to be close to the boatswain's summons for manning the sails to alter course in face of storms, and monotonous rations of salt pork and beef, hardtack, and stale water.

This perfunctory shipboard "chow" abetted the most dreaded hazard of all—*mal de loanda,* or scurvy (scorbutus), announced by stiffness and swelling of limbs, jaundice, bleeding gums and loss of teeth, general listlessness and apathy, depression, and near certain merciful death. Often during the almost routinely extended Pacific cruises, up to three-fourths of a ship's crew could expect to come down with scurvy, and at least half the sufferers would perish. During the 1740s the three-ship Anson expedition, which circumnavigated the globe, lost seven hundred seamen out of a complement of over a thousand from scurvy. Relief for scorbutic sufferers came in 1747, when the Scottish naval surgeon James Lind found that treating afflicted sailors with lemons and oranges produced dramatic cures. Gradually ships' commissaries came to stock fresh fruits and vegetables, along with lime, orange, lemon, and grapefruit juices. Other effective remedies included sauerkraut, a dehydrated soup (forerunner of the bouillon cube), spruce beer, and wine and brandy rations with water.[2]

Navigators from Spain and Portugal, and to a limited extent from England and Holland, pioneered in exploring the Pacific. Initially they concentrated their pelagic probings on its central and southern margins, although Spanish and English mariners eventually entered the northern and eastern segments. However, their discoveries and colonial establishments in all areas of this ocean are germane to the Pacific Basin frontier study, because the information provides foundation knowledge for explaining the eventual economic, political, and diplomatic-military expansion by Anglo-Americans beyond the confines of their continental territory.

A papal bull issued in 1493 and the Treaty of Tordesillas, 1494, divided the world outside Europe between Portugal and Spain.

This assignment ceded virtually all of the earth covered by the Pacific Ocean to Spain; for centuries Spaniards considered it their national "Mar del Sur," and they regarded intruding aliens as trespassers.

Both Spain and Portugal moved promptly to acquaint themselves with their new territories. Of particular interest to both nations was finding a water route to tap the rich trade of Southeast Asia and adjacent islands to feed their expanding post-Renaissance economies. Overland commerce in oriental spices, gems, porcelains, textiles, and tea was monopolized by Arab traders and Venetian merchants.

Portuguese explorers sailed past the Cape of Good Hope into the Indian Ocean and were the first to arrive on the Pacific's western rim. They established bases on the islands near the China coast, and by purchase from Spain added to their western Pacific empire the nearby Moluccas, or Spice Islands, five tiny volcanic extrusions on the equator, source of the world's supply of cloves and several other prime seasonings. Thereafter the Portuguese were content to play the role of suppliers of mace, pepper, cloves, nutmeg, ginger, and cinnamon to the insatiable European market.

Spaniards, denied use of the Cape of Good Hope–Indian Ocean route to the rich oriental trade depots by the Portuguese monopoly, began a search for alternative access. Their peregrinations made them the principal explorers of the Pacific, eventually leading them into what later became the Anglo-American portion of this huge region.

The first Spaniard to behold the Pacific was Vasco Núñez de Balboa, while exploring the Isthmus of Panama in 1513. He named it the South Sea. Ferdinand Magellan commanded the first Spanish expedition, five ships and 265 crewmen, into the Pacific. This Portuguese navigator in the service of Spain set a course down the South Atlantic, discovering the strait bearing his name, which opens on the South Sea. Magellan explored several archipelagoes, including the Ladrones (Marianas), paying particular heed to Guam, which became a leading support base for Spanish maritime traffic in the western Pacific. In early 1521 Magellan discovered the Philippine archipelago. There hostile natives ambushed him and several crewmen. Eighteen survivors and one ship proceeded into the

Magellan's Voyage of 1519–22

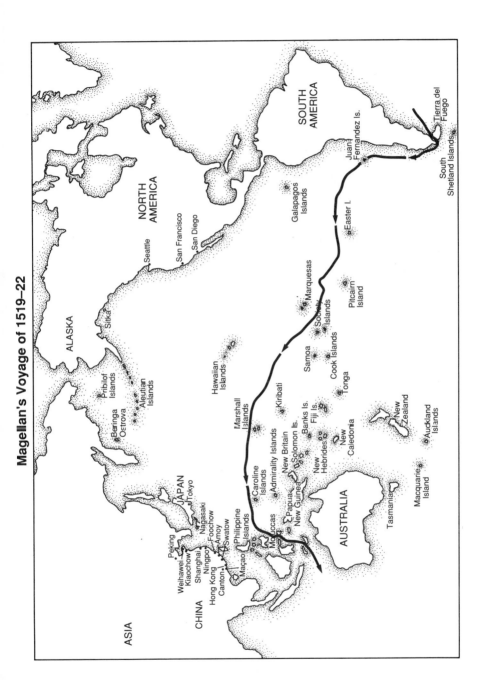

ASIA

CHINA

Peking
Weihawei
Kiaochow
Shanghai
Ningpo
Hong Kong
Canton
Amoy
Foochow
Swatow
Nagasaki
JAPAN
Tokyo

Macao
Philippine
Islands

Moluccas

New Guinea
Papua
New Britain
Admirality Islands
Solomon Is.
Banks Is.
New Hebrides
Fiji Is.
New Caledonia
Caroline Islands

AUSTRALIA

Tasmania

Macquarie Island

New Zealand
Auckland Islands

Tonga
Cook Islands
Samoa
Society Islands
Kiribati
Marshall Islands
Hawaiian Islands

Pitcairn Island
Marquesas

Easter I.

ALASKA

Pribilof Islands
Beringa Ostrova
Aleutian Islands

Sitka

Seattle
San Francisco
San Diego

NORTH AMERICA

Galapagos Islands

SOUTH AMERICA

Juan Fernandez Is.

South Shetland Islands

Tierra del Fuego

Indian Ocean, cleared Africa, and continued north in the Atlantic to Spain, becoming the first Europeans to circumnavigate the earth.

Thereafter most Iberian exploration of the Pacific took place from Spain's colonies in North and South America. The west coast ports of Navidad and Acapulco in Mexico, Callao in Peru, and Valparaíso in Chile were the principal embarkation points. Workmen in American shipyards and docks constructed the crafts and refitted and maintained them for probing Pacific waters.

Thus supported, colonial navigators and crews began the systematic reconnaissance of their South Sea, searching for a water passage through the North and South American continents, for the so-called lost southern continent that ancient geographers had named "Terra Australis Incognita," and for resource-rich islands to enhance the empire's commerce.

American-based Spanish explorers discovered the Marquesas, Santa Cruz, New Hebrides, the Philippines, and several other island groups. The Philippines, strategically situated adjacent to the Asian mainland, exceeded all other Spanish island discoveries as a trade entrepôt. Therefore in 1565 Miguel Lopez de Legazpi began the colonization of Cebu in the Philippine archipelago. A baffling problem for Spanish ship captains had been the return to the home ports of Navidad and Acapulco. The track to the Philippines was easy along the path of the trade winds to Guam and thence to Cebu, but contrary winds and currents made return by the same route next to impossible. The solution was provided by Legazpi's navigator, Andrés de Urdaneta. In 1565 he found that by setting a course from Cebu into the North Pacific and then turning east, the prevailing westerlies carried his ship to the upper latitudes of North America, where offshore currents and winds made the passage to Mexican home ports relatively easy. Urdaneta's discovery made further colonization of the Philippines attractive. In 1570 Legazpi sent troops north to Luzon. A year later he established his headquarters there on a wide and spacious harbor, which he named Manila.

Thus Manila became the great Spanish marketplace in western Pacific commerce, receiving camphor, beeswax for candles, nutmeg, cloves, cinnamon, mace, and pepper from Borneo, the Moluccas, Siam, and Java; cotton cloth and ivory from India; and silk, porcelain, carved exotic woods, and tea from China. Japanese products also occasionally appeared in the Manila warehouses. Eventually much of the Philippine commerce fell under the control of Chinese merchants residing in Manila. The Mexican *peso* that paid for these goods "established a monetary standard for the east coast of Asia" that endured for centuries. By 1600 Spain ranked as the wealthiest nation in the world with the grandest empire, and much of this nation's power and affluence was derived from the Pacific.[3]

Shipbuilding, a thriving industry in American ports, where workmen constructed exploration vessels for South Sea expeditions, was also established in the Philippines. Spanish trade officials designed a special carrier craft called the Manila galleon, from 350 to 500 tons, with a deep draft to accommodate expanded cargo holds. Chinese and Malay workmen laboring in the yards at Cavite on Manila Bay used hardwoods from the islands to construct these strong, slow-moving crafts, called "castles in the sea."[4]

Each year two Manila galleons laden with cargoes of gold, silver, tobacco, sugar, cotton, cowhides, grain, and dried meat sailed from Acapulco ahead of the trade winds on the four-to-six-month voyage to Manila. There ship captains made the exchange for oriental products and prepared for the return to Mexican ports, another four to six months at sea, propelled by the more northern westerlies.[5]

Spanish navigators from Acapulco and Navidad also began to explore unknown segments of their ocean. Their missions varied. Some searched for fabled islands of wealth or supported overland expeditions moving up the coast into California and other lands of the northern frontier of New Spain. Others searched for a water passage through the continent (the mythical Strait of Anián) after 1565, explored the coast for sites for mainland stations to break the long trans-Pacific passage of the Manila galleons and protect them against English freebooters, and investigated reports of English colonies intruding on Spain's territories on the northern Pacific coast.

An early oceanic reconnaissance occurred in 1538–1539, when Francisco de Ulloa led three vessels north from the Mexican Pacific ports. One of his ships reached the head of the Gulf of California, proving that the ribbon of land forming the gulf was a peninsula and not an island, as had been speculated. He also reconnoitered the outer coast of the peninsula. To support Francisco Vásquez de Coronado's expedition to the northern frontier of New Spain in 1540, Viceroy Antonio de Mendoza ordered Hernando de Alarcón to lead a two-ship supply group. Sailing from Acapulco, Alarcón reached the head of the Gulf of California and proceeded up the Colorado River for eighty-five leagues. Two years later, Juan Rodríguez Cabrillo sailed from Navidad. He found San Diego Bay and the Santa Barbara Channel, where he died. His pilot, Bartolomé Ferrelo, sailed north in 1543 and explored the Oregon coast. Then in 1567 Alvaro de Mendaña sailed from Callao in Peru into the south Pacific and found the Solomon Islands. He eventually reached the westerly wind belt and, using that and the Japanese Current, explored along the California coast before returning to home port.

Several naval expeditions from Acapulco searched the northern California coast for Sir Francis Drake and other English raiders who were active in the eastern Pacific after 1570. And in 1594 Sebastián Rodríguez Ceremeño sailed from Acapulco to survey the California coast for a port to succor the Manila galleons. First he sailed to Manila and returned with the galleon, exploring Trinidad Head, sixty-five miles south of the California-Oregon boundary and other points along the coast. Close by Drake's Bay, he charted the coastline at a place he named Bahía de San Francisco. Near there storms drove the galleon onto shoals, where breakers battered it to pieces. Additional surveys of the California coast for a suitable harbor and colony site included those made by Sebastián Vizcaíno. In 1596 he explored the east coast of Baja California with a three-ship squadron. Spanish officials in New Spain were planting small support settlements on the peninsula preparatory to occupying Alta California. Vizcaíno resumed his reconnaissance of coastal California in 1602, charting the coast from Cape Lucas to Cape Mendocino. One of his vessels reached a point on the coast at forty-three degrees north. The crew discovered Monterey Bay, and they recommended it as a colony site and galleon station. Then in 1611 Vizcaíno turned to broader Pacific explorations, searching for fantasy-rich islands, his quest extending to the Philippines and Japan; along the way he discovered several small islands of little resource or commercial value.

Increasingly during the pioneer period of Pacific Basin exploration, and certainly after 1550, competing nations in Europe— England, France, and Holland—began to challenge the Portuguese-Spanish monopoly of the colonial world. The French were the first to confront the Portuguese and Spaniards. During 1529 Jean and Raoul Parmentier navigated their trading vessel into the western Pacific in search of stations to enable France to enter the lucrative spice trade. They reached Sumatra and negotiated for a cargo of local products. Thereafter French political and commercial groups became so preoccupied with continental affairs that representatives from this nation did not return to the Pacific until after 1700.

The Dutch also rank among the pioneer Pacific explorers, and accounts of their discoveries and colonial establishments in the western Pacific provide vistas of understanding for twentieth-century Pacific events. By 1581 navigators and traders from Holland began to ignore the Portuguese-Spanish monopoly claim. Holland's chief interest was in the rich trade of Java and adjacent islands. The Dutch also established a trading colony in Japan, at Deshima. Abel Tasman and other sea captains ranged over the western Pacific in search of additional trade territories, discovering New Zealand, the Fiji Islands, New Guinea, and Australia, which they named New Holland.

Businessmen in Amsterdam formed the East India Company to manage the Dutch commercial empire in the western Pacific. Company rules banned entry into the Pacific via the Cape of Good Hope around Africa and the Strait of Magellan around South America, the only known accesses at the time, without authorization. Another group of Dutch businessmen chartered a rival company and prepared to defy the East India Company monopoly. In 1615 they sent a two-ship expedition commanded by William Schouten to the Pacific. Schouten sailed into the south Atlantic, probing the tip of South America for an alternative entry into the South Sea. He patiently tested the turbulent waters south of the Strait of Magellan and finally found a passage leading into the Pacific, which he named Strait of Le Maire, after the company's founder, and Cape Horn, from his birthplace, Hoorn, in Holland.

Trading and plantation interest in their western Pacific island empire rather completely engaged the Dutch during the seventeenth and eighteenth centuries. Thus except for occasional discoveries of islands incidental to their thriving local commercial activities and buccaneer raids on Spanish shipping, Dutch interest in this water hemisphere focused on its western margins.

Englishmen, after Spaniards and Portuguese, were the most tenacious pioneers in the Pacific Basin, and they were the fiercest and most threatening of the intruders to Iberian hegemony there. This was particularly true in the eastern Pacific along the California coast, although late in the period of pioneer exploration they also became entrenched in the western Pacific. John Oxenham led the way. In 1575 he directed an expedition that first raided Spanish settlements in the Caribbean and then crossed the Isthmus of Panama to prey on Pacific-coast towns. Spaniards eventually captured the intruding Britons and executed them.

Next came the intrepid Elizabethan Sir Francis Drake. He had a twofold mission to perform in the eastern Pacific: to raid New Spain's treasure-rich Pacific-coast towns, and to determine the feasibility of a plan conceived by Sir Humphrey Gilbert to found an English colony on the Pacific coast at what Gilbert speculated would be the Strait of Anián, which he believed would connect with the St. Lawrence River on the eastern margins of the North American continent. Drake entered the Pacific by way of the South American access, his men plundered several Pacific-coast towns, he explored the California coast, including Drake's Bay, and named the area New Albion. But he found no water passage. Then Drake navigated his *Golden Hind,* laden with Spanish bullion, across the Pacific and on to home port, the first Englishman to circumnagivate the earth.

In 1586 Thomas Cavendish followed Drake's path into the eastern Pacific to raid Spanish shipping. In California coastal waters he captured, plundered, and burned a Manila galleon. A fourth English freebooter, Richard Hawkins, led a raiding expedition into the Pacific in 1593, but Spanish naval patrols had become increasingly vigilant; a squadron from Acapulco captured Hawkins and his crew and committed them to prison. When released, Hawkins wrote a book about the eastern Pacific, among the first of a long list of works describing this exotic region.[6]

English explorers were also active in the western Pacific during the era of pioneer reconnaissance. Their discoveries provided the foundations for future trading stations and colonies there, which blossomed into a rich and powerful nineteenth-century British Pacific empire. In 1591 James Lancaster opened trade with several islands off the Asian mainland. Additional expeditions by Lancaster between 1601 and 1603 founded English trading stations in the Moluccas. And by 1610 David and Henry Middleton had expanded English island and mainland posts to include an economic beachhead in Japan.

By 1600 Europeans were acquainted with the eastern and western margins of the Iberian South Sea. Yet its central and northern portions remained unexplored, and even the southern section still required considerable mapping and charting refinements. After 1600 much of this was attended to. European nations claiming dominion there consolidated their hold on colonial establishments. They enlarged their Pacific territories through additional exploration and settlement. To their mercantilist-imperialist quest they increasingly added scientific observation and reporting, which substantially increased the body of information about the Pacific Basin. And the period after 1600 was also a time of entry of additional outside nations into the race for oceanic empires.

CHAPTER FIVE

In the Wake of the Pioneers

So vast is the Pacific Basin that it required an additional two centuries of exploration after 1600 before navigators from the intruding nations achieved a comfortable acquaintance with its character. Increasingly those European nations excluded by the papal division of the Pacific Basin ignored Portuguese-Spanish claims to hegemony over the vast region. And just as their minions contended over North and South America, Africa, India, and adjacent islands for imperial position, they also probed the Pacific. Their early attention had been largely concentrated on its eastern and western margins, using the intervening water as a highway.

After 1600, however, several changes occurred. Portuguese representatives, content to exploit their colonial holdings on the basin's western margins, did little additional reconnaissance work. The Dutch for the most part followed the same course, except for occasional limited exploration to enhance their well-established empire in the western Pacific. The French, only slightly interested in the Pacific Basin in the pioneer period of exploration, after 1600 substantially increased their activities there, which became an enduring colonial interest.

A new colonial proprietor, Imperial Russia, entered the northern rim of the Pacific Basin in this period. However, Britons did most of the exploring there and established foundations for a rich nineteenth-century empire. Spaniards, the Pacific Basin pioneers who from the papal donation claimed most of it as national territory, continued their exploration and empire extension, largely for defensive purposes against European competitors.

During this two-century period after 1600 improved marine technology was applied to Pacific Basin exploration. Enlarged knowledge of its geography led to better maps and charts. Significantly, Spaniards guarded their navigation information. English, Dutch, and French freebooters often purloined charts, logs, maps, and other valued maritime information with gold and silver treasure from captured Spanish ships. In this time the chronometer emerged, a godsend for determining longitudinal position. Shipbuilders constructed larger, stronger, more seaworthy sailing craft. They increased hold capacities up to two hundred tons and applied copper and lead sheathing to the lower hull sections to guard against toredo infestation and barnacle encrustation, and to reduce hull slashing by submerged rocks and coral pinnacles. The British navigator James Cook demonstrated the utility of the lowly collier, a slow-moving but brute-strong sailing vessel designed to haul coal, for use in Pacific exploration.

Interest quickened in the Pacific Basin's environment. Thus increasingly expedition rosters included scientists and cartographers, who examined its meteorology, astronomy, and flora and fauna; and artists, vital in a prephotography age for preparing sketches and paintings of marine scenes and landscapes. These latter-day maritime expeditions to the Pacific also included hydrographers, who studied current and wind patterns, measured the depths of bays and future harbors, and charted reefs, other navigational hazards, and straits. As national leaders came to appreciate the Pacific Basin's strategic value, they directed their marine representatives to seek out prospects for resources that might strengthen home economies, a water passage through the western hemisphere to replace the long and dangerous passage around South America or Africa, the elusive southern continent of "Terra Australis Incognita," and military sites.

Also in this two-century period there was an improvement in crew welfare, as experience demonstrated the essentials for long sailing stints in Pacific waters. Larger holds provided greater cargo space for stowing reserve provisions and water. The cooper (barrel maker) became an indispensable member of each ship's crew. His wooden barrels, fitted with airtight covers, maintained the quality of flour, rice, beans, bread, water, and salted meat over long voyages. The aforementioned use of antiscorbutic foods checked scurvy outbreaks. And crewmen used deck space to pen hogs, goats, sheep, even an occasional cow, and crates of chickens for fresh eggs, milk, and meat.

Toward the close of this intensive two-century race for position in the Pacific Basin, two significant developments occurred. One was the near outbreak of war between Great Britain and Spain over the issue of control of the Pacific Basin's eastern margins. And more important for this part of the world's future, the entry of the youthful United States, further complicating the increasingly tangled, intensely competitive international situation there.

As indicated, for the two-century period between 1600 and 1800, the Dutch, like the Portuguese, were largely content to concentrate on developing their rich colonial holdings in the western Pacific. A notable exception was Jacob Roggeveen, who retired from colonial service after making a fortune in Dutch East India Company operations and devoted himself to searching for the so-called lost southern continent, the discovery of which had to that time been denied explorers. In 1722 the Dutch East India Company provided Roggeveen with three ships for his quest. From Holland Roggeveen entered the Pacific via the Strait of Le Maire and sailed to sixty degrees south, where large ice floes forced him to abandon the search. Returning to warmer latitudes, Roggeveen discovered Easter Island, describing in his journal its tattooed native people and their huge stone statues. Roggeveen also came upon several undiscovered islands in the Tuamotu and Samoan archipelagoes.

After supporting a century of raiding Pacific Spanish shipping by their privateers, French officials began in 1700 to sustain serious searches for colonial stations in that water hemisphere which, in geographical scope, exceeded their North American empire-building activities. Thus were formed foundations for a Pacific Basin empire that has endured into the twentieth century.

The many French exploratory ventures there in the eighteenth century generally crossed in southern waters, turning north at the Asian mainland to approach North America over the Spanish galleon return route. An exception to this exploration pattern occurred in 1700, when Captain Jacques Gouin de Beauchesne led a two-ship expedition to explore the Pacific Basin's southeastern quadrant for trade and scientific information. He negotiated the dreaded Strait of Magellan and sailed north along the South American littoral, visiting several Spanish coastal cities before turning west 575 miles to the Galápagos, islands administered by officials at the Spanish colony of Peru. Other French Pacific Basin reconnaissances in this period included Pierre Frondat's exploration of the territory between the Japanese islands and the California coast, and Forgeais de Laugerie's examination of a course between Formosa and Valparaíso.

These expeditions escalated Gallic interest in the Pacific Basin and led to formation of the French East India Company, the agency to direct founding a commercial empire there. One of the first company-sponsored expeditions was assiged to Lozier Bouvet. In 1739 he sailed south of the Cape of Good Hope and explored several ice-bound islands situated north of Antarctica before turning north into the Indian Ocean and thence to the Pacific. The two most important expeditions in the eighteenth century to confirm French colonial rights in the Pacific Basin were led by Chevalier Louis Antonine de Bougainville and Jean-François Galaup de la Pérouse.

Bougainville, a court favorite, received two important maritime assignments, both reflections of enlarging French interest in the Pacific Basin. The fascination with the region was increased by the prospects for profit which, it was hoped, would rehabilitate the lagging French economy and near-destitute royal treasury following the disastrous Seven Years' War and crippling Treaty of Paris of 1763. Pacific Basin advocates in France claimed opportunities for profit there equaled "all that has been produced by America. . . . What opportunities for trade in furs, silks, spices, medicines, dyes, gold and jewels."[1]

In 1764 the French court commissioned Bougainville to check British entry into the Pacific via the Tierra del Fuego passages by taking possession of the guardian Falkland Islands and settling French colonists and a military garrison there. Claiming territorial rights from prior explorations, officials of both Spanish and British governments protested this French beachhead in the far South Atlantic, the Spanish adding to their claim the contention that the Falklands were an extension of South America, which, excluding Brazil, was exclusively an Iberian continent. Sustained diplomatic pressure finally forced the French to withdraw from the Falkland Islands.[2]

Bougainville's next maritime assignment was to make an extensive examination of the Pacific Basin, seeking the Strait of Anián, the "Terra Australis Incognita," and stations for a Pacific empire. For this mission he was assigned two ships (a twenty-six-gun frigate and a smaller supply ship) and four hundred crewmen. The ship's complement included the naturalist Philibert Commerson, who would observe flora, fauna, and native peoples; and the astronomer Pierre Antoine Vernon, who would test new methods for determining longitude.

Departing French waters in late 1767, Bougainville's expedition stopped off the coast of Brazil. On the beach Commerson came upon a flowering shrub with gaudy red blossoms, which he named "bougainvillea." Proceeding into the South Pacific, Bougainville first searched for the lost southern continent without success, then turned north and made a landing at the island of Tahiti. The British navigator Samuel Wallis had preceded Bougainville there by nine months.

The French visitors were enthralled by the exotic delights of this South Sea haven and titillated by its beauty and lovely people, particularly the women. Commerson exulted over the discovery of "natural man," who seemed "free of every prejudice . . . the gentle impulses of instinct not yet corrupted by reason." Bougainville called Tahiti New Cytherea after the Greek island Cythera where Aphrodite, the goddess of love and beauty, rose from the sea. Disregarding the earlier British stop there, Bougainville claimed the island for France, and the popularization of Commerson's view of the place produced the enduring myth of paradise in the South Seas.[3]

From Tahiti Bougainville ranged over the lower Pacific, coming upon an archipelago he called "The Navigators," which became Samoa; then the New Hebrides; the Great Barrier Reef off Australia's northeast coast; the Solomons; the Bismark Archipelago; the island of Bougainville; then Batavia. The Pacific expedition, out two years and four months, returned to France in 1769. Publication of the expedition accounts and reports on flora, fauna, and native peoples, added much to knowledge about the Pacific Basin and increased French interest there. However, clear French title to Tahiti was not confirmed until 1847, when Great Britain withdrew its claim. Bougainville's was the first French expedition to circumnavigate the earth.

Intensive colonial rivalry between France and Great Britain continued for the remainder of the eighteenth century, and nowhere were their competitive efforts more apparent than in the Pacific Basin. Increased British activity there, due primarily to the territorial revelations of the century's premier navigator, Captain James Cook, goaded French officials to match their adversary's successes.

One of the most notable French Pacific explorations after Bougainville was mounted by La Pérouse. In 1785 he was placed in command of two frigates and commissioned to range over the Pacific, searching out and exploring all islands missed by Cook. Passing through the Strait of Le Maire, he stopped at Valparaíso then proceeded to Easter Island, where expedition scientists studied the environment and La Pérouse distributed seeds and goats to the natives. From Easter Island he sailed to the Hawaiian archipelago, already exposed by Cook, avoiding Tahiti because, in his view, it was already "well known." Expedition scientists studied the island of Maui much like they had Easter Island, before La Pérouse proceeded north for a visit to the settlements in Russian America. He then turned south and explored and charted portions of the coast to California, where he paused in the Spanish ports. La Pérouse then set a course for the Asian mainland, visiting the Marianas and stopping at Cavite in the Philippines to repair his ships and take on supplies before proceeding to Macao. He spent considerable time near the Asian mainland, exploring the Formosan littoral then coasting the Japanese home islands, charting several harbors and straits in the archipelago. Next he sailed southeast to Samoa, visited the Tonga Islands, and anchored in Australia's Botany Bay, where he left letters, ships' logs, and accumulated expedition notes, charts, and maps with British authorities for delivery to France, which, as events developed, was a fortuitous step. La Pérouse then sailed into the southwest Pacific to his doom. His two ships and crewmen were battered to total destruction on the wicked reefs of Vanikoro Island in the Santa Cruz archipelago. No sign of the wreck or knowledge of the crew's melancholy fate were revealed until 1827, when searchers found remnants of his ships' hulls. La Pérouse's expedition reports, notes, maps, and charts were published in France and constituted a valuable increment to Pacific Basin knowledge, and his crewmen were among the first to use the marine chronometer to determine longitude by correlating local time with the time of the zero meridian.

Two additional French expeditions of note ranged over the Pacific before 1800, both searching for new colonial territory and for signs of La Pérouse's expedition, one by Etienne Marchand, the other by Antoine de Bruni de'Entrecastreaux. Marchand with a single vessel departed home port in 1790 and proceeded into the Pacific by way of the Strait of Le Maire. He explored the Marquesas and took possession of five islands in this group for France. Then he sailed to the Northwest Coast, traded with Indian hunters for a cargo of furs, and proceeded to Macao by way of the Hawaiian Islands and Marianas. Marchand found no trace of La Pérouse; he reached home port at Toulon during the late summer of 1792.

Bruni d'Entrecastreaux commanded a two-ship Pacific expedition to seek colonial territory for France and search for La Pérouse. He departed Toulon in late 1791 on a course by now familiar to French mariners via the Strait of Le Maire into the South Seas. After spending considerable time on the island of New Caledonia, d'Estrecastreaux explored islands in the central and western Pacific, coasted New Guinea, then turned to the Moluccas. Finding neither promising colonial territory nor sign of the lost Frenchmen, he sailed south to the west coast of Australia and carefully examined the coast of Tasmania and the surrounding waters and islands. Failing to find a single clue as to the fate of La Pérouse's expedition, he returned to France.

Competition among European imperial nations for access to Pacific Basin territory and resources was heightened around 1700 by the entry of Russia. By this time Russian explorers and fur traders had crossed Siberia to the Pacific shore. Vitus Bering, a Danish navigator, was commissioned by the Russian court in 1728 to explore the waters east of the Siberian coast. He traced the littoral north of Kamchatka and the strait that bears his name. Then in 1741, with Aleksei Chirikov, he led a second Russian expedition of two ships. Their assignment included searching for new territory to accommodate Russian expansion and to watch for a water passage through the American continent. They founded the town of Petropavlovsk and then sailed west. Soon after leaving port a violent North Pacific storm separated Bering and Chirikov. Bering did sight the North American mainland but later lost his ship in another storm. He and his crew were stranded on a bleak, rockbound island; several, including Bering, perished from scurvy. The survivors eventually were able to fashion a raft and return to Kamchatka in the summer of 1742.

Chirikov's ship successfully explored the Northwest Coast down to approximately the fifty-fifth parallel before returning to home port. Crewmen had obtained several hundred sea-otter pelts from native hunters. These dark, luxurious skins provoked keen interest among local fur traders, the *promyshlenniki*. They came to prefer the more attractive and profitable sea otter to the popular Siberian sable pelt, and the prospect of a rich sea-otter harvest drew them to the east. They literally swarmed around the northern rim of the Pacific Basin, landing first in the Aleutians, mercilessly exploiting the Aleuts (rated the finest of native hunters), and quickly exterminating sea otters in that island chain. Thereupon they moved entire Aleut villages eastward to new hunting grounds on the offshore islands. The bonanza trade in sea-otter pelts led to formation of a score of fur companies operating in the northern Pacific. These were consolidated in 1799 into the Russian-American Company. Company officials placed Aleksandr Baranov in charge. He ruthlessly and vigorously enlarged the Russian presence in the North Pacific, eventually establishing satellite settlements south to California and the Hawaiian Islands.

As early as the 1760s, colonial officials in New Spain, eternally committed, it seemed, to sustaining the royal stance, braced by papal donation, that this maritime province was an "Iberian Lake," became alarmed at reports of the increasing traffic of competitor empire-building European nations in the Pacific Basin. They calculated at the time that the most pressing threat to Spanish hegemony over the eastern Pacific was posed by agents of Russia, reportedly driving south from their settlements in the Aleutians in quest of fur territories. Spaniards responded by occupying Alta California.

In 1767 Visitador General José de Gálvez directed the construction of a naval base at San Blas, a port on the Gulf of California, to support this action. Fray Junípero Serra, president of the Franciscan missions of Baja California, was commissioned to form a line of missions in Alta California. Gálvez believed that Christianizing the Indians "would lead to settlements thwarting any Russian colonies" along the California coast.

Colonists for the Alta California settlements—soldiers, missionaries, and settlers—recruited from the towns of Baja California, were divided into two parties. One group set out for Alta California aboard two ships; a second group went by land. Gaspar Portolá, governor of Baja California, was in charge of the military and settler component of the column; Serra was in charge of the Franciscan missionaries. The sea and land parties converged at San Diego Bay, where in 1769 they founded a mission, presidio, and lay settlement. Portolá and an exploring party marched north along the coast in search of Monterey Bay, which they missed initially, failing to recognize it from the land. As a result they continued north and discovered San Francisco Bay, before returning to Monterey and San Diego. Portolá led a second expedition to Monterey in 1770, where Franciscans and soldiers founded a mission and a presidio.

In 1776 Captain Juan Bautista de Anza led a party of 150 settlers, missionaries, and soldiers to San Francisco Bay. The land between San Diego and San Francisco was gradually filled with towns, missions, presidios, farms, and ranches. San José, in the Santa Clara Valley near the head of San Francisco Bay, was founded as a lay settlement in 1777; near mission San Gabriel, Spanish settlers founded Los Angeles in 1781. By 1782 this Alta California frontage on the Pacific Basin's eastern margin consisted of presidios at San Francisco, Santa Barbara, Monterey, and San Diego; San José and Los Angeles were pueblos, or lay towns; and there were nine missions between San Francisco and San Diego. Monterey became the capital of Spanish Alta California.

Indians of southern and central California for the most part submitted peacefully to Spanish rule. The Franciscans found bringing them under their *regula* rather easy. Padres selected mission sites on the basis of location, soil quality, water availability, and pasturage, and gathered Indians from their scattered settlements. Franciscans taught Native American neophytes Christian doctrine, agriculture, and vocational arts. The number of Indians at each mission varied from a few hundred to two or three thousand. Through the years the California missions with strict Franciscan oversight and productive Indian labor developed irrigated fields for grain and other crops and pastures supporting large herds of cattle and sheep. By both civil and ecclesiastical law, these wealthy mission estates, with their riches in irrigated fields, crops, and livestock, were the property of the Indians, held in trust by the Franciscan padres.

Missions so dominated the lives of these Native Americans that they came to be called "Mission Indians." The total number of baptisms of California Indians performed by Franciscan missionaries during the period of Spanish dominion in this portion of the Pacific Basin (1769–1822) amounted to about ninety thousand.

Spanish occupation of Alta California placed an Iberian barrier athwart Russian expansion down the Northwest Coast. This initiative, however, was not enough to discourage the entry of an even more aggressive imperial foe—Great Britain. British navigators were the most tenacious, daring, and successful explorers coursing over the Pacific Basin during the period between 1600 and 1800. In the seventeenth century, their role was less as explorers and more as corsairs and privateers preying on Spanish shipping. English marine raiders used uninhabited Pacific islands off the Peruvian and Mexican coasts as bases for strikes against Iberian colonial galleons.

Most notorious of the Pacific Basin buccaneers was William Dampier. His oceanic peregrinations included a raiding cruise during 1686 across the north Pacific from Mexico to Guam. Returning to England he wrote two books—*A New Voyage round the World* (1697), detailing his Pacific Basin adventures, and *Voyages and Descriptions,* which included a maritime treatise, *Discourse of Trade-Winds,* which demonstrated his ability as navigator and hydrographer.[4]

Dampier's writings popularized the Pacific Basin as a potential province for British colonial expansion. Admiralty officials commissioned him to conduct maritime surveys of the Australian and New Guinea coasts in the southwest Pacific. Between 1689 and 1700 he discovered and named the island of New Britain, Dampier Strait, and the Dampier Archipelago. Soon after 1700 and during the war with France and Spain, Dampier was assigned the command of two Pacific-bound ships fitted out by British merchants as privateers. Prowling the eastern Pacific, one ship stopped at Más Atierra Island in the Juan Fernández group, and Alexander Selkirk, who had quarreled with the captain, was put ashore. Subsequently that ship was disabled by a large hull leak and was captured by a Spanish naval squadron. Dampier in the second vessel took a Spanish prize to Macao before returning to England.

In 1708 Dampier signed on as pilot of a privateer. The following year his ship anchored off Más Atierra Island to rescue Selkirk. Selkirk's sojourn in the Juan Fernández Islands supplied the basis for Daniel Defoe's *Robinson Crusoe* (1719).[5]

Each year after 1700, English private and public interests became more serious about colonial prospects in the Pacific Basin. Their goals in this regard were to find ways to crush the presumptive Spanish monopoly of the South Seas and negate Spanish and Portuguese attempts to control access to the Pacific Basin, all the while seeking a direct route to rich Asian markets. This was a continuation of the "Tudor dream" of finding an unencumbered, direct road to Cathay by searching out North America's east coast for the Northwest Passage from the Atlantic, connecting in the continental heartland with the Strait of Anián debouching into the Pacific, which earlier had been probed by Cabot, Frobisher, Davis, Chancellor, Willoughby, and Drake. British mariners were no less committed to testing the theory of the presence of a southern continent, believed situated near the South Pole with considerable of its territory extending into temperate latitudes, making it habitable. The English scientific community, led by the geographer Alexander Dalrymple, urged a thorough maritime reconnaissance of the antarctic region to determine the theory's validity.

Added to these motivations for enlarged British activity in the Pacific Basin was pressure from commercial interests anxious to expand trade territories. Primarily this came from the wealthy and powerful British East India Company, whose directors envisaged "rich promise of undiscovered lands and new markets," a network of Pacific Basin trading posts, "through which the teeming population of a world new to Europe might receive British manufactures in exchange for their natural resources" and "based on an alliance with coloured peoples instead of settlement by European colonists."[6]

Four imperial wars against France and Spain after 1685 diverted British attention from these colonial expansion objectives, although even during the recurring military contests British activity in the Pacific continued. In 1740 Commodore George Anson led an eight-ship squadron through the Strait of Le Maire to retaliate against Spanish naval impositions on British shipping. Lurking off the Peruvian and Mexican coasts, Anson's raiders took several prizes then sailed to Tinian in the Marianas and on to Macao on the China coast for refitting his ships. Before returning to England in 1744, Anson plundered several treasure-laden Manila galleons.

Also during these imperial wars, British planners conceived schemes to expand their dominion over the Pacific. Parliament approved a measure granting twenty thousand pounds to the first British subject on a British ship to find a water passage between Hudson's Bay and the South Sea. British planners were also anxious to break the presumptive control of passages into the Pacific around Africa, the Cape of Good Hope, and around South America, the Straits of Magellan and Le Maire. British empire officials considered occupying the Falkland Islands as a base for protecting the latter Pacific access and supporting southern maritime explorations for "Terra Australis Incognita."

By the Peace of Paris, 1763, Great Britain emerged supreme in the imperial contest, and colonial advocates prepared to establish what has come to be called the "Second British Empire," largely centered in the Pacific Basin. The first postwar effort to initiate this process occurred during 1766, when Samuel Wallis and John Byron commanded two expeditions to resume explorations in the Pacific.

Wallis, with Philip Carteret, was to reconnoiter archipelagoes in the South Pacific. Byron's mission was to reenforce the British claim, established by Sir Francis Drake, to New Albion, situated on the Northwest Coast, and to search for the western entrance to the continental passage. Wallis explored the Tuamotus group and the Society Islands, pausing at Tahiti for a month to allow his crew to recover from scurvy and taste the delights of this South Sea paradise. Wallis named Tahiti "King George III Island." Carteret discovered Pitcairn Island, rediscovered the Solomons, and also found New Ireland and the Admiralty Islands. Byron missed his objective, made no discoveries of importance, and returned to England a failure.

In the wake of the Wallis-Byron Pacific explorations came James Cook, acknowledged a marine surveyor "of extreme thoroughness and precision," and hailed as the premier navigator of history. Cook carried out three extensive reconnaissances of the Pacific Basin, each with a specific mission.

During the 1760s Cook surveyed the coasts of Labrador, Nova Scotia, Newfoundland, and the St. Lawrence estuary. His first Pacific assignment came during 1768, from the British Admiralty and the Royal Society. Astronomers calculated that the planet Venus would cross the face of the sun on 3 June 1769; they favored the newly discovered island of Tahiti as the optimum site for observing the planet's transit. Cook was placed in command of this expedition to serve the causes of science and the British empire because, in addition to supervising the astronomical observation, he was directed to explore New Zealand and search for new Pacific territories. Proceeding to the Pacific via Cape Horn aboard the *Endeavor,* Cook reached Tahiti on 10 April 1769. Scientists aboard observed the predicted transit of Venus, then Cook explored the Polynesian islands adjacent to Tahiti, naming the group Society Islands, before proceeding to New Zealand. He spent six months surveying this large island and the eastern coast of Australia, then returned to England via the Cape of Good Hope, reaching home port on 13 July 1771.

Cook's second Pacific excursion was expected to determine the validity of the many-centuries-old theory posed by geographers concerning the presence of an unknown habitable continent in the southern hemisphere. For this purpose Cook planned to circumnavigate the earth with two ships, the *Resolution* and the *Adven-*

ture, as close to the South Pole as conditions would permit. Approaching Antarctica by way of the Cape of Good Hope, he sailed to a record-setting seventy-one degrees ten minutes before glaciers and the polar ice pack forced him to retreat. Cook kept his expedition on this mission for nearly three years, making three hazard-filled thrusts to the very edge of the formidable south-polar ice pack before pulling back to milder latitudes. He also continued explorations in the South Pacific for additional landforms, discovering the Marquesas, and doing additional charting and mapping of the Society Islands, New Hebrides, and New Zealand. After the third polar reconnaissance, Cook became convinced that "Terra Australis Incognita" was a mythical entity, the product of a detached, perhaps overactive collective imagination.

James Cook's third Pacific Basin mission was to make an exhaustive examination of the Northwest Coast, to determine the existence of the theorized Strait of Anián. This reconnaissance was also expected to reenforce the British claim to New Albion, established by Sir Francis Drake in the late sixteenth century, and "to determine its strategic relevance to British imperial interests." And Cook was to continue exploring, mapping, and charting known and unknown land areas in the water hemisphere. A coordinating expedition was to approach North America from the west coast of Newfoundland and trace Baffin and Hudson's bays, exploring their rivers and inlets into the interior, searching for the Atlantic threshold of this mythical water passage through the continent.

Cook, in command of the *Resolution* and the *Discovery,* sailed for the Pacific via the Cape of Good Hope during July 1776. His crew included Midshipman George Vancouver, Crewmen Nathaniel Portlock, George Dixon, and John Ledyard, and the sailing master of the *Resolution,* William Bligh, all to figure prominently in the Pacific Basin's unfolding imperial drama.

Cook spent two years coasting Tasmania, New Zealand, and the Friendly Islands before proceeding on a northwesterly itinerary, in the course of which he discovered, during January 1778, an archipelago he named the Sandwich Islands, for the Earl of Sandwich, first lord of the Admiralty. Kaua'i was the discovery island. After coasting several islands in the archipelago and taking on food, water, and wood for the ships' galleys and resting his

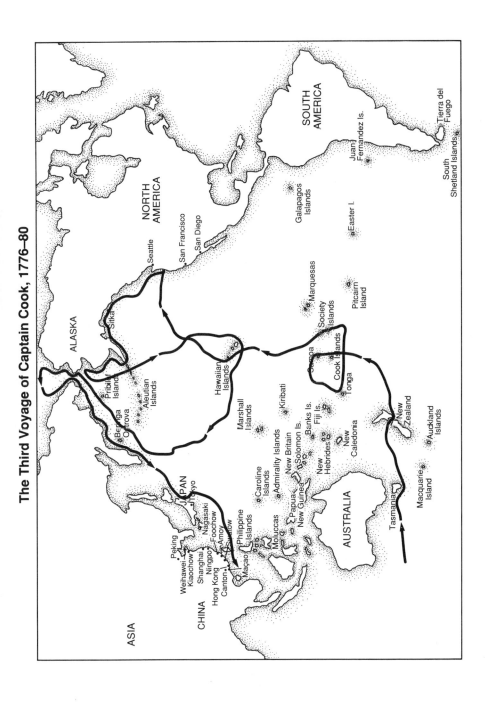

The Third Voyage of Captain Cook, 1776–80

crews, Cook proceeded to the Oregon coast, traced out Nootka Sound on southwest Vancouver Island, then explored the coast of Russian America. He breached the Bering Strait and continued his search for the Strait of Anián along the Arctic coast. While in the northland, Cook visited Russian traders on Unalaska in the Aleutians.

Returning to the Sandwich Islands during January of 1779, Cook explored Maui and the largest island in the group, Hawai'i. Anchoring his ships in Kealakekua Bay on Hawai'i's west coast, Cook went ashore on 14 February to recover property seized by natives. Hawaiians ambushed the Europeans; Cook and four marine guards were slain. Captain James Clerke took command of the expedition and, resuming the search for the sea passage, proceeded north through the Bering Strait into the Arctic Ocean, until severe storms forced him back into the Pacific. Clerke died of consumption, and crewmen buried him on the Siberian shore. Captain John Gore then took command of the ships and sailed to Macao. There crewmen sold sea-otter pelts, obtained from native hunters on the Northwest Coast, to Chinese merchants for one hundred Spanish dollars each. After refitting his ships at Macao, Gore continued to England, arriving there on 4 October 1780.

Cook's third Pacific expedition had been out of home port over four years. As in the case of the two preceding oceanic excursions headed by the now deceased grand mariner, this one also produced substantive results. His calculated peregrinations had revealed a new archipelago—the Sandwich Islands—destined to become in a few short years the "Crossroads of the Pacific." He and his successor in command of the expedition had disproved the existence of the long-sought Strait of Anián. Cook's explorations along the Northwest Coast strengthened British claims to the area and "made it possible for the future Dominion of Canada to extend to the Pacific coast." And the seemingly insignificant sale of sea-otter pelts by expedition crewmen to Chinese merchants at astonishingly high prices precipitated a rush of traders from several nations, including the infant United States, to the source of this bonanza on the Northwest Coast, where conflicting national claims nearly led to war between Great Britian and Spain.[7]

Thus a pattern evolved for periodic imperialistic surges in the Pacific Basin. Serendipitous discoveries of natural resources—earlier it was fur, gold, fertilizer, and pelagic riches, particularly whales; later it was petroleum—and strategic military sites have precipitated, even forced, actions by nations seeking an advantageous position well into the twentieth century, often out of historical context in time and national intent. In the late eighteenth century, the magnet drawing agents of Great Britain, Russia, France, the infant United States, and even Spain to renewed activity, was the sea otter. Before 1800 its pelt became a prize item in Pacific Basin commerce and a *cause célèbre* in international rivalry for pre-eminence on the Northwest Coast. Russian promyshlenniki with their forced Aleut hunters had been harvesting sea-otter pelts in the North Pacific for over thirty years, but the British were responsible for popularizing this new source of personal and national wealth.

Crewmen from the third Cook Pacific expedition returned to home port in October 1780. At the time Great Britain was at war with France, Spain, and the insurgent North American colonies, and royal officials attempted to restrain expedition members from publishing reports of recent Pacific discoveries and the bonanza market at Canton for sea-otter pelts. Nevertheless three unsigned reports appeared before the first official journal of the third Cook Pacific expedition was issued in 1784, a year after the conclusion of the American War of Independence.

Merchantman Captain James Hanna was the first British trader to reach the Northwest Coast, anchoring his *Harmon* in Nootka Sound in 1785. He traded with local Indian hunters for a cargo of sea-otter pelts and sold them in the Canton market for twenty thousand Spanish dollars. When Hanna returned to Nootka the following year, aboard the *Sea Otter,* he found six English ships from ports in the British Isles and India in the sound, their crewmen ashore trading for furs. The ships were there under authority of licenses issued by the British East India Company, which from 1600 on had held a monopoly of the trade between the Cape of Good Hope and Cape Horn, and two additional crown-chartered companies, functioning in a subsidiary role to the East India Company—the South Sea Company and King George's Sound or London Company. Their captains included Nathaniel Portlock and George Dixon, officers of Cook's third Pacific expedition, James

Colnett, and John Meares, each to figure in the international drama unfolding on the Northwest Coast.

These merchantman captains regularly visited the settlements in Russian America and trafficked with Nootka, Kwakiutl and Haida Indians, superb pelagic hunters much like the North Pacific Aleuts and Tlingits. But these traders had the additional mission of contributing to the establishment of the so-called Second British Empire. Home officials supported them in the consummation of a "blueprint" for supremacy in "trade and dominion" in the Pacific Basin, an expanding triangular network reaching from China to the Northwest Coast, with the newly discovered Sandwich Islands as an intermediate support station. These pioneer traders on the Northwest Coast envisaged permanent colonial depots there to provide furs, naval stores, foodstuffs, and havens for resettling convicts similar to the Australian experiment. Colnett carried aboard his ship *Argonaut* a party of over twenty Chinese workers to build a trading settlement at Nootka.

The French, with 150 years of years of experience in the fur trade of North America's continental interior, also surveyed prospects for participating in the Northwest Coast sea-otter pelt industry. La Pérouse ranged over the northern Pacific during the mid-1780s, mapped portions of it, and visited the Russian settlements there. He established a French claim to Lituya Bay in Russian America, naming it Port des Français, as a possible future Gallic colony site. While in the northern Pacific, he stopped at Kamchatka and posted certain of his journals for delivery to officials in Paris. Then he proceeded to Spanish California, stopping at Monterey, where he shared his northern Pacific maps with Spanish officials and advised them that Russian traders were preparing to move down the coast toward San Francisco. La Pérouse's reports became warnings for officials in New Spain, which led to the ultimate confrontation with the colony-planting intruders in Nootka Sound. And in 1790 Etienne Marchand carried a cargo of pelts from the Northwest Coast to Macao.

La Pérouse's warnings were not idle rumors. In 1786 Grigorii Shelikhov, a principal stockholder in the leading trading company of Russian America, directed his agents to proceed toward California. And during the late 1780s, Russian navigators probed the coast southward for trade and settlement sites, goaded by recent British and French visits to their northern colonies and by the threat of Spanish occupation of Northwest Coast fur territory. ,

Even the young United States became involved in the contest for a share of the Pacific Basin bounty. Americans as British colonial subjects had become acquainted with the Pacific as crewmen aboard British trading ships, whalers, and privateers. Soon after the Revolution, American ships increasingly entered Pacific waters. Formal maritime activity there began in 1784, when Robert Morris and several other American investors sent the *Empress of China* with a cargo of ginseng from New York to Canton via the Cape of Good Hope and the Indian Ocean passage. Ginseng, a plant that grows wild in New England and other parts of the United States, was used by Chinese physicians as a curative. The return of the *Empress of China* with silk and tea augured a promising future for the American mercantile enterprise in the Pacific Basin.

A book by John Ledyard, the *Journal of Captain Cook's Last Voyage to the Pacific Ocean,* stirred additional interest in the American business community. Ledyard, a native of Connecticut, left his studies at Dartmouth in 1773 at the age of twenty-one for the sea. In London three years later he enlisted in the British marines to accompany Cook's third voyage. When his ship returned to England, he refused to serve against the rebelling colonies. Finally British naval authorities impressed him for service on a man-of-war bound for America. Ledyard jumped ship on Long Island and settled at Hartford. There he wrote of his Pacific adventures, stressing the prospects for wealth in the Northwest Coast fur trade and recounting the easy sale of sea-otter pelts in the Canton market, each skin bringing a hundred dollars. Many Americans read Ledyard's book. Joseph Barrell, a Boston financier, joined several businessmen to fit out the 212-ton *Columbia* and the 90-ton *Lady Washington* for a Northwest Coast trading venture. The two ships sailed from Boston during September of 1787, with John Kendrick, a whaler and privateer commander during the Revolution as captain of the *Columbia,* and Robert Gray, also a privateer commander during the Revolution, in charge of the *Lady Washington.* The two ships entered the Pacific via Cape Horn and reached Nootka Sound during September of 1788. The Americans wintered there, trafficking with local Indian hunters for pelts and witnessing a grand and decisive confrontation between Spain and Great Britain for momentary suzerainty over this portion of the Pacific Basin.[8]

Interestingly even Spaniards, although increasingly uneasy over alien intrusion in territory they claimed, also became involved in the sea-otter trade. From their commercial links at Manila with the Chinese mainland, they were aware of the high Chinese esteem for these exquisite furs. Franciscan padres, eager for an export product to improve mission support, encouraged their Indian communicants to hunt sea otters along the California coast. When the Manila galleon of 1783 left Acapulco with a cargo of over seven hundred sea-otter pelts from the California missions, businessmen in Mexico became interested in the industry. They formed the Philippine Company to exchange pelts for Chinese quicksilver, essential for refining gold ore extracted from the Mexican mines. They also urged officials in New Spain to establish trading posts in the richer fur territory of the Northwest Coast so they could more readily profit from the pelt trade and also check intruders. The Spanish bureaucracy stifled this businessmen's attempt to use commerce to confront the interlopers. And as matters worked out, the Spanish eventually were forced to resort to military and diplomatic action in their attempt to achieve this exclusion.

Spanish explorations in the Pacific became increasingly defensive in the face of recurring reports of Russian, French, and British activity, primarily on the Northwest Coast. As early as 1774, officials in Mexico sent Juan Pérez at the head of a maritime expedition to explore to sixty degrees north latitude to reenforce the Spanish claims to the upper Pacific Basin and to take possession of portions of the northern territories by planting inscribed plates and crosses at selected locations. Thus Spain continued in its determination to maintain the Pacific Basin as a grand Iberian lake, basing its title on the clerical division of the world in 1493 and "prior discovery and symbolic acts of possession." Pérez proceeded north to the lower limits of Russian America, then searching out sites for future settlements he coasted south, discovering Vancouver Island and the expansive anchorage situated on the island's west coast, future focus of a great military and diplomatic confrontation.[9]

A follow-up to the Pérez expedition came in 1775, when Bruno de Hezeta and Juan Francisco de la Bodega y Quadra explored the coast north of Monterey. Their mission was to reach at least sixty degrees north, regarded as the northern limit for the Strait of Anián. Illness among the crew forced Hezeta to turn back before reaching his objective, but he did find the mouth of the Columbia River. Bodega was able to proceed to fifty-eight degrees north and found an anchorage that came to be known as Bodega Bay.

In 1779 Ignacio de Arteaga and Bodega were directed to search over the North Pacific for the Cook expedition and to try again to reach sixty degrees north. The Spaniards found only Russians in the North Pacific as they explored points on the northern coast including the Kenai Peninsula and islands near Kodiak; they finally reached sixty degrees north but discovered no passage through the continent.

These defensive reconnaissances climaxed in May 1789, when a Spanish naval force of two ships commanded by Don Esteban José Martínez entered Nootka Sound. He found three British merchantmen and the two pioneer American vessels to the Northwest Coast, the *Columbia* and the *Lady Washington,* anchored in the sound. Martínez did not challenge the American ships but commandeered the three British ships and sent them under guard to the Mexican naval base at San Blas. His crewmen also seized a trading post on the beach erected by John Meares, ran down the British flag, and raised the Spanish ensign. Martínez also declared the Pacific coast from Cape Horn to sixty degrees north latitude Spanish territory.

Word of the Spanish action at Nootka Sound eventually reached British officials in London. They expressed appropriate indignation, prepared the British navy for combat, and confronted Spanish representatives with the choice of war or prompt restoration of ships and crews, indemnity for crewmen, and recognition of the right of British subjects to trade and establish settlements on the "unoccupied coasts" of America. Awesome British sea power and the very real threat of retaliation forced Spanish officials to accept the British demands in the so-called Nootka Convention. Thus Spanish claims to much of the Pacific Basin "based on prior discovery and symbolic acts of possession" clearly were ineffectual, because Spain was unable to support them "from a position of strength."[10]

The Nootka Sound Convention marked the beginning of Spain's retreat in the Pacific Basin, although the process was slow and unfolded by stages; major withdrawals occurred in 1821–22 and 1898. But for the time being, Spanish officials in those colonies facing on the Pacific, in spite of the setback at Nootka, continued to support explorations and to maintain some Spanish presence in the basin. From Mexican, Peruvian, and Chilean ports, Spanish ship captains explored the island adjacent to Tahiti, and church officials located missions there staffed by clerics. But Spanish colonial attention increasingly concentrated on the Philippine development, with Guam as a support base for the maritime lifeline between Manila and Acapulco. Spanish ships came to pause at the Sandwich Islands, to break the monotonous Pacific crossing and to restock their stores of pork, poultry, fruit, wood, and water. Spaniards also continued to explore the Northwest Coast. In 1791 Alejandro Malaspina, seeking the Strait of Anián, mapped much of the upper Pacific littoral.

Having won Spanish acknowledgment by the Nootka Sound Convention of the right of "open access" to unoccupied portions of the Pacific Basin, Great Britain continued for the remainder of the eighteenth century to explore and develop plans for a colonial establishment there. Captain Arthur Phillips in 1787 led a fleet of eleven ships laden with convict colonists from the British Isles to Australia. After Lieutenant John Watts discharged the 102 female convict passengers aboard his ship at Port Jackson, he made an extensive exploration of the Pacific, which included discovery of the Kermandec Islands and Tongareva, with a stop at Tahiti.

By 1785 British whalers, manned with skilled Nantucket crewmen, had entered the Pacific via Cape Horn in search of new whale fisheries. Beginning off the Patagonian coast, they worked along South America's rim watching for islands and isolated mainland stretches for stations to take on wood and water and to repair ships. In response to whaling interests' requests, British naval authorities in 1793 directed John Colnett, commander of the Royal Navy ship *Rattler,* to explore, map, and chart the west coast of South America and adjacent islands and watch for commercial and military base sites. Colnett examined the Pacific littoral from Patagonia to Lower California. In his view the Galápagos were "ideal" for a whaling station and a trading and military base. The Colnett mission was an irrefutable manifestation of late-eighteen-century British intent in the Pacific Basin.

Another series of British surveys of the Pacific Basin before the close of the eighteenth century grew out of attempts at breadfruit transplanting and mutiny. The Dampier, Anson, and Cook reports praised the food value of the breadfruit, yield of a tree native to the South Pacific. The fruits are from four to eight inches in diameter, and when roasted resemble bread. This led plantation operators in the West Indies to encourage the introduction of the plant there to feed field-workers. William Bligh, a member of Cook's third Pacific expedition, was placed in command of the breadfruit transplanting project; its roster of forty-four officers and men assigned to the *Bounty.*

The *Bounty* sailed from home port in late December 1787, entering the Pacific via the Cape of Good Hope and the Indian Ocean and stopping at New Zealand before arriving at Tahiti. The *Bounty* crew worked on this island paradise for six months collecting suitable breadfruit nursery stock. The *Bounty* sailed for the West Indies in early April 1789, Bligh intending to explore the Tongan archipelago en route. Shortly thereafter Fletcher Christian and a portion of the crew rebelled, seized Bligh in his cabin, and forced him and eighteen crewmen into the ship's launch. Then the mutineers took the *Bounty* back to Tahiti. Several remained there, while others navigated the *Bounty* to Pitcairn Island, burned the ship, and established a colony there. Bligh and the loyal crewmen in the open longboat proceeded on a westerly course through the Fiji Islands to Timor and eventually reached England on a Dutch ship. Bligh, with Royal Navy support for the breadfruit transplant scheme, returned to the Pacific with two ships during 1791. He explored atolls in the Tuamotus before stopping in Tahiti for breadfruit stock. Resuming his Pacific explorations, he coasted several of the Tongan islands, the Fijis, and Melanesia before setting a course for the Cape of Good Hope. En route Bligh stopped at St. Helena for a breadfruit planting. He delivered a large stock of breadfruit trees to Jamaica in early February 1793; the plantation workers rejected the fruit, preferring bananas (plantains) as their staple.

During 1790 Royal Navy authorities sent the *Pandora* with 160 men and 24 guns under Captain Edward Edwards to search for the *Bounty* mutineers. Entering the Pacific at Cape Horn, Edwards explored beyond Easter Island and found small Ducie Island and Tureia Island but missed Pitcairn Island, the mutineers' haven. Later Edwards discovered Marutea and Tureai islands. On Tahiti his crewmen found 16 mutineers: 2 were slain and 14 surrendered. Marine guards chained the 14 prisoners aboard the *Pandora* and Edwards continued his search for the remainder of the mutineers, discovering several additional islands, including Chatham and Upala, as well as islands in the eastern Samoan group and Rotuma and Amoda in the Santa Cruz archipelago. A fierce storm battered the *Pandora* on the Great Barrier Reef; 31 crewmen and 4 prisoners perished. Survivors in longboats reached Timor. From there a Dutch ship carried them to Batavia and eventually to England. Of the 10 surviving prisoners, 4 were acquitted, 3 were pardoned, and 3 were hung from the yardarm of the *Brunswick* in Portsmouth Harbor.

Eighteenth-century British explorations of consequence were concluded by George Vancouver between 1791 and 1795. Also a member of Cook's second and third Pacific expeditions, his mission was to proceed to the Northwest Coast with two ships, the *Endeavor* and *Chatham,* and there explore and map the land area, chart the waters, select sites for colonies and military stations, and once and for all determine the existence of the Strait of Anián. Vancouver's ships departed England on 1 April 1791 and entered the Pacific via the Cape of Good Hope and Indian Ocean. He stopped first at New Zealand, then proceeded to the Sandwich Islands. Besides mapping and charting portions of the archipelago, he concluded an agreement with Kamehameha, a powerful island leader, for the British annexation of Hawai'i, a commitment Vancouver's government failed to honor.

Vancouver continued to the Northwest Coast. He spent three summers there carefully examining every possible access into the interior, concluding at the end of this exhaustive reconnaissance that the Strait of Anián was a myth, the product of extravagant hopes. His mapping and charting extended along the California coast, including the San Francisco and Monterey harbors. In late December 1794, Vancouver completed his examination of the eastern rim of the Pacific Basin and returned to England.

By this time Great Britain was locked in a desperate war with France that continued for twenty years. It so absorbed British resources, manpower, and attention that colonial leaders were forced to set aside for over a generation their dream for a Pacific Basin empire.

In that interim, late-arriving Americans came to dominate the rich trade between the Northwest Coast and Canton. Gradually their interest in the Pacific Basin enlarged to the extent that they came to regard it with the same proprietary assumptions they were applying to the North American continent. And as they had done on the mainland, they exploited the Pacific Basin. In their seemingly irrepressible expansion, Americans tapped the Pacific as a source of national strength and as a source of the frontier myth.

Orange Harbor, Tierra Del Fuego. In Charles Wilkes, *Narrative of the United States Exploring Expedition during the Years 1838, 1840, 1841, 1842,* vol. 1 page 120.

A Night Dance by Women in Hapaee (engraving after John Webber, 1784). In *Illustrations to Cook's Voyages.* (Courtesy Alaska and Polar Regions Department, Rasmuson Library, University of Alaska Fairbanks, acc.# B0082.)

Tahitian natives on the beach. In Wilkes, *Exploring Expedition*, vol. 2 page 8.

Broom Road, Tahiti. In Wilkes, *Exploring Expedition*, vol. 2 prior to page 85.

A native throwing a boomerang, New South Wales. In Wilkes, *Exploring Expedition*, vol. 2 page 192.

A view of Karakakooa, in Owyhee (engraving after John Webber). In *Illustrations to Cook's Voyages*. (Courtesy Alaska and Polar Regions Department, Rasmuson Library, University of Alaska Fairbanks, acc.# B0082.)

Tamméaméa, Roi des îles Sandwiches, c. 1815. In Louis Choris,
Voyage Pittoresque Autour de Monde (1822). (Courtesy Alaska and
Polar Regions Department, Rasmuson Library, University of Alaska
Fairbanks, acc.# B0083.)

Port d'hanarourou, c. 1815. In Choris, *Voyage*. (Courtesy Alaska and Polar Regions Department, Rasmuson Library, University of Alaska Fairbanks, acc.# B0083.)

La Reine Kinau, Dans D'une Rue D'Honolulu, Capitale Des Îles Sandwich. J. Masselot was the artist and Bichebois the lithographer. (Courtesy Honolulu Academy of Arts, gift of Mrs. Charles M. Cooke, 1927 neg. no. 5731.)

The southeastern part of Honolulu in 1826, with palace of Kamehameha III in foreground. Watercolor by an unknown artist. (Courtesy the Baker Collection, Bishop Museum, Collection, neg. no. CP 29158.)

An Aleut man and woman. In Choris, *Voyage*. (Courtesy Alaska and Polar Regions Department, Rasmuson Library, University of Alaska Fairbanks.)

Pali, Oʻahu. In Wilkes, *Exploring Expedition,* vol. 3 prior to page 391.

A pride of sea lions in the Pribilof Islands of Russian America illustrates the fur wealth of the Pacific, 1815. In Choris, *Voyage*. (Courtesy Alaska and Polar Regions Department, Rasmuson Library, University of Alaska Fairbanks.)

Ououluk principal établissem.^ᵗ sur l'île d'Ounalachka.

Aleut hunters in a bidarka near Unalaska. In Choris, *Voyage*. (Courtesy Alaska and Polar Regions Department, Rasmuson Library, University of Alaska Fairbanks.)

The harbor of St. Paul on Kodiak, Russian America, 1804. In Urey Lisiansky, *A Voyage Around the World* (1814). (Courtesy Alaska and Polar Regions Department, Rasmuson Library, University of Alaska Fairbanks.)

Russian Fort Ross, Bodega, California, 1843. From a sketch by the "King's Orphan."
In Samuel C. Upham, *The Far Western Frontier: Notes of a Voyage to California Via
Cape Horn, Together with Scenes in El Dorado in the Years 1849–50* (1878, rpt. 1973),
page 557.

The town and port of Yerba Buena, in San Francisco Bay, 1843. From a sketch by the "King's Orphan." In Upham, *Far Western Frontier*, page 553.

Old Glory marks Canton's American factory in the early 1800s. In this compound, factors traded for cargoes while sampans brought in tea. From an oil painting by an unidentified Chinese artist (M5214). (Courtesy Peabody & Essex Museum/Peabody Museum Collection, photo by Mark Sexton, neg. no. 6969.)

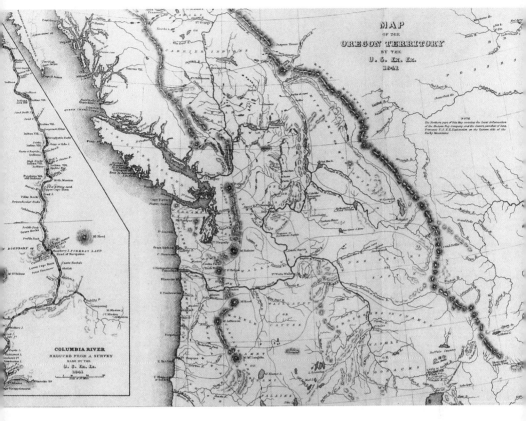

A map of the Columbia River and the Oregon Territory, 1841. In Wilkes, *Exploring Expedition,* vol. 4 prior to page 291. (Courtesy Alaska and Polar Regions Department, Rasmuson Library, University of Alaska Fairbanks, acc.# A1693.)

Astoria, Columbia River. In Wilkes, *Exploring Expedition,* vol. 5 prior to page 113.

CHAPTER SIX

The Yankee Advent

Americans were latecomers to the Pacific Basin, arriving there in the 1780s, but in less than a century they came to dominate its eastern margins and to exercise considerable economic, diplomatic, military, and even cultural influence over much of the remainder. Portuguese and Dutch colonial builders were the pioneers in the western Pacific, but the sixteenth and seventeenth centuries must be designated the era of Spanish dominion in this vast water hemisphere; the eighteenth century was the time of unquestioned British supremacy, with some French and Russian competition. But the escalating preoccupation of European nations with the continental tension and conflict growing out of the French Revolution and beginnings of Gallic conquest diverted essential imperial attention and application by the Pacific Basin's erstwhile principals and left an open path for Americans to enter.

In their early *entrada* period, Americans concentrated on the Pacific Basin's eastern margins, the continental littoral from Russian America to Patagonia (maintaining a prudent distance offshore in those proscriptive Spanish colonial waters) and west to Hawai'i. However, from the beginning of their arrival in this new frontier area, Americans maintained a commercial relationship with the flourishing trading community at Canton, and even attempted to enter the recluse kingdom of Japan. The Americanization process that quite soon would transform North America's continental heartland, and also engage a substantial portion of the Pacific Basin, was yet in its nascent stages. Thus the period from 1784 to 1800 for American pioneers on the broad bosom of the Pacific was a time of discovery and of adjustment to this exotic marine continent, of feeling their way. But this was no less an important time for the Pacific Basin's future, in that it was during this entrada period that the vital American presence, which laid foundations for subsequent Yankee claims and suzerainty, was established.

Prospects for sharing in the rich commerce of the Orient initially lured Americans into the Pacific Basin. Colonial America as a component of the British Empire had been expected to serve as a source of raw materials and foodstuffs for the imperial market, which had the effect of curbing the rise of any appreciable industry. After independence Americans were desperate for markets to absorb their lumber, grain, beef, hides, iron, wood, hemp, simple manufactures, and furs. Principal markets for American products in colonial times had been British home ports and West Indian plantations. After independence American access to them was limited, and trade outlets in France and other European nations were erratic and uncertain.

Colonials knew of far-off places. American seamen served as crewmen on British merchant and naval ships. Fishing fleets and whalers from New England ports ranged over the Atlantic. Colonial traders delivered foodstuffs and lumber to West Indian plantations, they ventured to Portugal, coasted Africa's western shore, and called regularly at Mediterranean ports. And during the frequent Anglo-French wars, colonial ship captains prowled Atlantic and Mediterranean waters as privateers preying on Gallic shipping. Americans had generations of shipbuilding and navigational experience. New England yards produced a number of strong, seaworthy craft for the East India Company. But colonials were excluded from the Pacific, by the suppressive British East India Company monopoly and monopolies held by its collateral companies, from commerce between the Cape of Good Hope and Cape Horn. Of course following their secession from the British Empire, Americans were no longer bound by this prohibition.

American businessmen's attention to Asian ports, centering on Canton, as markets for their exports was drawn from several sources. Certainly John Ledyard's *Journal,* describing Captain James Cook's third Pacific expedition and setting forth the bonanza of commercial prospects therein, provoked considerable interest in the Yankee mercantile community. And during their nearly two centuries as a colonial outpost of the British Empire, Americans had become well aware of the yield of Asian markets. Although the East India Company monopoly excluded them from this commerce, they were consumers of oriental products and goods. By 1700 tea had become a popular colonial beverage. At the time China was the source; tea and other exotic products were delivered to American ports in East India Company ships. Also during the eighteenth century, the oriental motif became exceedingly popular in Europe; it was smart for affluent householders to include Chinese lacquerware; porcelain bowls; delicately colored urns; exquisite wood carvings; wallpaper; textiles of brocade, silk, and cotton; and inscrutable oriental figures. This sinological preoccupation reverberated even into colonial America—commanding pagoda figures gave an exotic cast to the governor's palace at Williamsburg.

Soon after the close of the American War of Independence, Yankee entrepreneurs began to plan China trading ventures. In late 1783 the *Harriet*, a 55-ton sloop laden with a cargo of ginseng, which grew wild in North America, sailed from Boston for the Orient. In colonial times Americans had gathered and stowed this herb aboard East India Company ships bound for the Far East. At the Cape of Good Hope, the *Harriet* was intercepted by a British East Indiaman laden with tea; the captains exchanged cargoes, and the *Harriet* returned to Boston.

The next American trading ship committed to the oriental trade was the *Empress of China*, a 350-ton vessel used as a privateer during the war and still fitted with guns, stuffed with a cargo of ginseng, furs, raw cotton, and lead. Robert Morris and Daniel Parker were the principal financiers. The *Empress* sailed from New York, 22 February 1784, on a course via the Cape of Good Hope and Indian Ocean into the Pacific, arriving at Canton on 28 August 1784. There the ship exchanged the cargo for tea and other Chinese products and returned to the states, reaching New York on 10 May 1785, the first American ship to dock at a Far Eastern port. The venture's backers made a 20 percent profit on invested capital.

The *Empress of China* supercargo—a passenger aboard who does not participate in the operation of the ship but who looks after the business interests of the venture backers—was Samuel

Shaw. His reports to investors and Congress on this first trans-oceanic crossing to the western rim of the Pacific Basin yielded interesting and useful information for the public and for future trading expeditions. Shaw noted that in the beginning, Chinese officials at Canton had difficulty distinguishing between British and American traders, finally calling the latecomers "the new people."[1]

Shaw explained in his reports that Whampoa was the anchorage for Canton; Canton was the only port Chinese officials permitted foreigners to enter. Downriver on the estuary was Macao, the Portuguese Far East station leased by the Portuguese government and business interests from the Chinese government. Shaw identified British, Dutch, Portuguese, and French traders present at Canton, adding that Prussian and Swedish ships docked there occasionally. Trade was controlled by the Co-Hong (Yeung Hong Sheung), the Canton merchant guild, an organization of thirteen Chinese businessmen who held a monopoly of the trade at Canton. Stringent rules set by government officials forfade alien residence in Canton. Foreign business houses, called factories or *hongs*, were situated outside the city wall. Shaw noted that the most substantial hong in the compound was that of the British East India Company, which monopolized commerce for its countrymen. Chinese officials permitted American traders to build a factory or hong to service their trade. Chinese law prescribed that aliens could reside at their factories only during the winter trading season and required that they return to Macao for the summer.

Shaw added for his American readers that the Chinese regarded Westerners as "troublesome barbarians" or tributary people, uncivilized, not to be considered equals; thus their concentration in a single port in a crowded compound. Aliens were not permitted to enter China beyond the designated area at Canton.

Chinese officials maintained an attitude of superiority over Westerners and insisted on their nation's self-sufficiency, although their merchants did trade some across Asia for bullion and Russian furs. They believed "trade was more important to . . . Europeans than to China." Therefore because "Europeans were the ones seeking to trade, the imperial government and its agents possessed a most effective sanction" to arbitrarily "terminate the trade if their demands were not complied with." In addition the government of China refused to establish diplomatic relations with other governments on the "Western pattern."[2]

Shaw observed that ships approached Canton by stopping first at Macao, on the estuary below the trade center. There the ship captain was required to hire a Chinese pilot for the passage upriver to the anchorage at Whampoa, situated about fourteen miles below Canton. In addition the trader was required to engage an interpreter, who according to Shaw spoke only broken or "pidgin" English. Aliens were expected to pay bribes and all manner of special assessments to "port people," one of the principal ones being the *hoppo* or superintendent of commerce, a Mandarin, who expected the grandest present of all.

The return of the *Empress of China* and Shaw's reports generated wide interest in the Orient, and after 1785 the number of American ships dispatched to western margins of the Pacific Basin increased each year. When Robert Gray, en route to circumnavigating the earth, arrived in Canton in 1789, he counted seventy alien trader ships in the Whampoa anchorage, fourteen of them American. These early China trading ventures are reported to have saved Robert Morris and other American financiers from bankruptcy for a time.

When Shaw returned to China in 1786 aboard the *Hope,* he accomplished several important things for America-China commerce. These included erecting the first American commercial house at Canton and establishing the first American consulate in the Pacific Basin. The Congress of the Confederation had commissioned Shaw as American consul, with the stipulation that he was to serve without pay or fees.

Shaw also helped reduce the problem of limited exchange goods facing Americans trading at Canton. Chinese officials' unyielding position of self-sufficiency and scorn, even contempt, for the products of aliens attempting to traffic for oriental goods limited the opportunity for commercial success at Canton. American traders were at a particular disadvantage. Their home market desired the products of China, especially tea, as well as silk, fine carvings and figures, porcelains, and lacquerware. To pay for these was the problem. The American nation was rich in raw materials and foodstuffs, but poor in specie, which the Chinese preferred from aliens in payment for their goods. American traders found only a limited market at Canton for North American ginseng, because Chinese physicians favored this herb grown in north China and Korea. Chinese merchants expected gold and silver in coin or bar to address the balance of trade. This was a problem for all traders at Canton whose nationals, like Americans, had become committed consumers of tea, silks, and other exotic products from this portion of the Pacific Basin. And they expected their traders to supply these products. This drain of specie from the West to China was not reversed until the late 1820s, when traders found the enlarging Chinese appetite for opium exceeded their lust for specie. British East India Company agents during the 1790s had already begun importing small quantities of opium from India into Canton.

Resourceful American traders found ways at least to diminish the specie drain to the Orient. Shaw, a shrewd businessman, demonstrated one way to accomplish this. En route to China on the *Hope* in 1786, he stopped at Batavia and received permission from the Dutch governor general to exchange his cargo for items more receptive at Canton. This became a regular practice, which Shaw called "coasting." American vessels laden with domestic raw materials and foodstuffs stopped at island ports on the western rim of the Pacific Basin to exchange lumber, furs, hides, grain, iron, and simple manufactures for spices, textiles, and other goods more attractive to Chinese merchants.

A productive coasting territory was Australia (New South Wales) at Port Jackson (Sydney). Subjects in the recently established penal colony there were perennially short of tools and provisions. The British East India Company monopoly between the capes worked in a negative way for the "down under" colonies. No other British supplier was permitted in this vast trade arena and, with its other commercial enterprises, the company was unable to supply the needs of Australian colonials. Australian officials, desperate for supplies, permitted Americans to provide them but protested their dependence on the Yankees for "survival." Traders received local products and both specie and British bills for their cargoes, which they in turn carried to China to purchase oriental goods for the American market.

Another way American traders improved their exchange in the China traffic, at least temporarily, and increased their specie supply was serving as carriers for Europe. During the long, destructive wars between France and Great Britain beginning in the mid-1790s, and until federal embargoes and finally United States involvement in the war from 1812 to 1815, American shippers nearly monopolized the carrying trade for European markets, including the transport of tea and other products directly from China to Europe. This service increased the American specie supply, much of it committed to settling accounts with Chinese suppliers of goods for the American market.

For a time the most compelling way Americans addressed the troublesome Chinese "indifference" to trade with aliens, an approach that also reduced considerably the punitive specie drain, was drawing on those rich Pacific Basin resources attractive to Chinese merchants. The most productive of these resources was the nonpareil sea-otter pelt, yield of the so-called Northwest Coast fur trade. The sea otter, *Enhydra lutris,* yielded a prime skin (the "cutsark"), when stretched for drying measuring about five feet long and twenty-four to thirty inches wide, covered with many very fine hairs, about three-fourths of an inch long, having a jet black, glossy surface, and exhibiting a silver color when blown upon. William Sturgis, an old Northwest Coast fur man from Boston, commented that "excepting for a beautiful woman," he regarded sea-otter pelts "as among the most attractive natural objects that can be placed before him." This pelagic pelt traffic was similar to the land-based fur trade and was no less strategic than its continental counterpart in discovering new territories, calling public attention to them, establishing a vital American presence therein, and engaging the national interest as preliminaries to economic imperialism and the fur territories' possible ultimate absorption under the American aegis.[3]

In addition to searching for new products to trade in China, American frontiersmen casting over the broad ocean expanse occasionally discovered new lands. Yankee trader ships, after breaching the dreaded Cape Horn portal, often set an angular course toward Hawai'i before proceeding to the Northwest Coast, a path that led through the Marquesas. Most of the islands in this archipelago had been discovered and were marked on mariner maps and charts, but American navigators found several unknown islands on this course. Joseph Ingraham, first mate on the *Columbia* during its initial voyage to the Northwest Coast, later captain of the brigantine *Hope* on a Pacific trading venture, while negotiating the Marquesas in early 1792 came upon seven islands not shown on Spanish and British maps, which he claimed for the United States. He named them Washington, Adams, Federal, Lincoln (for a New England politician), Knox, Franklin, and Hancock. Josiah Roberts on the *Jefferson,* navigating on a similar track to the Sandwich Islands during 1792, coasted the Marquesas and found four unidentified islands he named Massachusetts, Resolution, Adams, and Jefferson. Then in 1798 Edmund Fanning on the *Betsey,* sailing on a course from the Chilean coast (where he took on a cargo of fur-seal skins for Canton), with a stop in the Marquesas for wood, water, and food stores, found near the equator two unidentified islands, which he named Fanning and Washington.

An epochal discovery laden with portent for American territorial interest in the continental Northwest and the eastern rim of the Pacific Basin was made by Robert Gray during his second stint on the Northwest Coast. During 1792 while coasting the *Columbia* in the shoal-ridden waters below Vancouver Island, he found and entered a broad estuary and traded with native hunters to a point twenty miles upstream. Gray named this mighty river Columbia. The Spaniard Bruno de Hezeta had found its mouth earlier, but Gray was the first to make a recorded entry over its dangerous bar. Already this outstanding American navigator had joined that select coterie of mariners that included Magellan and Drake.

American ship captains ranging over the Pacific Basin also contacted points of future economic, diplomatic, and even military consequence. Regularly Yankee captains called at Valparaíso and other South American Pacific ports. The first American vessel to anchor in Spanish California waters was the *Otter* of Boston, captained by Ebenezer Dorr, which entered Monterey harbor in 1796 for provisions. And John Kendrick, Gray's trading mate on the Northwest Coast, did some wandering over the Pacific with the *Lady Washington*. During 1792 he approached the southern shore 301of the Japanese home island of Honshu and anchored there for several weeks, attempting to open the closed kingdom to American commerce, a feat not accomplished for another sixty-two years.

By the close of their pioneer period in the Pacific Basin, American maritime frontiersmen, like their continental counterparts in confronting the North American heartland, were becoming adjusted to the grandeur, expanse, challenge, and prospects of their awesome milieu. They had increased in numbers and activity in such a startlingly short time, that they dominated the fur trade on the Pacific Basin's eastern margins and were well established in the rich oriental commerce on its western margins. In 1800 over one hundred American ships cleared Canton, and in volume of trade Yankees ranked second only to the British. Certainly their ever-increasing peregrinations over its waters were acquainting Americans with the basin's vast aquatic interstice. And already these maritime pioneers were conceiving grandiose dreams of permanent settlements in the basin, all of this a supportive and productive setting for launching those ad hoc expansion entities (maritime fur frontier, maritime trader frontier, missionary frontier, agrarian frontier, and military frontier) that in less than a century would combine to integrate vast portions of the Pacific Basin under American dominion and exert a pervasive influence over that portion of the water hemisphere outside direct American hegemony.

CHAPTER SEVEN

The Maritime Fur Frontier

Foundations for twentieth-century Anglo-American supremacy in the Pacific Basin were established by the fur men. They were the first from the United States to exploit its natural bounty, they seeded the essential American presence, and their economic success attracted collateral frontier groups. Subsequent collective appeals from these vanguards of American imperialism to their home government for support and protection activated reluctant nationalizing currents that eventually led to annexation of much of the eastern margins of the Pacific Basin and diplomatic-economic-military domination over much of the remainder. The fact that California, Oregon, Washington, Hawai'i, and Alaska are states in the American Union is compelling evidence of the certain work of the fur frontier and other Americanizing entities that shortly became implanted in the Pacific Basin.

The natural bounty sought by the Americans was sea-otter pelts, seal skins, and furs and hides from mainland-dwelling animals. The sea otter, at this time the most esteemed quarry of the Pacific Basin wilds, was distributed over a range extending from the Aleutians across the North Pacific and down the North American littoral to Lower California. Besides the large size, incomparable beauty, and utility of sea-otter pelts, there was the added advantage of the cool temperature of the Japan Current that bathed the sea-otter habitat and made shedding in summer unnecessary; the pelts remained in prime condition year-round. Fur seals were distributed throughout the Pacific Basin's eastern rim from Antarctica to the lower Arctic and on islands adjacent to the South American and North American coasts. Furs from mainland-dwelling creatures became important in the last stages of the Pacific

Basin fur frontier, after 1820, as intensive hunting drastically reduced the sea-otter population.

American businessmen became interested in the Northwest Coast fur trade as an adjunct of the China trade, since furs would reduce the domestic specie drain for oriental goods and products. John Ledyard had explained in his *Journal* how one might fuse the two enterprises. Several American financiers had experience in backing frontier ventures in the continental West, including the fur trade. The first maritime traders to the Northwest Coast were supported by a group of businessmen led by Joseph Barrell, a Boston merchant. He and five associates fitted the *Columbia* and *Lady Washington* for the initial venture in the Pacific Basin. They placed John Kendrick in command of both the *Columbia* and the expedition and named Robert Gray captain of the *Lady Washington*. Both were seasoned New England mariners; each had commanded a privateer during the War of Independence.[1]

The expedition departed Boston in 1787 and proceeded to the Pacific by way of Cape Horn. Once on the trading grounds, Gray took command of the *Columbia* and Kendrick moved to the *Lady Washington*. Centering their trade at Nootka Sound, crewmen from both ships trafficked on the beaches with Indian hunters, exchanging cloth, abalone shell, axes, sheets of copper, bars of iron, buttons, beads, mirrors, guns, knives, powder, shot, chisels, pots, and pans for sea-otter pelts.

In 1789 Gray with a cargo of furs aboard the *Columbia* sailed for Canton. He stopped at the Sandwich Islands to refresh the crew and replenish stocks of food, water, and wood. He purchased 150 live hogs, which crewmen penned on the deck; hogsheads (barrels) of cured pork; and other foodstuffs. Proceeding to Canton, which required a nine-week sail, he exchanged the fur cargo for tea and other oriental products, then set a course for Boston via the Indian Ocean and Cape of Good Hope. The *Columbia* docked in home port during early August 1790. Gray brought with him a native of the Sandwich Islands who, arrayed in feather cloak and "gorgeous" feather helmet shaped like that of a Roman soldier, attracted large crowds in Boston. In 1791 Gray sailed for the Northwest Coast to rejoin Kendrick.

Hard on the heels of Robert Gray and William Kendrick, the

pioneer fur men from the United States in the Pacific Basin, came other Americans. In the beginning they were intruders on territory claimed by other nations. Spain by authority of late fifteenth-century papal dispensation and treaty, claimed all of the Pacific Basin's eastern waters and rimland. Soon after 1700 agents of Imperial Russia challenged this claim by coursing from bases in Siberia over the Aleutians with fur-trading settlements. A territorial interstice commonly called the Northwest Coast, extending roughly from southern Russian America to just above San Francisco, the northernmost Spanish settlement on the Pacific, in a sense had been opened to all nations by the so-called Nootka Sound Convention of 1790, which grew out of a British challenge to Spanish claims of hegemony over this portion of the Pacific Basin. Eventually Americans ranged from the Aleutians to Lower California in search of sea-otter pelts, but during the formative years of their fur frontier, their exploitive attention centered on the Northwest Coast.

Initially American frontiersmen were contested in this new fur territory by Spanish, British, French, and Russian interests. British and French activity in the North Pacific declined drastically after 1800, due to their extended involvement in the continental wars of the Napoleonic Era. British fur men continued intermittently to traffic on the Northwest Coast until around 1815, when they became the most formidable competition for the Americans. However, during the formative years of the fur trade there, the serious challenges to Americans came from Russians and Spaniards.

Following a destructive sweep across the Aleutian Island chain, which annihilated the sea otter there and nearly exterminated the resident Aleuts, Russian promyshlenniki moved eastward onto islands off the mainland coast. The first permanent Russian settlement in North America was established in 1784 on the island of Kodiak by Grigorii Shelikhov and a party of traders. Shelikhov's manager at Kodiak was Aleksandr Baranov. Baranov established a technique of fur gathering, whereby each promyshlennik brought under his control a band of Aleut hunters. Russian fur men, each with his retinue of Aleut hunters, were carried in small ships from Kodiak into the coastal bays and inlets; the Aleuts were set ashore to collect furs and picked up when their quotas had been met.

In 1799 the Russian imperial government chartered the Russian-American Company and granted it a monopoly over the trade in the colony. Baranov was appointed resident manager. Saturation hunting soon obliterated the sea otter and other fur-bearing animals on Kodiak and adjacent islands, forcing Baranov to seek new fur territory. Sitka became the favored station in the expanding string of Russian settlements.

Baranov imported agricultural workers, seeds, livestock, and implements from Russia and attempted to develop an agricultural colony at Sitka. The Russian-American Company was perennially short of food, and Baranov hoped to produce sufficient grain and beef to sustain the scattered settlements. The agricultural colony failed, mostly because of unfavorable soil and climate conditions. In 1802 Tlingit Indians massacred Russians and Aleuts at Sitka. With the help of naval vessels, Baranov recaptured Sitka and dispersed the Tlingits in 1804. He then moved his headquarters from Kodiak to Sitka.

The continuing problem of providing food for the fur hunters led Baranov to seek grain and other essentials from the Spanish settlements in California, from Hawai'i, from intruding Yankees, and eventually to extend Russian settlements down the Pacific coast threateningly close to San Francisco. This move particularly intensified the Spanish–British–American–Russian contest for fur territory on the Pacific Basin's eastern rim.

One motive for intensifying Spanish coastal reconnaissance and patrol activity north of San Francisco, as the pace of foreign trespass increased in the North Pacific during the middle and late eighteenth century, was to seek out sea-otter hunting grounds and, where possible, eject intruders poaching on territory claimed by Spain. The Nootka Sound Spanish-British confrontation, the strong British response that nearly brought on a global conflict, and the ultimate convention settlement, occurred in no small measure because Nootka Sound, the focus of the Northwest Coast, was the Pacific Basin rimland's richest sea-otter hunting ground.

The Spanish sea-otter pelt industry centered in California coastal waters, the pelagic mammals hunted largely by mission Indians. Soldiers, settlers, and padres at the missions were permitted to deal with the Indians, as individuals or trading companies, for the pelts.

However, Franciscan fathers dominated the annual pelt harvest, directing their mission charges on the hunts. Between 1786 and 1790 nearly ten thousand sea-otter skins, with a value of $3,120,000, were collected from California hunting grounds.[2]

By virtue of Spain's exclusionist mercantilist system, the Philippine Company maintained a "tenacious hold" on Asian commerce and monopolized the selling of oriental goods in America. Trading companies could obtain free hunting privileges in California for taking sea-otter pelts or trading with Indian hunters for them, but they were prohibited from participating in the exchange for oriental goods and their subsequent sale, which reduced the value of their enterprise. Thus the Philippine Company franchise permitted only limited involvement in this potentially rich fur traffic; it throttled initiative and had the effect of preventing Spaniards from achieving their commercial potential. And as a result the sea-otter population in California coastal waters was never seriously diminished by local hunters, making it an attractive poaching territory for daring American fur men.

While the number of Britons on the Northwest Coast declined drastically after 1800, a few remained to compete with the Americans for the region's fur riches. However, they like the Russians and Spaniards suffered from the strictures of royal franchise. To engage in the Pacific Basin fur trade, a British subject was required to obtain a license from the British South Seas Company, which held a monopoly over commerce in the eastern Pacific Basin, and a license from the British East India Company which held a monopoly over commerce in the western Pacific Basin, which included the Canton market. Several Britons evaded these bothersome and expensive stipulations by masquerading their ships with altered registry. One changed the names of his two ships on the trade course between Canton and the Northwest Coast to *Felice* and *Iphigenia,* and each flew the Portuguese flag. The owner of the *Loudoun* placed it under Austrian registry, with the name *Imperial Eagle.* And the owner of the *Mercury* shifted his vessel to Swedish registry with the name *Gustavus III.*

American fur men experienced regular difficulty transacting their business on the Northwest Coast because of competition from Spaniards and Russians, in part because of the advantage provided by their land-based settlements relatively close to the sea-otter hunting grounds. And Britons were a continuing concern because of their sustained if diminished tenacity in maintaining some level of participation in the fur trade there and the ever-present threat of their return to the Northwest Coast in strength, which eventually materialized. But Americans also benefited from their competitors' monopolistic mercantile systems, which suffocated individual initiative. Yankee frontiersmen in the Pacific Basin functioned as individual entrepreneurs or as agents of small, independent companies, nourished by eastern capital, and in which they maintained an owner's share in the risk and the profit.

Several hundred Americans followed Gray and Kendrick to the Northwest Coast, where they formed the fur frontier that functioned there from 1800 to about 1840. Their enterprise yielded private and public benefits, the prospects from which had been dramatically demonstrated during the pioneer period (1787–1800) of Yankee activity in the Pacific Basin. The maritime fur industry provided bonanza profits for many of the participants. It yielded for specie-scarce Americans one of the very few products at the time esteemed by Chinese merchants at the Canton marketplace. And the promise of adventure and personal fortune attracted national attention to the Pacific Basin, seeded an American presence that drew increasing numbers of frontiersmen from the United States, flared the Americanizing process over this water hemisphere, and established the basis for the nation's territorial claims to portions of it, including the strategic Northwest Coast.

Of the hundreds of Americans drawn to the Pacific Basin's maritime fur trade, those who loomed most prominent were William Sturgis; Jonathan, Nathan, and Abiel Winship; Benjamin P. Homer; Richard Cleveland; Joseph O'Cain; and William Shaler. Just as Jedediah Smith, Joseph Reddleford Walker, George Yount, and other continental-based fur men opened paths in the wilderness that became concourses for expansive Americans rushing westward in their wake, even in some cases providing helpful maps and journals, maritime fur men mapped and charted the oceanic wilderness and marked the sailing courses for those who would follow them. Several were so smitten by the Pacific Basin's promise for personal and civic success that they wrote and published appealing promotional accounts illuminating the resources and prospects for consummation of the American Nation's mission. These include Shaler's *Journal of a Voyage from China to the Northwestern Coast of North America Made in 1804* and Cleveland's *Narrative of Voyages and Commercial Enterprises.*[3]

While maritime fur men performed many of the same functions as the continental-based fur men, they differed in some important respects. One of the most conspicuous was that of failing to form a subculture analogous to the wilderness "mountain man" that emerged among their land-based counterparts. To account for this, one must regard comparative time spent in place and profession for the two groups. Land-based fur men often remained for a lifetime in a broad fur territory as a hunter-trader, while maritime fur men on the average made only three to five sorties to the Northwest Coast for cargoes of pelts for the Canton market. Each then returned to his home port, for the most part in New England, with a grubstake to establish a business; or he turned to exploiting other resources of the rich Pacific Basin bounty.

Pacific Basin fur men followed the modus operandi established by Gray, Kendrick, and other Northwest Coast pioneers. They continued to rely on the tested and proven 200–250-ton brig-type vessels, the durable craft capable of challenging turbulent North Pacific waters and manned with a crew of twenty to twenty-five seamen who, when in fur territory, also served as hunters and traders for pelts. On the voyage out, the holds were laden with trade goods calculated to please Native American hunters. Experience had demonstrated the importance of clearing home port, generally Boston, in autumn to take advantage of the quieter waters of Antarctic summer. Negotiating the treacherous antipodes passages into the Pacific, the captain would set a northwesterly course to the Sandwich Islands for refurbishing his ship, reprovisioning the larder, and resting the wearied crew before proceeding to the Northwest Coast.

Nootka Sound on Vancouver Island continued to be the favorite anchorage for Yankee maritime fur men. There they might secure the ship in a protected bay and on the beaches construct small sailing craft, shallops, carried out in frame form on the deck of the supply ship. Manned by ship's crewmen, these coasted the beaches and inlets, the men hunting sea otters and trading with Indian hunters for their catch. To fill the supply ship hold with three thousand pelts, at the time regarded as essential for a paying voyage to the Canton market, they then ventured out of the sound, casting north toward Russian America and south toward Spanish California, collecting sea-otter pelts from Indian hunters or themselves hunting for them. It has been estimated that "Hardly is there a point on the coast from 30° to 60° which is not visited" by the Yankee fur men. To accumulate the three-thousand-pelt quota, a captain and crew generally were out of home port for from two to three years.[4]

Maritime fur men found it economical of effort and time, whenever possible, to depend on Indian hunters for pelts. Curing the furs to withstand the long period of storage and passage to the Canton market, maintained in prime condition, required special processing care, at which Northwest Coast Indians were also expert.

Traders included iron, beads, glass items, copper, coarse woolen goods, axes, knives, nails, and firearms and ammunition in their ships' stores for trafficking with Native American hunters for sea-otter pelts, but they found it to be "more of a game of chance, so fickle and whimsical were the native traders, so peculiar and varying their ideas of value." In the early years, goods valued at from two to fifty cents each fetched an otter skin. One fur man received sixty "fine skins" for a handful of spike nails, and there is an account of a Yankee exchanging a small chisel for two hundred skins on the Queen Charlotte Island beach. Throughout the years of the sea-otter-pelt industry, iron in all forms (chisels, weapons, axes, hatchets, and nails) was the staple commodity, with other trade items in descending order of esteem, "depending in good measure on fancy and caprice."[5]

Tlingits, the Kolosh people residing on the southeastern littoral, the unremitting enemy of the Russians, welcomed American fur men, but the Yankees found them to be the shrewdest of all traders on the Northwest Coast. To obtain their furs, Americans often had to offer for a single pelt six yards of heavy woolen cloth, a pail, a cup, a mirror, knives, scissors, and two handfuls of beads; or three or four pounds of gunpowder and six to eight pounds of lead; or a gun with ten cartridges, powder, and an ax. By the late 1820s, Americans had to offer five to six large blankets for a sea-otter skin. Yankees were favorites of the Tlingits, not only because they supplied firearms (even a small cannon), but also because they taught the Kolosh how to use the weapons, which they regularly turned on their enemy, the Russians.

Risks for Yankee adventurers in the Northwest Coast commerce were great, but the returns on investments often were prodigious; it was not unusual for a two-year venture in the eastern Pacific Basin to yield a profit of $200,000 in the Canton market. Prices at Canton varied between 1800 and 1840 from $15 to $150 per pelt, depending on supply and quality, the range generally $50 to $80 per pelt. William Sturgis, a maritime fur man from Boston, reported a return of $284,000 on an investment of $50,000 from a single venture to the Northwest Coast. Over a hundred American fur vessels were involved in the Northwest Coast commerce by 1818. Most of the ships were from Boston, although occasionally one turned up from New York, Philadelphia, Providence, Bristol, or Salem. The year 1811 was rated a "good year" for the fur men, when fifteen American ships carried eighteen thousand sea-otter pelts, valued at over half a million dollars, to Canton.[6]

Shipwreck in angry, storm-lashed waters; crippling injury from hazardous duty; and illness, even death, from disease were constant threats to the well-being of maritime fur men working the Northwest Coast. But no danger matched the ever-present peril of reprisal attack by local natives. It was claimed that seldom "did an American ship complete a voyage through the Pacific without the loss of some of her men, by the treachery or the ferocity of the natives . . . and several instances have occurred of the seizure of such vessels, and the massacre of their whole crews. . . . It may be truly said that one party had often to suffer for wrongs inflicted by another; and on both sides were instances of unprovoked outrage."[7]

British-Canadian fur men blamed the reckless, short-sighted, at times even rapacious, practices of Yankees in their dealings with Native Americans for precipitating Indian retaliation. Alexander Mackenzie, a Northwest Fur Company official, explained that the Pacific fur trade "is at present left to American adventurers, who without regularity or capital, or the desire of conciliating future confidence, look altogether to the interest of the moment. They therefore collect all the skins they can procure, and in any manner that suits tham, and having exchanged them at Canton for the produce of China, return to their own country." He and other British-Canadian fur men accused the Yankees of "practicing every species of fraud and violence in their dealings with the nations of the coasts."[8]

Two retaliatory incidents suffice to illustrate the propensity of some American fur men of treachery and the cruelty of blind surrogate vengeance by exploited Native Americans. During 1802 the *Boston* rode at anchor in Nootka Sound, near the village of chief Maquinna, as the captain and crew prepared to trade for sea-otter pelts. Maquinna and his people had suffered repeated indignities, even death, at the hands of Yankee fur men. On one occasion crewmen raided his household while he was absent, took his furs, and abused his women. Traders had fired on canoes and killed twenty of his people. On another trading occasion, Maquinna received a faulty firearm from the ship's captain in a fur exchange. The tribal leader protested, and the captain cursed him. Maquinna understood some English, particularly profanity. His rage mounted but he held his peace and plotted vengeance. And the opportunity presented itself when the *Boston* anchored near his village. Maquinna and a party of warriors were permitted aboard to trade their sea-otter pelts. At his signal the Indians drew secreted knives and hatchets from the bundles of furs, turned on the crew, and killed all but two. They beached the *Boston*, carried off the cargo and fittings, then burned the vessel.

In 1811 the *Tonquin* and crew suffered a similar fate, when Indian hunters were permitted aboard to trade their sea-otter pelts. Eventually it was learned that the unprovoked attack on the *Tonquin* was due to an earlier incident involving the captain and crew of the *Mercury*. During 1810 the ship's captain engaged twelve Nootka Sound Indians to join in a sea-otter hunt along the California coast. When the mission was completed, rather than return the Indians to their village as he had promised, the captain abandoned them on an island off the California coast. When the survivors made it back to their home village, the community was outraged by their report, and they fell upon the first vessel to enter their waters—the *Tonquin*—seizing the ship and killing the crew.

The Sandwich Islands, situated about two thousand miles west of the Pacific Basin's eastern rim, came to play a vital support role in the Northwest Coast fur trade. This archipelago also became a strategic link with the Pacific Basin's western rim in the rich oriental trade. During their pioneer period in the Pacific Basin, Americans competed with British, French, and Russian representatives for resources, position, and influence there and seeded an ever enlarging presence, which eventually became a matter of serious national interest. Significantly it was the maritime-based fur-trade frontier that initiated the Americanization process in the Sandwich Islands.

The utility of this archipelago in the pelt trade was demonstrated in 1785, when two British traders, Nathaniel Portlock and George Dixon, spent twenty days refitting their ships in the languid island bays before proceeding to the Northwest Coast. They were in the islands while La Pérouse explored Maui. By 1787 six ships rested in Hawaiian waters, all connected with the Northwest Coast fur trade. Robert Gray was the first American to stop there, in 1789, to restore his crew and food stores en route to the Canton market with a cargo of sea-otter pelts.

Reception of haoles (outsiders) by the natives was uncertain and varied for some time. Hawaiians ambushed Captain James Cook and several crewmen on the beach at Kealakekua Bay; Cook was slain in the attack. And natives annihilated everyone aboard the *Fair American* while it was anchored near Kawaihae. John Young, a crewman from this ill-fated vessel, was ashore at the time and escaped the fate of his shipmates. During the 1790s three circumstances improved the reception of haoles by native Hawaiians: the visit of Captain George Vancouver to the archipelago and his admonitions to island chiefs concerning the treatment of visitors; the expanding influence of Kamehameha, ambitious chief of the island of Hawai'i and increasingly pro-Western in attitude; and the presence and influence of Young and another seaman who had retired to the beach, Isaac Davis. Both were British subjects, had adopted the native life-style, married Hawaiian women, and had advanced in rank and power to equal many of the island chiefs. Their influence on Hawaiian leaders did much to reduce threats to visiting ships and crews.[9]

The haole population grew. Ship captains customarily left a portion of their crews in the islands to gather native products, while they proceeded to the Northwest Coast to trade for furs. By 1794 the island haole community numbered over a dozen and included English, Americans, Irish, Portuguese, Genoese, and Chinese.

Kamehameha observed that he could use the skills of foreigners, particularly artisans, to build his power. He intended to conquer and integrate the islands of the archipelago into a single kingdom, a feat he accomplished in 1795. Ruling as Kamehameha I, he welcomed haoles, assuring them protection. The new king decreed the repair of ships at the enlarging yards at Honolulu (on Oʻahu) and Kealakekua (on Hawaiʻi) and their provisioning a monopoly, the income of which enhanced the royal treasury. Thus soon after 1800, the Kingdom of Hawaiʻi "formed the hub" of Pacific Basin maritime traffic, providing a haven for maritime fur men and linking the Northwest Coast and Russian America with the Canton market.[10]

Increasingly American fur men wintered in the delightfully mild archipelago, repairing their battered ships, resting their crews, curing furs and preserving them from vermin, and reprovisioning for a fresh sortie to the Northwest Coast or the passage to Canton. Island springs provided fresh water, the forests wood for ships' galleys, the beaches salt for seasoning rations and preserving freshly slaughtered beef and pork; island farms yielded fruits, yams, breadfruit, taro, and sugarcane. Native sennit, made from coconut husks, supplied a strong line for replacing frayed rigging and cables. However, the most valued resource of the Hawaiian kingdom were the kānaka. Wise in the ways of the sea, these Polynesian seamen made excellent crewmen. Captain Jonathon Thorn of the ill-fated *Tonquin,* on his course toward the Northwest Coast, stopped in the Hawaiian Islands for provisions and left ten "indifferent sailors" there, replacing them with sixteen kānaka. Thorn concluded a contract with Kamehameha I to pay each Polynesian crewmember ten dollars per month and to supply him a suit of clothing each year. These fresh crewmen were placed under the charge of an elder Polynesian, his pay to be fifteen dollars per month.[11]

The intensive demand American fur men placed on native hunters and their own hunter-crewmen for more and more pelts led to virtual extermination of sea otters in that portion of the Northwest Coast adjacent to Nootka Sound, forcing the Yankees to range over a larger territory on the Pacific Basin's eastern rim. This extended quest for furs brought them to Spanish California and Russian America. For several years after 1800, American maritime fur men had occasionally tested the certitude of Spain's mercantilist system, which excluded aliens from commercial contact with the colonies. Coasting the California littoral, they noted Indian hunters taking sea-otter pelts, most of them directed by padres at the mission settlements from San Francisco to Lower California, and they found the Franciscans generally willing to trade the pelts for textiles and metal goods they carried aboard. However, they frequently came under the surveillance of Spanish officials, which had the effect of discouraging commercial contact. Therefore Yankee fur men working California waters for clandestine trade sources, when virtually "caught in the act" by vigilant royal officials, resorted to dissimulation by claiming to be short of water, wood, and provisions and appealed for permission to enter port and resupply.

Spanish officials, generally hospitable, provided the claimed needs, but oftentimes the weight of suspicion was so heavy that they ordered their sergeant's guard to inspect the cargo. More often than not this revealed bales of sea-otter pelts acquired in California waters. Thus matters reached the point where officials would provide food and other needs but took the precaution of placing a guard detail aboard to watch the crew while in port and ordering the captain to depart as soon as his ship had been provisioned and to touch at no other Spanish port.

Several American fur men, besides misrepresenting their motives for appearing in Spanish territory in the first place, further complicated relations with Spaniards in California by committing ungracious or unfriendly acts. The maritime fur ship *Otter* was reported to have attempted to anchor at Monterey "against the will of the officials"; being rebuffed, as a parting retaliatory insult, her captain discharged several convict stowaways from Botany Bay on the beaches nearby. Even more insulting was the action of the captain of the *Alexander,* who, after being hospitably received at Monterey and supplied with food required for continuing his passage to the Northwest Coast, slipped away without paying for the provisions.[12]

Excursions for sea-otter pelts north of Nootka Sound by Yankee maritime fur men eventually brought them into territory claimed by Imperial Russia. They established contact with the coastal-dwelling, deadly Tlingits (the Kolosh), traditional enemies of the Russians, and by patient bargaining with these singularly shrewd Native Americans obtained high-quality furs, albeit at the highest prices in trade goods paid on the Northwest Coast.

American fur men working North Pacific waters also contacted Russians at Kodiak and Sitka. Finding Aleksandr Baranov, resident manager of the Russian-American Company, perennially short of food to sustain his promyshlenniki-led Aleut hunting brigades, visiting ship captains began to include in their cargoes from home ports grain, flour, sugar, dried and pickled beef and pork, and other foodstuffs, which they traded to Baranov for furs. They also carried beef, pork, fruits, and vegetables from the California mission settlements to the Russians. In addition Yankee captains transported Russian-American Company furs to Canton and sold them in the market there under American auspices for higher prices than Russian traders received at Kyakhta, situated on the Chinese-Siberian border, the only point where Chinese officials permitted Russian products to enter the Celestial Empire.

These two arrangements between Russian officials and Yankee ship captains led to a third, which lasted nearly ten years. American fur men in reconnoitering California waters had noted that even though mission-supported Indian hunters harvested sea-otter pelts each year, they had not appreciably diminished the thickly populated rafts of these marine mammals; the California coast represented perhaps the richest sea-otter hunting grounds remaining on the Pacific Basin's eastern littoral.

Thus beginning in 1803, Boston ship captain Joseph O'Cain proposed to Baranov that he be permitted to use Aleut hunters, rated the best in the Pacific Basin, in California waters in return for a share of the catch. Baranov and O'Cain struck a contract, and later that year the Bostonian sailed south to the sea-otter range near San Diego. His crewmen sent the Aleuts in their highly man-ueverable bidarkas, which had been stacked on the ship's deck in passage, into bays and inlets well screened from Spanish surveil-lance. In six months O'Cain returned to Kodiak with eleven hun-dred furs taken by the Aleut hunters from California coastal waters, which he divided with Baranov. O'Cain also had aboard seven hundred additional pelts he had accumulated from trading with mission padres. This arrangement between American fur men and Russian-American Company officials, Yankees carrying grain and other food to Russian America, trading foodstuffs for pelts, using Aleuts to harvest sea otters along the California coast, and trans-porting Russian furs to Canton, continued until around 1812. The mild climate off the California coast enabled Aleuts to hunt year-round. Several American ship captains followed the pattern es-tablished by O'Cain, and they and their New England financial backers profited handsomely from these surreptitious sorties into California coastal waters. During 1811 alone it was reported that 150 bidarkas, each manned by two Aleuts, skimmed across the waters between Bodega Bay and San Francisco searching out the elusive sea otter.[13]

This initiative to expand the fur frontier along the Pacific Bas-in's eastern littoral brought the Yankee intruders additional profits and extended the life of the industry there, but it also provoked the envy, concern, and eventually response of competing nations. A serious attempt by American Fur Company agents to establish a settlement on the Columbia in 1811 may be regarded as the principal precipitant of a renewal of the international contest for primacy on the Northwest Coast, which rather soon spread into the north-central Pacific and the Kingdom of Hawai'i. John Jacob Astor, head of the New York–based American Fur Company, may be regarded as the original protagonist in this unfolding interna-tinal drama.[14]

Astor became interested in the Northwest Coast fur traffic through his participation in the Canton trade, which he entered around 1800. In the troubled decade of continental and maritime conflicts preceding the War of 1812, Astor maintained a fleet of four ships on the route between New York and Canton, each vessel laden with furs collected from North American interior pelt zones, bales of cotton, cochineal (a red dye), ginseng, and seal skins. In 1800 his ships carried 30,500 seal skins to Canton, in addition to kegs of bullion. One American Fur Company venture to China included 51 kegs of specie, valued at $140,000. It has been calculated that each of Astor's ships returned to home port with oriental cargoes that would yield at least a $200,000 profit. Astor collected in his New York harbor warehouses large quantities of Asiatic textiles, chinaware, nankeens, spices, silk, and taffeta, which he transshipped to markets in France, Germany, Italy, and England when these nations' ports were free of imperial interdict, blockade, and embargo caused by the continental wars.[15]

This China trade exposed Astor to the Northwest Coast fur frontier, and he began to conceive a scheme for integrating it into his commercial empire. At no time did he journey to the Northwest Coast; rather he depended on reports brought back to him by his perceptive sea captains. Increasingly they stopped on the Northwest Coast to trade for sea-otter skins on the passage from New York to Canton, with a rehabilitative stop in Hawai'i. Their trading excursions along the Northwest Coast eventually brought them into contact with Russian-American Company officials. On one North Pacific sortie, American Fur Company ship captain John Ebbets, an experienced China trader, arrived at Sitka just in time to rescue several Russians and Aleuts from Tlingit fury and thus prevented the annihilation of the colony's population. Understandably this action won favor with Baranov. Ebbets and other American Fur Company agents then began to deliver annual shipments of foodstuffs to the ration-short Russians and to transport their furs to the Canton market.

All the while Astor worked on a grand scheme to bring under his control a major portion of the North American fur trade, both continental and oceanic. Following up the advantage of his American Fur Company's strategic relationship with the Russian-American Company, Astor negotiated a commercial pact with Russian officials in Washington by which the American Fur Company and Russian-American Company peremptorily divided the Northwest Coast fur territory. The signatories agreed to ban the sale of firearms and ammunition to natives, except where required for hunting, and that the American Fur Company serve as exclusive carrier of Russian furs to the Canton market and supplier of provisions to the Russian American colony. Each company would cease trading or dealing with outsiders and attempt to exclude independent fur men and agents of other nations from the Northwest Coast fur trade.[16]

The second part of Astor's design for achieving ultimate preeminence in the North American fur trade called for occupation of his assumptively assigned portion of the Northwest Coast. In the North American interior fur trade, Astor found British-Canadian fur-company agents an increasing threat to American Fur Company operations. He saw the rapid thrust of Montreal-based fur men across the continent as only a prelude to their return to the Northwest Coast. And he found that to fill his fur needs for the Canton, European, and domestic markets, he was required to purchase furs at Montreal, at times amounting to three-fourths of his annual market demand. One irony of this was that most of the furs he purchased in the Montreal market were taken by brigades of the royal-chartered Northwest Company and Michillimackinac Company, working on United States territory. This tribute to alien companies led Astor to conceive the plan to attempt to bring "the whole of the United States trading territory under his control, . . . even as far as the Pacific Ocean." He envisaged a line of fur-trading posts positioned from Saint Louis to the Northwest Coast along the Lewis and Clark path to the Pacific. Astor's plan had a nationalistic aspect in that he expected to oust "British influence from the trans-Mississipii area."[17]

During 1810 Astor completed arrangements to effectuate his scheme. The New York legislature granted a charter for the Pacific Fur Company. Two expeditions, one by land from Saint Louis, the other by sea (with trade cargo and the fur brigade aboard to sail from New York to the Columbia and establish the plan's westernmost post, to be named Astoria), were formed. While the overland section collected at Saint Louis, Astor dispatched the *Tonquin*, a 290-ton brig with ten guns, a crew of twenty-one, and thirty-three passengers—the fur brigade, captained by Jonathon Thorn, a United States Navy lieutenant on leave—from New York harbor on 8 September 1810. Following the Cape Horn route, the *Tonquin* arrived in Hawai'i on 10 February 1811, reprovisioned, and departed on 1 March for the Northwest Coast, reaching the mouth of the Columbia three weeks later. The fur-brigade workers selected a site for Astoria on the south bank of the river on Young Bay, near the site of Old Fort Clatsop. They constructed cabins, a large warehouse, and small shipyard for constructing coasting schooners, then set to work collecting furs from local native hunters.[18] Thorn sailed into Nootka Sound, anchored, and permitted Indian hunters to board with their furs. The natives turned on the crew, captured the ship, burned it, and massacred the ship's company.[19]

The War of 1812 intruded to destroy Astor's dream of a continental–Northwest Coast fur-trade empire. Most of the supply ships he sent to succor the Pacific Company brigade at Astoria were wrecked in turbulent seas or anchored in neutral ports to avoid capture and prize confiscation by British privateers and naval marauders working the Pacific. British naval supremacy during the conflict (1812–15) forced a suspension of virtually all activity on the Northwest Coast by Americans on their fur frontier. Many Yankee adventurers retired to Hawai'i or Canton for the duration.

The war stirred both British and Russian fur interests to expansive activity, the British sustained by naval power, the Russians driven by the inability of American ship captains to meet their needs, particularly the delivery of food for the Russian America colony and the transport of Russian furs to Canton.

Astor's fear of a British-Canadian fur-industry sweep across the continent to the Pacific was confirmed in 1811, when a flotilla of Northwest Company agents descended the Columbia to Astoria; thereafter frequent contact and near collision occurred between the parties contesting for the Northwest Coast fur bounty. Sustained by well-managed support stations in the Columbia outback, the intruder population increased in the succeeding months.[20]

During 1813 the Northwest Company agent received word of formal hostilities between Great Britain and the United States and informed the Astorians. With no support and the threat of military conquest by enemy naval forces, Astorian managers sold the post to Northwest Company agents for $80,500. Later that year the twenty-six-gun warsloop *Raccoon,* commanded by Captain William Black, entered the Columbia. On 12 December Black took formal possession of Astoria, raised the British flag, and renamed it Fort George.[21]

American fur men returned to the Northwest Coast after the war, to find the British had arrived in strength, were entrenched at Fort George, and were now able to compete favorably through the advantage of their land-based fur network over the Yankee's tenuous and far more extended ship-sustained fur frontier. Astor attempted to recover Astoria, but to no avail. And with the demise of his Pacific Fur Company, there also passed the principal American attempt to establish a strangling monopoly of the fur trade in the Pacific Basin similar to those maintained by the Russian-American Company and the British South Seas Company–British East India Company. Had Astor's plan succeeded, it would have severely impaired trade access for free American traders. But on their return, the Yankees found the enlarging and ever-strengthening British-Canadian fur enterprise on the Northwest Coast a competitive force of unanticipated magnitude.

The Northwest Company during the 1790s supported continental explorations by its agents for new pelt zones. First Alexander Mackenzie led an expedition across the Canadian west in 1793 to the Pacific. Others followed his route, and the Northwest Company followed up these reconnaissances by establishing a line of support stations and recruiting skilled Iroquois and Abenaki hunters from eastern Canada for service in the far-western fur brigades. Once on the Pacific coast, the Northwest Company imported kānaka to man their small coastal vessels, which ranged over an ever-widening territory along the Northwest Coast from the Columbia to the Bering Sea. British-Canadian fur men were just as pleased with the Polynesians' versatile performance as the Americans were, finding that they were "honest and trustworthy and willingly perform as much duty as lies in their power." Besides being singular seamen, they were useful as divers. One report explained "little of our effects are lost beyond recovery which accident now and then consigns to the bottom of the water in our perilous navigations; and it is next to impossible for a person to get drowned if one or more of them are at hand; in that element, they are as active and expert as the reverse on dry land, and on every occasion they testify a fidelity and zeal for their master's welfare and service."[22]

While the enlarging British-Canadian fur enterprise on the Northwest Coast each year after 1815 became more threatening to American preeminence there, Northwest Company officials for some time found themselves, much like Russian-American Company fur men, dependent on Yankee sea captains for transport of their annual pelt catch either to Canton or London, because of the suffocating monopoly of the South Seas–East India Company monopoly. For several years Americans engaged in the Northwest Coast fur trade transported supplies to British-Canadian stations on the Northwest Coast from London and carried their furs to Canton, consigned to American trading companies there; proceeds from these sales the Yankees then took to London for deposit with Northwest Company officials and for cargoes of supplies for British Pacific posts.

Competition on the Northwest Coast intensified in 1821, when the Northwest Company and Hudson's Bay Company merged. The consolidated Hudson's Bay Company functioned from Fort Vancouver, situated on the Columbia near the mouth of the Willamette River. Fur brigades from this post ranged both into the interior and along the Northwest Coast, crowding both Yankee maritime and continent-based fur men.[23]

Russian-American Company officials also attempted to become more competitive with the enlarging American fur establishment in the North Pacific. They sought to reduce their dependence on Yankee maritime fur men for shipping and provisions. And they contemplated extending their fur range into the rich Northwest Coast preserve. Their particular objective was to occupy Nootka Sound, but the prospect of stiff native resistance there discouraged fulfillment of the plan. Count N. P. Rezanov, a court inspector of the Russian America colony, visited San Francisco in 1805–6 to purchase provisions for the Russian settlers. Impressed by the enormous tract of unoccupied, potentially productive land north of San Francisco, blessed with a mile climate, Rezanov concluded that a colony there would enhance Russian interests. His goal was to control the Pacific littoral from Russian America to the Gulf of California and "drive away the Bostonians from this trade forever." He concluded that "From the Columbia we could gradually advance toward the south to the port of San Francisco, which forms the boundary line of California . . . and in the course of ten years we should become strong enough . . . to include the coast of California in the Russian possessions."[24]

Shortly thereafter Spain, beset by domestic chaos and colonial insurgency, became impotent as an overseas empire proprietor. Russian officials during 1812 took advantage of this Iberian prostration by consummating Rezanov's plan for the California colony. That year ninety-five Russians and eighty Aleuts landed on the New Albion shore near Bodega Bay and began construction of Fort Ross, which became the principal Russian settlement on the lower Pacific coast. Russia's California pioneers increased to five hundred; their principal export to the northern warehouses were grain, dairy products (butter and cheese), beef, pork, and furs. Aleut colonists with promyshlenniki foremen hunted sea otters and seals on the northern California littoral, while local Pomo Indian conscripts performed the fieldwork on the Fort Ross colony farms.[25]

Russian officials also showed strong interest in the Hawaiian Islands, both as a source of provisions for sustaining the Russian America colony and as a strategic oceanic outpost. Naval officers who commanded several early nineteenth-century Pacific expeditions reconnoitering the archipelago's waters strongly urged annexation of the islands. These included the Krusenstern exploration of 1803–6 and the Hagemeister expedition of 1806–9.[26]

Baranov was aware of the value of the Hawaiian Islands to Russia's Pacific Basin establishment. Generally lacking seaworthy shipping before 1815, he largely depended on American maritime fur men for provisions and the carriage of company furs to Canton. On those rare occasions in the pre-1815 era when he had access to a seaworthy Russian ship, he often dispatched it to the archipelago for a cargo of foodstuffs.

During the War of 1812, several American maritime fur traders sold their vessels to the Russian-American Company rather than risk seizure by British naval and privateer squadrons prowling the

Pacific. With reliable and adequate shipping, Baranov prepared to establish a colonial beachhead in the Hawaiian Islands. He assigned the venture to Georg Schäffer, a German physician employed by the Russian-American Company.

Russian officials received concessions from the royal Hawaiian government to open plantations on Oʻahu and Kauaʻi in 1815, and Schäffer observed the resentment of certain island chiefs at the consolidation of power and formation of the kingdom of Hawaiʻi over the archipelago by the Kamehameha family. The head man of Kauaʻi, Kaumualiʻi, appeared to Schäffer to be particularly restive and committed to some form of independent direction for Kauaʻi. Thus the Russian-American agent proceeded to concentrate his efforts for a colonial foothold there by exploiting Kaumualiʻi's separatist leanings. Eventually he struck a pact with the island politico, whereby Kaumualiʻi pledged allegiance to Czar Alexander I; he granted to the Russian-American Company exclusive trading privileges with Kauaʻi, permitted the Russians to construct factories and fortifications and open plantations on the island, promised to supply natives to erect these facilities and work on the plantations, and, further, to supply from his native farms those additional foodstuffs required by the northern colony.[27]

Americans in Hawaiʻi, alarmed by this intrusion, warned royal Hawaiian officials that Schäffer's pact with Kaumualiʻi jeopardized the kingdom's sovereignty. Hawaiian officials ruled the agreement void and ordered the Russians to evacuate the Kauaʻi establishment. The Russian government supported the Hawaiian government in its stance and disavowed Schäffer's action with the statement that "the Sandwich Islands will remain what they are—the free port and staple of all the navigators of the seas. But should any foreign power conceive the foolish idea of taking possession of them the jealous vigilance of the Americans, who possess the almost exclusive commerce of these seas, and the secure protection of England, would not be wanting to frustrate the undertaking."[28]

For the time being, Russian colonial officials' imperial dreams of expansion in the Pacific Basin were aborted. During 1818 Russian colonists on Kauaʻi returned to Sitka. Then, slightly over twenty years later, Russian officials liquidated their Fort Ross colony, vending improvements and occupation rights there during 1841 to John Sutter for an estimated $30,000. Most of the California colonists retreated north to Russian America. And thereafter, with the Spaniards scrubbed from the Pacific Basin by diplomatic retreat and wars of independence, the contest for hegemony in the basin's northeastern quadrant devolved on the resilient Britons and the increasingly entrenched Americans.

American maritime fur men continued to range the Northwest Coast for sea-otter pelts, but with gradually diminishing success, due to the decline of the fur-animal population, the result of sustained and ever intensified harvesting to meet the insatiable Canton market demand. Accelerated Russian and British maritime fur collecting on the Northwest Coast after the War of 1812 additionally contributed to the sea-otter population decline. This progressive *Enhydra lutris* depletion caused some Yankee fur men to turn to harvesting fur seals. These animals, quarry of marine hunters on an intermittent basis since the 1790s, were distributed over a much wider range than sea otters, found on the eastern Pacific Basin littoral and islands from the Bering Sea to Antarctica and along its periphery to islands off the southern shores of Australia and New Zealand. One reason marine fur men gave less attention to the fur seal than the sea otter as a pelt source was the substantial difference in market value; a prime sea-otter pelt might bring eighty to a hundred dollars on the Canton market, a seal skin only one to two dollars. Therefore maritime fur hunters, for the most part, filled their ships' holds with seal skins only when they could not, for various reasons, obtain cargoes of sea-otter pelts.[29]

American fur men on the Northwest Coast hunted sea otters, but they preferred to use skilled Indian and Aleut hunters for killing the animals and processing the skins. When seals were their quarry on the other hand, they largely did the hunting and processing themselves. They hunted seals along the South American and North American coasts and adjacent islands. Crewmen from the hunter ships went ashore for extended periods, camping in temporary huts and often subsisting on penguin eggs. Seals formed thickly populated colonies, sometimes of several thousand each, on the Pacific Basin's sandy beaches and rock shores. Hunters found it relatively easy to slay great numbers of these slow-moving creatures in a day's work. Besides skinning the animals, they rendered oil from the carcasses in large pots heated by driftwood fires.

A prime seal-hunting zone was the island of Más a Fuera in the Juan Fernández archipelago off the Chilean coast; on that island alone, American marine fur hunters had collected an estimated 3,000,000 seal skins by 1807. Another favorite seal hunters' rendezvous was the Farallon Islands off the California coast. There during the period 1809–12 American hunters garnered over 150,000 seal skins; each carcass also yielded one or two gallons of high quality oil.[30]

The seal-industry phase of the American maritime fur frontier in the Pacific Basin contributed to national recognition and prestige through extensive discovery and exploration. In their search for seal colonies, American maritime fur men occasionally came upon unknown geographic areas. Thus in 1820–21 when twenty American ships ranged southern antipodal waters in search of fur seals, at least one Yankee captain is reported to have been the first to cross the "antarctic threshold" and land on Antarctica.[31]

In 1822 the American maritime fur frontier finally obtained a land base on the eastern Pacific Basin littoral. Up to that time, Yankee fur men had for the most part worked the coastal areas for skins from aboard ship. Their supply line, from New England and the Kingdom of Hawai'i, obviously was extended, tenuous, and expensive to maintain. And they faced a logistical disadvantage in competing with land-based Russian and British fur men. In 1821 Mexico (New Spain under the Spanish Empire), achieved independence, and the following year the new nation extended its dominion over the former Spanish Pacific province of California. This marked the end of the exclusionist mercantilist policy there.

Gradually fur men established themselves in California ports and hunted openly along the coast for sea otters and seals. Several fur men settled in the California coastal towns as suppliers for the maritime hunters and as dealers in furs, providing storage and grubstaking fur men for one-half the catch; a leading pioneer pelt dealer serving the maritime fur frontier from a land base in California was William Goodwin Dana at Monterey. Of course for several years Yankees had to compete with Russian and Aleut hunters working coastal waters from their Fort Ross colony north of San Francisco. Also the Mexican government adopted a code of laws regulating the fur trade that required hunters to obtain licenses from the new provincial government; it included a stipulation that favored Mexican citizens in the fur trade.[30]

Opening California to aliens additionally influenced the progression of the American fur frontier in the Pacific Basin. Soon after Mexican independence, beaver hunters from the American continental fur frontier arrived in California. Jedediah Smith's brigade reached there in 1826, and Isaac Galbraith of his group remained to become a sea-otter hunter. During this period the wanderer James Ohio Pattie also hunted sea otters in California waters. Other continental fur-frontier celebrities, including William Wolfskill, George Yount, Ewing Young, and Nathaniel Pryor, reached California during the late 1820s and 1830s to participate in sea-otter hunts. The continental fur men found that the "sport was exciting and the returns profitable." These deadly marksmen hired kanakas off the California beaches, there awaiting assignment to ships' crews, paying each sixteen dollars a month to swim out and retrieve sea otters they shot.[33]

By the 1830s the effectiveness of the Americanization process in the northeastern quadrant of the Pacific was evident. Planted there by its pioneer carrier, the maritime fur frontier faced more handicaps and barriers than its continental counterpart and thus had been unable to perform with the efficiency and promptness of the latter. But it functioned, albeit at a slower pace, and by the 1820s had demonstrated substantive results similar to those accomplished by the more familiar land-based fur frontier. It had seeded an enduring American presence on the Pacific Basin's eastern rim and had established an abiding and enlarging economic and political interest there. Pioneers, mainly from New England, had been drawn to the Northwest Coast and had become acquainted with the region and its resources. While the maritime fur trade dominated their attention, they had observed the region's abundant wildlife beyond sea otters, its great forests, and mineral and agricultural prospects. Thus in the later years of the Pacific fur trade, Yankee ship captains came to include salmon in the fur cargoes drawn from Northwest Coast commerce.

These maritime pioneers laid the foundations for subsequent United States territorial claims to the Northwest Coast. While they established no confirming, permanent land bases until the California entrada after 1822, nonetheless they made several attempts. And these aborted efforts surprisingly figured with considerable weight in later negotiations with nations competing for dominion over the Northwest Coast. John Kendrick, with Robert Gray, the American maritime fur pioneer on the Northwest Coast, was also a stirring nationalist. This "adventurous mariner" concluded purchase agreements with local Indian leaders in the Nootka Sound area for land, with the intent of forming settlements. He is reported to have sent the documents confirming these transactions to the United States government in Philadelphia. Then during 1810, Jonathan, Nathan, and Abiel Winship, along with Benjamin P. Homer, New England captains of the *O'Cain* and *Albatross,* conceived a plan to found a settlement on the Northwest Coast. They prepared for the venture in the Kingdom of Hawai'i by taking on their ships construction materials, breeding herds of hogs and goats, twenty-five kānaka workers. The expedition crossed the dangerous Columbia estuary passage and prepared to construct the settlement ten miles inland at Oak Point on the south bank of the river. Floods and Indian hostility forced early abandonment. The final effort by maritime fur-frontier pioneers to establish a land base on the Northwest Coast was the ill-fated Astoria venture in 1811.[34]

This enlarging if tenuous Yankee beachhead on the Pacific Basin's eastern littoral elicited protective responses by the pioneers' home government. Thus when British Northwest Company officials, concerned over the growing American presence on the Northwest Coast, which they eventually expected to occupy and convert to a private fur preserve, prepared to send an armed force to eject the Yankees, nationalizing currents were activated. Astor learned of this early threat to his Astoria establishment from Canadian sources and appealed to Secretary of State James Monroe for protection, pointing to the "commercial and political importance" of a station on the Columbia to the United States. Federal officials fitted out the frigate *John Adams* for a cruise to the Northwest Coast, but before they launched the mission naval needs in the

North Atlantic, growing out of the early stages of the War of 1812, required a change of orders.[35]

After the war Astor expected that Astoria would be restored, because he concluded that the Treaty of Ghent, the pact ending the War of 1812, seemed clear in stipulating that the United States had "a right in the Columbia River." During 1815 Secretary of State Monroe notified British officials in Washington that the United States intended "immediately to reoccupy the post at the mouth of the Columbia." But no immediate action was taken; Astor abandoned his hopes of recovering Astoria, and he liquidated the Pacific Fur Company. Nevertheless American nationalizing influences were moving toward the Northwest Coast.

Proceeding under the clause of the Treaty of Ghent that stipulated *status quo ante bellum,* during 1817 the president appointed James Biddle, captain of the sloop *Ontario,* and J. B. Prevost as commissioners to preside over the recovery of territory claimed by the United States on the lower Columbia. Biddle left Prevost at Valparaíso, Chile, to conduct United States business and proceeded to the Columbia, where on 9 August he "took temporary possession of the country on that river, in the name of the United States." Later Prevost arrived, lowered the British flag, and raised the American flag over the territory adjacent to Astoria. Of course the post Astor's workmen had erected in 1811 remained the property of the Northwest Company.[37]

The legacy of the maritime fur-trade frontier continued to manifest itself. Several diplomatic agreements concluded between 1818 and 1828 consolidated the American claim to a sizable territorial enclave on the Northwest Coast. In 1818 an American-British convention established the principle of joint occupation, open to subjects and citizens of both nations on the principle of equality, of the territory west of the Rocky Mountains. In 1819 Spain and United States, by the Adams-Onís treaty, agreed on the western boundary for the Louisiana Purchase. Its far-northwestern limit was set on the forty-second parallel, the present California-Oregon boundary. Spain ceded its claim to territory north of that line to the United States. This pact removed one of the major claimants from the Northwest Coast contest. The Northwest Coast was further delimited in 1824 and 1825, when Russian officials concluded conventions with American and British diplomats, respectively, stipulating that the southern boundary of Russian America terminated at fifty-four degrees forty minutes and excepting the Russian colony on the California coast at Fort Ross.

The U.S. Congress also contributed to the flow of nationalizing currents into the Pacific Basin. In 1821, at the urging of Representative John Floyd of Virginia, the United States House leadership appointed a select committee to investigate American interests in the area of the Northwest Coast. It recommended the establishment of a United States military post in Oregon and organization of a territorial government.

Maritime fur pioneers were the Yankee vanguard in the Pacific Basin. But in their very close wake came other American frontiersmen, including whalers. They ranged over a much wider pelagic territory than the fur men, discovered new lands, exploited the sea-mammal fisheries most intensively, seeded an additional American presence in the basin, and consolidated national gains there.

Pacific Basin Whalers as Frontiersmen

Frontiers, those expansion entities and agencies that Americanized both the continental heartland and adjacent water hemisphere, were formed by congeries of restless adventurers, each group engaged in a particular quest. As on the continent, American frontiersmen coursed over Pacific waters searching for personal or public advantage. They all served the national purpose: the private, material seekers (be they fur men, gatherers, whalers, miners, agrarians), all lusting for fortune, status, and fame; and the civic-minded, nonmaterial seekers (military men and missionaries), striving for personal fulfillment through public service or by enlarging Christendom. They established an American presence in far-off places; increased individual and public wealth; and eased access to material, human, and security resources.

Whalers were a part of this expansion process. In the context of American continental development, they most closely resemble the buffalo hunters, who, by prodigal slaughter, nearly exterminated the vast western bison herds for hides. Whalers demonstrated the same mindless destruction toward Pacific Basin pelagic mammals, nearly extirpating several whale species in less than a century of intensive maritime hunting. Whalers also resembled maritime fur hunters, in that they were ship-bound and highly mobile, plundering one whale fishery after another, often absent from home port for a period of three to five years accumulating a full cargo of mammal products. And as in the case of the maritime fur industry, whaling centered on Boston for primary capital support, although nearby New Bedford, Nantucket, and Martha's Vineyard were the leading whaling ports. Whalers established an American presence and national interest in the Pacific Basin just as maritime fur men did.

The principal differences between them, in addition to methodology and industry technology, were range, quarry sought, market, and mythology. The maritime fur trade evolved over a limited territory, focusing on the Northwest Coast and adjacent areas. In contrast Pacific Basin whaling ranged over a vast territory from Antarctica north to the Arctic and from the North and South American western littoral to the Japanese and Siberian coasts southwest into Australian and New Zealand waters.

Whales, warm-blooded mammals (cetaceans), breathe with lungs and suckle their young. Males are called bulls, females cows, and the young, calves. Maritime hunters observed nine species of whales in Pacific Basin waters, and of these they sought the sperm, bowhead, right, humpback, and gray. The sperm whale was the most esteemed. Found in all oceanic waters but most populous in the Pacific, it measured from thirty to seventy feet in length, weighed thirty-five to sixty-five tons, and yielded several useful products. Crewmen might render out up to two thousand gallons of fine, light oil (valued for illumination and lubrication in the incipient industrial age) and extract huge teeth, which they found were always attractive trade items (as ivory) in bartering with Pacific islanders for wood, food, and water. The sperm whale's huge skull alone encased a reservoir containing up to five hundred gallons of spermaceti, a very fine, light oil. Crewmen drew out the spermaceti by the bucketful, heated it slightly to prevent spoilage, then stored the liquid in sealed casks. It produced long-burning, almost smokeless, high-quality candles. Occasionally while processing a sperm whale's carcass, crewmen found ambergris, a whale secretion formed around indigestible material in the intestines. When exposed to sun and air this "soft, black and evil smelling mass . . . hardened and began to exude a pleasant smell." Ambergris was used as a fixative for perfume, a spice, and an aphrodisiac, and was rated as more valuable than gold. One whaler captain is reported to have sold eight hundred pounds of ambergris for ten thousand dollars.[1]

Next in desirability were bowhead and right whales. Smaller than the sperm whale, these two species were valued not only for oil but also for baleen, a comblike strainer in the mouth that trapped minute marine food animals. Bowhead baleen grows up to fourteen feet long, right-whale baleen up to eight feet long. Crewmen separated the baleen pieces and, after processing them, sold them for three dollars a pound. Before the advent of flexible steel, baleen was widely used in chair springs, buggy whips, fishing rods, bustle supports, and corset stays.

One cetacean generally avoided by American maritime hunters was the blue whale, the largest creature extant, reaching lengths of nearly one hundred feet and weights of two hundred tons, equal in bulk to an estimated thirty-three African elephants. Whalers found the blue too large, too swift, and too powerful to conquer with hand-thrown harpoon technology. An alternative in the quest for mammal oil when whales were not to be found during certain seasons was for whalers to kill and render walruses, seals, and sea elephants on the beaches.

Marine hunters, much like their counterparts the continental frontiersmen, believed they were waging a contest against a hostile nature, stocked with all manner of threats to human life and barriers to the consummation of Christian purpose. Matching the land-based hunter's hazards of deadly wild animals, dense forests, forbidding deserts and mountains, and at times hostile Indians were the Pacific Basin frontiersman's perils of an ambivalent sea, hidden shoals, the eternal prospect of shipwreck and starvation, equally hostile island aborigines, and hull-smashing charges from enraged pelagic leviathans. Cetaceans have awed humans from earliest times; their gargantuan proportions and fabled strength had embued them with a negative metaphysical quality as the ultimate epitome of evil, with an accompanying mythology. Through the ages, encumbered with "fundamentalist beliefs," people had perceived "the huge mammals . . . as the incarnation of evil." Herman Melville's Captain Ahab denounced Moby Dick, the great white whale, as "'the gliding great demon of the seas of life.'" In deference to New England's thriving nineteenth-century whaling industry, local clergy rationalized the marine hunter's slaughter of Pacific Basin mammal herds with the Old Testament license from the book of Isaiah, that the "Lord with his sore, and great, and strong sword, shall punish Leviathan the piercing serpent, even

Leviathan that crooked serpent; and he shall slay the dragon that is in the sea." Many impressionable crewmen stalking these giant beasts from their tiny whale boats in churning Pacific waters admitted a sense of medieval wonder, of cosmic fear, at the near-supernatural aura they perceived emanating from their quarry.[2]

Whaling was a demanding enterprise requiring specialized equipment, tools, techniques, and skilled crewmen. As in the case of maritime fur men, whale hunters were based on oceangoing craft. During the Pacific Basin's bonanza whaling era (1820–60), all types of vessels were used to stalk the giant pelagic mammals. However, the most numerous and efficient whale ships were of sturdy, brig-type construction. Of all the vessels navigating Pacific waters, whale ships were the most durable. Often these craft had to be at sea from three to five years to accumulate a full cargo of whale products, performing in differing climates and punishing, destructive elements—blistering heat; frigid cold in battering ice and crushing glaciers; raging gales; hull-slicing submerged shoals and coral tips; and the silent, sinister invasions of a ship's timbers by hordes of sea termites, the teredos.

Whaleships had to be especially strong to accommodate the giant whale carcasses once they were secured alongside by the crew for butchering, and with positive balance to enable crewmen to hoist heavy slabs of blubber on deck for rendering. The whaleship's length averaged 120 feet, with a 30-foot beam (width) and a depth of 18 feet; it was rated between 300 and 350 tons. It was three-masted, its hull copper-sheathed. Most whaleships were constructed in New England yards from local woods: a frame of oak and yellow pine, decking of yellow pine, hull cover generally of tough cured oak, and spruce masts extending over 100 feet above the deck. Three-fourths the distance up the masthead was the crosstree perch for the whale watch. Five to six whale boats, the attack craft, were suspended from davits on the outer rails. The Yankee whale boat was 28 feet long and 6 feet wide, propelled by oars each 18 feet long, and with a steering oar in the stern 2 feet longer. A coil of harpoon line, several hundred feet long, encased in a tub, lay near the center. This attack craft, light, swift, and maneuverable, was double-ended (pointed at bow and stern), to enable crewmen to reverse direction quickly to escape the thrashing of a wounded whale. It was crewed by five men on the oars, a boatswain to steer, and the harpoon man.

A crewman standing watch for whales on the crosstree perch, in a fairly calm sea, could sight quarry up to six miles distant. Two signs were particularly productive. One was circling petrels, gulls, and other marine birds, often anticipating a whale breaking water; they feed on the same swarms of krill as do the baleen whales. The other sign was a ten- to twelve-foot-high column of moisture geysering from the ocean, indicating a whale surfacing for air. The watch required much patience and concentration after the first sighting, because some time might elapse before the whale reappeared; it could swim underwater ten miles or more before resurfacing for air, along the way perhaps diving 500 to 2500 feet to forage on cuttlefish, octopus, or squid (in the case of a sperm whale).

The lookout's call, "Thar she blows," stirred furious action on the deck below. Crewmen lowered the attack craft, and the boatswain, harpooner, and oarsmen went after the whale. The harpoon man, standing in the bow with feet braced for the killing thrust as the boat drifted nearly to within an arm's length of the giant cetacean, struck his weapon (a razor-sharp point of malleable iron fitted to a shaft attached to the tub rope) deep into the whale just in back of the head. The harpoon line hissed through its ferrules as the wounded mammal submerged into the ocean deep, drawing boat and crew in a "Nantucket sleigh ride" over the water, until the whale expired and surfaced. Then crewmen attached a heavy fiber line or chain to the flukes (the broad tail) and drew the carcass to the ship, securing it to the hull, head aft.[3]

Butchers, working on a platform just above the whale and using flensers (razor-sharp cutting spades fitted with handles twenty feet long), sliced great slabs of blubber from the carcass. Workmen raised these slabs by windlass to the deck, cut them into small pieces, and fed them into try-pots (huge iron kettles, each of 250 gallons capacity), for rendering. Brick enclosures around the pots, filled with water, cooled the wooden deck and contained the try-pot fires. Men tending the pots drew out flakes of rendered blubber, resembling huge pork cracklings, for fuel to maintain the intense heat required to separate the oil.

An essential whaleship crewmember was the cooper, or barrel maker. He fashioned the thirty-gallon casks in which whale oil was stored. During most of whaling's bonanza age, oil sold for forty dollars a barrel; a full whaling vessel cargo consisted of from twenty-five hundred to three thousand barrels of sperm oil.[4]

Crewmen labored from two to three days at butchering a whale. Harbor residents claimed a whaleship's arrival was announced from several miles out by its characteristic stench from whale offal and blood, blubber grease, and oil spoilage. Crewmen saved their urine in deck barrels; with its ammonia content, it was the only available solvent for removing whale grease from clothing.

Americans had hunted whales in the Atlantic from earliest colonial times. Nearly two centuries of intensive harvesting by both Yankee and European whalers had drastically diminished the Atlantic whale fishery by the end of the eighteenth century; by the 1780s whalers were flanking the Falklands and searching out the ice- and glacier-bound northern rim of Antarctica for whales. The first whaling ship to enter the Pacific was the *Emilia*, a British vessel, under Captain James Shields. During 1789 his crew negotiated the dreaded Cape Horn passage and coasted the Chilean littoral; they discovered the "on-shore fishery" and became the first outsiders to kill sperm whales there. Shields returned to home port with a cargo of prime sperm oil. However, British whaling activity in the Pacific was limited for several years by the South Sea Company and East India Company monopolies between the capes, which required a special and expensive license for noncompany British subjects to enter and exploit resources of this assigned domain. Thus Shields's entry was regarded as more of a geographic reconnaissance than a commercial sortie. British whalemen exploited the Pacific Basin fisheries but, until the 1830s when the monopolies were abolished, only on a controlled, licensed basis. Thus as in the case of other Pacific Basin commercial enterprises, Yankees, not bound by these monopolistic restrictions, enjoyed an early and strategic advantage.

American hunters closely followed the Britons into the Pacific. These Yankee whale hunters, no less pioneers than maritime fur men, were prime carriers of American culture into the Pacific Basin; they established private and public interests there, and established a vital national presence. But while fur men worked only a limited territory on the Pacific Basin's eastern rimland, centering on the Northwest Coast and peripherally Russian America and California, and reaching to Hawai'i and Canton, whalers explored every nook and cranny of this water hemisphere in their quest for sea mammals.

The first Yankee whaler to clear Cape Horn hailed from Nantucket, the *Beaver,* captained by Paul Worth. The *Beaver* departed home port during August of 1791 and returned in February 1793 with a cargo of sperm oil. Six American whalers were in the *Beaver*'s wake, and before 1800 almost fifty Yankee vessels ranged along the coast and adjacent islands of lower South America in search of sperm-whale herds. This first Pacific whale fishery, the "on-shore," focused on the Juan Fernández and Galápagos Islands. These small islands provided havens from storms as well as water, wood, and some food. Crewmen hunted giant tortoises on the Galápagos and found their meat a welcome change from the monotonous ship rations of hard, moldy bread and salt beef and pork. The first American post offices in the Pacific Basin were covered boxes nailed to posts sunk in island beaches, which crewmen used as letter drops. Men on homebound ships collected this mail and delivered it to post offices in New England ports. Before the War of 1812, American whaling captains also maintained limited contact in the ports of Chile and Peru, where Spanish officials occasionally permitted them to anchor for reprovisioning and vessel repair.

Naval warfare during the War of 1812 in the Pacific Basin slowed the industry. Many American whalers either berthed in neutral ports or rushed to the safety of home ports for the duration. Most of the few whalers that persisted either were sunk or seized and confiscated as prizes by British naval squadrons prowling the Pacific. But Americans achieved some revenge on the Britons by the retaliatory strikes on British shipping in the Pacific Basin by David Porter and the crew of the USS *Essex.*

American whalers returned to the Pacific Basin after the war and gradually extended their hunting range from the southeastern quadrant's "on-shore fishery" into equatorial waters around the Gilbert Islands, founding a new whale territory they called the "middle-ground fishery." Continuing their reconnaissance of the central Pacific's mammal habitat, Yankee whalers eventually entered waters adjacent to the Hawaiian archipelago during 1819.

A year later they discovered the rich Japanese whale fishery, and in 1822 crewmen from thirty American ships hunted whales on Nippon's western margins; the next season, sixty Yankee ships appeared for the cetacean harvest. Whalemen then edged into the North Pacific and in the following decade confirmed the presence of large herds of sperm whales from Kamchatka and the Okhotsk Sea, off the Siberian coast, to Kodiak in Russian America. Breaching the Bering passage, they proceeded into Arctic waters searching for baleen-bearing bowheads. Explorations southward revealed large accumulations of whales around the Carolines, Philippines, and Indonesia. And late in the decade of the 1830s, American hunters found another whale territory, extending from Australia and New Zealand into upper Antarctic waters.

Having established that whales were present in virtually every segment of the Pacific Basin, American whalemen after 1840 hunted them on a seasonal circuit. Captains of the New England whaling fleet sought to make the Cape Horn run into the Pacific during the Southern Hemisphere's summer, to reduce the risk of marine disaster from storms and heavy seas. They first hunted out the "on-shore fishery," then sailed west into the "middle-ground fishery" in the waters around the Society, Samoan, and Fiji islands. From there they followed a course north of the equator into the Hawaiian ports of Honolulu, Lahaina, and Hilo for ship repair, reprovisioning, and discharging their accumulated whale-oil cargoes in company warehouses, for transshipment to Boston or the European market. By then the Northern Hemisphere's milder seasons had arrived, and the fleet moved west to the Japan whaling grounds. Then they searched the waters off the Siberian coast, proceeded into Russian American waters, and negotiated the Bering Strait into the arctic whale habitat.

Tracing whale-herd migrations southward along the Northwest Coast, Yankee captains often paused for a hunt in California waters before returning to Hawai'i for ship repair, reprovisioning, and discharge of oil and baleen cargoes. As the Southern Hemisphere summer approached, whaling fleets cast off for hunts in

Whaling Expedition from New Bedford to the Hawaiian Islands, 1856-57

Philippine waters and from there to the Australian, New Zealand, and Antarctic hunting grounds.

Whaling ships, often out from home port for three to five years, required periodic repair. Crews had to be rehabilitated occasionally from long periods at sea; ship captains had to replace deckhands because of desertion, illness, death, and other causes. Ships' stores and supplies of fresh water had to be renewed. And large quantities of firewood were required for processing whale oil at the try-pots. Thus whalers made frequent stops at islands and rimland ports.

They found some anchorages more reliable and productive than others. Whaler captains rarely stopped at Siberian or Russian American ports because of the perennial shortage of supplies there. Spanish colonial ports on the Pacific from Chile north to Mexico, including California, were closed to aliens by restrictive commercial policy, although occasionally Yankee captains were permitted to enter these anchorages. After independence from Spain, these new nations opened their ports; however, the Mexican government during the late 1820s assessed a $2.25-per-ton tax on each vessel entering its harbors from San Francisco to Acapulco.[5]

Favored whaler refuges among Pacific Basin islands included the Galápagos, Samoan, Caroline, Society, and Fijian archipelagoes and northern New Zealand. In each island group, Yankee sea hunters established small supply stations, which they occupied mostly on a seasonal basis, although some crewmen became permanent settlers.

The principal "on-shore fishery" anchorages were in the Galápagos. During 1832 José Villasmil, a United States citizen from New Orleans, received a charter from the government of Ecuador to found a colony on Charles Island in the Galápagos group, which he named Floreana for Ecuadorean politician Juan José Flores. The two hundred Floreana colonists, recruited from among retired soldiers and convicts, were to supply vegetables, fruit, wood, and water to whalers and other maritime craft calling at the island. Villasmil was characterized as a person of "mild disposition, very polite without affectation . . . a man of middle age, understands different languages, and the necessary solid information to carry his prospect to a happy and honorable conclusion." Villasmil's biographer naively claimed that "Pecuniary compensations are beneath his sentiments." He concluded that Floreana, under Villas-mil's "patronage, will be a great resort for . . . whaleships." The colony founder, perhaps innocent of the sailor's prodigal taste for strong drink and his well-known worldliness, banned "the use of ardent spirits" there; he expected Floreana to "become an important station for a seaman's chaplain."[6]

The Society cluster contained several heavily used whaler anchorages, including Papeete on the island of Tahiti. Widely acknowledged as "Pearl of the Pacific," Papeete was a prime supplier of whaleship needs from productive orchards and gardens, as well as of sexual satisfaction for shipbound crewmen. Visited by Spanish, British, and French mariners for nearly four centuries, Tahiti was finally annexed to the French Empire in 1843. As was their custom on arriving in the Hawaiian Islands, crewmen also frequently jumped ship at Papeete, and old seamen often retired there.[7]

The waters around the Fiji Islands abounded in sperm whales through nearly three decades of hunting, and several small land areas of this archipelago were used as bases for Yankee whaling operations. One report of 1856 revealed that "A number of Americans reside and do business in these islands, and whaling vessels frequently resort to them for supplies."[8]

Several Yankee sea hunters rated Sa Vai'i in the Navigator (Samoan) Islands as ideal, the most eligible for whalemen "of all Pacific stations for refitting and taking on supplies of provisions, wood and water which it affords in great abundance, and of excellent quality." Americans anchoring there announced that "for a musket the natives give 13 hogs, or 800 to 1000 yams; and great quantities of fowls, cocoanuts, bananas, etc. may be purchased for a few pipes, flints, and blue glass beads."[9]

In the far-western Pacific, Yankee whalers found Japanese ports closed to them, with a single reported exception, until they were opened by a United States naval force in 1853–54. However, they established alternative havens in that part of the basin.

A favorite far-western Pacific support base for many years was in the Bonin group, situated five hundred miles southeast of Japan. Port Lloyd on Peel Island with a deep, safe anchorage, was the most widely used station in this archipelago. Whaler captains had stocked the island with hogs, sheep, and goats. Fish were abundant in offshore waters. And during the late 1820s, a group of Americans from Massachusetts and Vermont and Polynesians from the Hawaiian islands, thirty in all, had colonized the area around Port Lloyd. The settlers grew sweet potatoes, onions, cabbages, and other vegetables and raised livestock for sale to the Yankee whaling fleet hunting in Japanese waters each season.[10]

American whalemen also established several small settlements on the Bay of Islands, situated near the northeast coast of New Zealand. Abundant fresh water, wood, and a variety of foodstuffs made this cluster of remote support stations a favorite stop for Yankee whalemen working the far-southwest Pacific. Forests reaching to the beaches supplied tall, straight trees for fashioning masts to replace those battered and splintered by Pacific storms. Maoris, the Polynesian native inhabitants, were an esteemed resource, too: both the receptive women, desired by the restless Yankee seamen; and the sturdy men, skilled as navigators, recruited as replacements for diminished crews. Ship captains set up repair stations in several harbors and on the beaches. These whaler settlements were populated by aged and ailing crewmen, deserters, escapees from the nearby British penal colony, and mestizos (mixed-blood offspring of Maori women and Yankee hunters). Americans began to abandon their whaling settlements on Bay of Islands in 1840, when British officials annexed the area to the empire and assigned agents there who established law and order, set up courts, and levied port and anchorage fees and tonnage duties.

Around 1850 the number of ports was increased for the Yankee whaling fleet in the Pacific Basin by action of the Spanish government. For some time empire officials had gradually relaxed the long-standing ban on alien access to colonial ports. At midcentury the royal government opened them to the ships of most nations, including those flying the United States flag. Thereafter Yankee whaler captains made extensive use of ports in the Philippine Islands and Guam for ship repair and replenishing commissary stores. Then in 1853 Commodore Matthew C. Perry, braced by an American armada bristling with heavy guns, entered Nippon's forbidden Yedo Bay and forced reluctant Japanese officials to open certain ports to outsiders and provide succor for shipwrecked seamen. Up to this time the shogun's subjects had tortured and imprisoned aliens cast upon their shores. And after Mexico ceded California to the United States in 1848, Yankee hunters occasionally called at San Diego, Monterey, and San Francisco. Certainly the ports in the Philippines, Guam, and the West Coast of the United States, as well as the whaler settlements in the Bonin, Navigator, and Fiji islands and on the Bay of Islands rendered valuable support for the Pacific Basin.

The first Yankee whaling fleet to reach the Kingdom of Hawai'i—two battered ships from New Bedford—anchored in Lahaina harbor during 1819. Within two years over one hundred whaling vessels had called at Hilo on the island of Hawai'i, Kawaihae on the island of Kaua'i, and Honolulu on O'ahu. At first American captains seemed to prefer Lahaina, but because its harbor flared into a huge, open roadstead, they increasingly patronized Honolulu, with its more protected anchorage. By 1835 it had become the Pacific Basin's principal whaling station and held this position until the demise of the industry in the 1870s.

The whaling industry, another herald of the American "march of civilization and wealth" into the Pacific Basin, transformed the Kingdom of Hawai'i, drastically altering its economy, producing substantial demographic change, and establishing an irrepressible and indisputable national interest in the archipelago. Great numbers of native Hawaiians settled in the port cities. The urbanization surge was most apparent in Honolulu; island business leaders acknowledged that the Yankee whaling fleet "made Honolulu" in the modern business sense. Throughout the 1840s and 1850s, during recesses between North and South Pacific hunts, four hundred vessels anchored in the Hawaiian ports, most of them at Honolulu, debouching three to four thousand pleasure-starved seamen into its narrow, shop-lined streets.[11]

Ship service and supply became the principal local industry. The crewmen of each ship required 650 different items (from food, whale line, and harpoons, to medical supplies) to sustain them on extended cruises through the Pacific Basin. New England firms dealing in whale products and ship supply established branch businesses in Honolulu and included ship's chandlers, sail lofts, warehouses, and offices of merchants dealing in oil, whalebone, and marine insurance. Yankee shipwrights constructed a yard in the harbor to restore whalers battered by fierce Pacific storms and hull-smashing attacks by maddened whales.[12]

The whaling industry also altered the Hawaiian countryside. Many small farms, for centuries adapted to sustaining households, became commercial plantations producing vegetables, fruits, livestock, and poultry for fleet commissaries. Yankee foremen ran gangs of native woodcutters in the Hawaiian forests, collecting fuel for whaler try-pots. Other crews filled casks with fresh water for shipboard use. Foodstuffs, cords of wood, casks of fresh water, and livestock and poultry accumulated at dockside each recess in whaling operations. Hogs and poultry were penned on deck for use as needed; cattle were slaughtered and preserved by smoking or pickling in casks of heavy brine.

Urbanization precipitated by the whaling industry included altered town appearances. Honolulu, Lahaina, Hilo, and other ports were transformed from villages of thatched huts to reproductions of New England communities. Honolulu particularly took on the aspects of a "thriving American town. The frame houses . . . the churches and schools which had been set up by the missionaries who had followed closely after the whalemen, as well as the stores and taverns and grogshops gave Honolulu a familiar air for all its exotic background of tropical vegetation and native life. 'Could I have forgotten the circumstances of my visit,' wrote one visitor, 'I should have fancied myself in New England.'"[13]

Mark Twain, on assignment for several California newspapers in the Kingdom of Hawai'i during 1866, wrote that "The whaling trade . . . centers in Honolulu. Shorn of it this town would die— its business men would leave and its real estate would become valueless. . . . Sailors always spend all their money before they leave port. . . . It is said that in the palmy days of whaling, fifteen or twenty years ago, they have squandered as high as a million and a half in this port at the end of a successful voyage."[14]

The recently established and growing missionary frontier in the Pacific Basin rated whalemen a "most pernicious influence." This was particularly noticeable in the Hawaiian ports, favorite resorts in the basin. Yankee sea hunters on shore leave, according to missionaries, were "boisterous, pleasure-seeking rabble," with interests "no higher than the grogshop and the brothel." Brawls they "entered upon with real zest."[15]

To check the carousing, disorder, and chaos caused by periodic visits of the whaler fleet, missionaries applied their influence over Hawaiian court officials to adopt a code of "blue laws," another New England implant, which closed grogshops, gambling houses, and brothels in the Kingdom of Hawai'i and imposed fines and incarceration for violation. After enduring months of hardship and danger at sea, Yankee whalemen arrived in Honolulu ready for an erotic frolic. Dismayed and enraged at finding the resorts padlocked, on several occasions they rioted, intimidating law-enforcement officials to relent. Yankee sea hunters forcing their will on this newly Christianized community resembled another frequent nineteenth-century protest against imposing civic morality on the continent. Texas cowboys, after a long and dangerous trail drive from southern ranches to northern railheads, discouraged local interference with their long-anticipated carnal adventures by taking over a Kansas cow town; "treeing the town," they called it.

Sometimes visiting French and British seamen joined the Yankees; once even sailors from a United States warship participated in violent protest of the restrictive new laws. The thirsty, pleasure-bound international mob threatened to burn the homes of missionaries, whom they blamed for the denial of what they regarded a natural right of access.

Jaded, weary, and broke from their week-long orgy, crewmen turned to refurbishing their ships for the next hunt. Whaler captains, besides watching over the stowing of support cargoes, had to muster crews; they found this an increasingly difficult task, because many seamen failed to appear on the appointed day. Throughout the age of Pacific Basin whaling, New Englanders dominated the industry as captains, mates, and in the early years, crewmen. However, as whaling expanded and became more competitive, and as the search for sea mammals intensified, the composition of crews changed, which had an alterative effect on Pacific Basin demography.

The treatment of crewmen by ships' officers varied, but because of the nature of the enterprise, with all its vicissitudes, even on the best-managed vessels discipline was stern and conditions trying. The riotous, reckless, even abandoned, life-style Yankee recruits adopted as whaler crewmen caused many captains, probably influenced somewhat by nineteenth-century New England reform, to run "temperance ships," banning the consumption of alcoholic beverages at sea. However, virtually every vessel's hold contained casks of liquor for trading to islanders for food, water, and wood. Also some wives accompanied their captain husbands, to avoid the three-to-five-year separation of the typical cruise. Crewmen derisively called such ships "hen frigates," but as a general rule their treatment was more temperate when a woman was aboard.

In the American maritime community, most whaleships were rated as "floating hells" when compared to trader vessels. Cruel treatment by ships' officers; long periods at sea without respite in harsh, insanitary, and miserably uncomfortable conditions; thick layers of rancid whale grease splattered on decks and bulkheads; the eternal stench of rotting offal; indifferent rations; incredibly destructive storms; and shipwreck on uncharted islands, with the very real prospect of slow death over the cooking fires of exultant cannibals—all these were pointed to as the principal causes for the abnormally high number of desertions from these vessels. One American consul assigned Pacific Basin duty calculated that during the 1850s, as many as four thousand American seamen jumped ship in the Pacific each year, most of them from whalers. The captains of these craft became reluctant to anchor in certain ports, for fear of "losing half their crews."[16]

J. Ross Browne, an American writer who signed aboard a whaler in 1842, was appalled at the treatment ships' officers inflicted on deckhands. He wrote a narrative of his adventures and an exposé of what he concluded to be conditions in the American whaling fleet, *Etchings of a Whaling Cruise* (1846). "There is no class of men in the world who are so unfairly dealt with, so oppressed, so degraded, as the seamen who man the vessels engaged in the American whale fishery . . . the condition of this oppressed class is a reproach to our country—a disgrace to the age of civilization in which we live."[17]

At best, the life of a whaleman is fraught with dangers and hardships. His duties differ widely from those of the merchant seaman; his compensation is more uncertain; his enjoyments are fewer, and his risk of life greater. Many of the comforts of the one are denied the other. . . . From the time he leaves port he is beyond the sphere of human rights: he is a slave till he returns. He sees little of the pleasures of shore life. He is frequently six or eight months on a cruise without seeing land. All this time he is subject to severe labor, the poorest and meanest fare, and such treatment as an ignorant and tyrannical master, standing in no fear of the law, chooses to inflict on him. On the cruising ground he not unfrequently stands from four to six hours a day at the masthead, under the scorching rays of a tropical sun, or exposed to the cutting blasts of a frigid zone. He has also his tricks at the helm night and day. At times when there has been a run of luck, he is out in the boats, toiling with his oar from six to ten hours on a stretch, and for weeks he has but four or five hours' rest out of twenty-four. Covered with oil, suffocating under the fumes of try-works, in imminent and perpetual danger of life and limb, he thus toils on, conscious that the proceeds of his labor are not for him. . . . He is flogged for the most trifling offense, cursed when he strives to please, trampled and spit upon without the power to resent the indignities. Remonstrance is a course to which he dare not resort. The officers, eager after promotion, cringe to the captain, and are ever ready to win a word of approbation by bestowing upon their inferiors in rank the choicest epithets in the calendar of vulgarity and blasphemy, and to show by word and deed that they are qualified, by every heartless and brutal attribute, for the discharge of their duty. It is painful to trace his career to its close. With a crushed spirit, he finds himself once more in his native land. But he is penniless and degraded. Who is to befriend him? Who to console him? He seeks oblivion in the rum-bottle—falls into the snares of a wary and designing set of agents, and is shipped again, to waste away his manhood in the service of others. . . . Such is the life of a whaleman.[18]

With such morbid prospects, his fate assured, how do we account for the at least moderate success by recruiters in luring Yankee youths from their native land? Certainly the promise of adventure, of exciting, even erotic, experiences in the languorous South Seas denied them by their prosaic, repressive Puritan society, was a compelling inducement. Added to this was the chance to make one's fortune by sharing in the expedition profits at the end of the three-to-five-year cruise, pledged to each crewman as a part of the recruitment pitch. Clearly this attraction dimmed after a few months at sea aboard a "hell-ship."

The proportion of Yankees in whaling crews gradually diminished, as tidings of the dreadful reality of whaling-fleet service was broadcast about the New England ports. This forced captains to turn to other manpower sources. By 1846, the peak year for Pacific Basin whaling, the American fleet there consisted of 736 vessels, and the Yankee crew population had declined to the point that captains increasingly mixed their crews; "Men from many climes were to be found on the New Bedford whalers." On the way out from home port to the Pacific, whaler captains stopped in the Azores to take on Portuguese seamen and at west-coast African settlements for a sprinkling of black deckhands. Chilean and Peruvian seamen might be gathered from the west-coast ports of South America. Then crews were completed with Polynesians from Tahiti, the Marquesas, Samoa, Hawai'i, and New Zealand. And as the whaling territory extended to the Northwest Coast, a few Eskimos and North American Indians began to appear in whaler crews.[19]

The most favored mariners were recruited from the Hawaiian Kingdom. By the 1850s over six hundred kānaka, described as the nonpareil seamen of the Pacific Basin, "tractable and ingenuous," were engaged for whaler service. Court officials made their employment a royal monopoly, requiring whaler captains to post a bond in the amount of ten dollars, increased to one hundred, then to as much as three hundred dollars, with the pledge to "return each man within three years."[20]

The Yankee whaler-crew presence in the Pacific Basin and its changing composition had substantive effects on the region's demography and culture. Retired and deserting crewmen often became permanent settlers in the islands and rimland settlements. They married native women, these unions yielding a multiracial population. Blending Yankee whaler crews with Portuguese, African, American Indian, Eskimo, and Polynesian seamen ultimately added to the Pacific Basin's enlarging genetic mix. Besides voluntary exile from the "hell-ships" on the part of retired and deserting seamen, many sailors were set ashore by shipwreck or forceful expulsion by callous, greedy captains, to avoid the payment of profit shares promised them at the conclusion of the cruise.

The immense scope of operations carried out by the American whaling fleet in the Pacific Basin during the nineteenth century exposed much of it to an escalating force of influences—most of them pernicious. Whalemen have been charged with spreading "a lurid trail of demoralization, dissipation, and disease" throughout the Pacific. Indigenous peoples, with no natural immunity to measles, smallpox, and venereal infections carried to them by the peripatetic seamen, endured incalculable suffering and drastic population decline. And their material and nonmaterial cultures also were casualties of the rarely positive contact process with the alien lifeways of the Yankee intruders.[21]

Granted its accumulating pejorative image, whaling made an immensely valuable contribution to the nineteenth-century American economy; its positive, supportive, material influence generated and sustained other industries. Sea-mammal products marketed in the United States and around the world, particularly oil as an illuminant, increased in annual value from about $6 million in the 1830s to over $10 million in the 1850s. An additional fifty thousand workers were employed in shipbuilding, vessel repair, provisioning, manufacturing equipment and supplies, and other supportive enterprises, all of which substantially increased the value of the industry in the American economy.[22]

Gradually, as European governments abrogated monopolistic charters limiting access to Pacific Basin resources, Yankee whalers faced growing competition. British, French, Belgian, and German (a single ship, the *Mozart* from Bremen) whalers after 1835 increasingly ranged the basin in search of mammal herds. However, the Americans, with their strategic knowledge of the region, long-standing experience there, and massive fleet, maintained supremacy throughout the effective life of the industry, that is, to the mid-1870s.

Whaling began to decline soon after 1860. Escalating demand for sea-mammal products until midcentury assured attractive prices and encouraged steady enlargement of the Pacific Basin whaling fleet. All of this, added to increased hunting by European whalers, placed a destructive pressure on sea-mammal populations, and the annual yield began to decline. Cetaceans never reached the threshold of extermination, as was the case for bison on the North American continent, but their numbers decreased to the point that wider-ranging searches with reduced results increased expedition costs.

Some sign of trouble in the industry appeared during the 1850s, when whalers were distracted by several Pacific Basin gold rushes. The strike in northern California in 1848 set off the great Gold Rush of 1849, the first massive human drift by land and sea to the Pacific Basin's eastern rimland. Subsequent discoveries of gold in Australia continued the process of shifting populations in the Pacific region and around the world. Crewmen, including those aboard whalers, abandoned ship to seek their fortunes in the Pacific Basin El Dorados. Drastic crew losses forced whaler captains to turn even more to non-Yankee replacements. And some captains found it more profitable during the 1850s (with the bonanza-induced inflated value of food, supplies, equipment, and human transportation in the Pacific Basin) to transport men and goods to the California and Australian mines than to hunt whales.

Of greatest impact on the future of whaling was the discovery of an alternative source of illumination and lubrication. In 1859 drillers struck petroleum in shallow wells at Titusville, Pennsylvania. Refined into grease for lubrication and rock oil, coal oil, or kerosene for illumination, the fossil fuel was marketed at a lower price than whale oil.

And ironically, from wealth generated by whaling, as well as the maritime fur trade and other exploitive frontier enterprises in the Pacific Basin, New England entrepreneurs were capitalizing the "safer and more lucrative" New England industries of textiles and shoe manufacturing. This drain and diversion of Yankee capital, which for generations had been invested in whaling, had a sapping effect on the sea-mammal industry.

The American Civil War also intruded into the Pacific Basin, contributing to the progressive decline of whaling there. After 1861 Confederate raiders prowled the seas in search of Union shipping; the *Shenandoah* ranged from Patagonia to the Bering Straits. On its first sortie, southern crewmen captured thirty-eight Yankee whalers and put the torch to thirty-four of them. Additional Yankee whalers were appropriated by Union officials, loaded with stone, and sunk across Confederate harbor entrances to strengthen the federal blockade.[23]

After a short postwar recovery, the American whaling fleet in the Pacific Basin was dealt a crippling blow from which it was unable to recover. In 1871 a major portion of the fleet collected north of the Bering Straits in Arctic waters, searching for bowhead whales. An early onset of the winter freeze crushed perhaps fifty ships in the ice; twelve hundred surviving crewmen, on foot on the floes and succored by Eskimos, finally reached ice-free beaches to the south. There they were picked up and carried to Honolulu.[24]

By 1885 whaling as a maritime frontier enterprise had completed its cycle. It had done much to expand American private and public attention beyond the continental limits. Certainly of all American frontiersmen coursing the Pacific Basin in the nineteenth century, none covered more pelagic territory than the whalemen. Their wanderings blazed new courses for navigators; they explored a greater number of islands, discovering several not recorded on mariners' maps; and called at virtually every rimland port. Captain Charles Wilkes, commander of the American naval expedition exploring the Pacific Basin during the early 1840s, commented that the United States whaling fleet whitened "the Pacific Ocean with its canvas."[25]

The Yankee whaler's Pacific-wide quest for cetaceans generated a corpus of useful maritime information that Matthew Maury, United States Navy oceanographer, used in his research concerning winds, currents, and landforms of that water hemisphere. His primary source was the large number of whaler logs accumulating at New Bedford and other New England ports. In turn his published reports, containing a digest of this information, provided useful guidance for American navigators manning whalers and other ships sailing Pacific waters.

We have seen that whaling stimulated urbanization on the Pacific islands; altered the basin's demography in ethnic composition and numbers; was instrumental in the formation of several settlements; and through crew desertion, exile, and retirement, scattered American colonists throughout the region. During 1818 Nantucket whaleman David Whippey "jumped ship," the *Francis,* in the Fijis. Because of his valued building skills and other talents,

Whippey became the favorite of the king of Ambow Island, who named him ruler of nearby Ovalau Island. Whippey took several Fijian wives, had many children, and was later appointed United States vice-consul in the Fiji archipelago.[26]

Whaling encouraged an increasingly diversified and commercial economy on many Pacific islands. This included stock raising, notably the range-cattle industry on the island of Hawai'i, and the beginning of regional plantation agriculture, in this phase devoted largely to producing foodstuffs for whaler commissaries.

Many Yankee whaling captains submitted letters and reports to New England newspaper editors regarding uncharted islands discovered, locations of shoals and passages, and general conditions in the Pacific Basin. Their published messages maintained reader attention on the Pacific Basin, its people and resources, contributed to popularizing this frontier region, and enlarged the nation's knowledge of its prospects for private and public benefit.[27]

Appeals by whaling-industry officials for federal assistance and protection in this aquatic wilderness led to the activation of those inevitable preliminaries to American expansion so familiar on the continent: among other things, the gradual buildup of naval forces in the Pacific to guard whalers from attack during international conflicts and to discourage depredations by islanders on whaler ships and crews while anchored in remote archipelagoes seeking food and water. Ultimately this produced a two-ocean navy, limited in the Pacific but of strategic value, particularly for American military operations on the Pacific Basin's eastern rim during the Mexican war (1846–48).

Nationalizing currents were also at work during the 1850s, when federal officials finally responded to whaler appeals for protection against the dreadful treatment the Japanese inflicted on shipwrecked crewmen, and the shogun's determined stance to seal off the island kingdom from alien entry of any sort. During 1853–54 Commodore Matthew C. Perry led American naval forces into Yedo Bay and accomplished what is known as "the opening of Japan" by extracting from reluctant Nipponese officials a treaty containing assurances of hospitable treatment of Yankee visitors and access to several ports.

Yet another evidence of the whaling industry as precipitator of nationalizing currents in the Pacific Basin was the appointment of United States consuls and vice-consuls for service at several ports and in the island settlements. Their function was to look after local American interests and adjudicate maritime questions.

Nonmaterial influence of the whaling frontier in the Pacific Basin includes contributions to American literature and folklore. This vast water continent is one of the world's richest sources of literary themes, exploited by writers from the times of earliest European entry; it has yielded a vast store of nonfiction and fiction. Whaling, as one of the region's most colorful and exciting enterprises, has been a prime contributor. Herman Melville, a crewman on the Yankee whaler *Acushnet,* "jumped ship" at Nuku Hiva in the Marquesas in 1842. Following a fulfilling sojourn among hospitable islanders there, he made his way to the Kingdom of Hawai'i, and thence to his home in the eastern United States. Melville used his experiences to write *Moby Dick* (1851), his best-known work, judged the ultimate treatise on Pacific Basin whaling.[28]

Crewmen aboard the whalers, with all their reported depravity, were creative. They composed a corpus of folktales and songs, many of them bawdy, to pass evenings on the "bounding main." And they developed a folk art, scrimshaw, using sea-mammal teeth and jawbones as their medium. The scrimshaw artist, called a scrimshander, carved the ivory surface with jackknife and sail needle, then applied a mixture of whale oil and lampblack to darken the incised composition. Intricate design, delicate construction, and in some cases surprising aesthetic application, have made scrimshaw pieces esteemed as unique folk art in certain museums and among private collectors.[29]

Whaling, like the maritime fur-traders' frontier, planted an enlarging American presence and proprietary interest in the Pacific Basin. Its legacy has been hailed as "America's greatest adventure in the western ocean," and it is claimed that whalemen were of greater influence on Pacific Basin peoples "than all the world's naval and merchant seamen combined."[30]

Other American maritime pioneers followed in the whalers' wake. One group of Yankees who at times challenged whalemen for scope of territory covered were the gatherers—collectors of cargoes of sandalwood, bêche-de-mer, tortoiseshell, pearls and oyster shell, guano, and lumber for the teeming markets on the Pacific Basin's western rim and around the world. They also established an American presence and contributed to the growing national interest in the marine territory west of California.

CHAPTER NINE

Yankee Scavengers
in the Pacific Basin

Fortune-seeking Americans drawn to the Pacific Basin during the nineteenth century included, besides maritime fur men and whale hunters, a group of itinerant pioneers who searched this water hemisphere for natural products. These Yankee gatherers marketed most of their varied cargoes on the Asian shore, chiefly at Canton and in the enlarging Australian marketplace. They delivered a few South Sea products to American and European markets. For the nation's future in the Pacific Basin, these adventurers established an American presence and interest there no less significant than those of the maritime fur men and whalers. Like the other American maritime pioneers, they were ship-bound; but they differed from most in that they were unspecialized in their economic quest, and they were not restricted to a limited exploitation territory, as were maritime fur men. Like the Yankee sea hunters, they ranged all over the western ocean in search of natural products, and in their peregrinations for profitable cargoes they exposed uncharted islands, passages, and anchorages. They too scattered American influence, positive and negative, throughout the Pacific Basin.[1]

South Sea bounty collected by these Yankee pioneers included bêche-de-mer, tortoiseshell, mother-of-pearl, shark fins, edible bird nests, grain, fish, salt, coal, sandalwood and other exotic woods, and crude construction lumber for Asiatic and Australian markets. Copra, copper, cowhides and tallow, arrowroot, vanilla, spices, and guano they delivered to American and European markets. Yankee scavengers also carried on a ghoulish traffic in native bondage labor for Pacific-island plantations, as well as the dried, tattooed human heads.

These maritime frontiersmen used a wide range of vessels in their business, including the schooner (a fore-and-aft-rigged ship having two or more masts and of from 50 to 150 tons burthen) and the square-rigged brig of 350 tons capacity. To accommodate the bonanza guano trade in later years, Pacific Basin gatherers directed New England shipwrights to enlarge transport vessels to from 900 to 1200 tons capacity. Most of these later ships plying Pacific Basin waters were of brig construction; however, by mid-century these pioneers also used swift clipper ships and even some steam-powered vessels to collect products and transport them to markets.

Yankee gatherers might begin their collecting circuit for Asian and Australian markets in the North Pacific, sailing to the Northwest Coast for salmon and construction lumber (from the redwood forests of northern California and softwood stands along the Oregon-Washington coast) and grain and flour from California and Oregon farms and mills. On the way to Canton and Sydney markets, collector-ship captains frequently called at Christmas Island, to send crewmen ashore to gather salt. Reports circulating in Atlantic-coast ports were that "For years the sun has been making salt in the lagoons" there "and whole shiploads of beautiful crystals could be obtained without trouble."[2]

After stops for tortoiseshell, bêche-de-mer, shark fins, edible bird nests, sandalwood, and coir (also called *kyar,* a stiff fiber from coconut husks, used in making ropes and mats) in the Fijis, they proceeded to the Tuamotu and Cook islands. These waters sustained pearl-bearing oysters with their mother-of-pearl, the milky, iridescent internal layer in oyster and abalone shells used at the time to make buttons and ornaments. While crewmen waded the shallow lagoons in search of shellfish, ship captains dickered with native divers to probe the richer oyster beds at depths of from five to ten fathoms. Shallow waters rimming portions of the Hawaiian Islands yielded pearl-bearing oysters and mother-of-pearl. As in the case of other valuable local natural products, Kamehameha I decreed pearl and shell collecting a royal monopoly.

Proceeding westward on their collecting circuity, Yankee gatherers often anchored offshore from dense forests of the Philippines and other tropical archipelagoes to trade with native woodcutters for *koa, 'ōhi'a,* and several mahoganylike woods used by Asiatic craftsmen to fashion furniture and paneling and to carve totems, curios, and fetishes. New Zealand forests furnished tall, straight, strong conifers, which Yankees sold as ship masts.

The gatherers' circuit for Pacific Basin products marketable in the United States and Europe was narrower. Leading items were kauri gum, the resin from pine trees found in New Zealand and on Espiritu Santo in the New Hebrides, used in the manufacture of linoleum and varnish; guano, a prime fertilizer, from the arid equatorial islands; copper ore from Chile; arrowroot starch, vanilla, and spices from the Pacific Basin's southwestern tropical islands; cowhides and tallow from California and Hawai'i; and copra, dried coconut meat (oil pressed from copra was converted to soap and candles). By 1850 copra had become one of the most valuable natural products moving in Pacific Basin commercial channels.[3]

Yankee scavengers paid Pacific Basin natives for products and services with trinkets, cloth, hardware, guns and ammunition, whiskey, and sea-mammal ivory. Above all other items offered, islanders esteemed whales' teeth most, because they ascribed to them "magical qualities" and wore them as ornaments. Collectors obtained these from the whalers.[4]

The most sought-after Pacific Basin natural products, because they consistently were the most profitable, were bêche-de-mer, sandalwood, cowhides and tallow, and guano. Bêche-de-mer (French, from the Portuguese *bicho-do-mar,* in Malay *trepang,* also known as sea slug, *dri,* sea cucumber, and "fish," in the Fijis) is a large holothurian, soft-bodied distant relative of the starfish, esteemed as a food additive by Asians, primarily in soups. Bêche-de-mer is widely distributed over reefs and ledges in the warm, shallow waters of the central and southern Pacific Ocean; the richest grounds are in the Fijis, followed by New Caledonia and the New Hebrides. It is usually harvested in shallow water at low tide, in about three feet of water, although the best are found at depths of from one to three fathoms, requiring divers for harvesting.

New England scavengers, primarily men from Salem, came to dominate bêche-de-mer collecting in the Pacific Basin. Around 1812 they discovered it to be a profitable item in the Canton market.

Primacy in this pelagic industry by New Englanders in the Fijis resulted in the application of efficient, systematized collecting and processing operations, involving large numbers of native workers. To obtain exclusive collecting rights and the required labor force on a particular island, Yankee ship captains often had to negotiate elaborate arrangements with local monarchs, including gifts of arms and ammunition and alliances requiring support from the ship's cannon in wars of conquest against neighboring islands. David Whippey, the New England castaway and Fijian court favorite, with his command of the local language and native ways, was strategically useful in establishing and maintaining his fellow countrymen in the Fijis for bêche-de-mer collecting.

Gathering a cargo of bêche-de-mer began with native divers harvesting holothurians in reed baskets, carrying them to the beach, soaking them in pits filled with seawater, to remove surface slime, then boiling them for brief periods in iron kettles described as about the size of New England sugar-maple vats. Next native workers slit and cleaned them and carried them to the smokehouses, thatched buildings about one hundred feet long and fifteen to thirty feet wide, sealed along their low eaves with dirt embankments. Smoke from green-wood fires in pits the length of the smokehouse, tended by natives, engulfed the dressed and stretched "fish"; in about a week they cured out "hard as shoe leather and rattled as they were bagged and stowed aboard ship."[5]

Bêche-de-mer sold in Asian markets for from ten to twenty cents a pound, or fifteen to twenty-five dollars a picul (133 1/3 pounds). In the early years of sea-cucumber collecting, Canton was the principal market; by the 1850s merchants at Hong Kong were purchasing large quantities of the "fish"; and Yankee gatherers also began marketing it at Manila in the Philippines, after Spanish colonial officials relaxed the ban on commerce with aliens, this move due in part to avoid the increased port fees on the China coast. Throughout the age of scavengers in the Pacific Basin, New Englanders remained paramount in bêche-de-mer collecting. By 1834 fourteen ships from Salem coasted the Fijis for "fish" cargoes; a report on Pacific Basin commerce just before 1860 announced that bêche-de-mer was still being harvested there, and that Yankees continued to dominate the traffic.[6]

Sandalwood ranked with bêche-de-mer as a prime trade item in Asian markets. *Santalum album,* a highland Indo-Malayan parasitic tree, yields a fragrant wood. Stands often grow in nearly inaccessible locations, so that cutting and transporting it to the beaches for loading aboard ships was dangerous, exhausting work for native timber crews and the haole overseers.

Sandalwood was used by many Pacific Basin peoples. Hawaiians and other Polynesians mixed its aromatic extract with coconut oil and used the lotion as a body rub; but the Chinese made the widest use of it. Artisans drew from its core, which varied in color from brown to yellow to red, a dyestuff and a fragrant oil used in perfume, and they carved pieces of sandalwood into fans, totems, fetishes, and furniture. Household use included burning it as an insect repellent, a pleasant-smelling incense, and a fumigant to purge rooms of disease. Physicians used extract of sandalwood to concoct a healing compound. And Buddhists honored deity idols by burning joss sticks (sandalwood slivers); joss papers, saturated with sandalwood oil, were burned at funerals and other observances.[7]

India's Malabar Coast and Timor in the Indonesian archipelago had been traditional suppliers of sandalwood for Asian markets, but centuries of intensive exploitation had by 1800 virtually exhausted these sources of the aromatic wood. Wide-ranging newcomers, most of them Yankees (but joined by a few gatherers from Australia, New Zealand, and the French and Dutch Pacific Basin colonies), searched for new sandalwood sources. They found the plant widely dispersed in highland locations on several Pacific Basin subtropical archipelagoes, including the Fijis, Marquesas, New Hebrides, and the Hawaiian Islands.

Collectors found that difficulties in accumulating cargoes of sandalwood were offset by the profits. For several years they were able to obtain great quantities in the forests of Fiji and other island groups for one cent a pound and to sell it at Canton for thirty-four cents a pound. Scavenger-ship captains established small sandalwood-collecting settlements in the islands, much as the whalers were doing, populating them with crewmen (and their island-women companions), to supervise native gangs in cutting and delivering sandalwood to the anchorages. This commerce flourished from about 1800 into the 1860s, although the bonanza period was over by 1830. Early profits were unprecedented in the Asian trade; the captain of the Boston ship *Hunter* in 1812 negotiated for a cargo of Fijian sandalwood for eight hundred dollars in trade goods and sold it at Canton for eighty thousand dollars.[8]

Fijian sandalwood-traffic protocol included application of the ubiquitous Pacific Basin "taboo." An island monarch would pledge his retainers to a particular Yankee captain to cut and deliver to the anchorage a cargo of sandalwood and seal the deal with a "taboo," or ban, on the "sale of wood to other ships in the meantime." The collector, returning eighteen months later, would find the contract "scrupulously observed."[9]

Intensive harvesting had, by 1820, virtually exhausted Fijian sandalwood supplies. Meanwhile American collectors were turning to the Hawaiian Islands for cargoes of this popular Asian market item. Several Yankee scavengers had been working this source from the 1790s, but never with the intensity they applied in Fiji, largely because Kamehameha I had made the sandalwood trade a royal monopoly, requiring that he share in the profits of this industry.

Close royal control of the sandalwood traffic limited participation and had the effect of excluding most independent gatherers. Thus in 1812 Jonathan and Nathan Winship and William Heath Davis concluded a pact with Kamehameha I, granting them exclusive access to the Hawaiian kingdom's sandalwood preserves for ten years, with the king to receive one-fourth of the value of the sandalwood marketed each year. The Winship-Davis combine sent five sandalwood-laden vessels to Canton, before the threat of seizure by British naval forces roaming the Pacific during the War of 1812 forced suspension of shipments. When it was safe to resume their enterprise, the Winships and Davis found that Kamehameha had repudiated the contract, due, it was claimed, to the influence of resident Britons. Soon after 1815 a group of American businessmen, Bryant & Sturgis Company of Boston and the John Jacob Astor Company of New York, gained control of the Hawaiian sandalwood trade.[10]

The royal share Americans paid in goods, ships, and specie; the annual value of the sandalwood carried in their ships from the Kingdom of Hawai'i exceeded half a million dollars. On all the islands except Kaua'i, local chiefs served as agents for the royal government and were required to meet annual quotas of sandalwood. They impressed both native men and women to cut and carry packs of *Santalum* to the beaches. By 1827 over five thousand Hawaiians were working to meet a royal assignment of fifteen thousand piculs (one thousand tons). The court treasurer received a credit of four dollars for each picul.[11]

Kamehameha I guarded against the reckless exploitation of his kingdom's resources. A shrewd negotiator, braced by the counsel of John Young and other loyal court haoles, he was reported to "drive hard bargains" with Yankee businessmen. The most civic-minded of the early Hawaiian monarchs, he used sandalwood income to construct internal improvements, including roads and port facilities; to accumulate a merchant fleet of six vessels, which he assigned to the China trade for royal benefit; and to increase his personal power.

Kamehameha I died in 1819 and his successor diverted the sandalwood income to indulging sybaritic tastes. This led to wasteful, nonproductive, and escalating expenditures. Imports to Honolulu for use by the royal family included fancy liquors, gourmet foods, exquisite textiles, musical instruments, military regalia for parade display, and luxury barges. In 1820 Kamehameha II purchased through local New England interests *Cleopatra's Barge,* the 191-ton Crowninshield yacht of Salem, Massachusetts, for $90,000. Court officials renamed it *Haaheo o Hawaii (Pride of Hawai'i).*[12]

Three dreadful consequences followed this hedonistic orgy. Their increased pressure on island chiefs for larger sandalwood harvests to support their prodigal life-style predictably led to "unregulated cutting," which destroyed the "best and most readily available sandalwood," leaving only marginal stands. Mindless disregard by the royal court and island chiefs for commoner well-being, simply for the sake of meeting increased sandalwood quotas, had a drastic impact on the kingdom's demography. Forced labor, both of men and women, weakened large numbers of native workers, leading to permanent crippling or premature death, and contributed substantially to the shocking nineteenth-century decline of the native Hawaiian population.[13]

161

Independent collectors, excluded by the royal monopoly, obtained some sandalwood from clandestine negotiations with readily corruptible island chiefs. Their most productive source was on Kaua'i, where Kaumuali'i marketed the fragrant wood from his territory to suit his personal interests in defiance of the royal government's ban on commerce outside the pale of the monopoly assignment.

However, reckless, "wasteful" cutting throughout the Hawaiian archipelago had so diminished sandalwood stands by 1830 that no amount of forced labor could meet the demand. The result was that Yankee scavengers joined British collectors, based in Australia and New Zealand, and French and Dutch collectors, from their Pacific Basin colonies, in harvesting the limited supply of sandalwood in the Marquesas and New Hebrides.[14]

Yankee scavengers prospered in the sandalwood trade and, as was the case for whalers and other Pacific Basin pioneers, their wide-ranging quest had substantive future effects on their nation's westward commitment. They too confirmed the Anglo-American frontier process. They added to the knowledge of this water hemisphere, established an enlarged American presence by forming small island settlements for servicing the scavenger fleet, founded mixed bloodlines through liaisons with island women, and generally contributed to the Americanization of the Pacific Basin.

Other Pacific Basin products Yankee collectors found profitable were cowhides and tallow. European and American maritime pioneers introduced cattle and horses into the islands and on the eastern rimland. Beef cattle particularly flourished on the island of Hawai'i and in California. Gatherers harvested some hides and tallow from Hawaiian Island herds, but California ranches furnished most of these products.

Central and southern California, by virtue of their mild climate and vast tracts of nutritious natural forage, were unsurpassed as stock-raising territory. Cattle there were descended from stock introduced by Spanish clerical and lay settlers in the eighteenth century. The animals had been permitted to range freely, receiving little ranching attention except at seasonal roundups for branding; by 1820 these semiwild cattle numbered well over half a million head.

Mexico achieved independence in 1821 and extended its dominion to the Pacific coast province of California the following year. Yankee ship captains had clandestinely worked the California coast in Spanish times for sea-otter and seal skins and trade with missions and civil settlements; after independence aliens were permitted to trade openly. For several years under the Mexican regime, their primary cargoes consisted of cowhides and tallow.

Most products Yankee scavengers "ransacked" from the Pacific Basin's rich bounty they marketed at Canton. However, hides and tallow they delivered to New England ports, the hides to sustain the booming local shoe, boot, and harness industry, the tallow for soap and candlemaking.

The Pacific Basin has been an enduringly rich literary source. Its exploration, colonization, military and diplomatic legacy, and sustained economic exploitation are but a few of the themes developed by its community of admiring writers. The scavenger industry is no exception. Among other works, it generated Richard Henry Dana's *Two Years Before the Mast* (1840), a maritime classic, accomplishing for hide-and-tallow collecting what Herman Melville's *Moby Dick* achieved for whaling.[15]

Dana artfully blends hardships endured by seamen aboard ships coasting the California littoral for hide-and-tallow cargoes with the color, adventure, and mystique of this region during the early nineteenth century. *Two Years Before the Mast* contains accounts of *vaqueros* slaughtering cattle and curing the hides. The lack of harbors on the California coast required the delivery of dried hides in crude, two-wheeled *carretas* to an *embarcadero* (rendezvous on the beach), often flanked by towering bluffs, the packs of hides lowered on ropes or simply thrown down to the thin ribbon of shore. There crewmen stacked several stiff hides on their heads and waded into the pounding surf to longboats rocking a safe distance from the shoal-ribbed beach. Waiting deckhands then ferried the hides to the mother ship, anchored one to three miles out at sea.

Ships of several nations called at the embarcaderos for California cattle products, although Yankee-registered vessels were most numerous, followed by those of British registry. Dana related that it required from two to three years for a ship to accumulate a cargo of from twenty to thirty thousand hides. Once their holds were packed with the reeking cowskins (vaqueros rarely scraped the inner surface clear of flesh), the captains sailed to San Diego. There crewmen unloaded the hides and transported them ashore to processing works, huge vats of salt solution manned by kānaka who lived in settlements around the harbor. This additional attention prepared the hides for the long voyage to Atlantic-coast markets.[16]

Mission cattle herds, each at the time of independence numbering in the tens of thousands, supplied most of the hides and tallow in the early years. When secularization occurred during the 1830s, the number of privately owned ranches increased; by 1842 there were ninety-two ranches between San Luis Obispo and San Diego. They became the principal source of hides and tallow for the collector fleet, although missions continued to furnish a substantial quantity each year.[17]

Collector-ship captains expended very little cash in purchasing hides and tallow, using goods that they stocked aboard each vessel, much like a seagoing general store. They paid in goods an average of two dollars for each hide (called "California bank-notes") and six cents a pound for tallow. These California products doubled in value in New England markets.[18]

The reciprocal value to Mexican California of hide-and-tallow collecting is affirmed by the conclusion that it yielded "virtually its only source of wealth. . . . From the sale of hides and tallow . . . Californians obtained almost everything they made use of in the way of clothing and manufactured articles. Similarly, government officials, whether civil or military, derived almost all public funds for salaries and other necessary ends from the revenue received directly or indirectly from the trade."[19]

And this phase of gathering by Yankee maritime pioneers abetted the Americanization process in this strategic segment of the Pacific Basin's eastern littoral. The hide-and-tallow trade, a primitive but profitable enterprise, drew a trickle of Yankee immigration to San Diego, Monterey, and San Francisco—agents, brokers, shipping representatives—to service the collector fleet. These commercial support enclaves became, as was the case in other parts of the Pacific Basin, vanguards of progressively enlarging American communities. And their presence augured the ultimate appearance of absorbing, integrative nationalizing currents—diplomatic, military, and political—by their home government.

In the declining years of the hide-and-tallow trade, around 1850, Yankee scavengers found another Pacific Basin product to sustain their collecting enterprise. This was guano, dried bird excrement used by European and American farmers as fertilizer. Traditionally they had applied animal manure and limestone to increase agriculture production. Guano was rated much higher as an agricultural supplement; one ton of it equaled fifteen to twenty tons of farm manure or limestone.[20]

Myriads of fish-eating seafowl—boobies, albatrosses, fish hawks, cormorants, pelicans, and gannets—populated the Pacific Basin's littoral and islands, using the land areas for roosting and nesting and feeding on the surrounding rich marine life. In much of the Pacific Basin, tropical rains washed the excrement away; in some coastal areas (Chile and Peru) and islands, however, particularly those situated in the doldrums, where rainfall is less than twenty inches annually, it accumulated to depths of several feet. One Pacific Basin authority concludes that "The guano formed from bird waste is an excellent fertilizer. Each bird deposits several dollars' worth of guano each year, making the birds among the most valuable in the world."[21]

European and Latin American capitalists opened the Peruvian and Chilean guano beds around 1812; by 1850 annual exports from these coastal fertilizer pits amounted to about fifty thousand tons. They marketed guano at from thirty to forty dollars a ton until midcentury, when British interests formed a cartel and hiked the price to about sixty-five dollars a ton. Fortuitously, relief for agrarian consumers came about the same time, with the discovery of new Pacific Basin guano deposits by Yankee maritime prospectors.[22]

The first reported discovery of an unclaimed Pacific Basin guano source by an American occurred in 1832, and it came about purely by accident. During Captain Michael Baker's trading cruise that year, one of his seamen, a young man named Warren Wilbut, became seriously ill. On his deathbed Wilbut drew from Captain Baker the promise that he would be interred on land rather than by the customary burial at sea. About the time of Wilbut's demise, crewmen sighted an island; they anchored, and a party went ashore in a longboat to dig Wilbut's grave. They found the island covered with the "most remarkable kind of soil," a fine, white, dusty material, which choked the men as they dug the grave. It proved to be an accumulation of guano several feet thick. The discovery was hailed in the United States as "marvelous," and the "basis of food for millions."[23]

Baker Island became the bonanza for this phase of the scavenger industry. As word spread, Yankee mariners scoured the mid-Pacific for other guano-bearing atolls. They found Britons and Frenchmen prospecting there, too, and heated disputes erupted over title to certain islands. The Americans appealed to their nation for succor, and supportive nationalizing currents came their way in two forms. First a vessel from the United States Pacific Squadron was dispatched from San Francisco, during 1855, to survey the guano-bearing atolls and protect American claimants "in their territorial rights." And the following year Congress approved an act "to authorize Protection to be given to Citizens of the United States who may discover Deposits of Guano." The law permitted a ship captain to assign United States sovereignty over any unclaimed island he found to contain deposits of guano. And he was allowed to mine the fertilizer under legal protection against others. The procedure for establishing American title and exclusive use by the discoverer included planting a staff with the American flag on the island, placing copies of an affidavit declaring the rights of the discoverer in two glass bottles and burying them on the atoll at remote distances, and posting two additional copies in public view.[24]

Braced by these protections, Yankee scavengers prospected widely over the central Pacific for guano-bearing islands; as a result of several years of intensive exploration, by 1870 they had discovered and applied United States sovereignty to seventy of them. Baker, Howland, Johnston, and Jarvis islands were the most productive. Interestingly, of the natural resources Yankee scavengers "ransacked" from the Pacific Basin and marketed in the United States, none received the attention and applause accorded guano. Editors rated the maritime-fertilizer industry a signal contribution to the "national welfare" and "The importance of the discovery of guano islands, and the value of that fertilizing agent, can hardly be over estimated. . . . In their voyages of discovery our countrymen have been singularly fortunate, and may be said to have obtained the lion's share of these valuable islands."[25]

Most of these new American possessions were devoid of vegetation and potable water. For the most part, each was a tiny atoll surrounded by a forbidding coral reef, treacheorus shallows, and pounding surf, offering no easy shoreline docking or close-in anchorage. Captains of guano-carrier vessels found it best to anchor from one to three miles out, and even at that distance, slipped cables from the press of wicked currents and impetuous winds caused frequent wrecks on the island shoals.

Yankee collectors constructed the most elaborate mining works on Johnston Island, where guano, described as a fine powder resembling snow, covered an area of fifty acres to a depth of five feet. Ship captains established tent settlements around the deposits, brought in provisions and water from the Samoan and Hawaiian islands, and hired kānaka, described as the "best kind of laborers, being quiet, and good strong fellows," to work the pits. Native laborers constructed a jetty five hundred feet long, extending from the guano diggings into the shallows beyond the reef, and fitted it with rails, over which moved small wooden cars drawn by mules. A lighter, bargelike craft with mast and sail and of eight- to ten-ton capacity, transported fertilizer from the jetty to the ship. Each day the Johnston Island crew mined and loaded forty-five tons of guano.[26]

Scavengers occasionally included humans in the cargoes they collected from the Pacific Basin. As nineteenth-century American, British, French, Dutch, and German maritime pioneers developed mining, lumbering, plantation agriculture, stock raising, and other primary industries in the region, they required increasing numbers of unskilled workers. Collectors met these labor needs by supplying two classes of workers—contract and blackbird.

Workers recruited under the contract-labor system had some protection against exploitation and ill treatment, in that their home government required a commitment from the employer stipulating transportation to the work site, the wages and maintenance provided on the job, and repatriation at a specified time. The government of the Kingdom of Hawai'i under Kamehameha I imposed such a system to protect kānaka employed on ships and in the maritime fur trade, whaling, mining, and other Pacific Basin industries. As the demand for labor increased, the Chinese and Japanese governments each formulated a contract-labor system to protect the thousands of their countrymen recruited for service on Pacific Basin plantations, in the mines, lumbering, and in railroad building. Ship captains transported workers from home ports to the designated employer, who paid for each laborer's passage from an advance on the labor contract.

Blackbird labor was involuntary servitude. Blackbirding was a Pacific Basin colloquialism for the forcible seizure of natives, their confinement in chains aboard ship, and eventual sale to plantation, mine, or lumbering proprietors. This sordid enterprise was reminiscent of the Indian slave hunting during the eighteenth century by British traders based at Charleston, South Carolina, who captured interior tribesmen and sold them in the Charleston slave market as field hands for the Caribbean plantations.

Blackbirders preyed on native peoples residing on remote Melanesian, Micronesian, and occasionally Polynesian islands. The Solomon Islands were rated as prime sources for blackbird labor. It was claimed that blackbirders preferred aborigines from islands where missionaries had been at work, because "the docility taught" by the clerics made these natives "more tractable to the fields."[27]

Blackbirders used various ruses to capture unsuspecting islanders. Commonly a collector-ship captain anchored his vessel in a quiet cove and lured curious natives aboard with promises of presents. Crewmen seized the unsuspecting visitors, shackled them, and cast them below decks. In addition parties of armed crewmen roamed the island beaches and interior, hunting able-bodied men. Shackled captives were hauled aboard, crammed into dark, evil-smelling, insanitary bilge compartments, and held there until delivered to some distant mine, mill, or plantation, for an unthinkable ordeal of dawn-to-dark labor. It is estimated that each year between 1863 and 1900 at least fifteen hundred native men were delivered to the Australian plantations alone. Proprietors paid collector captains varying sums for able-bodied hands; Samoan plantation managers offered one hundred dollars per head.[28]

Labor hunters from Peru and Chile ranged over eastern Polynesia for workers to man the guano mines of coastal South America. Their pitiless slaving reduced the population of Easter Island by two-thirds.[29]

As was the case for continental-based frontiers, the remoteness from surveillance by law-and-order forces enabled maritime frontiersmen largely to do as they pleased, each becoming a law unto himself, virtually free from civic restraint. And just as Americans "ransacked" the rich continental environment in the most reckless, abandoned fashion, so did Yankee maritime pioneers, as scavengers, in unison with whalemen and fur traders, plunder with a seeming vengeance the South Seas' enormous human and material bounty.

British naval forces operating out of Australian and New Zealand ports attempted to monitor contract labor and watch for blackbirding in the Pacific Basin's southwestern quadrant, but even this designated marine territory was so vast that violators were largely unnoticed. An occasional American naval force prowling the Pacific might discourage excessive exploitation momentarily, but scavenger captains regarded this policing as only temporary interference with otherwise unfettered access to Pacific riches. American consuls stationed at Papeete in Tahiti, Apia in Samoa, and Honolulu in the Hawaiian Islands, and settlements in the Fijis also attempted to curb the rapacity of these maritime frontiersmen, but with no noticeable effect.

However, with all their recklessness and depravity, Yankee scavengers contributed, though admittedly less than other maritime frontiersmen, to the Americanization of the Pacific Basin. They discovered and applied United States sovereignty to island territories, plotted new maritime routes, and enlarged American presence in the basin by the tiny collector settlements they established on remote islands. They enhanced American interest in the Hawaiian Islands and coastal Mexican California, and they introduced what became an enlarging interest in Samoa by using the islands of that archipelago as support bases.

Certainly one group of Yankee pioneers who contributed substantially more to the Americanization of the Pacific Basin than scavengers were the representatives of an older, more stable expansion entity—the maritime traders.

The Maritime
Trading Frontier

Maritime trading, with agriculture, survived for a longer period as a Pacific Basin frontier enterprise than any other commercial venture established there by American pioneers. Every Yankee adventurer was a trader of sorts. Maritime fur men exchanged guns, ammunition, hardware, textiles, beads, and baubles with native hunters for the sea-otter pelts they marketed at Canton. Whalers traded manufactured goods and sea-mammal ivory to islanders for wood, water, and food. And scavengers collected Pacific Basin bounty from islander workers, paying the natives in goods.

Thus during pioneer times in the Pacific Basin there was only limited Yankee specialization; one might be a fur man for one voyage, a scavenger the next if he discovered the value of an island product in the Asian market, and a sea hunter when whaling became a bonanza industry. Among those early-day adventurers who tried their hand at several enterprises before becoming maritime merchants were William Shaler and Richard Cleveland, both of whom wrote books emphasizing the personal and public prospects for Americans in the Pacific Basin.[1]

The gradually enlarging community of Yankee sea merchants formed an identifiable frontier or expansion entity in this water hemisphere much like that on the continent, which, with the furmen's frontier and miners' frontier, was drawing American dominion westward, ever closer to the Pacific shore, absorbing the interstitial territory. The maritime trader's continental counterpart was the frontier merchant like Josiah Gregg, the Santa Fe trader, who ranged from Mississippi Valley entrepôts in mule-drawn freight caravans to the Río Grande, eventually establishing himself commercially and planting the American presence in strategic enclaves from Taos and Santa Fe to El Paso and into Chihuahua. The maritime trader accomplished the same purpose in the Pacific Basin, from San Diego, Monterey, and San Francisco to Honolulu, Apia, and in diminishing waves of influence on to Sydney, Manila, and Canton.

Marine traders eventually became distinguished from fur men, whalers, and scavengers, because rather than marketing raw products, their cargoes consisted largely of manufactured, consumer goods. As the nineteenth century advanced, the oceanic consuming public served by the maritime traders became varied. And it contrasted dramatically, from sophisticated co-hong merchants at Canton, who displayed a surface attitude of commercial indifference, to an ever-enlarging and warmly receptive island consumer constituency of natives, missionaries, planters, and tiny settlements of beached seamen and escaped convicts from the New South Wales penal colony. Traders supplied the China market from large cargo ships, the island market from small coasting schooners. On most of the island trader ships, the captain's cabin was "fitted up as a variety store" for buyers to come aboard and shop. And crewmen by marine tradition were permitted to carry in their sea chests "a little property . . . called a venture," to trade on their own when ashore. If they found the "market uncommonly supplied," they waited for a more promising port.[2]

The maritime traders' entry into Pacific Basin commerce dated from the early days of the republic (the *Empress of China* first tapped the fabled riches of Cathay in 1784), and their initiative helped assure the young republic's future. Its economy had been severely battered by the recent War of Independence; the nation was suffocating under an awesome debt in excess of $50 million. Because at that time its production yielded only limited manufactures and consisted largely of raw materials, commerce would have to be its primary means for recovering private fortunes and establishing public solvency. But accustomed markets for American raw products were limited or closed. Great Britain refused to open its home ports on a free and equal basis to American shipping. Yankees could trade there, but only on suppressive, unilateral terms. And the British West Indies colonies, a lucrative trade source during colonial times, were virtually closed to Yankee suppliers. France also restricted American trade with its West Indies colonies. Spain continued its exclusionist mercantilist policies and refused to negotiate a reasonable commercial treaty with the United States. And prospects were dim for any substantial trade with other European nations.

Thwarted to the east, Americans turned west to overcome their nation's economic malaise. Cathay and the tradition of its "fabulous" riches had been a mythical attraction for the West even before Marco Polo's peregrinations through the Orient. The draw of exotic Cathay was fueled in the American mind by latter-day accounts by John Ledyard, Shaler, Cleveland, and others.

By this shift in the mercantile path, Yankee maritime traders eventually generated profits, oftentimes of immense proportion, and helped produce national prosperity. They were abetted in this double-edged recovery by four timely developments: (1) A willingness by British suppliers to extend generous credit, albeit with punitively high interest charges, for the purchase of manufactured goods (hardware, textiles, leather goods, gin, glass, guns, and ammunition); this provided traders with goods, some of them acceptable at Canton, and most of them esteemed at ports of call en route to Canton, which traders exchanged for other products or specie. (2) The discovery and use of "chain trading" en route to Canton, where at each exchange the maritime merchant profited or enhanced the value of his cargo. (3) The disappearance of most other maritime carriers for Europe during the protracted Anglo-French wars, beginning soon after 1790. And (4) the application of improved marine technology, notably the clipper ship.

Easy credit from British suppliers was a godsend for near-destitute Americans. Their first ships to Canton, the primary market throughout the Pacific Basin's pioneer period, 1784–1861, carried cargoes of ginseng collected from the American wilds. The holds of the *Empress of China* were packed with barrels of this herb. Chinese merchants accepted it only reluctantly, because they favored Korean ginseng; they preferred specie as payment for the tea, silk, and porcelain Yankee traders carried to home and European ports. This insistence on gold and silver for settling transactions created a specie drain in the United States and had a deleterious effect on the struggling home economy. Maritime fur men and scavengers had found the means, drawn from Pacific Basin resources, to meet this problem, but maritime merchants dealing in nonlocal products faced a handicap. This finally was eased by access to European manufactured goods obtained with British credit. During a two-year period in the mid-1780s, Americans purchased $30 million worth of goods on credit from British suppliers.

"Chain trading" was another way Yankee traders accumulated goods and products negotiable in the Canton marketplace. Their ships laden with European trade goods and some grain and other locally produced items, trader captains made for Spain and Portugal as first links in the chain, for a limited exchange permitted by these nations' restrictive mercantilist rules, then to Gibraltar for the sale of goods and grain for specie. A circuit of Mediterranean ports on the European, Levantine, and African shores brought aboard wine, olive oil, leather goods, and textiles. The Levant became increasingly strategic in the American-Chinese commercial network; at Smyrna Yankee ship captains traded for Turkish opium, which Chinese importers came to treasure more than specie. Returning to the Atlantic and coasting West Africa, American merchants stopped at Capetown, Mauritius, Bombay, and Batavia for exchanges before calling at Macao. At that point Chinese pilots guided the Yankee ships up the Pearl River to the Whampoa anchorage and the Canton wharfs, where cargoes were transferred to the American factory. Each stop in the chain trade involved a negotiation that enhanced expedition profits, all the while accumulating a wider range of goods. Thus the character of the cargo might change several times and its Canton value progressively increase.

Maritime traders' fortunes improved appreciably soon after 1790. Aside from the benefit of achieving access to marketable goods for Canton buyers, Yankee sea merchants received an unexpected advantage from the outbreak of the Anglo-French wars during the 1790s, which extended to 1815. England and France, diverted from customary peacetime enterprises of industry and commerce, were engaged in titanic combat on land and sea. Naval and privateer vessels of each preyed on shipping of the other; this enabled American maritime interests to become the prime carriers for Europe. It was a hazardous and costly advantage, however, because Yankee traders suffered from peremptory seizure of ships and cargoes and impressment of crews by both French and British sea raiders. And toward the close of the hostilities, American shipping was restrained by a national embargo and, finally, United States entry into the war, aligned against Great Britain. But for the most part it was a bonanza time for American traders. They achieved maritime preeminence, a position they maintained until the Civil War. American maritime interests prospered from commerce to all ports of the world, and particularly those in the Pacific Basin, becoming second only to Great Britian and its powerful East India Company in the Canton market and surpassing all competitors in the remainder of the Pacific Basin. By 1805 American traders were carrying to China goods valued at $5,300,000 and importing from there goods valued at $5,100,000. In addition, before United States involvement in the War of 1812, many of the commodities from Canton were reshipped from the United States to Europe. In some years over half the tea carried by Yankee traders from Canton was reshipped to Europe.[3]

Yet another reason American traders were able to establish mercantile primacy in the Pacific Basin generally and in the difficult but rich China trade second only to Great Britain, while at the same time making a substantial contribution to lifting the young nation out of its economic doldrums, was maritime traders' ready application of improvements in marine technology. Americans had built superior sailing vessels from early colonial times. Environmental conditions, particularly in the northern colonies, drew people to the sea, creating a reservoir of skilled seamen for all types of maritime duty. Pine and oak forests yielded shipbuilding essentials, responded to by an incomparable community of marine designers and shipwrights. Every New England estuary of any size had a shipyard. In colonial times Yankee shipwrights constructed tough, sturdy craft for North Atlantic fisheries; swift schooners, barques, scows, and brigs for the West Indies and Mediterranean trader and for smuggling; and East Indiamen, huge, slow moving 1000-ton cargo carriers for the British East India Company.

Most Yankee traders used the 300-ton square-rigged brig in the China trade; for the growing island trade they used the 50- to

150-ton schooner. As Pacific Basin commerce expanded, American marine designers conceived several new ship types; the two most widely adopted by Pacific Basin traders were the Medford and the clipper. The Medford was a miniature East Indiaman, a 500-ton craft with a crew of 18, one-half as large as the East Indiaman with its crew of 125, developed in Medford, Massachusetts. With neater bow and compressed hull, the Medford under sail was twice as fast as the East Indiaman; it became a heavily worked carrier of the New England manufactures that arose after the War of 1812, from that region's industrial revolution—textiles, leather goods, and hardware. In addition Medford ships became popular carriers of English goods for British exporters, to the chagrin of English shipping interests. This carrier trader to Pacific Basin markets was well developed by the 1830s.

But the most exciting sailing ship of the nineteenth century was the clipper. As Great Britain and other European nations recovered from war and resumed the competitive commercial contest with Yankee maritime merchants, Americans sought more speed and capacity from their trader craft than current vessels provided. There had been so-called clipper schooners and clipper brigs since 1812, the term *clipper* denoting speed and "smartness." Several marine designers contributed to the evolution of the clipper ship: John W. Griffeths, chief draftsman for Smith and Dimon of New York; and Donald McKay, New York trained but employed as a master builder in New England yards. The clipper ship has been described as built and rigged for speed. It was generally larger than older-style sailing vessels, with sharper bow and stern, longer in proportion to its width, and "more heavily sparred than the full-bodied, bluff-bowed ships" of earlier generations. Sailors called it the "greyhound of the sea." The *Rainbow,* 750 tons, was the first clipper built in New York; however, Boston "carried the clipper ship to its ultimate perfection." Eight clippers were built and sailing on Pacific waters before 1850.[4]

Yankee obsession with the clipper ship and the conviction that it was the ultimate in oceanic transport so mesmerized American traders that they either became oblivious or indifferent to a companion development in marine technology—the steam-powered ship. Americans were prompt to apply steam power to inland water transport, with domestic shippers maintaining steamboats on the Mississippi River and its tributaries before 1820. But maritime interests adamantly held to wooden hulls and sail, over steel hulls and steam power. This sentimental devotion to the sailing ship worked to their disadvantage, because British shippers, with no predilection for sailing vessels, adapted their trader fleet to steam at once, progressively improved this type of marine transport, and after the American Civil War surpassed Yankees in the size and efficiency of their merchant marine fleet.

In the period between the California gold rush and the Civil War, American businessmen established steamer service between Panama and San Francisco and eventually to Honolulu. And the American Navy gradually added steam-powered warships to the Pacific squadron before 1861. But for the remainder of the pioneer period in the Pacific Basin, Yankee traders for the most part held to sailing craft.

Pacific Basin navigation was improved by the periodic upgrading of charts and maps, revised from reports, letters, and logs of trading vessels, as well as whaler, scavenger, and maritime fur ships. Several mainland newspapers published ship captains' letters, reports of islands discovered, and hazards to navigation. Typical of the newspaper reports published primarily for the maritime constituency was an 1854 letter from Captain Upshur of the barque *Orion,* in the New Bedford *Daily Mercury Marine Journal:* "Saw a shoal extending from E. to W. about 2 miles from Clipperton Rock with heavy breakers ... most dangerous place for vessels, who should always give the Rock a wide berth." Christmas Island had become a trader ship graveyard; the Boston *Daily Evening Traveler,* on 7 December 1864, warned in its column "Notice to Mariners," that "Vessels from San Francisco to Sydney should give this Island a wide berth—at least 100 miles—for I know of four or five wrecked there, and the masters all stated that they were forty or fifty miles to the eastward. But there is a strong westerly current." During 1847 the whaleships *Mozart* and *Maria Helena,* the *J. C. Fremont,* a lumber ship, and the Danish barque *Zorgen Lorentzen,* with a cargo of oats and wheat, were destroyed on Christmas Island. And a warning report published in the Boston *Daily Journal,* 23 October 1850, submitted by Samuel C. Jones, mate of the *Harrison,* revealed that Clipperton Rock was "marked doubtful" on the charts of the North Pacific: "There is a reef off the north end extending a quarter of a mile, another off the south end, half that extent. They must be near the surface as the sea was very smooth, and the breakers could be seen very distantly from the ship's maintop. As this rock is liable to be fallen in with vessels from California for Peru or Chile, the writer submits this information for the benefit of navigators who may be bound to California."[5]

During their pioneer period in the Pacific Basin, American traders established a commercial network that focused on five primary market points, each requiring special attention to local protocol, product preference, and exchange technique: China; Australia and New Zealand; the Pacific islands; the American littoral, from Bering Strait virtually to Tierra del Fuego; and Japan, after 1854. Like the land-bound Santa Fe trader, the maritime merchant established a vital American presence at market points that produced an alterative impact in the local economy, as well as in institutions and life-style. In each trade constituency, besides introducing occidental goods, Yankee adventurers also planted cultural seeds that germinated with variant force. In some places they were so strong that annexation was the ultimate fate; in others they produced a mild to strong adoption or at least an imitation of American ways.

The most profitable market and the one receiving major attention from maritime traders during their pioneer period in the Pacific Basin was the Chinese emporium at Canton. However, to Americans as well as British, Portuguese, and other nationals who preceded them on the Asian coast, the situation there was little short of bizarre. The Chinese operated from the ethnocentric position that their civilization was superior, while the remainder of the world was barbarian. They regarded all nations as tributary, their subjects or citizens as "foreign devils." Chinese officials claimed that they had no need for the goods and products traders offered them; besides, these items were inferior. Thus in the age of the so-called "Old China trade," the period before 1842, alien traders had to submit to the arbitrary rules and at times daily "whims" of Chinese officials and the co-hong, the merchant guild. Portuguese traders in 1577, with Chinese "sufferance," established a station at Macao and from there were permitted to conduct a restricted trade with the mainland. Russian traders were permitted to do business at the Siberian border settlement of Kyakhta.

Beginning in 1784 Americans, like the earlier Europeans, found that they could trade only at the pleasure of the Chinese imperial government, which restricted all alien commerce to the South China port of Canton. Yankee newcomers observed that besides the British, present under the auspices of the East India Company, there were French, Portuguese, Spanish, Dutch, Swedish, Danish, and German traders, all seeking a share of the rich Asian commerce. British agents at Canton in particular scorned the newcomers, claiming Americans would never succeed in the China trade without a settlement base in the East Indies close to Canton. Yankee maritime traders ignored this gratuitous speculation, and by 1790 twenty-eight of their ships cleared Canton; by 1800 over one hundred called there, and they ranked second only to the leader, Great Britain, in volume of trade.[6]

Americans promptly learned the suppressive rules Chinese officials applied to alien traders. Only during the summer trading season could they reside at their factories, adjacent to the city of Canton; the remainder of the year they were expected to stay at Macao. Under no circumstances were women permitted in the factories. Because the Chinese imperial government regarded all other nations as inferior, it refused to negotiate any sort of diplomatic agreement with Western nations. Thus traders had no treaty rights to protect them. Chinese edicts banned aliens from the city of Canton, their movements restricted to the trade area or compound set aside for foreign factories. "These buildings were rented from the hong merchants, and were situated on a plot of ground in the suburbs which extended a quarter of a mile along the north bank of the [Pearl] river." The factories, thirteen in number, were "handsome houses built in the European style, on the margin of the river. . . . They were generally of two stories, the lower being used as warehouses. They were whitewashed, and with their respective national flags displayed on a high staff above them, made a very pretty appearance."[7]

Americans conducted the China trade by independent companies, no single company becoming dominant or monopolistic, as was the case for the British and several other European mercantile interests. Throughout the pioneer period in the Pacific Basin, occasional "single-voyage ventures" were characteristic of the Yankee presence there. Traders concentrating on the Canton marketplace were based in several Atlantic-coast ports. Businessmen at Charleston and Norfolk sent only one vessel each to the Orient during the pioneer period. Baltimore interests were limitedly involved there. Philadelphia, America's largest city at the time, maintained a strong interest in the China trade, but New York and several New England ports, including Boston, Providence, and Salem, were the leaders. By 1825 five large American firms (Perkins and Company of Boston; Archer Company, and James Oakford Company of Philadelphia; and the Astor Company, and T. H. Smith Company of New York); as well as three smaller Boston firms (James P. Sturgis Company, Joseph Peabody Company, and Augustus Heard Company) pressed the East India Company for primacy in the oriental trade.

To purchase Chinese teas, silk, and chinaware, Yankee traders increasingly resorted to chain trading to obtain the required specie, largely Spanish milled dollars, which they acquired in the limited trade permitted in Spain and Portugal, in the more open exchanges at Gibraltar, and in the West Indies and Manila trade. English bills of exchange, from the enlarging European carrying trade, also became increasingly popular in the Canton market. Richard Cleveland, a pioneer American trader there, confirmed that this medium was readily "substituted for Spanish dollars, which formerly were indispensable to the prosecution of this trade." The growing preference for English bills of exchange at Canton is explained by the rapidly expanding popularity among Chinese consumers of "foreign mud," supplied largely by the British East India Company.[8]

American cargoes offered for sale in the Canton marketplace continued to include ginseng as well as bar iron, steel, gin, rum, cheese, simple manufactures, European trade goods, hardware, and some textile and leather goods. John Jacob Astor found Canton a prime outlet for furs, particularly beaver and muskrat, collected by his continental-based American Fur Company trappers. Astor's pelts are said to have "furnished the oil" for his "Aladdin's lamp" of fortune.[9]

However, it was opium, the "foreign mud," that became the pièce de résistance of the China trade for both American and British adventurers. It also became the catalyst that changed Asian trade patterns and transformed Chinese society, government, and relations with the West.

Chinese merchants had imported limited amounts of opium for centuries, and local physicians applied it in the healing arts. Portuguese and Dutch traders had been the early suppliers of this narcotic, collecting it from the principal sources—India and Turkey. Until around 1800 its use in China had not "constituted a major social or economic problem." By that time, however, the British East India Company had become the supplier of steadily increasing quantities of the drug. Chinese officials discovered its deleterious effect on subjects and issued decrees forbidding the importation and use of opium.[10]

British and American traders, unwilling to pass up the opportunity for certain profit and a means to eliminate the punitive specie drain, ignored this ban. By 1833 East India Company agents were importing each year from India opium valued at $14 million, this traffic providing over 50 percent of the value of British imports into China. And it is claimed that this grand old company had "come to depend on its [opium] sale for financing the government of India."[11]

Most American traders included Smyrna opium in their cargoes bound for Canton. Its advantage as a trade item included easy access to a cheap supply, its "high value in small bulk," and its aid in easing the specie drain. In spite of its illegality, Americans and Britons evaded port rules in connivance with local officials and were the major suppliers. Yankee ship captains in 1805 delivered 102 chests of opium to Canton; by the close of the 1820s this had increased to nearly 1500 chests a year, valued at over $2 million, representing one-tenth of American imports to China.[12]

American firms investing heavily in the Asian opium trade included Perkins and Company, Stephen Girard Company, Russell and Company, and Joseph Peabody. John Jacob Astor's China-bound ships also carried opium in their holds. So profitable was the opium traffic that for a time "every Boston and Salem merchant who could get it" carried the drug to Asia.[13]

Olyphant and Company of New York was reportedly the only American trading house at Canton that refused to participate in the opium trade, but rival merchants claimed "their motive was not so much moral as practical. They feared that a traffic forbidden by the Chinese government, however countenanced by its officials, would breed trouble. They were right."[14]

Court officials at Peking, alarmed at the widespread public addiction to opium, the morbid physical and social damage the drug inflicted on the populace, the corruption of port agents ostensibly enforcing the ban on opium imports, and the drain of specie from the Chinese economy to procure the drug, finally acted decisively. During 1838 they appointed Lin Tse-hsu special commissioner, with orders to stamp out the importation of opium. Lin moved with dispatch on the trader settlement at Canton. He placed the factories under siege, confiscated several million dollars worth of opium, and destroyed it.

British retaliation set off the so-called "Opium War." Naval squadrons blockaded portions of the Asian coast. During June 1840 a British army landed at Hong Kong, defeated the Chinese defenders, and captured Whampoa, Canton, and Shanghai. British commanders forced several capitulation agreements from vanquished Chinese leaders, culminating in the definitive Treaty of Nanking, concluded on 29 August 1842. This pact, which ended the Opium War, required China to cede Hong Kong to Great Britain, opened the ports of Canton, Amoy, Foochow, Ningpo, and Shanghai to foreign trade, granted Great Britain the beginnings of extraterritorialty over its subjects in China, and assessed the Chinese government reparations in the amount of $21 million, in Mexican dollars, to pay for the opium confiscated by Commissioner Lin and the costs to Great Britain of conducting the war.[15]

During the hostilities Commodore Lawrence Kearny, in command of the American frigate *Constitution*, maintained a protective presence near Canton, to guard American residents of the trader community. He warned Yankee traders that he would not "countenance" the opium trade under the protection of the United States flag.[16]

While there was no overt American involvement in the Opium War, officials in Washington, with China prostrate, sensed the opportunity to elicit a diplomatic advantage for United States interests in the western Pacific Basin. President John Tyler appointed Caleb Cushing, a Massachusetts congressman, to head the China Commission, its purpose to attempt to establish formal diplomatic relations with the Celestial Kingdom. Up to this stage in the Pacific Basin's American pioneer period, United States officials had concluded only one treaty with an Asian nation. Edmund Roberts in 1833 negotiated a pact with the leaders of Siam, pledging that nation to levy no tariff duties and to abstain from interference with foreign trade. Roberts's Siamese treaty was ratified by the United States Senate in 1835.[17]

Cushing reached the Asian coast aboard the USS *Brandywine*, one of a three-ship squadron. Pausing at Macao he continued to nearby Wanghia on 3 July 1844, where he negotiated the treaty of the same name. By its terms citizens of the United States were permitted to reside in the five treaty ports with full trading privileges. The Treaty of Wanghia also extended extraterritorial jurisdiction over nationals. A consul in each treaty port and a United States commissioner were to be accredited.[18]

Under the auspicious stipulations of the Wanghia pact, Yankee traders joined other aliens in settlements formed in the treaty ports; most Americans moved to Shanghai, which replaced Canton as the principal trade center on the Asian mainland. Opium, still illicit, persevered as a profitable commodity in the China trade for British and American merchants. Increasingly Yankee traders came to concentrate on tea (black and green) and silk as prime cargo material for home and European markets. Tea imports into the United States rose drastically after the Treaty of Wanghia, from nearly 7 million pounds annually to over 20 million pounds. Swift Yankee clipper ships of the "tea fleet" also became the principal carriers of this cargo to England and continental markets before 1861.[19]

In addition the enlargement of trade access on the China mainland led American traders to look on the Celestial Kingdom less as a supplier of exotic consumer products for American and European consumers and increasingly as a market for the surging production of textiles, leather goods, and hardware pouring from expanding United States industries. By the 1850s, the final decade of the American pioneer period in the Pacific Basin, the annual value of Yankee exports to China exceeded $10 million; imports mounted to nearly $30 million. American traders increasingly penetrated China's vast heartland with river steamers, delivering manufactured goods to interior markets and bringing out tea and silk to the bustling Shanghai harbor for transshipment via the clipper fleet to Atlantic depots.[20]

Throughout the American pioneer period, the China trade received primary attention from Yankee traders. However, at the same time, maritime merchants from the United States were establishing trade in other parts of the Pacific Basin, modest when compared to the opulent Canton ventures, but economically significant and profitable enough to hold their interest. And as in the case in China, each market territory also became a seed bed for American culture.

One portion of the Pacific Basin receiving Yankee traders' attention early in the 1780s was in the southwestern quadrant, at New South Wales, the future Australia (at Port Jackson, later Sydney), and at New Zealand's North Island settlements. Australia's early role in the empire was that of a penal colony. Ubiquitous Yankee traders took advantage of the repressive East India Company monopoly, which prevented noncompany-affiliated British suppliers from providing the struggling colony with essentials, and appeared with cargoes of tools, clothing, food, and much-esteemed alcoholic beverages. Yankee ship captains also carried Australian products to Canton. From this trade they obtained specie and British bills of credit, which they applied to purchases in the Chinese market. By 1840 American traders also dominated the New Zealand trade, particularly around the North Island settlements, the primary supply stations for the Yankee whaling fleet that ranged the southwestern Pacific Basin.

The most prosperous time for American traders engaged in the down-under traffic was during the Australian gold rush of the 1850s. Yankee sea captains transported thousands of goldseekers, supplies, provisions, and mining equipment to Australia. But American commerce in Australia and New Zealand waned toward the close of the American pioneer period, as colonials there increasingly turned to wool and grain production. These staple exports competed with American grain and wool for international markets, and Australian and New Zealand imports, because of empire trade favoritism, became increasingly British oriented.

Pioneer sea merchants also worked the bays and inlets of the basin's scattered island in "general store" schooners, searching for trade outlets. Cargoes included umbrellas, shoes, saddles, hats, dried codfish, lumber, rice, Lowell cottons, German glass, guns, ammunition, tools and hardware, needles and thread, medicines, gravestones, blankets, and rolls of denim. These itinerant traders found that the spread of plantation economies in the islands and the appearance of retail settlements for planters, missionaries, and native consumers provided a modest but generally profitable market for their goods. Their commercial network served three classes of islands: colonies of European empires, including Batavia (Holland) and the Philippines and Guam (Spain); islands on the verge of being integrated into imperial spheres (Samoa and Tahiti); and the independent Kingdom of Hawai'i.

On Batavia and other Dutch Pacific islands, Yankee traders traded their goods for hemp, tobacco, indigo, sugar, and spices. Several American merchants also established stores on these islands, stocking their shelves from visiting schooner stores and dispensing the goods to colonials and native workers on Dutch plantations.

In the Spanish colonies of Guam and the Philippines, American traders profited from the Spanish government's policy of gradually relaxing its exclusionist mercantile rules. Their commerce was concentrated at Manila, where they exchanged manufactured goods for indigo, sugar, hemp, coffee, and rice for the Canton markets. Americans also increasingly used Manila as a base for cargo storage, to avoid the escalating port levies at Canton. This practice reached such proportions in the days before the 1844 Treaty of Wanghia, that Russell and Company and several Yankee traders established branches of their firms at Manila.

Tahiti and Samoa were representative of the second class of island markets for Yankee traders. The principal port on Tahiti was Papeete, with a superb, nearly landlocked harbor, the periphery described as "white crescent beach, border of palms, orange and banana trees, half concealing white cottages and thatched huts" set against a backdrop of "verdure-clad mountains and slum-brous . . . surf on barrier reefs." Papeete served the South Pacific trade as Honolulu did the Central and North Pacific, as a boun-teous emporium where trader schooners restocked for supplying the scattered South Pacific island network. Merchants ashore also carried a wide range of goods and supplies for whaling and scav-enger ship and crew needs. Apia's exquisite harbor was described as "one of the best in the Pacific . . . capacious, well protected . . . a good entrance and sufficient depth of water for large vessels. An experienced pilot is at hand." It was the site of the first trading settlement in the Navigator, or Samoan, archipelago. American trading schooners supplied merchants ashore with goods required by plantation crews, missionaries, and native consumers, and cap-tains of whaling and scavenger ships calling there. Apia merchants were "prepared to furnish vessels with all such stores as are gen-erally in demand, and will take drafts at reasonable discount."[21]

Several harbors in the island kingdom of Hawai'i, including Lahaina on Maui and Hilo on Hawai'i, were favored ports of call for all manner of Pacific adventurers. But the premier urban and trade center for the archipelago was Honolulu. By 1830 this Cen-tral Pacific city "had become an important commercial port, from which trading operations radiated somewhat like spokes from the hub of a wheel, to Manila, Canton, Kamchatka, the coasts of North and South America, and the South Seas." Yankees domi-nated the trading community there. Most had begun their Pacific ventures as peripatetic traders making the island rounds, finally settling at Honolulu to benefit from its excellent harbor and stra-tegic commercial location. Besides the enlarging demand for man-ufactured goods from the local Hawaiian court, nobility, commoners, and growing haole community, there was the ever-increasing busi-ness of supplying the needs of the Pacific whaling fleet based at Honolulu and the emerging plantation agriculture and stock-raising enterprises on all the islands of the archipelago.[22]

Yankee traders were challenged by British, French, and on one occasion, Russian traders for preeminence as mercantile leaders in the Hawaiian Kingdom. Britons posed the greatest threat. Their ships delivered dried salmon, lumber, spars, wheat, and flour from Hudson's Bay Company stations on the Northwest Coast (primarily Fort Vancouver in the Columbia River valley) and manufactured goods from England. British agents in Honolulu had as their goal "to drive all Yankees off the islands and out of the Pacific." However, the Hudson's Bay Company and the two other British commercial houses at Honolulu "never seriously endangered" American primacy in the Hawaiian trade.[23]

Yankee traders came to use Honolulu as an entrepôt to supply their ships coasting the North and South American littorals. One of their profitable markets had been the North Pacific string of Russian and Indian settlements, but during the 1830s Russian-American Company managers assigned this commerce to Hudson's Bay Company agents. This forced the Hawaiian-based Yankees to concentrate on more southerly trade centers from California to Chile.

The laws of the Indies banned aliens from the Spanish colonial trade, but from their earliest days in the Pacific Basin, Americans had vended goods in Spanish-American settlements, by smuggling (if the local commandant was honorable) or, as was often the case, with official approval for a price. William Shaler and other pioneer maritime merchants found several post commandants "most diverted," that is, cooperative, for a share of the trade profits.

Those commandants who resisted temptation and conscientiously enforced the exclusionist trade rules were concerned, because the "Boston men," in addition to offering attractive goods to Spanish colonials, also were carriers of "subversive" ideas of democracy, freedom, and republicanism. After 1812, as the independence movement spread across Latin America, Yankee traders (*contrabandistas*) supplied large quantities of arms and ammunition to insurgents and made "enormous profits" from the traffic. John Jacob Astor, ever alert to prospects in Pacific Basin commerce, also engaged in the arms-supply business. However, he took the precaution of providing his ship captains with documents attesting that the vessels were "cleared for Canton and the Northwest Coast," to guard against his company being charged with gunrunning, should Astor-owned ships be intercepted by royalist patrol boats.[24]

After Latin American independence, the Pacific coastal towns of Callao, Valparaíso, Concepción, Paita, Coaquimbo, and Guayaquil were profitable import centers for goods delivered by Yankee traders. An estimated 250 American ships called there each year; 150 American vessels docked at Valparaíso alone in 1845. These Latin American ports became prime markets not only for hardware but also for New England textiles and Chinese silks.[25]

Honolulu-based Yankee traders became regular visitors to Mexico's Pacific ports after that nation achieved independence in 1821. For their cargoes of hardware and textiles they received Mexican dollars that, like the antecedent Spanish specie, became the Pacific Basin's principal exchange medium. They also called at San Diego, Monterey, and San Francisco, when the Mexican government relaxed the long-standing Spanish trade restrictions on the California coast.

San Francisco, the former Yerba Buena, became the great port of upper California after United States naval forces occupied it during the Mexican War. The 1848 Treaty of Guadalupe Hidalgo, which ended that conflict, brought the upper California coast north to forty-two degrees under American dominion. A treaty with Great Britain, negotiated two years earlier, assigned to the United States that portion of the Northwest Coast encompassing the Oregon Country's Pacific frontage, the strategic Columbia River valley, and the hinterland up to the crest of the Rocky Mountains, north to forty-nine degrees. This opened to sea merchants a trade territory previously monopolized for many years by exclusionist Hudson's Bay Company practices.

The discovery of gold in northern California in 1848 and the subsequent rush had a galvanizing effect on Pacific Basin demography and economy. The burst of settlement and drastically increased consumer needs created a sudden, huge demand for maritime traders' services—as carriers of goldseekers and as suppliers of provisions, tools, equipment, and machinery for the evolving mining frontier.

The fifth Pacific Basin trade focus for Yankee maritime merchants was Japan. Leaders of this island kingdom had closed their nation to contact with the external world except for the lone Dutch station on the island of Deshima. They adamantly refused appeals by outsiders for leave to approach Nippon. Increased trader and whaling-vessel traffic to China and the North Pacific fishery followed a path near the Japanese home islands. Frequent shipwrecks in coastal waters and the callous, even cruel, treatment inflicted by the Japanese on survivors generated appeals from American maritime interest for redress. Finally, United States government officials responded by placing Commodore Matthew Culbraith Perry in command of a naval task force (a four-ship squadron) with orders to proceed to Japan, there to urge leaders in the strongest terms to yield from their closed national stance.[26]

The American ships anchored in Yedo (Tokyo) Bay on 8 July 1853. Perry persistently pressed reluctant officials there to accept a message from President Millard Fillmore. When they finally agreed, Perry told them he would return soon for an answer. During early 1854 the commodore returned to Yedo with his gun-bristling squadron; on 31 March 1854 he negotiated the Treaty of Kanagawa. This was the first pact between Japan and another nation, and in effect it began the opening of the island kingdom to the West. It provided for permanent peace between the two nations, opened two ports (Shimoda and Hakodate) to American ships, assured humane treatment for shipwrecked seamen, established an American consulate, and gave the United States most-favored-nation status.[27]

Consul General Townsend Harris, on 29 July 1858, concluded a commercial treaty with Japanese leaders that opened additional ports to American traders and delegated extraterritorial jurisdiction to the United States over its nationals. Thus by Commodore Perry's unyielding confrontation with Japanese leaders and Consul Harris's commercial negotiations, American maritime traders gained access to the Japanese market. Initially the volume of this commerce in no way compared to that of any single Chinese port. However, it provided the foundation for an ever-increasing economic intercourse with Japan in the post–Civil War period.[28]

As the pioneer period came to a close around 1861, there was a noticeable change in the cargoes American maritime traders delivered to Pacific Basin consumers. For the "steady market" in the island-colonial-plantation zone, kerosene, tinned foods, hardware, tools, seeds, machinery, and cheap textiles were the items schooner captains stocked. For the larger markets on the China coast (besides the familiar textiles, hardware, wine, rum, and gin, as well as opium), Yankee traders stowed heavy equipment, especially railroad locomotives, rolling stock, and steel rails. For the Hawaiian market and to some degree the Pacific islands generally, they delivered horses from California ranches.

Relations with Russian America during the 1850s improved, and Yankee traders were permitted to return to Sitka and other North Pacific settlements. The American-Russian Commercial Company, incorporated in 1853 by San Francisco merchants, began to invest in northern salmon processing, coal mining, and ice gathering.

Yankee traders began the ice traffic on a limited scale soon after 1815. New Englanders developed ice-carrying ships, insulated with pine sawdust, and engaged agents to promote the use of ice in Pacific Basin ports for iced drinks and making ice cream. They erected ice-storage houses in Honolulu, Canton, Papeete, Apia, and later at Shanghai, San Francisco, Valparaíso, Concepción, Callao, and Guayaquil. At first ice for Pacific Basin consumers came from New England ponds, but during the 1850s Russian America supplied it, via American traders, at twenty-five dollars a ton.

The maritime trading frontier, in common with other Americanization entities at work in the Pacific Basin during the period from 1784 to 1861, produced both personal and civic benefits. Its commerce yielded profits that provided "much of the capital" that financed "New England's industrial revolution" and contributed to national prosperity, which in turn diminished the stifling national debt and provided profitable outlets for the expanding range of American products. Meeting the maritime traders' transport needs made shipbuilding a leading home industry, encouraged ship-design innovation (leading to, among others, the swift, romantic clipper ship), and enabled the United States to achieve and maintain international maritime supremacy for two decades before the Civil War.[29]

As in the case of other American frontiers at work in the Pacific Basin, representatives of the maritime traders' frontier established a vital presence and drew their home government's attention to the water hemisphere, which in turn activated nationalizing currents. These mercantile adventurers were joined by fellow citizens in other frontiers, other Americanization entities. One that rapidly transformed portions of the Pacific Basin beginning in 1849 was the mining frontier.

Ship *Bowditch*, built at Newbury, Massachusetts, 1823, a whaler from 1832 to 1856 and later in the guano trade, from a watercolor by Montardier (M5132). (Courtesy Peabody & Essex Museum/Peabody Museum Collection, photo by Mark Sexton, neg. no. 16176.)

"A whaling station on the California coast." Wood engraving after a drawing by Frenzeny that appeared in *Harper's Weekly*, 23 June 1877. In Lawrence Dinnean, *Nineteenth Century Illustrators of California Sights and Scenes: A Selection of Works by Pioneer Graphic Artists with an Introduction and Notes by Lawrence Dinnean* (1986), page 51.

The Rotch whaling fleet off the island of Hawai'i, including the ships *Enterprise, William Rotch, Pocahontas* and *Houqua,* 16 December 1833. From a colored aquatint in the Lothrop Whaling Collection (M21,751). (Courtesy Peabody & Essex Museum/ Peabody Museum Collection, photo by Mark Sexton, neg. no. 24,932.)

"Brig Pilgrim," from an original oil painting by William S. Thompson, nephew of Captain Francis A. Thompson. (Courtesy Santa Barbara Historical Society, neg. no. x.2.78.44.)

194

The Confederate raider *Shenandoah* in June 1865 attacks and destroys Yankee whaling vessels off Cape Thaddeus in the Arctic Ocean. (Courtesy the New Bedford Whaling Museum, neg. no. 5168.)

Biche De Mar House. In Wilkes, *Exploring Expedition,* vol. 3 prior to page 221.

A trading scene in Apia. In Wilkes, *Exploring Expedition*, vol. 5 page 22.

Harbor at Pago Pago. In Wilkes, *Exploring Expedition*, vol. 2 page 71.

A view of Sydney, New South Wales. In Wilkes, *Exploring Expedition,* vol. 2 prior to page 157.

The ship *Flying Cloud* rounding Cape Horn. Painting by J. K. Tudgay.
(Courtesy, Peabody & Essex Museum/Peabody Museum Collection, neg. no. 3833.)

A view of Chilkoot Pass. (Courtesy Albert J. Johnson Collection, acc.# 89-166n, Alaska and Polar Regions Department, Rasmuson Library, University of Alaska Fairbanks.)

A woman mining on the beach in Nome, Alaska. (Courtesy Albert J. Johnson Collection, acc.# 89-166n, Alaska and Polar Regions Department, Rasmuson Library, University of Alaska Fairbanks.)

A dog sled delivers U.S. mail to Lake Bennett. (Courtesy Albert J. Johnson Collection, acc.# 89-166n, Alaska and Polar Regions Department, Rasmuson Library, University of Alaska Fairbanks.)

"Californian's Throwing the Lasso (at Mission San Jose)," after an original drawing by William Smyth, of HMS *Blossom*. Published in Capt. Frederick W. Beechey's *Narrative of a Voyage to the Pacific and Beering's Strait* (1831). The plate was engraved by F. Finden. In Dinnean, *Nineteenth Century Illustrators,* page 27.

Santa Rosa, California, c. 1857. Full plate lithograph from sketches by Grafton T. Brown. Lithographed by Kuchel and Dresel. In Dinnean, *Nineteenth Century Illustrators,* page 53.

Hale Kea, the Manager's House, Parker Ranch, Hawai'i.
Photograph by John S. Whitehead.

The Reverend Hiram Bingham and Syþil Moseley Bingham. Oil painting by
Samuel Finley Breese Morse, 1819. (Courtesy Yale University Art Gallery, gift of
Hiram Bingham, B.A. 1898, neg. no. 1945.237.)

The Reverend Asa Thurston and Lucy Goodale Thurston. From the original ambrotype, about 1864. (Courtesy Hawaiian Mission Children's Society, Honolulu, Hawai'i, neg. no. N-697.)

Kaahumanu and the Reverend Hiram Bingham recommending Christianity at Waimea, O'ahu, 1826. Wood engraving by B. F. Childs after a sketch by Hiram Bingham. (Courtesy Hawaiian Mission Children's Society, Honolulu, Hawai'i, neg. no. N-1336.)

The Baldwin House, in Lahaina, Maui, was home to one of Hawai'i's early missionary families. Photograph by John S. Whitehead.

CHAPTER ELEVEN

The Mining Frontier

The Pacific Basin is rich in minerals; its islands and rimland yield gold, silver, tin, phosphorous, copper, iron, chromium, mercury, tungsten, platinum, manganese, lead, zinc, nickel, cobalt, antimony, asbestos, bauxite, diamonds, and the fossil fuels coal and petroleum. All of these resources help sustain the world's mercantile-industrial establishment. In addition Pacific waters contain magnesium and traces of other minerals. While most of these resources were not exploited until recent times, the mining frontier evolved quite early in the region's discovery period, energized by the feverish quest for gold and silver.

Spaniards were the first imperial intruders to tap the Pacific Basin's precious-metal bounty. Soon after 1521 they began to extract gold and silver ores from rich mines situated in the Pacific cordillera, a highland spine extending from western Mexico to southern Chile, where Native Americans had dug for centuries before the European advent. Pioneer Spanish navigators ransacked the South Seas from the basin's eastern rimland to the China coast for additional sources. However, only the Western Hemisphere mines met the Spaniards' lavish expectations; specie from the American colonies enabled Spain to maintain political, diplomatic, military, and even ecclesiastical domination of Europe and a large portion of the colonial world for nearly four centuries.

In 1848 Anglo-Americans established the second Pacific Basin mining frontier, their initial bonanza strike occurring on the eastern rim in recently acquired California. The Yankee miner was a frontiersman, self-serving as well as aiding national expansion, a role much like that performed by the fur man, the wilderness merchant, and other adventurers on the Anglo-American frontier.

He customarily occupied the forefront, often crowding the fur man for the leading position in the American westward advance.

Mining had been a serious Anglo-American enterprise since late colonial times, with prospectors searching the wilderness for riches in gold and silver and the crude but essential lead, salt, and other resources. They found gold in North Carolina and Georgia, lead in Illinois, Iowa, and Missouri, and salt in Indian Territory. Their discoveries often set off stampedes or rushes, demographic bursts that created urban pockets in the wilderness and accelerated absorption and political integration of primal territories into the national life. And these prospector-adventurers touched fellow Americans, drawing many of them into the mining-frontier experience. The excitement, lure of quick wealth, and titillating attraction of the roaring, worldy mining camps spawned by these occasional strikes provided many pioneers with a cherished relief from their otherwise dull, drab, agrarian, church-centered lives.

However, the mining frontier's grandest moment occurred in the Pacific Basin where the initial strike of 1848, besides yielding incomparable wealth to some, set off substantial, far-reaching economic, social, and political reverberations throughout the water hemisphere and on into the world at large. The Pacific Basin's post-Spanish mining frontier evolved in a three-step process, from the initial point in rimland California, southwest to Australia, then north to British Columbia, and ultimately to Alaska.

Yankee occupation of the Pacific Basin from 1784 to 1848 had been slow but sustained, carried forward by maritime fur men, scavengers, sea-mammal hunters, and maritime merchants. The discovery that established the second great mining frontier, which became the activating force that drastically accelerated the region's development and political integration, occurred on 24 January 1848 on the upper edge of John Sutter's grant in northern California. Sutter, a Swiss, seeking his New World fortune in such places as Indiana, New Mexico, Oregon, the Hawaiian Islands, and Russian America, reached California in 1838. He petitioned for and received from the governor of Mexican California a grant of eleven square leagues (ca. fifty thousand acres) on the lower Sacramento River. Sutter named his gargantuan estate New Helvetia, stocked it with cattle and horses, planted orchards, and opened grain fields. When the Russians departed Bodega Bay, he purchased most of their equipment.

During late 1847 Sutter directed an employee, James W. Marshall, a carpenter and millwright from New Jersey and a California resident for two years, to construct a water-powered mill. Marshall, accompanied by workmen and equipment, selected a mill site about fifty miles above Sutter's settlement, near the forested slopes of the Sierra Nevada, on the American River in a broad valley the Indians called Coloma. First Marshall's crew erected the mill structure, then with shovels, plows, scrapers, and blasting powder, the workmen excavated the millrace. As water flowed through the diversionary channel, Marshall noticed bright yellow flakes suspended in the current. He dipped out several particles of the hard material that, after tests, proved to be gold. Tidings of this discovery, which became the Coloma Placer, galvanized the Pacific Basin, and in less than a year affected virtually all the world.[1]

During their colonial preeminence, Spaniards had been so preoccupied with their productive gold and silver mines in Mexico and other bonanza points southward along the coastal cordillera that they gave little attention to prospecting Alta California. During the Mexican period, Francisco López found placer gold in Feliciano Canyon, forty miles north of Los Angeles. Miners worked those diggings until 1848, when they exhausted the deposit. Prospectors also discovered a vein of cinnabar (mercury ore), required for refining precious metals, near San Jose in 1846.

Ironically the bonanza riches of Mexican California were revealed in the same year that Mexico was ceding this portion of the Pacific Basin to the United States. American military forces had completed the conquest of California and Mexico, Mexican leaders had capitulated to United States army commanders in Mexico City, and commissioners representing the two nations were drafting the peace settlement culminating in the Treaty of Guadalupe Hidalgo, by which Mexico ceded the Southwest, including California, to the United States.

Americans had been collecting on the Pacific Basin's eastern rim in Mexican California since 1822, some as farmers, others as stockmen, hide-and-tallow dealers, retired continental and maritime fur men, whalemen, political adventurers, and shopkeepers and artisans. Recent arrivals were soliders, sailors, and marines from the army of conquest, serving as an occupation force until the cession treaty of 1848, when they became an enforcement arm of the American military government.

News of the Coloma Placer nearly depopulated the coastal settlements. Workmen, ministers, lawyers and judges, clerks, crewmen from ships anchored in the harbors, all abandoned their tasks and rushed to the American River. Even soldiers deserted their posts in occupied California. Officers reported that on muster they found that twenty-six troopers at Sonora had "gone over the hill," twenty-four at San Francisco, and twenty-four at Monterey. One soldier on a three-week furlough claimed that he found fifteen hundred dollars' worth of gold in the California placers, "more than the government would pay him for a five years' enlistment."[2]

Tidings of Marshall's find coursed along the Pacific Basin's channels of commerce, northward around its eastern rim to Oregon, coastal Canada, and Russian America, thence southward to Mexico, Peru, and Chile, and west to Tahiti, Hawai'i, Australia, New Zealand, and China. At least four thousand men were working the placers before the close of 1848, and ten thousand were en route from around the Pacific Basin—experienced miners from Mexico and Chile, fur men from the Northwest Coast, Hawaiians, Chinese, Australians, New Zealanders, and farmers from Oregon. Boosters there lamented the manpower drain, claiming their territory was nearly depopulated of males; two-thirds of the men rushed to the California diggings.[3]

The human mix of forty-eighters included Mormons; two streams of Latter-Day Saints entered the goldfields. One group came from the Mormon Battalion that marched with General Stephen W. Kearny's Army of the West from Fort Leavenworth into New Mexico and thence to San Diego. Veterans of the Mormon Battalion scattered over this portion of the basin's eastern rimland; some reached San Francisco and the northern settlements, including New Helvetia, and several were employed by Sutter. Marshall's Coloma sawmill crew included Mormon workmen, who pioneered in the Coloma Placer. Another Mormon stream, numbering two hundred, came to the Pacific Basin's eastern rim by ship, refugees from the Illinois scattering, conducted by Sam Brannon. He became a leading entrepreneur in northern California, establishing a hotel, newspaper, and store at San Francisco and several stores in the goldfields. The Mormon presence and influence in the early development of the mining frontier in northern California is confirmed in the names of several camps—Mormon Gulch, Mormon Bar, Mormon Island, and Mormon Diggings.

The founders of this mining frontier, who called themselves forty-eighters so as not to be confused with forty-niners and other latecomers, found gold with ease and regularity that first year; 1848 was truly bonanza time. With the primitive technology of knives to pry gold from the crevices of ore-bearing rocks, pans to sift gold from watered sand, and a few sluices to separate ore from gravel, they averaged sixty dollars' worth of gold a day; some struck it rich. Two men from the emerging camp of Hangtown made sixteen thousand dollars in one week; a group on the Yuba made seventy-five thousand dollars in three months; and north of Coloma, in a ravine, a miner made twenty thousand dollars in six weeks. The forty-eighters found rich placers all along the American River and its tributaries and came up with an estimated $10 million worth of gold that first year.[4]

News of their good fortune spread beyond the Pacific Basin to the Mississippi Valley and the eastern United States. Newspapers in those parts published accounts of the California mines during the summer of 1848; the New York *Herald,* on 19 August, was one of the first to print a letter relating the Coloma bonanaza. During the preceding June, Thomas Larkin, former United States consul at Monterey, transmitted a report and gold samples that arrived in the eastern United States in September. And that summer Colonel R. B. Mason, military governor of California, visited the goldfields and in August sent an official report of the strike, with gold samples, to President James Polk. Polk incorporated Mason's report in his message to Congress, providing official recognition and confirmation.

These notices precipitated a national gold fever. One citizen described his symptoms:

a frenzy seized my soul; unbidden my legs performed some entirely new movements of polka steps—I took several—houses were too small for me to stay in—; I was soon in the streets in search of necessary outfits; piles of gold rose up before me at every step; castles of marble, dazzling the eye with their rich appliances; thousands of slaves bowing to my beck and call; myriads of fair virgins contending for my love—were among the fancies of my fevered imagination. The Rothschilds, Girards, and Astors appeared to me but poor people; in short I had a very violent attack of the gold fever.[5]

The lure of the new El Dorado swept like an epidemic through New England, the Middle Atlantic States, and the South; it coursed into the Old Northwest, Old Southwest, the Mississippi Valley, and intruded into the Texas and Indian Territory settlements. Its tidings seeped across the Atlantic and galvanized the adventurous in the British Isles and mainland nations. During 1849 they joined the hordes rushing out to the Pacific Basin to seek their fortunes. Forty-niners came to be called argonauts, after the hardy ancients who joined Jason in his search for the legendary golden fleece.

The greatest outpouring came from the United States. For that first year estimates on the number of Americans undertaking the westward journey vary from fifty to a hundred thousand. At least half of them approached the Pacific Basin by land. During the winter of 1848–49 they began to gather at emigration points on the eastern termini of the overland trails—the border towns of Westport, St. Joseph, Council Bluffs, Van Buren, and Fort Smith. San Antonio was a popular launching point for argonauts from the South. Those gathering at Westport had a double choice. They could follow the Oregon-California Road, which crossed the Rocky Mountains at South Pass, on to Fort Hall, there branching, with the southwest fork conducting traffic toward the Humboldt and up to the Sierra crossings; or they could venture over the well-established traders' concourse to Santa Fe, thence down the Río Grande to Doña Ana, west to the valley of the Gila, and along that river to the Colorado, into California at San Diego or Los Angeles, north to San Francisco, and from there into the Sierra goldfields. At Council Bluffs they had the choice of proceeding along the Mormon Trail to Great Salt Lake, thence over the Nevada deserts into the Sierra Nevada and down the Pacific slope. In 1849 a column of soldiers commanded by Captain Randolph

B. Marcy marked a road from Fort Smith to Santa Fe, with an alternate cutoff, the Doña Ana Road, southwest to the Gila and along that established line of march to the Pacific. The San Antonio Road to California led to El Paso, eventually leading into the Gila Valley to the Colorado River crossing and into California.[6]

Maps and journals generated by the explorations of Jedediah Smith and other partisans of the continental fur frontier, and the official reconnaissances of the American West during the 1840s by Captain John C. Frémont, provided timely guides for travelers venturing across the continent to the Pacific Basin. Most Americans chose the Westport–South Pass–California–Oregon Road. However, the six-month crossing required careful attention to seasonal timing—starting in the spring when plains grasses were sufficiently mature to sustain livestock, and reaching the Pacific Basin before deep snows closed the Sierra passes. The advantage of the southerly routes was their being open to travel throughout the year, but all overland passages had their hazards. Uncertainty of water and pasture and scarcity of game and fuel were perennial threats to those hardy adventurers electing the continental crossing. And their peril was heightened by the fact that every trail to the Pacific Basin trespassed on the domains of powerful and often hostile Indian nations.

The sea also fed a stream of goldseekers into the Pacific Basin's first mining frontier. Maritime argonauts had several choices. Favored were bookings on record-setting ships of the smart American clipper fleet, vessels that often covered the eighteen thousand miles from home Atlantic port to San Francisco in ninety days.

Carrying adventurers to the Pacific Basin proved so profitable that shipowners converted several merchantmen and whalers to crude passenger craft, cramming up to 250 persons aboard, at $150 per passenger. On either transformed merchantmen or whalers, goldseekers could expect an ordeal of six months' duration. Even so, during December 1848 and January 1849, sixty-one of the converted ships, each packed with Pacific Basin passengers, departed Atlantic ports.

Many adventurers traveled aboard vessels of the newly established steamship line, consisting of two three-ship fleets of coal-burning side-wheelers, one in the Atlantic and one in the Pacific.

From Atlantic and Gulf ports these ships delivered mail and passengers to the Isthmus of Panama. Indian boatmen moved travelers, baggage, and mail to the headwaters to the Chagres River. From there mules transported passengers and cargo down to the Pacific port of Panama, for reembarkation on the San Francisco–bound steamer. Alternate crossings to Pacific waters used by argonauts were established in southern Mexico and Nicaragua. In addition American businessmen financed the construction of a railway across the forty-seven-mile-wide Isthmus; completed in 1855, it transported travelers between the oceans for a twenty-five-dollar fare.[7]

Few adventurers arriving in northern California to form the Pacific Basin's second great mining frontier were experienced miners. Only a scattering of veteran prospectors from the southern Appalachian goldfields and the Illinois, Missouri, and Iowa lead mines were present. However, the lack of mineral know-how was no handicap for most of these men; two factors offset this limitation.

One was the consuming ambition of virtually every argonaut to strike it rich, make his fortune, and liberate himself from the near inevitable fate of most midnineteenth-century men—consignment to a lifetime of mindless toil, from dawn until dark, eking out a bare living. For some it was in a dark, dim, debilitating eastern factory; for most, it was on farms, each exacting its toll of punishing, backbreaking labor. To escape this ordeal, most argonauts were prepared to apply great energy and physical labor for what they expected would be a brief time, to reap the reward of quick wealth and merciful deliverance from their fate.

The other factor was the character of the mineral fields exploited during the early phase of this mining frontier. Gold was easily accessible, dispersed in what prospectors called "placers."

Placer gold was found in the form of nuggets, particles, flakes, and dust, free mineral in the sense that it had broken from the parent lodes or veins in the Sierra and, washed by creeks and rivers draining the highlands to the hills and lowlands, had lodged in sand and gravel beds and in soil along the banks of streams. Thus placer mining required little skill but considerable patience and physical exertion.

In addition placer mining could be accomplished with simple, even primitive, technology. These mining pioneers applied common sense and trial-and-error methodology, and they imitated the experienced prospectors. Those from Georgia introduced the pan for the exploitation of ore-bearing sands, and they and lead miners from the Mississippi Valley diggings introduced the sluice, rocker (or jig), and cradle to separate the ore. And the miners learned to "crevice" gold, that is, gouge nuggets from rocks with knives and pry bars.

Pioneer miners working the northern California placers applied the pan; pry bar and knife; pick and shovel; and sluice, rocker, and cradle to collect the mineral. Gold, which is seven times denser than most associated materials, was easy to separate from sand, gravel, and soil. Washing the ore-bearing material from the streambed or from pits along the bank in a shallow pan or sluice separated the nonauriferous material and concentrated the gold. The sluice, rocker, and cradle was a series of troughs fitted with cleats, or baffles, nailed to the trough floor; the troughs were pitched so as to drain water washing over the ore, which miners shoveled into the sluice. The cleats trapped the denser gold, as the wet sand and gravel flowed through the sluice.[8]

Miners generally formed partnerships, because exploiting a placer required at least two workers. They also impressed local Indians (some native crews numbered up to twenty-five), including former neophytes from the San José Mission. Argonauts also hired kanakas to excavate prospect pits and work the sluices.

The living pattern of this Pacific Basin mining frontier was urban. Miners clustered in settlements of tent and log-shanty shelters near the placers. The Pacific-facing Sierra slopes were eventually dotted with these crude camps. Some had a life of only a few weeks or months; as placer gold petered out, resident miners abandoned the site, moving on to more promising diggings. When prospectors, eternally scouring this Pacific Basin wilderness in quest of the "mother lode," happened onto a promising placer along some isolated creek, the tidings inevitably spread through the settlements, precipitating a "stampede." Miners freely abandoned their nondescript camps, and these later became relics, or "ghost towns." Goldseekers would then gather around the new placer and another camps would evolve. Pacific Basin mining settlements took on evocative, symbolic names—Red Dog, Fiddletown, Humbug, Poverty Hill, Hangtown, Yuba, Chile Junction, San Andreas, Chile Gulch, Rich Bar, Mormon Island, Sonora, Rough and Ready, Grass Valley, Brandy Flat, Mariposa, Rabbit Creek, Mormon Gulch, and Tuttletown. A few mining camps managed to achieve permanent status because of an enduring mineral deposit or their role as support center for peripheral settlements. Mining-camp survivors of the gold rush that metamorphosed into permanent communities included Sonora, Columbia, Placerville, Marysville, Oroville, Mariposa, San Andreas, and Jackson.

The mining frontier was urban and more populous than the fur and mercantile frontiers, or even than the agrarian frontier. The demographic fruits of this rush into the Pacific Basin surpassed all previous outpourings of American pioneers. From 1848 to 1852, California's non-Indian population increased from less than 8000 to over 250,000.

The basic unit of this mining frontier was the "poor-man's camp"—prospectors working singly or in partnership on a small grubstake with simple equipment. Before the law and other customary American institutional fixtures arrived, the burgeoning population created land-tenure challenges and law-and-order problems. Every Anglo-American frontier or expansion entity had its peculiar legal system: maritime traders, whalers, collectors, and other seaborne adventurers were subject to admiralty law; the military frontier applied martial law; the missionary frontier used sectarian or canon law. Mining-camp residents met their early regulatory needs by forming the extralegal miners' court and private law-enforcement apparatus, the vigilante committee. These patterns and precedents for regulating mining-camp society were applied in other parts of the Pacific Basin to which the mining frontier subsequently expanded.[9]

When prospectors found a productive mineral field, they met in town assembly, organized a mining district, and adopted laws to regulate their industry and protect their lives and property. The miners' code included rules determining the "number of running feet of river bottom each claimant was entitled to and the distance up the hills on either side that claims might go; they decided how much work the finder must do to establish a claim and how much to hold it. They recorded on their informal books the claims and transfers and did the work so well that when laws caught up with the prospectors, it was generally enough to give legal effect to the agreements already in force." Much of this locally derived mining law fashioned in the Pacific Basin miners' camps was incorporated into federal statutes in 1866.[10]

If the economic side of mining-camp law maintained the principle of traditional American equity, by contrast its human side was saturated with bigotry, prejudice, and ugly exclusionism. The population of this mining frontier was mixed. Anglo-Americans were the vast majority, but they were joined in the diggings by resident Indians, argonauts from Europe, Hawaiians, Samoans, Malays, Chileans, Peruvians, Sonorans, Australians, New Zealanders, and Chinese. It has been estimated that one in every five miners was from China.

Indians suffered the most from Yankee xenophobia. In the first year or so of this Pacific-slope mining frontier, Native Americans either mined for themselves or worked as employees of Anglo miners. However, they gradually became objects of the most cruel persecution. Expansive Anglos ignored Indian land rights and regarded land as theirs "by right of conquest." Indians were considered interlopers, as were Chinese and most other foreigners. In some parts of California, Americans even carried out a calculated genocide on the natives. The decline in Indian population was shocking; from an estimated 150,000 in 1848 to about 30,000 in 1861. The first session of the California legislature in 1850 enacted a statute titled "Act for the Government and Protection of Indians." It provided that Indians could be impressed into legal indenture for forced service and labor, a practice particularly applied to children and young women, the latter primarily as concubines. And the outright sale of Native American captives was common in California from 1850 until 1863, when the act was repealed to conform to the national emancipation proclamation. It is estimated that 10,000 Indians were indentured or sold for forced labor before the repeal of this statute.[11]

Miners' assemblies also adopted ordinances regulating so-called alien activity in the goldfields. Chinese and Polynesians were forbidden to enter several placer districts. And in those where these immigrants were tolerated, they could only mine abandoned claims and rework tailings.[12]

When Mexican miners at San Andreas and Sonora found rich placers, Anglo miners invaded their claims, drove off the Hispanics, and appropriated the diggings. Chilean miners suffered the same fate at Chile Gulch and Chile Junction, where the so-called Chilean War was fought between these South American miners and Anglo invaders seeking to take over their rich placers.

In this Pacific Basin bonanza, wealth was easily gained and just as easily lost. Essentials in food, clothing, equipment, and entertainment were scarce and oppressively expensive. Through every gold camp there pulsed a current of desperation; each man was driven by selfish fear of losing out to his neighbor in the intensively competitive quest for quick riches. One forty-niner's description illustrates the heterogenous composition of the typical "poor-man's camp" on this mining frontier.

> Take a sprinkling of sober-eyed, earnest, shrewd, energetic New England businessmen; mingle with them a number of rollicking sailors, a dark band of Australian convicts and cutthroats, a dash of Mexican and frontier desperadoes, a group of hardy backwoodsmen, some professional gamblers, whisky-dealers, general swindlers, or 'rural agriculturalists' ... and having thrown in a promiscuous crowd of broken-down merchants, disappointed lovers, black sheep, unfledged dry-goods clerks, professional miners from all parts of the world, and Adulamites generally, stir up the mixture, season strongly with gold fever, bad liquors, faro, monte, rouge-et-noir, quarrels, oaths, pistols, knives, dancing and digging, and you have something approximating to California society in early days.[13]

This mining frontier included few women. Far and away the favorite of the gold camps was María Dolores Eliza Rosanna Gilbert, Countess de Landsfeld, better known as Lola Montez. Billed as a dancer and actress and acknowledged as an overpowering seductress, Lola Montez was characterized by the male casualties of her charms as tempestuous, temperamental, violent, and irresistible. She arrived at San Francisco in 1851, her advent having been announced several weeks beforehand. The docks of the port were jammed with men lusting for a glimpse of this "distinguished wonder."

The first stage of this Pacific Basin mining frontier had been a veritable bonanza. During the period of productive placer mining, 1848–55, an average of $65 million worth of gold had been extracted each year. However, by the mid-1850s, miners were encountering increasing difficulty finding free gold in the Sierra placers. Much gold remained, but its extraction required mining on a larger scale and the capital to finance expensive hydraulic equipment, dredges, and drills and explosives for the excavation of deep shafts and tunnels to expose the ore veins—the mother lodes that had fed the gold dust and nuggets into the placer deposits along the creeks and rivers.

As the placer gold played out, some argonauts turned to other pursuits. They went to work as day laborers for the mining companies formed to exploit the quartz-ore deposits. Others returned to their homes, some with a stake, others broke. Many remained in California and became ranchers and farmers or took up the vocations and professions they had followed before being smitten with the gold mania.

Others, still obsessed with the El Dorado quest, scattered over the continental West, opening new mining districts in Nevada, New Mexico, Arizona, and Colorado. They went north into the Columbia River region, opening mines in western Washington Territory and preparing the way for the discovery of Idaho, Montana, Wyoming, and Dakota bonanzas. The more adventurous ones joined the stampede to the Australian mines to help form the third Pacific Basin mining frontier. Others searched the eastern rim of the Pacific Basin, sampling the ocean-bound waters draining British Columbia's highlands for gold, eventually reaching coastal Alaska; there they would find increasing evidence of the mineral riches that would support the fourth Pacific Basin mining frontier.

The Pacific Basin's third mining frontier, formed on the ocean's far southwestern corner, in Australia, was an extension of the second. The down-under mining frontier bore many characteristics of its antecedent, but came to display certain distinctive qualities. This is a case where the dynamics of Anglo-American imperialism as applied to the Pacific Basin were cultural rather than political;

the territory, although transformed by the mining-frontier process, was not absorbed into the American community.

Geologists rate the western two-thirds of Australia as a mineralized zone. It contains gold, silver, lead, zinc, tin, copper, tungsten, related minerals, and extensive coal deposits (both bituminous and lignite). Copper was among the first of these resources to be exploited, with the mines at Burra Burra worked in the 1840s. Gold had been noted as early as 1839. The knowledge of this and subsequent reports of finds in 1841, 1846, and 1848 were suppressed by colonial government officials at Melbourne, "for fear of 'agitating the public mind.'" These administrators were committed to keeping settlers engaged in the bucolic enterprises of livestock and grain production.[14]

Even the lure of California placers became threatening to Australian leaders. During 1848 nearly 700 Australians undertook the three-to-four-month passage to San Francisco, crammed 100 to 175 per ship. Two years later 3,500 set out for California; and in 1851, when the east-bound emigration peaked, 6000 Australians booked passage for the goldfields. Australian exporters also shipped great cargoes of processed meat, livestock, grain, forage, and lumber to the Sierra goldfields. While public and private interests welcomed this bonanza market for Australian products, they feared that the manpower exodus would bring decline, even ruin, to the colony. Therefore, to check the population drain, they were prepared to relax the ban on making public the reports of gold deposits at home.[15]

An Australian goldseeker particularly attentive to the gold-bearing geology in the territory exploited by the California mining frontier was Edward H. Hargraves. He observed its curious match with terrain he had roamed over as a stockman in New South Wales. During 1851 he returned to Australia and ventured into the Blue Mountain region to examine streambeds in the manner he had learned in the California placers. Hargraves found unmistakable gold sign. He reported the discovery to colonial officials in Melbourne; they appointed him commissioner of crown lands, paid him a reward of ten thousand pounds, and released an official report of the strike to Australian newspapers. For a time Hargraves returned to New South Wales to share skills learned in the California placers with local men turned prospectors.

Tidings of the down-under El Dorado reversed the flow of men and products from the Pacific Basin's eastern rim to Australia. New Zealanders, Chinese, Malays, Maoris, Hawaiians, Europeans, and Americans from all parts of the United States, including experienced California miners, joined Australians in the New South Wales and Victoria mining districts. Ships of the Yankee merchant marine, world leader in the decade of the 1850s, dominated the carrying trade for the Australian gold rush, delivering thousands of goldseekers and tons of mining equipment and supplies. In 1858 seventy-three American vessels, most of them the swift clippers, docked at Sydney.[16]

Nearly 95,000 goldseekers disembarked at Melbourne alone in 1852, more than had arrived in San Francisco in the first year of the California gold rush. The combined population of New South Wales and Victoria in 1850 was 265,000; by 1860, fed by the influx of miners, it had increased to 887,000. Of the first 100,000 immigrants arriving in New South Wales and Victoria, about 10 percent were Americans. In all the camps of the two districts, the actual miners numbered 200,000, with the remainder support people and hangers-on.[17]

This mining frontier accommodated American prospecting skills and the mining technology and methodology that argonauts had fashioned in the California mining frontier, but they were adapted, where required, to local conditions. "Diggers," as goldseekers were called in the Australian mining districts, adopted the familiar pan and sluice, rocker, and cradle to separate free gold, but the scarcity of water complicated these applications. When it was not accessible in a creek or river near the diggings, miners hauled water in barrels or diverted it from creeks and rivers via canals into storage ponds near the diggings. They also hauled gold-bearing ore in horse-drawn wagons to water for separation.

Surface placer mining, common in the California goldfields, was limited in the Australian diggings, because much of the free gold was covered with a soil, gravel, or rock overburden of varying thickness. Therefore miners excavated prospect shafts, commonly to a depth of eight to ten feet in promising locations. The New South Wales and Victoria landscape soon was pitted with these shallow prospect shafts. Miners often excavating shafts, with a horse- or steam-powered hoist to lift the dirt, from two to three hundred feet deep, and followed the ore veins laterally in drifts from the shaft openings. In several camps gold was found to be so widely dispersed on a claim that miners excavated a small open pit, locally called a paddock mine. Deeper shafts required more than a single miner or a partnership. Large crews were needed to move dirt and bail or pump water from underground workings; a mine fifty to three hundred feet deep might require up to twenty workers. Thus when a favorable prospect turned up at a deep level, the claim owner commonly sold shares to raise the capital required to proceed.[18]

The living pattern in this mining frontier also was urban; workers clustered in tent camps. As in other aspects of this Australian frontier, the Anglo-American–California influence was conspicuously present in the camp names—Yankee Hill, California Gulch, Eureka, Jim Crow, Buffalo, and Hangtown. Locally derived camp names included Ballarat, Bendigo, Forest Creek, Mount Malaga, Devil's River, Pennyweight Gully, Dead Horse Gulch, Ovens, Napoleon's Creek, and Polish Flat. The most populous camp, with peripheral settlements, was Bendigo, with twenty thousand prospectors working the pits.[19]

In contrast to the mining frontier in California, where personal sovereignty was supreme, the Australian mining frontier was initially a controlled entity. As the bonanza there escalated, the British colonial bureaucracy at Melbourne issued ordinances for the governance of mining districts and created a corps of agents to enforce these rules. They included the requirement that each miner purchase a permit; only permit holders were allowed to prospect and mine gold in the New South Wales and Victoria fields. Colonial inspectors roamed the camps checking worker permits. Those without current credentials were arrested and placed in the camp jail. Also present in each camp was a special commissioner, who received the gold produced there. He issued a receipt for the value of the gold to the mine owner, redeemable in cash.

An officer in command of a squad of mounted and foot police

maintained order in each camp and escorted gold shipments to Melbourne in a two-wheeled armored cart drawn by four horses. The colonial commissioner in each camp adjudicated disputes over claims. Colonial mining law prescribed that a miner could work a claim twelve feet square, set off on the corners with stakes, locally called pegs. Thus rather than "staking a claim," diggers "pegged a claim." The mining code required continuous work; if none was performed within a twenty-four-hour period, the claim could be taken over by another miner. The police squad assigned to each camp was expected to guard the workers and their property against raids by predatory highwaymen, or "bush rangers." Black Douglas and Red Jack became legendary robbers, somewhat in the fashion of Joaquín Murietta, the fabled Hispanic folk hero of the California mining camps.

Life in the camps was coarse, the labor taxing, and diggers driven by the same feverish competitive effort that dominated the Sierra mining districts. Camps in this extension of the Pacific Basin mining frontier were rated as "no havens of gentility," but rather places "fit only for Negroes, Chinamen, deserting seamen and ex-convicts," by no means "a place for a decent man. He would have to work himself to death and grow wild." However, the harsh life there was tempered a bit by the occasional appearance of itinerant vaudeville and dramatic troupes. The "notorious" Lola Montez, after devastating denizens of the California mining frontier, proceeded to Australia and titillated standing-room-only audiences all the way from Melbourne to Ballarat with an erotic dance she called "the spider."[20]

The controlled character of this mining frontier was altered rather quickly, with the diminution of colonial oversight and the application of miner sovereignty due in no small measure to the American presence in the miner population as well as to the higher expectations of returning Australians, exposed to self-determination in the California goldfields. Americans, while never numerically dominant in the Australian mining frontier, exercised a great deal of influence. Their skills in finding gold-bearing locations, their mining technology and experience, were readily applied and adapted as required by local conditions. But in the estimation of Australian leaders, the intruding Yankees brought with them a reputation for "lawlessness, revolutionary background, aggression against Mexico, and crusading to save the world." Colonial officials were apprehensive that they carried the virus of Manifest Destiny, and that they would form plots in the gold camps to stir up an Australian independence movement. A prominent Australian reminisced that Yankees were called by some "Young Americans," advocates of an intense belief in "capitalistic progress and romantic individualism." When "California diggers came here in the 50's to the gold fields, they talked and taught freedom and self-government."[21]

Colonial bureaucrat apprehensions were accurate. Very soon American miners joined disaffected Australians, most of them fresh from the self-governed camps of California, to protect the unfamiliar restraints and impositions. They formed activist organizations including the Independent California Rangers' Revolver Brigade. During 1852 these groups began mass protests, initially denouncing the miners' levy as "Taxation without Representation" and calling it "Robbery." The Sierra emigrants raged that "in California this state of things would soon be altered, and that in a summary way."[22]

In 1854 the scattered protest-reform associations coalesced at Ballarat into the Australian Reform League. Australian and American spokesmen demanded several changes in mining-camp laws, as well as certain alterations in general colonial policy. The Ballarat platform called for abolition of the miners' tax, changes in mining-camp governance, and application by the colonial government of what locally were called Chartist principles of suffrage extension and parliamentary representation, in addition to opening crown lands to settlement.[23]

At mass meetings on 29 November 1854, miners burned their despised mining licenses. Three days later, at Eureka, the demonstrators raised a blue flag bearing the Southern Cross (the mariners' celestial guide, a southern constellation having four bright stars in the form of a cross) as the emblem of their defiance of colonial authority. Insurgent leaders declared that the banner was "of their own choosing, and which absorbs nationalities." The inevitable confrontation with colonial troops occurred on 3 December 1854, at the Eureka stockade. In the gunfire exchange, thirty miners and four soldiers were killed. Officials installed martial law in the camps, but eventually eased control and redressed grievances, including attention to the miners' tax. In addition the miners' insurrection is credited with obtaining for Australian citizens the adoption of the so-called Australian ballot, hailed as the "safeguard of democracy."[24]

Order returned to the camps, workmen resumed gold production, and before the decade of the 1850s closed, Australian mines were outproducing those in California to become the world leaders. The Pacific Basin mining frontier down under gradually dissipated, as deeper, more costly operations replaced placer and shallow-pit mining. Diggers, the entrepreneurs of this frontier, remained to work the deep-shaft mines as day laborers or went on to search for a new El Dorado; some succeeded on a limited basis in New Zealand and several other Pacific Basin outposts.

The fourth and final Pacific Basin mining frontier was established in Alaska and western Canada. Its ultimate development, a gradual process extending from the 1850s into the 1890s, came to a peak with the great stampede to the Arctic Circle diggings in 1898. A few survivors of the California and Australian mining frontiers were there to preside over the opening and development of this last of the Pacific Basin mining bonanzas.

Many argonauts, disappointed in the California goldfields but smitten by chronic gold fever, continued their restless quest, prospecting the eastern slope of the Sierra Nevada and venturing into the Great Basin and Rocky Mountains. Some joined the rush to Australia to help form the mining frontier there. Others continued exploring to the north, toward the Arctic Circle, along the eastern rim of the Pacific Basin. They would become the principals in the ultimate formation of the Alaskan mining frontier.

This fourth and final great rush was not the sudden, overwhelming demographic phenomenon the California and Australian mining frontiers had been. Rather it was the denouement of a series of modest placer strikes made along the Pacific Basin's eastern rim between 1855 and 1896. And this mining frontier was a multinational spectacle, situated as it was astride the Canadian-Alaska border.

Russian-American Company agents had found small quantities of gold in the coastal streambeds of their northern colony. Pioneer

American maritime traders working the North Pacific markets had observed Northwest Indians wearing gold ornaments. After the United States acquired Russian America and renamed the land Alaska in 1867, American soldiers on duty there found gold along the banks of the Yukon's tributaries. But for the most part, Alaska was an ignored, neglected land except as the special exploitive preserve of the Alaska Commercial Company (formed by a group of San Francisco businessmen) and other selective beneficiaries of franchises granted by supportive federal officials to tap Alaska's fur, salmon, seal, ice, coal, and timber resources.

Initially the secretary of war was in charge of Alaska; he governed the province with troops and martial law until 1877, when this assignment devolved to the secretary of the treasury. Thereafter for several years, the only sign of local United States authority was the collector of customs and the crewmen of a revenue cutter patrolling coastal waters.

Stages in the piecemeal evolution of the Alaskan mining frontier included the Fraser River strike in western Canada during 1858, which drew nearly twenty-five thousand men from the California goldfields. Small strikes continued northward along the Pacific littoral during the 1860s. A strike in western British Columbia in 1870 drew an additional thirteen thousand miners. And in the late 1870s, Yankee prospectors entered the Alaska panhandle, working small but rich placers on American territory. They found gold-bearing quartz formations along the Gastineau Channel in 1880, and Juneau became the principal settlement in this new mining region. Each northern discovery brought these frontiersmen closer to the fabulous placer that would finally activate the Alaskan mining frontier; the 1880 strike also produced a Yankee population increase that would not be denied its political expectations. Congress finally responded in 1884, by approving Alaska's First Organic Act, which provided for an appointed governor, judges for local courts, and a federal marshal. But rather than being designated a territory in the traditional pattern, Alaska was classed a "district." This response of nationalizing currents to frontiersmen's demands demonstrated the efficacy of personal and collective sovereignty in the American system and marked the beginning of at least some elements of civil government in Alaska, along with the diminution of the power and privileged status of federally favored business combinations.[25]

While substantial amounts of gold were extracted from the mines of Juneau and from streams along the Yukon in the 1880s and early 1890s, the great northern mining bonanza was yet to come. In 1896 a party of American prospectors working a stretch of the Canadian Yukon about a hundred miles east of the Alaskan border found the goldfield that became the incomparable Klondike; it provided the collective name for this fourth and final mining frontier. "On to the Klondike!" became the incessant, the unabating imperative for thousands of adventurers in the United States, Canada, indeed all around the Pacific Basin, Europe, and the world. The rush to the Klondike lasted from 1897 to 1900, peaking in the year 1898, when a hundred thousand goldseekers rushed northward.[26]

The triggering event was the widely broadcast landing of two ships, one in San Francisco, the other in Seattle, laden with cargoes of gold collected from the new bonanza. Writers characterized the Klondike rush as a "stampede," a "more descriptive word than 'rush,' implying not just the notion of a rush, but a headlong, heedless, mass movement of men like frightened cattle thundering before a rising storm," a "frenzied pouring of men into the North Country, thoughtless of what lay ahead."[27]

Some ninety-eighters went overland by way of Canada on the Edmonton route, an itinerary promoted by Canadian businessmen expecting to profit from the elaborate outfitting required to survive and function in the Northland. Thousands traveled by sea from San Francisco and Seattle. Many seaborne adventurers took passage on ships condemned to the scrapyard but hurriedly pressed into service; in these "floating coffins," passengers were crammed ten to a cabin, jammed into suffocating holds, "packed like so many herring," or bunked on deck and exposed to fog, rain, heat, and cold.[28]

One of the most heavily used gateways into the Klondike country was over the glacier-packed Chilkoot Pass. Each goldseeker was required by Canadian authorities to bring in a ton of supplies and equipment to assure survival and minimum mining needs. This often entailed the ordeal of climbing Chilkoot Pass forty times, each ascent with a fifty-pound pack. The Turnerian personal metamorphosis induced by frontier hardship occurred many times as Jack London testified; to survive, "Their hearts turned to stone—those which did not break—and they became beasts."[29]

In the years immediately before and after the Klondike strike, wide-ranging prospectors extended the field along the Yukon and its upper tributaries into Alaska and on out to the Bering Sea. Camps spawned by this very fluid mining frontier included Dawson City (which had a population of thirty thousand by 1900), Forty Mile, Circle, Eagle, Chicken, Star City, Nation, Seventy Mile, Livergood, Ruby, Rampart, Tanana, Crowfoot, Fairbanks, and Nome. The latter, on the Seward Peninsula near Bering Strait, was sited on the beaches and tundra where Anvil Creek empties into the Bering Sea. Over a two-year period, Nome accumulated a population of ten thousand.

The territory included in this mining frontier was the most difficult, demanding, and challenging environment yet encountered by American mining pioneers. The Arctic Circle's harsh seasonal cycle startled them and required considerable adjustment, as did the alternating extended periods of darkness and light. Bitter cold temperatures (averaging forty degrees below zero and at times reaching to seventy degrees below zero), cutting winds, snow, ice, and the brief period of milder temperatures (during June, July, August, and September) limited serious mining. A mining engineer surveying the Alaskan goldfields soon after the stampede concluded that they presented for the miner the most "formidable conditions."[30]

Northland goldseekers applied the pan and sluice, rocker, and cradle, along with other familiar technology, to local ore beds and adopted new ways where required. A prospecting device widely used there was the small, steam-driven churn drill, which tested the tundra for gold. Miners excavated the familiar prospect pits, shafts, and drifts to follow the ore courses; but thawing the permafrost (on the surface for placer work and underground in shafts and drifts) required wood fires and compressed steam.

All three later Pacific Basin mining frontiers had been international in character. This final one was no exception. The great strike that set off the Klondike stampede was made by American prospectors; a Russian mixed-blood found the Circle City field; Scandinavians discovered the Nome field; the rich Fairbanks placers were developed from the claim filed by an Italian, the news spread by a Japanese; and the Juneau mines were developed by a German, a Frenchman, and an Irishman.

In each Pacific Basin mining frontier, a vernacular evolved. Goldseekers in California were argonauts; in Australia they were diggers. In the North Pacific mining frontier, sourdoughs (from their perennial ration of sourdough bread and bad bacon) were the pioneers, the firstcomers, the miner elite. "Cheechakos," or tenderfeet, were the greenhorns, the latecomers.

Two kinds of law applied to this mining frontier. On the eastern side of the international boundary, a single Canadian code was in force; American law in various forms applied west of the boundary. Canadian law sought to maintain a controlled, structured society. Ordinances forbade miners to carry firearms. Saloons and houses of pleasure were permitted in the Canadian camps, but were required to close at stroke of midnight on Saturday, in deference to the Lord's Day. Goldseekers were required to purchase a "miners certificate" and to pay to the Canadian government a 10 percent royalty on gold they produced.

In the American camps there was a mix of controls. The secretary of war had returned several companies of troops to Alaska by the late 1890s, and military officers served as a source of authority, occasionally placing a camp under martial law if they found the miners excessively disorderly. However, most local questions of law and order were handled by miners' committees and juries, the latter determining the guilt and punishment of the accused. Theft, rated as the most serious offense on this frontier, was punished by whipping at the public post and banishment from the country.

Royal Canadian Mounted Police enforced Canadian law to the east. They were braced by three army units (the Royal Canadian Rifles, the Royal Canadian Dragoons, and the Royal Canadian Artillery), assigned duty on the border to reinforce the Royal Mounted Police "by a government concerned that the Americans in the Yukon (its boundaries still in dispute) might cause an insurrection that would lose the territory to Alaska and the United States."[31]

Whether a miner drew gold from his placer valued at fifty or a thousand dollars a day, he could be expected to spend it quickly and with abandon. Camps of this last Pacific Basin mining frontier offered a plethora of elegant satin- and velvet-shrouded seductions that surpassed anything the more primitive settlements of the antecedent California and Australian mining frontiers could provide: carpeted, mahogany-trimmed saloons; plush houses of chance; palaces of erotic pleasure; even restaurants offering San Francisco cuisine. All food in the Northland was scandalously expensive, but particularly fresh vegetables. Onions sold in drug stores as a scurvy cure for two dollars each. Prices at Dawson City were rated as the highest on the continent. In all major camps, miners paid thirty dollars a pint for champagne. The bizarre became the ordinary; prodigal spending, flaunting easy access to gold, became a competitive barroom sport. A favorite spectacle was the weekly auction of a prostitute for her weight in gold.

The Northland camps produced their quota of lurid and in some cases legendary characters. Tinhorn gambler Kid Kelly won the Monte Carlo at Dawson City "on the turn of a card." Big Alex McDonald was the acknowledged "King of the "Klondike." And the "girls" most in demand were Sweet Marie and Diamond Tooth Gertie.

This was the age of Barnum. Charlatans roamed the camps separating fools from their gold. Their offerings included pans for placer work fitted with a clocklike mechanism that, it was claimed, spared the miner hours of wracking labor squatting over a cold creek bed; and gophers trained to dig for gold in the frozen tundra.

This North Pacific mining frontier shared with the California and Australian frontiers several substantial contributions to national and international fiscal affairs. The Klondike field yielded about $300 million worth of gold, the California lodes $2 billion, and the Australian mining fields exceeded the production of both by several million dollars. The period from 1800 to 1900 was the specie century, when a phenomenal increase in gold and silver entered world monetary channels. Gold from the Pacific Basin mining frontiers, together with production from Siberia and South Africa, gave capitalism "a tremendous boost." The British economy, which had been in a state of progressive decline, "revived with spectacular suddenness." And the vanguard American mining frontier provided its nation's voracious economy, committed to continental conquest and development with a vast railway grid, with a timely specie infusion that enlarged the national fiscal foundation and gave it the elasticity required to match its expansionist capital demands.[32]

Of all the expansion entities carrying American dominion across the continent and into the Pacific Basin, the mining frontier produced the most pervasive effect and change. The so-called cultural imperialism of the Anglo-American presence in the Australian mining frontier was significant. And the rich California strikes encouraged a comprehensive mineral reconnaissance of the remainder of the Pacific Basin, producing additional gold discoveries and also exposing less attractive but nonetheless essential minerals. During the twentieth century, the United States and other nations have continued to mine the Pacific Basin. This mineralogical quest has brought to production new goldfields as well as deposits of tin, phosphate, copper, iron, silver, chromium, manganese, coal, tungsten, mercury, petroleum, platinum, bauxite, diamonds, lead, zinc, nickel, cobalt, antimony, and asbestos in the Caroline Islands, New Caledonia, the Fijis, Indonesia, New Zealand, the Philippines, and the Solomon Islands. The force of the mining frontier continues, eliciting certain inevitable and predictable changes in the native peoples and their natural and social environments.

The nineteenth-century mining frontiers produced a rush to the new mineral regions of fortune seekers, who rapidly populated many sections and stimulated essential supportive enterprises. Much of the Pacific Basin rimland and islands are arid and were unattractive to Anglo-American pioneers; under normal conditions settlements would have been slow and uncertain. The mineral strikes prevented this outcome, however, and the rate of occupation and development in some areas was little short of phenomenal. Such an accelerated peopling of portions of the Pacific Basin had an immense and immediate impact on American society and exerted strong pressure for nationalizing currents, to which a reluctant national government finally yielded.

The lure of gold and silver broke through the agrarian preoccupation of America and produced the rapid settlement of many areas that would have been passed over in the usual continental and oceanic frontier progression. Mineral discoveries led to unique patterns of occupation and urbanization of the wilderness. Miners who feverishly worked their claims from dawn until dark each day had no time to maintain traditional frontier self-sufficiency; they were dependent on others for food and other essentials. The mining towns thus generated supportive industries that had a further stimulating effect on the settlement and development of the Pacific Basin. Many of these supportive industries outlived the mining period to become permanent. The principal survivors were stock raising, farming, lumbering, some manufacturing (particularly the fabrication of mining equipment), mineral and food processing, and transportation (freighting on land and water).

The rapid population of the Pacific Basin's eastern rimland enhanced eastern interest in the continental West and Pacific Basin, generated nationalizing currents through the exercise of local popular sovereignty, and committed the nation to policies that contradicted its traditional isolationist stance. And the demographic draw of the mining frontiers provided the numerical basis and local public demand for the creation of new territories and political integration.

The heady ambience of the mining frontier, the flamboyance, daring, and desperate commitment of its partisans, produced a gallery of colorful characters and an incomparable literary legacy. Bret Harte for the California frontier; and Jack London, and Rex Beach for the Alaskan frontier transmitted through their writings unforgettable images of mining frontiers and their protagonists.

But if the mining frontiers had their positive side, they also had a negative one. Of all the Pacific Basin's exploitive frontiers, the mining and refining of minerals were ecologically the most destructive. Gold, silver, and other minerals plentiful in the Pacific Basin were extracted at an ever-increasing rate to feed the world's industries, depleting these irreplaceable resources, which had required millions of years to accumulate by natural processes. Each mining district in turn became a wasteland. Landscapes are pitted with prospect holes, deep shafts and tunnels; the surface scarred with dump piles and punctuated with vast depressions created by cave-ins, as supports in mined-out galleries rotted and collapsed. Forests near mines have been obliterated, leaving bare mountainsides exposed to the elements, the trees sawed into timbers and boards for mine cribbing, supports, and lumber for mill structures and mining-camp shelters. Great quantities of wood, sometimes converted to charcoal, were required to fire the steam boilers that turned the mine machinery and to smelt the minerals. Noxious fumes from smelter-furnace stacks injured trees, shrubs, and grasses, destroying plant life for miles around. Hydraulic and dredge mining washed and disturbed soils and rocks, fouled rivers, and eroded gullies. Mine and mill waters charged with deadly minerals and chemicals fed into creeks and rivers, killing fish, migratory waterfowl, and the land creatures that drank the poisoned waters.

By the 1840s yet another Anglo-American frontier had crossed the continent and was poised on the Pacific Basin's eastern rimland, preparing to follow the mining frontier. This was the agrarian, the farmers', frontier. It was the integrating and stabilizing force in the American nation's seemingly inevitable and unchallenged progression toward the setting sun.

CHAPTER TWELVE

The Agrarian Frontier

The American pioneer hero is epitomized in the farmer. Of the several Yankee expansion entities, or frontiers, that with incredible velocity swept across the continent during the nineteenth century, the farmers' frontier made the major contribution to establishing a more or less permanent national presence. This was primarily because of its demographic mass (probably 85 percent of the national population was rural and to some degree engaged in agriculture), and because American agriculture was notoriously exploitive of the earth's productive capacity, pioneer agrarians required fresh, new territories every generation or so. This lent a dynamic, restless mobility to the farming frontier. Even so, it customarily became more deeply entrenched in its territories and had a greater longevity than most of the other expansion entities. These pioneers, venturing as families, were primarily folk carriers of the Yankee life-style across the continent. This plus the magnitude of their numbers made them the most vital force in transforming the western landscape.

When, near the close of the first third of the nineteenth century, the farmers' frontier reached the Pacific Basin's eastern rimland, it did not stall, but it did slow perceptibly and took a more measured stride. While the frontier did not pervade the basin, it exerted its customary alterative impact in the rich valleys of California, Oregon, and Washington, and upon the volcanic-soil coasts of the Kingdom of Hawai'i.

Deceleration of the flow of this expansion entity was due to several factors endemic to the Pacific Basin. First was environment: the range of unfamiliar climates from frigid polar to languid tropical, differing soils, exotic plants, strange insect pests, the isolation

235

of the limited agricultural territories, and near unthinkable distances to markets. Additional deterrents included the presence of established agricultural economies, some several millennia old, the partitioned territories of European empires, prescriptive land systems, crop-shift imperatives, and limited labor resources.

The American farmers' frontier had confronted established agricultural economies on the continent in the Indian communities in the rich Mississippi Valley and its tributaries, and in the desert Southwest, where some peoples practiced irrigated farming. However, in most cases they were able to eject the Native American farmers and, with federal license, appropriate their lands. Yankee adventurers roaming the Pacific Basin beheld well-functioning agricultural societies in Polynesia, on several western archipelagoes, and on the Asian mainland; the most ancient they found in Japan and China.

As partisans of the American agricultural frontier prepared to enter the Pacific Basin, they observed the major deterrents to be the enormous environmental diversity and the imperial realities. Yankees were latecomers. Dutch, British, Portuguese, Spanish, Russian, and, to a limited degree, French subjects already had preempted much of the basin's prime island and rimland agricultural territory and were formulating an imperial planter's culture.

A recent study of sequestration of Pacific Basin territories and resources by intruder nations identifies these colonial agrarians as "sojourners" rather than settlers (people committed to more or less permanent occupation of a territory). Sojourners by this classification were missionaries, soldiers, traders, miners, and farmers on temporary leave from their respective homelands to discharge assignments or seek fortunes, occupying a transitory tenure, and subject to periodic turnover. In the agricultural territories claimed by intruder nations, only in Australia and New Zealand did a settler class (farmers and stock raisers) evolve. The study concludes that in the "Asian and Pacific Island territories the invaders failed, even in the conquered lands, to advance beyond the state of sojourner civilization." Furthermore, the sojourners "dug their own graves by introducing Western ideas, scientific knowledge and Western women who in self-defense promoted those false ideas of racial superiority and colour barriers which remain."[1]

The sojourners' evolving agrarian culture, based on plantation agriculture, included a colonial life-style with the agrarian-sojourner functioning as a manager-operator, indulged by native field and household labor, his limited tenure made bearable by importing cherished home comforts, and with a hybrid social life; the planters identified as a "broad-hatted, coatless, red-sashed, and leather-belted community." Each planter settlement was embellished with a "club . . . a pleasant house with balconies hanging over the water, and cool, open rooms for reading, writing, billiards, etc."[2]

Sojourner agrarians supervised the production of native and alien food and fiber crops on island plantations situated in the tropical and subtropical climate belts. Gangs of native field hands raised bananas, coconuts, sugarcane, citrus, papaya, breadfruit, yams, rice, and some wheat and barley for subsistence. Spanish planters introduced maize, white and sweet potatoes, and livestock (horses, cattle, sheep, and goats), and improved breeds of swine and poultry. European explorers, notably Cook and Vancouver, also distributed livestock, seeds, and plants about the basin.

Sojourner plantations yielded coffee, cinchona, cacao, tea, pineapple, cotton, sugarcane, and copra for export. Characteristically for nineteenth-century plantation agriculture, cultivation was intensive and highly exploitive of soil nutrients. Soil depletion commonly occurred on these holdings after two or three years, requiring heavy application of guano or the abandonment of old and the subsequent clearing of new fields.

The coconut palm's fruit surpassed all other Pacific Basin crops in export value. Called "lazy man's crop," coconuts ripen throughout the year, require no storage or processing, and are a prime source of nutritious food. Sojourner agrarians found that the meat of the coconut could be dried (a product called copra), then pressed to yield a multipurpose oil valued as an illuminant (when made into candles), as a cooking oil, and as a base for the manufacture of margarine, glycerine, and cosmetics. Initially copra production was a gathering industry. Natives collected coconuts from the wild, hulled and cracked the hard shells, chopped the meat into pieces, dried it in the sun (or, during the wet season, over slow-burning fires), then sacked the copra and awaited Chinese and European traders.[3]

By the 1840s sojourners developed a process for pressing copra locally, and its exploitation shifted from a gathering to a plantation industry. Within a short time, copra and coconut oil were the principal cargoes departing the island anchorages of southern Polynesia and the western Pacific. Traders shipped pressed oil or copra in barrels for later pressing, much as sea hunters had been handling whale oil for half a century.[4]

Coconut-palm plantations spread from Tahiti and Samoa to New Guinea, the Bismark Archipelago, and most other islands situated in the tropical climate belt. In addition, sojourner-managed plantations on these and other islands yielded cacao, citrus, cotton, coffee, tea, and sugarcane: the Fijis grew primarily sugarcane; Indonesia, coffee, tobacco, spices, tea, sugarcane, and cotton; the Philippines, sugarcane, tobacco, and cotton; and Australia and New Zealand, livestock, wheat, sugarcane, tropical and subtropical fruits, vegetables, and cotton.

Early Yankee adventurers in the Pacific Basin, scions of a predominantly agrarian society, were struck by its seemingly insuperable environmental and imperial deterrents to transplanting the farming frontier. Nonetheless several of these maritime pioneers, crewmen exiled on tropical island beaches, made some effort at farming by raising potatoes and other foodstuffs and vending their produce to commissary officers from the whaling and trader fleets. In addition, by 1850, the several American capitalists who had negotiated concessions for plantation sites in Indonesia and the Philippines were producing and exporting coffee, tea, and spices.

However, at no time or place in the Pacific Basin was the traditional farmers' frontier able to entrench and articulate itself with its customary form and vigor, to serve the nation as it had over much of the continent as the premier expansion juggernaut. Confronted with a multitude of deterrents as it prepared to enter the region, while it did not completely stall, it did slow perceptibly to take an altered, more measured stride. As was characteristic of Yankee expansion entities, however, the farmers' frontier, rather than being a monolithic structure, demonstrated a flexibility, adapted, and formulated a way to address the deterrents.

On its approach to the Pacific Basin, the American farmers' frontier first sought to establish itself on the eastern rim, in Oregon, Washington, and California. In modified form eventually it extended to Hawai'i, Samoa, Guam, the Philippines, and in the twentieth century, Alaska.

Aside from Hawai'i, the altered farmers' frontier achieved its greatest success on the eastern rimland. Here Yankee agrarians, confronted by a strong British presence centered at Fort Vancouver on the Columbia River, sustained by a lucrative fur trade, were forced to make their first substantive change in approach. The joint occupation and equal-use privilege in the territory between forty-two degrees and fifty-four degrees and forty minutes, extending from the crest of the Rocky Mountains to the Pacific, guaranteed by British-American conventions, was effectively negated by a deliberate British exclusionist economic imperialism. American fur traders and other vanguards had been effectively denied access. Thus to deflect British anxiety over American intent, the missionary frontier preceded the farmers' frontier into this new expansion zone, serving as a stalking horse for the latter. British managers at Fort Vancouver readily received American missionaries for the ostensible purpose of ministering to local Indians; the Yankee divines seemed to pose no economic or imperial threat.

The deceptively noncompetitive missionary frontier was energized in 1831 by four Indians from the Oregon Country who appeared in Saint Louis and declared that their people desired instruction by missionaries. Editors of religious publications transformed this into a plaintive heathen call from the Northwest wilderness. It became a holy charge, as pastors transmitted the tidings to their congregations. The mission boards of several religious bodies interpreted the Indian appeal as comparable to St. Paul's "Macedonian call."

The first religious body to respond with a definite plan for establishing missions in the new territory was a consortium of Methodist congregations in New England and New York. Their mission board raised funds and selected the Reverend Jason Lee to lead the Oregon Mission to carry the gospel to the tribesmen of the Pacific Northwest. Lee and the first group of mission workers departed New York in 1833.

Lee supervised erection of a mission school and church at French Prairie, in the upper Willamette Valley; the school became the headquarters for additional mission stations. The Methodist church at French Prairie ministered largely to employees of the Hudson's Bay Company at Fort Vancouver and their families. After three years the Methodist mission schools had an enrollment of nineteen students.

The Methodists were followed to Oregon in 1835 by Presbyterians sponsored by the American Board. This group commissioned Samuel Parker (clergy representative), Dr. Marcus Whitman (physician), and several mission workers. The Presbyterians established a station at Waiilatpu, near the junction of the Columbia and Snake rivers; it served as the center for several smaller mission stations located near tribal settlements. Roman Catholics also established missions at this time in the Northwest. The first stream of clerics came from Canada during 1838, guided by Hudson's Bay Company men. Shortly thereafter Roman Catholic missionaries arrived from Saint Louis; their most famous representative was Father Pierre Jean de Smet, who by 1842 had established the most successful Christian stations in the region, primarily in the Coeur d'Alene and Bitterroot mission districts. In the Oregon Country, Catholic missions far exceeded Protestant missions in sustained commitment, service, and results. More than to any other reason, this fact is attributable to the Catholics' single-mindedness in their charge. The Protestants were torn by mixed interests.

The Protestant missionary frontier in the Oregon Country became the precursor of American expansion and settlement. In order to activate their vocational-training program, the missionaries imported cattle, horses, and mules from California. They established flourishing orchards and broad fields of grain. These farms, undertaken to instruct a few Indian students in farming and stock raising, demonstrated the fertility of the soils and the generally favorable agricultural conditions existing in this Pacific Basin rimland.

Protestant missionaries have been accused of following an ambivalent course: of working for the Americanization of the Oregon Country while going through a charade of fulfilling the missionary charge to local peoples. Jason Lee has been called an expansionist, a missionary with "a colonizer's heart and a pioneer's shrewdness," intent upon importing New England values and that region's "superior brand of American culture to the Pacific." It is claimed that he conceived his true mission to be providing "New England farmers a foretaste of Heaven" by attracting them to the Pacific Basin's eastern rim. It is at least undeniable that mission staffs increasingly spent time developing farms and livestock herds for their personal benefit and to the detriment of their ministry to Indians.[5]

Missionary workers corresponded with families and sponsoring church congregations in the East, and their letters are replete with superlatives describing the bounty of the Oregon Country. Often these letters were shared with newspaper and magazine editors, who published them for a wider body of readers. Missionaries also regularly returned to the states to raise money to support their work in the new territory and to recruit additional workers for the missions. In 1838, four years after founding the mission at French Point, Jason Lee journeyed to the East on a fund-raising venture. He returned to French Point with fifty men, women, and children, certainly more than were needed for the Methodist mission staff working this Pacific Basin outpost.

Escalating public interest in the Oregon Country during the 1830s led to the organization of Oregon immigration societies in Massachusetts, Missouri, Ohio, Michigan, and Pennsylvania. The Oregon Provisional Emigration Society of Lynn, Massachusetts, sought to recruit several hundred "Christian families" to migrate to this Pacific wilderness, transform it, and lead the Indians to salvation. The first immigrants who had no missionary connection, numbering about thirty, gathered at Independence, Missouri, in 1841. They proceeded to the Pacific Basin's eastern rim over a route that came to be called the Oregon Trail. The next year a hundred ventured west; during 1843 a thousand Americans passed over the trail. Two years later this number swelled to three thousand and by the end of 1845, five thousand Yankees had arrived on the Columbia; this compared to a British resident population of about one thousand.[6]

The Americans promptly applied grass-roots democracy. At several public meetings between 1841 and 1843, pioneer delegates meeting at Champoeg organized a local government directed by a compact based on the Northwest Ordinance of 1787 and the

241

Iowa statutes and containing an antislavery clause. Representatives of this provisional government carried petitions to Washington, urging Congress to recognize their action and absorb the Pacific Northwest into the American community.

A strong Yankee presence and the articulate appeal from this segment of the Pacific Basin activated those essential nationalizing currents, familiar steps in the American expansion process. During 1846 American and British representatives concluded a pact providing for the end of joint occupation of the Oregon Country and for dividing it along the forty-ninth parallel; the territory below that line went to the United States, the territory above that line to British Canada. In 1848 Congress created the Oregon Territory. Five years later, in response to local appeals from the ever-enlarging farmers' frontier, Congress created the Washington Territory from the area north of the Columbia River. Oregon entered the Union in 1859, Washington in 1889. Religious, political, and economic interests there (other than agrarian), worked with the farmers' frontier to achieve these spectacular occupation, development, and political integration successes; but the primary force throughout was applied by the farmers' frontier.

In each segment of the Pacific Basin penetrated by the farmers' frontier, its partisans met anomalies in labor-access and land-tenure systems. Less apparent at first, by degree both surfaced in the Oregon Country. Thus one of the most revolutionary steps taken by Congress in distributing the public domain was applied to this Pacific territory by the passage of the 1850 Donation Land Act, which assigned to a pioneer who had settled there before 1 December 1850 320 acres and before 1 December 1853, 160 acres.[7]

During most of the nineteenth century, an age of limited technology, pioneers opening wilderness areas were largely dependent on human and animal power, because only limited applications of wind, water, and steam were available. Americans from colonial times forward had attempted to meet this need by the use of Indian bond servants, indentured workers, African slaves, and large families. The extension of African slave labor across the continent had become a bitter political as well as economic issue. The farmers' frontier here, in contrast to its stance in other Pacific Basin territories, was committed to eschewing use of slave labor in opening the wilderness, taking a stand to keep it "free soil" and thus derive the required work force from large families, hired help when it could be afforded, and labor exchange with neighbors.

In this segment of the Pacific Basin's eastern rimland, the farmers' frontier, with a substantive assist from the missionary frontier, had consummated its personal and civic missions. It had achieved modest prosperity during its formative years, as foodstuffs (particularly grain, livestock, and poultry) found their way into Pacific Basin commerce. The discovery of gold in adjacent California in 1848 provided a strategic and lucrative market for this produce.

California was the next segment of the Pacific Basin rimland to receive the alterative and integrative force of the Yankee farmers' frontier. Spanish administrators in New Spain had assigned the region's initial occupation to Franciscan missionaries. Between 1769 and 1823, clerics of this order established a chain of twenty-one missions, extending from San Diego to Sonoma. The mission as a primary expansion entity for Spanish colonial America introduced agriculture into California. The mission staff, often two padres supported by a squad of five or six soldiers from the nearby presidio, collected local Indians and resettled them at the mission, to become Hispanicized, a process that included instruction in horticulture and animal husbandry. Mission fields yielded vegetables, fruits, grain, and fibers; pastures sustained ever-enlarging herds of horses and cattle, as well as flocks of sheep and goats. Many of the mission fields were irrigated.

The California mission system survived Mexican independence in 1821, but during the 1830s, officials secularized the Franciscan properties. After assigning resident Indians the rights of Mexican citizens and one-half the mission land, livestock, and equipment (most of which the neophytes promptly lost to non-Indians), Mexican officials partitioned the residue of land into grants, some thousands of acres in extent, to individuals.

Meanwhile aliens in increasing numbers were appearing on the California scene. During 1812, as we have seen, Russian-American Company officials established a colony near Bodega Bay, designating it Fort Ross (or Russ); its purpose was to produce food for Russian fur brigades working the upper Pacific Basin's eastern rimland. Imported Russian peasants and Pomo Indians were impressed to tend the grain and vegetable fields at the colony.

Aliens from the United States, Europe, and points in the Pacific Basin also reached California in this era. One of the most notable in terms of nourishing the farmers' frontier in California was John A. Sutter, a German of Swiss citizenship who arrived in California in 1839. On application to Mexican officials at Monterey, he received a vast land grant on the American River near its juncture with the Sacramento. In addition Sutter purchased Fort Ross from the Russian-American Company.

There Sutter developed a thriving settlement complete with fortress, mill, shops, and general store, and named it New Helvetia. Situated at the terminus of most trails through the Sierra passes, New Helvetia became an important center for later American activity in northern California. For arriving farmer pioneers, New Helvetia's fields of grain, productive orchards, and herds of cattle, horses, and mules served as a promising demonstration of agrarian success.

Several American fur men and maritime traders had retired in California in the early days of Mexican independence, to engage in farming and stock raising. However, the first serious agrarians from the states, the true vanguard of the farming frontier, reached California in 1841. Their passage led over the Oregon Trail to Fort Hall, then turned southwest, skirting the northern edge of Great Salt Lake to the Humboldt River, across the Nevada Desert and the Sierra Nevada by way of the Walker (or Truckee) River, crossing at Truckee Pass into California's interior. This first immigrant party numbered about thirty-five. The immigration to California by Yankee farmers in no way matched that to Oregon; by 1846, the year of the American conquest of the Mexican Southwest, less than a thousand American farmers resided in California. However, their great success in the new land augured California's status a century later as a world leader in food production. The pioneer John Bidwell received a grant on Butte Creek, where he grew wheat and fruit with marked success. Other American agrarians were making similar progress in adapting to farming in the new area. Then ironically, in 1848 the event occurred that inflicted a brief setback on the farmers' frontier, only rather quickly to become an asset.[8]

In 1848, the year of the Treaty of Guadalupe Hidalgo, which concluded the war with Mexico and ceded California to the United States, John Sutter's employees found gold in a millrace diverted from the American River. The prospect of quick riches lured many recently arrived Yankee farmers to the goldfields. Grain was left to rot in the fields, orchards to wither, and mills stood idle from lack of corn and wheat, as transplanted husbandmen joined mechanics, sailors, and townsmen in the stampede to the Sierra placers. One observer said that "the proportion of labor employed for digging gold . . . was altogether too great for the true interest of California. . . . gold mania had blinded men's eyes to the surer profits to be derived from producing more useful commodities."[9]

As the gold excitement subsided, many farmers returned to their fields to produce food for the mining-camp market. A goodly number of them found in farming the El Dorado that had eluded them in the goldfields. For example near Sacramento in 1850, an acre-and-a-half truck patch yielded tomatoes worth eighteen thousand dollars. As more goldseekers abandoned mining for farming, an increasing volume of vegetables, fruits, and grain replaced the miners' monotonous fare of dried beans and salt pork. Until 1854 California suppliers imported wheat to feed the miners. Renewed agricultural production by 1855 yielded sufficient wheat so that no grain imports were necessary; in 1856 California's wheat surplus permitted the export of seventy thousand barrels of flour to Peru. Four years later these Pacific Basin rimland farms yielded nearly six million bushels of this grain, and by 1890 California ranked as the nation's leading wheat producer.[10]

Many European immigrants, attracted to this Pacific Basin rimland by the gold rush, joined the farmers' frontier to produce food for the mining camps. French, German, and Italian immigrants established vineyards and marketed their grapes in the Sierra settlements. American pioneers introduced cotton and the raising of silkworms.

In 1850 California had been Americanized (settled, developed according to the Yankee formula, and integrated into the Union), the certain and shared work of several expansion entities. Similar to the case of the Oregon Country, where the farmers' frontier, rather than dominating the expansionist drama as it had in regions to the east, had shared the Americanizing process with the missionary frontier, the farmers' frontier in California played a contributing role to the dominating miners' frontier. And these two expansion entities benefited from the alterative influence of the antecedent fur and maritime trading frontiers there. However, before the nineteenth century closed, the agrarian frontier eclipsed all others in sustained influence, although not without undergoing substantive changes in its economic and social profile, particularly in labor and land-tenure systems. These contrasted conspicuously with the systems that had characterized it in those eastern areas it had transformed so successfully.

Immigrants to this rimland outpost had imported African slaves in the early years of settlement, but at no time was slave labor a factor in the economy there. In fact, the state constitution by which Congress admitted California to the Union in 1850 banned slavery.[11]

Nevertheless, Californians practiced a form of involuntary servitude that mocked the antislavery clause of the state constitution. It permitted the impressment of thousands of local Indians into social and economic bondage. Local judges were authorized to assign male and female Indians to guardians, who supervised their "productive" labor in households and fields.[12]

The sheer size of agricultural properties in California also required a shift from the yeoman-style operation run by the freehold family (father, mother, and many children) to ever-larger irrigated commercial, even corporate, holdings, with labor provided by Indians and Asiatics and European contract workers. The use of this new labor force had become the common resort in Pacific Basin agriculture territories during the nineteenth century. In California there is a utilitarian connection between this trend and the migrant work force of the twentieth century, involving many races until around 1950, with the increasing resort to immigrant Mexican labor.

This novel land-tenure system was the result of Spanish and Mexican practices of territorial distribution, which set the tradition for large farm and ranch holdings. By the time of the 1846 conquest, much of central and southern California had been as-signed to Hispanics, Indians, and aliens.

Late-arriving Yankees protested this preemption that resulted in only a small amount of desirable public domain land being available for distribution to settlers under the land laws of the United States. In 1851 Congress responded with legislation that required all grantees "to present their petitions for verification within two years" before the United States Land Commission or forfeit their rights.[13]

This statute placed the "burden of proof" on the claimants. "They often were hard pressed to locate the carelessly drawn titles and maps of by-gone days. Friends testified for each other as to boundaries that were both vague and altered by use and claims by squatters. The Land Commission hearings went on for ten years, and court proceedings followed upon them." Some United States patents to Mexican grantees were not issued until 1872. In the process a great number of the Spanish and Mexican grants were annulled by action of the United States Land Commission and the conqueror's courts.[14]

True to the pattern of land tenure in the Pacific Basin, Hispanic and Indian grantees were stripped of their properties. But the tradition of large plantation holdings, involving from three hundred to several thousand acres, persisted in agriculture and stock raising.

The Yankee farming frontier, thus altered by its experiences in the Pacific Basin's eastern rimland, prepared to move deeper into the region: on to Hawai'i, Samoa, Guam, the Philippines, and (in the first third of the twentieth century) Alaska.

This expansion entity proceeded into the island interior at a measured, piecemeal pace, its first beachhead formed in the Ha-waiian archipelago, where it encountered an ancient, traditional Polynesian agrarian establishment. First observed by Westerners in the late 1770s, during the Cook Pacific reconnaissance, this island chain was fragmented into local chiefdoms. The native pop-ulation, at the time numbering at least three hundred thousand, was supported by a farming economy supplemented by fishing and interisland commerce. Each island chief was the acknowledged owner of the land; he distributed portions of his domain to lesser district chiefs, who in turn assigned subsistence parcels to peasant subjects.

Polynesian farmers produced taro, sweet potatoes, bananas, sugarcane, and arrowroot on terraced, irrigated fields located on the narrow, arable coastal strips. They tended herds of pigs and flocks of poultry, impounded mullet and other marine animals in ponds, and gathered breadfruit, coconuts, and other foods from a lush, tropical environment.

Each peasant family was required to render annual tribute in the form of chickens, pigs, and other foodstuffs to the local lord, and to labor one day each week on his estate. Western observers reported they had seen hundreds of men, women, and children working the local chiefs' taro plantations, some of the fields fifty acres in extent. Families failing to satisfy their local lord's demands could be punished by having their personal property seized and their houses burned.[15]

After the unification of the islands into the Kingdom of Hawai'i, by Kamehameha I, title to the land on the islands under his control was vested in him and his issue, a practice that lasted until 1848, when a new land distribution plan, known as the Great Mahele, began to replace this native Polynesian practice with Western fee-simple tenure. An added labor tax was assessed on Hawaiians following the formation of the Kingdom of Hawai'i; subjects were required to perform an annual "king's week" of labor on roads, royal plantations, fortifications, and other public works.

Hawai'i's climate, largely volcanic soils, exotic plants, uncertain labor supply, marketing obstacles, and a royal government that maintained a variant land-tenure system all combined to compel the Yankee farmers' frontier to undergo even greater change than had been necessary on the basin's eastern rimland. And its pace of development in this archipelago was slow; it did not mushroom as it had in its passage across much of the continent. In the Kingdom of Hawai'i, it proceeded through several stages, so that by the close of the century it was considerably different, although it still served the nation as a vehicle for extending American territorial dominion.

The farming frontier in the Kingdom of Hawai'i was by 1850, when it functioned as a generally successful economic enterprise,

a synthesis of Polynesian, maritime import, and missionary ad-
aptations, with a rich ethnic seasoning. Pioneer haoles settling in
Hawai'i during the 1790s were largely beached sailors; many married native women and became subsistence farmers. They copied
the Polynesian system of terracing and irrigating the slender arable
coastal strips, cultivating native plants and tending small flocks
of poultry and swine. Sea captains occasionally presented them
with seeds, plants, and livestock (horses, mules, cattle, sheep, and
goats) to stock their tiny farms. The missionary advent in 1820
enhanced the setting for the farming frontier. In addition to introducing Christian teachings, demonstration farms were established to instruct native converts in additional food- and fiber-
production techniques.

Americans dominated the early haole population, although
they were not the only new settlers. The most prominent early-
day farmer in the islands was a Spaniard, Francisco de Paula Marín.
He arrived in Hawai'i in 1791 and led all haoles in creating the
setting for the agrarian frontier. A premier horticulturalist, in his
gardens he raised pineapples, oranges, beans, cabbages, pumpkins,
tobacco, cotton, coffee, maize, peas, wheat, barley, tomatoes, tur-
nips, Irish potatoes, and grapes (from which he produced a "fine
wine"). He imported cattle, goats, pigs, poultry, pigeons, horses,
and mules from South America. And because he spoke English
"remarkably well," he frequently acted as one of the king's interpreters. By "his industry," Marín "had become a rich and useful
member of the community," and "amassed during a residence of
thirty years in the country" a considerable fortune. "His riches
and frugal habits of life were calculated to make him many enemies, and he was, in fact, universally unpopular." However, a
member of the 1825 Byron Pacific expedition paid him deserved
tribute, observing "To Mr. Marin's diligence as a farmer, the Sandwich Islands . . . may be said to be under some obligations for his
introducing and multiplying various kinds of animals, which in a
few years will be plentiful."[16]

As maritime traffic to and among the islands increased after
1800, Polynesian and haole farmers found outlets for garden and
livestock products, and they shifted increasingly from subsistence
to commercial production. The range of products offered to mar-

itime-trading and whaling-fleet commissary officers at the island ports also increased. Besides cargoes of fresh and salt beef and pork, Irish and sweet potatoes and yams, coconuts, breadfruit, pumpkins, taro, cabbages, bananas, pineapples, melons, and beans, they supplied crates of poultry. The Irish potato was the farm product most in demand; they sold by the barrel. By 1847 the maritime market annually took twenty thousand barrels.[17]

There was also a noticeable increase in the size of farms, many becoming plantations of from several hundred to thousands of acres in extent. Access to the land was obtained from the king as grants under lifetime lease tenure to favored haoles, or as assignments by island chiefs. More and more native Hawaiians spent less time farming on their own and entered the employ of these new plantation operators.

Additional commercial crops included coffee, oranges, rice, maize, crude sugar, syrup, molasses, and wheat flour. Marín had first demonstrated the feasibility of these crops in the island milieu.

Coffee, an esteemed Hawaiian export in the twentieth century, was carried to Hawai'i from Manila, Batavia, Yemen, and Brazil. Missionaries also distributed coffee plantings to native converts, in an attempt to provide them with a cash crop for their small farms. The first coffee plantation was established at the head of Manoa Valley on O'ahu in 1825, by an Englishman named John Wilkinson. The Hall estate on the island of Hawai'i included by 1846 an "extensive coffee plantation" of "many thousand coffee trees" and "after 5 years labor" proved profitable. At the same time the Titcomb plantation situated in the Hanalei Valley on the island of Kaua'i contained over fifty thousand trees about four years old, which yielded from 100,000 to 150,000 pounds of coffee each year.[18]

On the leeward, drier, portions of the islands, pioneer farmers found that grains (barley, wheat, and maize) flourished. And rice, popular and easy to keep aboard ship, adapted easily to the islands' wetter sections. Planters imported rice seedlings from South Carolina, and this grain replaced coffee as second to sugar in the established agrarian economy of the islands until around 1900. Wheat ranked with coffee and rice as a favored new crop for the islands, largely because of its easy conversion to flour. Seed for island wheat farms came from the Pacific Basin eastern rimland farms in Oregon and from the western rimland farms in Australia. Steam mills for processing wheat into flour were established on several islands. Flour previously came around the Horn to arrive at the Hawaiian market "in a damaged condition. It is only occasionally that a ship brings flour around the Cape perfectly sweet; it is more frequently sour, and often musty withal, and of course greatly deteriorated in money value as well as healthful qualities."[19]

The Kingdom of Hawai'i's sugar bonanza developed after 1850, although a limited amount of native sugarcane reached the maritime market before this. Native Hawaiians traditionally had raised sugarcane on their subsistence patches. Missionaries then added it to coffee and vegetables in their demonstration fields, to encourage converts to adopt it as a cash crop. Pioneer farmers processed small quantities of sugar in crude mills into molasses, syrup, and crude sugar for sale at the maritime market.

They also experimented with the production of cotton, silk, and indigo. Cotton received uneven attention as a commercial crop. Every decade or so a burst of interest in its production would surface, and at times promising crops resulted. It was most popular as a commercial crop in the islands during the American Civil War, when the Sea Island type was produced to offset the loss of the short-staple fiber from the American South. With the islands' limited arable land (scarcely one-fifth of the total land area), cotton could never compete with sugar as the premier cash crop.

Pioneer farmers attempted to establish sericulture in the 1830s. They imported silkworms and mulberry trees from China and the United States. Early prospects for success dimmed rapidly, due (according to some authorities) to drought, inexperience with this exotic industry, and the influence of missionaries. It was claimed that at least one large cocoonery, representing a heavy capital investment, failed because of "unsteady labor of natives . . . the worms had to be fed on Sundays (!) This did not exactly suit the rigid notions of the ecclesiastics that controlled the spiritual interests of the natives." This critic charged that missionaries forbade "natives employing a few minutes on the Sabbath to feed silkworms; and this was done on a penalty of excommunication, and the pains of an endless shower of hell fire beyond the grave."[20]

Pioneer farmers also expected indigo to be a commercial success when it was introduced into the Kingdom of Hawai'i in 1832 by a sea captain from Batavia. However, "the mania . . . subsided, and the plant left to take care of itself." One observer reported "hundreds of acres are covered with its dense growth, and it continues to overrun some of the most valuable lands on the islands. So obnoxious has it become, that I have heard agriculturalists wish that its introducer were compelled to uproot every plant by his teeth. There is no reason, however, why indigo, properly cultivated, should not become a very lucrative branch of exportation."[21]

Ranching was another valuable aspect of the farming frontier in the Kingdom of Hawai'i. Vancouver delivered the first cattle to the island during the 1790s. Richard Cleveland, a maritime trader, is credited with importing the first horses into Hawai'i. Other maritime visitors brought additional horses and cattle as well as mules, goats, sheep, and improved breeds of swine and poultry. Through the years much of the seed stock, left untended, increased in numbers and became a prime food source. It is claimed that Vancouver influenced Kamehameha I to arrange for a *kapu* (taboo) to be placed on the killing of cattle, so as not to interfere with herd increase. Eventually the monarch decreed that cattle, like the land, were crown property. Thus hunting cattle for hides, tallow, and beef required a license from the court.

Several pioneer haoles became stock raisers; some ranges they obtained from the crown were larger than the evolving plantations being carved from the archipelago. The largest in the islands, over two hundred thousand acres, was established by an emigrant from Massachusetts, John Parker. To work these ranches, proprietors imported Spanish and Mexican vaqueros from California to instruct native Hawaiians in ranching techniques. Hawaiian cowboys came to be called *paniolos* (from *Españoles*).[22]

Ranching was a strong contributor to the success of the farming frontier in the Kingdom of Hawai'i. Oxen, horses, and mules were essential for clearing and cultivating plantations, hauling equipment, turning the primitive cane presses, and, in the case of horses and mules, supplying land transportation. Beef, pork, mutton, and poultry were much in demand at the port markets for provisioning the trading and whaling fleets. And wool as well as goat and cattle hides were valued export commodities. As late as 1855, the value of livestock products produced on island ranches exceeded by 60 percent that of sugar.[23]

Soon after 1850 the hint of a decline in Pacific Basin whaling activity, with a concomitant reduction in demand for island food-stuffs, led farmers and ranchers to seek alternative markets. Fortuitously, the California and Australian gold rushes assured profitable outlets for Hawaiian products throughout the 1850s. These rim-land outlets, while not as conveniently situated as the earlier dock-side markets, acted as a supportive bridge connecting the Hawaiian agrarian frontier with its future enduring obsession, the production of sugarcane.[24]

By midcentury farmers in Hawai'i clearly were seeking a main-stay crop. Grains, coffee, fruits and vegetables, and livestock products were marketable, but had limitations as basic support crops. The rise of competitive agricultural territories in the Pacific Basin, market isolation, and declining capital interest combined to demand reconsideration of crop emphasis. Just as the southern United States had evolved a monocrop plantation system based on cotton, the Kingdom of Hawai'i became increasingly committed to a plantation system based on sugarcane. Island experience with cane production had demonstrated the islands' ideal environment for this universally esteemed sweetener, now less a world consumer luxury than a necessity.

Several obstacles to this transformation first had to be resolved. Powerful haoles applied their influence on the royal court and governmental agencies to elicit policies that smoothed the way. Two of the haole principals responsible for the momentous changes were Dr. Gerrit P. Judd and the Reverend William Richards. Both had come to the Kingdom of Hawai'i as members of the American Board mission, Judd as medical missionary, Richards as minister-teacher. Eventually Judd and Richards became influential counselors to Hawai'i kings; Judd served as prime minister of the kingdom for several years.

According to spokesmen for the farmers' frontier, the most serious obstacle to agrarian success was the land-tenure system, wherein title to the kingdom's land was vested in the monarch. The potential for capriciousness by the head of state in allocating land use to haoles, it was claimed, discouraged the large-scale plantation investment required by sugarcane production; advocates urged adoption of the Western fee-simple land-tenure system.

Judd, Richards, and other leaders fashioned a plan, called the Great Mahele; its application began in 1848. The Great Mahele abolished the feudal land system of Hawai'i. Another influential missionary leader, the Reverend Richard Armstrong, announced, "The government has lately granted fee-simple titles. . . . This gives the final blow to the old feudal system. . . . It is a point for which I have long contended and finally on my own motion it was carried by the King and Council." Categories of land reservations under the Great Mahele included crown lands (ca. 1,000,000 acres), government lands (ca. 1,500,000 acres), and kingdom lands (ca. 1,500,000 acres). Commoners received fee-simple title to small homestead grants, *kuleanas,* from the government reserve. The new system permitted haoles to purchase island land and hold it in fee-simple tenure. Outside developers created huge plantations under the new order; 213 haoles purchased over 320,000 acres before 1864, and by 1893 foreigners had obtained over 600,000 acres at about 92 cents an acre. In addition 72 aliens received access to over 750,000 acres of segregated crown and government lands through an annual lease payment of a few cents per acre. Claus Spreckels, developer of Pacific Basin sugar-refining facilities, obtained access to 24,000 acres of prime island sugar property. And the entire island of Ni'ihau, containing 61,000 acres, was purchased by a single haole.[25]

The principal casualties of this revolution in land tenure were Hawaiian commoners. Most were shortly dispossessed of their homesteads by debt, mortgage foreclosure, and other legal maneuvers applied by plantation proprietors. These Polynesian proletarians were not unlike their ethnic counterparts on the continent—American Indians dispossessed of their landed estates by the Dawes Act of 1887 and its exploitive aftermath. For native Hawaiians the Great Mahele became rather than the great "land division . . . the great eviction." Their resentment at haole success in this divestment was directed largely toward American Board missionaries and their offspring, "sugar missionaries," the ones "who stole the land and despoiled the Hawaiian people."[26]

An additional obstacle to achieving a plantation sugarcane culture was the shortage of labor. This enterprise required a large field-labor pool. Hawaiian agriculturalists therefore resorted to practices of planters on islands controlled by Great Britain, Holland, and France: they negotiated indentures and term contracts to recruit workers from the islands and from India. France had established a penal colony on New Caledonia; its eight thousand prisoners were assigned to labor on local plantations and public works. Blackbirding (the kidnapping of healthy island men as permanent field hands for island planters) also supplied workers.[27]

The native Hawaiian population was drastically weakened by years of the most punishing exploitation by sandalwood collectors, planters, and construction contractors and was devastated by Western diseases against which it had no natural immunity. Numbering an estimated three hundred thousand at the time of European contact in the 1770s, it had declined (as revealed by royal census) to sixty-seven thousand in 1860 and to fifty-one thousand in 1872.[28]

This demographic nadir was reached at the very time the farmers' frontier was preparing to achieve the "new order" through concentration on plantation sugarcane culture, with its concomitant increased requirement for field labor. As had been their strategy in removing the obstacle to fee-simple land tenure, leaders applied their ever-escalating influence, again receiving substantial support from powerful haoles holding key positions in the royal government to achieve a solution to the labor problem. They functioned collectively through the Royal Hawaiian Agricultural Society and the Planters' Society, each dedicated to advancing the agrarian cause in the kingdom, including the promotion in world markets of plantation products (with an emphasis on sugar), and to searching for solutions to the labor problem.

They triumphed again. In 1864 the Hawaiian Congress adopted a law creating the Bureau of Immigration to supervise importation of foreign laborers, regulate their contracts, and promote free emigration from abroad. The statute created the position of commissioner of immigration, whose duties included recruiting a work force from the Pacific Basin.[29]

The commissioner's first success was on the basin's western

rimland—China. Small parties of Chinese, locally called coolies, had reached the kingdom during the 1840s and were employed on coffee plantations. This first consignment of Chinese workers recruited by the royal commissioner numbered 522, and included 95 women, each signed to a five-year contract, at wages of four dollars a month, food and lodging furnished, with a two-dollar bonus at Chinese New Year. Thereafter, until the end of the century, an alien stream of Chinese, Japanese, Samoan, Korean, Filipino, and European (Portuguese, German, Norwegian) workers flowed into the islands to labor on the sugar plantations. Over 10,000 Portuguese relocated from Madeira and the Azores, but Japanese came in the greatest numbers; Filipinos, later arrivals, ranked next. The Hawaiian farm-labor recruitment program attracted 120,000 people over a fifty-year period. Contract stipulations varied as to term of service, committing the worker to a four-, three-, or one-year obligation, in some cases for the harvest period only. Planters lodged laborers in "camps" on the plantation grounds, each worker community supplied with a clinic, general store, and other minimal necessities, much like the isolated "company towns" in the mining, lumber, and mill settlements on the mainland. A diarist from a missionary family turned sugar planters transmitted to posterity a field scene of a company of

> Celestials . . . just from China. There are 38 men and 10 women all hired to work together in the field. They wear the Chinese costume which consists of wide trousers and a loose frock, the women dressing just like the men, only that their frocks are longer, coming to the knees. They appear more uncivilized than the natives, but it pains me to see the women thus employed in the field for they are small of stature and look slender—as though they could not endure much hardship. Whilst I am writing I hear them singing at their work.[30]

Having resolved the land and labor problems, the planters proceeded to bring to fruition the "new order" in Hawaiian agriculture. The enlarging labor pool enabled them to increase cane acreage. Scots, in demand on mainland ranches as managers in the emerging range-cattle industry there, were also recruited by island planters. Highly esteemed for their "legendary reputation for frugality and singleminded obsession with economic success," these "tough" overseers drove gangs of contract laborers to plow, cultivate, harvest, and process sugarcane. Labor crews tunneled mountains, constructed conduits, and opened ditches to bring highland water to thirsty fields.[31]

Capital for plantation expansion came from Honolulu and San Francisco investors, who for several decades had profited from outfitting Pacific Basin whaling and maritime trader fleets. Thus financed, plantation operators converted the water- and ox-powered mills that pressed the juice from cane stalks (some fourteen feet long and nine inches in girth at the lower joints) to more efficient steam power. And they constructed railroads to transport the raw cane to mills and the raw sugar to ports for carriage to refineries.

The American Civil War created a world sugar shortage and precipitated a sharp rise in price, conditions that aided the industry in Hawai'i. The number of plantations increased during the period 1860–66 from twelve to thirty-two; in 1860 island sugar exports amounted to less than 1,500,000 pounds; in 1866 they were 17,000,000. The value of sugarcane came to surpass that of all island products including livestock.[32]

The production of coffee, vegetables, and fruits continued, but competition for acreage caused a reduction in land devoted to other products. The pineapple, which was produced in prediscovery times on native farms and popular in the dockside markets for supplying trader and whaler fleet commissaries and for export to the California and Australian gold camps during the 1850s, continued to receive some attention; but it did not become the "golden fruit" and base of Hawai'i's second most important industry until after 1900.

Several men from the Hawaiian missionary community (missionaries and their adult sons) and haole businessmen surfaced as leaders in the agribusiness centered on sugarcane production. None, however, surpassed San Francisco sugar magnate Claus Spreckels in the achievement of sustained economic power and conglomerate control. It was claimed that for a time his Hawaiian Commercial and Sugar Company controlled the entire sugar output of Hawai'i through the domination of cane land, banking, transportation, and refining. He came to be called the "sugar king of Hawai'i," "uncrowned king of Hawai'i," and "the power behind the throne." His era of economic dominion extended from 1876 to 1893.[33]

Most Hawaiian raw sugar was shipped to refineries in San Francisco. As clipper and steam vessels increased their carrying range, they were relied upon to transport sugar to New York via Cape Horn, joining cargoes of Pacific Basin livestock, copra, and other island products and grain from California, Oregon, Washington, and Australian farms. By the 1880s Hawaiian sugar, both raw and refined, had become the primary product in the holds of these maritime carriers.

The planters enjoying this postwar prosperity found the future clouded by an additional obstacle. Their primary market was the United States. They had sought through the royal government a commercial pact between the Kingdom of Hawai'i and the United States that would extend favored treatment to Hawaiian agricultural products in the American markets. Treaties containing this indulgence were negotiated in 1855 and 1867. Both failed to be ratified in the United States Senate. Finally, on the third attempt in 1875, the desired pact was concluded by both nations. Hawaiian sugar received in American ports prior to 1875 averaged less than twenty million pounds; after the reciprocity treaty was ratified, the amount increased to approximately two hundred million pounds.[34]

The Hawaiian farming frontier had one more function to perform before the century closed. While this expansion concentrated most of its attention on Hawaiian culture and institutions, it was also in the process of exporting its influence, in a more limited degree, to the Samoan Archipelago, to the Philippines, and to Guam.

The altered monocrop plantation system went on to Samoa, the Philippines, and Guam; its impact was substantial on Samoa, slight on Guam and the Philippines. The latter territories came under American dominion near the close of the nineteenth century, as prizes of the Spanish-American War. The United States determined to retain Guam largely as a military station; environmental limitations and naval preemption of much of the land area (out of a total of less than 210 square miles) discouraged serious farming attention.[35]

In the case of the Philippines, soon after 1800 Spanish officials permitted Yankees to settle as traders at Manila. By midcentury several were engaged in plantation agriculture. After 1898, when the United States determined to prepare the natives of this archipelago for ultimate independence, Americans gave more serious attention to plantation enterprises there, growing copra, fibers, sugarcane, coffee, and fruits and vegetables. This interest extended well into the twentieth century.[36]

The most substantial American agrarian implant in the western Pacific was in Samoa. Well before 1850 American maritime traders and whaler captains had paused in the archipelago's commodious anchorages to refit their ships and take on wood, water, and provisions supplied by Polynesian farmers. Escalating competition for imperial advantage in the Pacific Basin during the latter half of the nineteenth century, precipitated largely by the belated entry of Germany into the region, focused attention on Samoa. In 1889 this led to a tripartite division of the islands by Great Britain, Germany, and the United States, with the latter assigned Eastern Samoa, centering on the harbor and settlement at Pago Pago.[37]

Well before the partitioning, beached Yankee seamen had settled Samoa to become pioneer farmers, joining the natives in supplying traders and whalers with fruits, vegetables, pork, and beef. The surge in demand for copra in Europe, beginning at midcentury, led to imperial interest and a revolution in island agriculture; along with the Society Islands, Samoa is the prime coconut-growing region of the Pacific. The German, British, and American settler populations increased there after 1850, bringing about a shift away from gathering wild coconuts to plantation culture of the coconut palm. In addition Samoan planters produced cotton, sugarcane, tobacco, nutmeg, and indigo for the Western market, as well as fruits and vegetables for the regional maritime market.[38]

The Yankee farmers' frontier had joined with the missionary frontier, the mining frontier, and, in a limited way, with the military frontier to bring American influence to a large segment of the Pacific Basin's eastern rimland. With the missionary frontier it had accomplished the same in the Kingdom of Hawai'i. Subsequently, as in the case of its limited extension to Guam and the Philippines, it joined with the military frontier to establish itself in Samoa. The American Navy, to adapt to the new marine technology and to fulfill its enlarged security mission in the Pacific Basin, required bases. The Samoan Islands contained splendid anchorages that, in the view of American naval commanders, made United States dominion over this archipelago essential.[39]

Thus the agrarian frontier and the military frontier joined to assure a strong American presence and to demonstrate a multiple interest in Samoa. Naval spokesmen urged prompt action by the national government to realize the military opportunity there. And from 1850 forward, several stateside newspapers promoted Samoa as a future bonanza territory for American agrarians. This is illustrated by a statement supplied by a sea captain familiar with conditions in the South Pacific, published at New Bedford: "Those who would emigrate here with a view of settling on the island, I would say, good land is to be obtained at a fair price, and there are no difficulties whatever attending agriculture. . . . The foreign population is at present increasing. Settlers would be welcomed . . . with every demonstration of cordiality."[40]

The American influence on Samoa followed a familiar course: divesting natives of their land and relentlessly exploiting them for labor and carnal satisfaction. By the 1870s the lure of agricultural fortunes in Samoa was so strong that speculation in plantation lands there was being handled by brokers in California. However, reports by United States officials in Samoa charged that this speculation had become an "iniquitous traffic," in that plantations were formed from tribal lands obtained from natives by the use of whiskey and firearms. Results included destitute Samoans divested of their lands and engaged in bloody, destructive intertribal wars.[41]

The final extension of the farmers' frontier in the Pacific Basin took place on its northeastern rim, in Alaska. Late in the eighteenth century, Russian colonial officials had introduced agriculture in this eastern imperial province, importing seeds, plants, livestock, and peasant workers from Russia. For the most part, their efforts were to no avail. Following the acquisition of Alaska by the United States in 1867, Yankees began the intensive exploitation of this territory's rich fur, mineral, timber, and fishery resources, but they gave little attention to agriculture. This was largely due to the region's harsh environment and climatic limitations: extended winters, an abbreviated growing season, and the vast permafrost interior. Not until the 1930s did Americans make a serious attempt to establish farms in Alaska. During 1935, at the nadir of the Great Depression, the Federal Emergency Relief Administration colonized two hundred families in the Matanuska Valley in an experimental farm settlement. The enterprise received considerable promotional publicity, but at the time reportedly failed to attract any substantial increase in farmer population; however, several transplanted families persevered and met with some success. Settling some ten thousand acres in the Matanuska Valley, these latter-day pioneers demonstrated that this subpolar territory, with its long hours of summer sun, could yield vegetables (cabbage, carrots, lettuce, beets, and potatoes), cereals (wheat, oats, barley, and rye), and hay for a prospering dairy industry.[42]

The farmers' frontier in the Pacific Basin served the national purpose by performing several customary expansionist functions. Joining with other frontiers, it created an American demographic presence, as well as contributing expectations of an organized pressure for absorption into the American political community. The result was the creation of five American states from Pacific Basin territories: California, Oregon, Washington, Hawai'i, and Alaska.

The agrarian frontier drastically altered native life-styles and institutions, methodically removing obstacles to its progress. And it affected Philippine institutions as the people of that archipelago prepared for ultimate independence. One of this frontier's most drastic impacts was upon Pacific Basin demography. First it contributed to the depopulation of the Kingdom of Hawai'i, then it repopulated the islands (largely from China and Japan) by importing laborers to meet its plantation needs. Ironically it has contributed to what might be called the reconquest by Hispanics of the California territory Mexico ceded to the United States in 1848, through the heavy demand of California agribusiness for Mexican field laborers.

Often paving the way for the farmers' frontier were Christian missionaries. While seemingly nonintrusive, the frontier of these pioneer men and women eventually had the most alterative influence of any of its antecedents or followers.

CHAPTER THIRTEEN

The Missionary Frontier

Christianity is dynamic, obsessively exclusionist, and vigorously peripatetic. And its proponents have maintained a bitter, competitive stance, as members of various religious orders and sects have strived for communicants. During the imperialist surge by European nation states after 1500, sovereigns, with papal imprimatur, carved the so-called heathen world into segments of empire. Christian missionaries, fired with the sanctified commission to go forth and convert the pagan, became a strategic part of the conquest process.

Ecclesiastical adventurers in Africa, Asia, India, North America, South America, and throughout the Pacific Basin have served as conditioning agents, preparing native peoples in these far-off territories for their ultimate absorption into the home nations' empires. Pious disclaimers to the contrary, most missionary ventures have been devastatingly successful from the imperial viewpoint.

The Anglo-American missionary frontier served the purpose of Yankee expansion in the Pacific Basin no less than its maritime trading and mining frontiers. But all three expansion entities were latecomers to the Pacific Basin. The imperial antecedents in this basin included the missionary frontiers established by the Spanish, Portuguese, Dutch, Russians, and English. The French also launched a missionary frontier to aid their nation's imperialist drive across the Pacific but, like the Americans, they were also latecomers.

The Christian gospel reached the Pacific Basin's western rimland late in the thirteenth century, following a punishing peregrination across Asia by the Franciscan missionary John of Montecorvino. He arrived at Peking, capital city of the Chinese empire, in 1295. Rome then sent seven Franciscans to work with

Montecorvino, but only three reached Peking. The Chinese mission functioned until 1368, when Ming dynasty officials suppressed it.

Jesuit missions reached the Pacific Basin in 1549, when Francis Xavier from Goa, India, landed at Kagashima, Japan, a Zen Buddhist stronghold. He converted 150 Japanese there, visited other settlements, and appealed for more Jesuits to enlarge the work in Japan. Xavier then visited Canton and died on a small island near Macao in 1552. The evangelization effort in Japan persisted with the arrival of additional Jesuits, six of them in 1561. By the 1580s they had established several churches and had won over 500,000 converts. Spanish-supported Franciscans and Dominicans from the Philippine colony later joined the Jesuits in Japan. Competition among these orders for converts and the involvement of Jesuits in government (a seemingly inevitable propensity of the order) caused the shogun to exile most missionaries and to persecute Japanese Christians with such cruelty that survivors went underground.

Portugal and Spain, as bitter imperialist rivals for hegemony in the western Pacific Basin, supported missionary establishments on the mainland, the Portuguese sponsoring Jesuits and Spaniards sponsoring Dominicans and Franciscans. The Jesuit Mateo Ricci pioneered by founding a mission near Macao. From there he and other Jesuits proceeded into China's heartland, first to Nanking and eventually to Peking. Franciscans and Dominicans from the nearby Philippine colony also appeared. By 1660 members of these three orders had won over 250,000 Chinese converts. But rivalry between Jesuits and Franciscans and Dominicans, along with their court intrigues, so annoyed the Manchu emperor that in 1724 he expelled "all but a few Jesuits who were permitted to remain in Peking because of their scientific attainments."[1]

Portuguese-sponsored missions did not extend much beyond the basin's western rim. Spain, however, committed to converting the Pacific into "the Spanish Lake," supported mission planting over a wide range of oceanic territory, along the basin's eastern rim from San Francisco to southern Chile. Of interest to Americans in their future westward surge, a significant number of these missions were established in Alta California, from San Diego to the Golden Gate, by Father Junípero Serra and a company of Franciscans beginning in 1769.

The Pacific Basin's interior also received the attention of Spanish-sponsored mission builders. Clerical pioneers planted a mission settlement on Guam, designated a port of call for the Manila Galleon. Native Chamorros violently resisted the padres, killing at least twelve, but disciplined application and courageous commitment finally led to a successful mission outpost.

Spanish adventurers and missionaries from colonial ports on the basin's eastern rimland also reconnoitered the islands of the South Pacific, the former for fortunes, the latter for heathens to save. In 1772, to counter threats of British expansion in the Society archipelago, two Spanish missionaries with a support party established a mission in Tahiti; it was abandoned in three years.

Of all the imperial nations carving empires from Pacific Basin territory, Holland was the least concerned with the spiritual status of its subject peoples. A Protestant nation dominated by the Dutch Reformed Church, it sent few missionaries to work among the natives of its rich empire in the basin's southwestern quadrant.

Aleuts and Indians in Russian America received missionary attention in 1793, when Empress Catherine II issued a ukase directing that Russian Orthodox priests be sent to the colony. The following year eight missionaries began work among the natives in the Aleutian Islands and on Kodiak. During 1795 they established a church on Kodiak and began agricultural experiments, in an attempt to relieve the threat of starvation there. The next year the first Orthodox priest was martyred; Father Juvenal was killed by natives at the mouth of the Kuskokwim River. Ships sent out from Okhotsk in 1799 to support the new missions sank with all missionary workers, supplies, and equipment lost. There followed a relaxation of the mission efforts, and by 1809 there was only one priest in the colony.

The intensive Russian Orthodox missionary effort on the northern rim of the Pacific Basin began in 1824, with the arrival of Ivan Veniaminov in the Aleutian Islands. He was friendly and dedicated; he learned the native languages, was respected by the Aleuts, and succeeded in converting many of them. In 1834 Veniaminov was transferred to Sitka, to attempt to convert the fierce Tlingits to Christianity. His poorest results were among these independent people; most of them remained dedicated to their tribal religion. Their leaders explained that over the years they had observed the terrible things the Russians had done to the Aleuts, and they were determined to reject Christianity. Veniaminov persevered and finally converted 102 Tlingits, built a church for them at Sitka, and established schools for their youth.

Veniaminov and other missionaries were able to give the Aleut, Eskimo, and Tlingit languages a written form and to publish books in these languages for use in the mission schools. He greatly extended the missionary horizons of Russian America; besides great success among the Aleuts and only modest success among the Tlingits, he also established missions among Eskimos. After Russian fur hunters moved into the Bering Sea, Veniaminov erected a northern headquarters at St. Michael, and from there missionaries penetrated the lower Yukon and Kuskokwim basins. From the schools Veniaminov established in the Aleutian Islands, on Kodiak, at Sitka, and other locations in Russian America, native youth, most of them of mixed parentage, went on to St. Petersburg to complete their educations at the expense of the Russian-American Company.

Above all else Veniaminov was a constant critic of Russian treatment of Native Americans. His regular reports to the court at St. Petersburg exposed the oppression in the colony, and his complaints brought investigations by the czar's agents; sadly for the native peoples, little improvement in treatment resulted. Following the purchase of Russian America in 1867 by the United States, Russian Orthodox missionaries continued their work in local churches, schools, and missions. As late as 1900 they were conducting six schools for native people in Alaska.

Pacific Basin religious diversity was additionally enhanced by the entry of British missionaries around 1800. Quite early in the British colonial establishment in Australia and New Zealand, Anglican and Methodist clergymen organized churches there; but British missionary efforts in the Pacific Basin really began in 1795, with the organization of the London Missionary Society. This ecumenical association, consisting of Methodist, Baptist, and other Protestant groups, committed itself to an outreach program for the Pacific Basin. The following year the society sent out thirty missionaries: ten to Tongatabu; eighteen to Tahiti; and two to the

Marquesas. Most of them were killed and eaten by island cannibals. The surviving five clerics concentrated their efforts of Christian conversion on the natives of Tahiti. The London Missionary Society sent reenforcements to the Tahiti mission, and by 1815 the workers there had converted three hundred Society Islanders. They preached to the natives; counseled them on conversion; reduced their Polynesian to written form; established a printing press; and published scriptures, hymns, and religious tracts in Polynesian.

In 1817 John Williams arrived at the Tahiti mission. His energetic application of London Missionary Society resources led to the founding of missions on other islands of the Society archipelago, and on the Cook Islands, Austral Islands, Loyalty Islands, New Hebrides, and eventually on Samoa and New Guinea. Williams stressed the training of native teachers. At the mission schools he established at Tahiti and Rarotonga, he prepared 490 natives to teach other islanders British culture and Christianity.[2]

Williams was particularly interested in converting the natives of the Navigator, or Samoan, archipelago. During the 1830s he reported that he was busily "stamping out idleness and lesser sins" on many islands from Tahiti to Samoa, "teaching natives to be happy," and "fighting Catholic and Polynesian heathenism."[3]

Apia, Samoa, had become a favorite port of call for sailors aboard ships plying South Pacific waters. Their well-being concerned Williams; on his initiative, the London Missionary Society erected a seamen's chapel there in 1849, which included a worship center and a reading room with newspapers and books. His purpose was "to counteract the temptations held out to seamen by the grog-sellers on shore."[4]

Williams solicited funds from English churches to finance the construction of a fleet of schooners to service the string of island missions. Some British missions prospered, while others suffered from fiercely resistive natives. Island cannibals captured, killed, and ate several English and Polynesian missionaries, aborting conversion efforts on some islands. Cannibals were notoriously active in the Marquesas, Fijis, and New Guinea.

The other serious threat to British missionary efforts in the Pacific Basin were the late-arriving French, using Roman Catholic missionaries as the vanguard for absorbing pelagic territories into their emergent empire. During the 1840s French expansionists began moving into the Society Islands, notably Tahiti, forcing a diminution of Protestant control of the people. In 1886 after years of suppression by French colonial administrators, the London Missionary Society withdrew completely from the Tahiti mission.

English missionaries ventured to the Pacific Basin's western rim in 1807, when Robert Morrison, a Methodist, reached China. British East India Company officials regarded Christian missions as a "pernicious distraction to commerce," and refused Morrison passage on their ships; an American merchantman delivered him to Canton. Morrison was banned from the British East India Company compound there and resided in the United States factory. It is said that Chinese officials and traders at Canton thought him to be an American.

As in the case of the French, Americans were delayed in establishing their missionary frontier in the Pacific Basin. A nation with deep religious roots, arrogating to itself the identity of "Christian nation," and no less exclusionist than its imperialist competitors, its delay in entering the Pacific Basin to share in the "heathen harvest" there was due largely to its continental preoccupation. The American missionary frontier had functioned from the early days of the republic, but for a generation it had been occupied with immediate concerns. The clerical frontiersman worked among the Indian tribes occupying territories west of the Anglo-American settlements, shaping the aboriginal communities to be receptive to the inevitable and imminent pioneer advance. And he colonized tribesmen ahead of the settlers, ostensibly to protect them from the corrupting influences of American settlements; nonetheless, he served the national purpose of removing Indians without the use of military force and eviction.

The American missionary frontier in the Pacific Basin had several characteristics that distinguished it from those formed by the religious establishments of other imperial nations entrenched there. First its diversity reflected the sectarian chaos of Protestantism in the United States. A principal segment was formed by an ecumenical association called the American Board of Commissioners for Foreign Missions (ABCFM), composed of the Congregational, Presbyterian, and Dutch Reformed churches. In addition Methodist, Roman Catholic, and Mormon missionary organizations answered the "Macedonian call." And later Baptist and other American religious bodies sent representatives to the Pacific. Second there was wide variance in time of entry into the Pacific Basin mission field, ranging from 1820 for the firstcomers to the 1890s and even into the twentieth century for latter-day entrants. Third, its geographic outreach was awesome. Yankee churchmen maintained the most extensive and far-flung outreach of all missionary frontiers supported by imperial nations working the Pacific Basin. From its eastern rimland American clerical pioneers carried the gospel to the islands of the central and northern Pacific, later to the islands of the southern Pacific, touching even the Anglican and Methodist provinces in Australia and New Zealand, then penetrating the basin's western rimland into Japan and China. And fourth the American missionary frontier surpassed all others as an alterative force. No other nation's missionaries did as much to plant and nourish Western civilization. The American missionary frontier also exceeded the nation's maritime trading frontier, the mining frontier, and all other expansion entities in its pervasive and enduring influence on basin peoples and cultures and in serving the national interest.

Congregational church leaders of New England first met at Bradford, Massachusetts, in 1810 to form the American Board of Commissioners for Foreign Missions (ABCFM); two years later they sent their first missionaries to India. Presbyterian and Dutch Reformed churches joined in support of ABCFM activities. Some of the American Board's best-known work was accomplished among the tribes of the southeastern United States (Cherokees, Choctaws, Chickasaws, Seminoles, and Creeks). Under the transformative tutelage of New England missionaries, these Indian communities came to be designated the Five Civilized Tribes. American Board missionaries subsequently accompanied the Five Civilized Tribes over their "Trail of Tears" during Andrew Jackson's exile of these Native Americans to the western wilderness.

American Board missionary pioneers venturing to the Pacific Basin chose to establish their first spiritual beachhead in the Sandwich Islands. This decision was derived from their contact with kānaka seamen serving aboard New England–based ships. Board officials established a Foreign Mission School at Cornwall, Connecticut, in 1817. In the Cornwall Foreign Mission School student body were American Indians as well as Pacific islanders, including five Hawaiians. A Polynesian who galvanized the Protestant constituency of America was Henry Obookiah (Opukahaia). He arrived in New Haven aboard a merchant vessel and lived with a sea captain's family. Later he came to the attention of Timothy Dwight, president of Yale College. Dwight converted Obookiah and matriculated him at the Cornwall Foreign Mission School, to prepare the youth for missionary duty in the Sandwich Islands. Sadly the Polynesian became infected with typhus and died. His memoirs, an appeal for the Christian transformation of his pagan people, were published in 1818, went through twelve editions, and "reached into thousands of homes to stir a missionary spirit throughout the land."[5]

The American Board's Hawaiian mission evolved from this surge of Christian solicitude and zeal. Hiram Bingham and Asa Thurston, both Yale graduates and Andover Theological Seminary students, were the first to volunteer for service with the mission. Shortly the mission family was completed: two ordained missionaries and their wives, five assistants (teachers and a farmer) and their wives, five children, and four Hawaiians. The Sandwich Islands missionary community drew up articles of faith and a covenant in the tradition of the Mayflower Compact, and sailed from Boston in October 1819 aboard the *Thaddeus,* a merchant vessel chartered by the Board. The missionary party arrived in the islands on 30 March 1820.[6]

These Yankee invaders were committed to challenging the traditional Polynesian socioreligious system, overthrowing the pagan deities, and substituting for their heathen society a New England brand of Puritan-steeped Christian culture. The islanders believed in an animistic pantheon, the principal deities being Kane, Lono, Ku, and Kanaloa. Kane was the greatest force in the Hawaiian universe, for he was the deity of light, in a sense the sun god. The Hawaiian myth of creation included the concept of Sky as the father and Earth as the mother. The religious system fostered idols representing the deities; these were placed in stone temples (*marae*) and households, as fetishes to ward off evil spirits. Priests, *kahunas,* presided over the religious system and ranked high in the Hawaiian social order, just below the king and royal family.

Missionaries found that their island charges followed the matrilineal mode of reckoning descent and had a hierarchial social organization, with clans that had rigidified into castes. The basic unit of Hawaiian society was the family, and several families in a clustered residence area made up a village. Yankee educators found that the islanders had no system of writing and that instruction and tradition were transmitted orally by village elders to the young. American Board representatives were shocked that islanders practiced plural marriage—both polygyny (more than one wife) and polyandry (more than one husband)—and among the *aliʻi* (ruling caste) brother-sister marriage was not uncommon.

Hawaiian government, an institution of considerable future concern and interest to the missionaries, was an extension of the social caste system. Island chiefs had become hereditary rulers, basing their right to rule on a claim of descent from the gods. They were supreme and exercised total power over their subjects. As earthly agents of the gods, even the land belonged to them; the use of it was a privilege bestowed upon the people by the benevolent royalty. Recently the monarch of Hawaiʻi had conquered the peripheral islands, created a unified kingdom, and installed himself as Kamehameha I. The kahunas ranked next in the social order. Their function was to preside over the religious system, placate island deities, foretell the future by divination, and assist the monarch in controlling the population by applying kapus, restraints and restrictions on individual action. Next in the island social order below the priests were civil agents, courtiers, and leaders of the army. Then came commoners: farmers, fishermen, artisans, and traders.

The American Board missionary advent could not have been more fortuitously timed; the ancient Polynesian life-style was undergoing drastic change. The catalyst was the ever-expanding presence and the pervasive, alterative influence of the haole community, largely Yankee: traders, whalers, adventurers, and seamen who chose to become more or less permanent residents. Hawaiians noted that haoles paid no heed to the ubiquitous kapus that encumbered and regulated native life, and that they suffered none of the punitive consequences the kahunas claimed were inflicted on those who failed to observe the sanctions. A malaise in religious attentiveness was apparent; pagan spirituality was declining as a force in the lives of the native population.

The ancient practice of requiring women to occupy a suppressed, secondary status was a casualty of the decline in Hawaiian religion. Kahunas taught that woman's heavenly ordained function was to occupy a degraded status and serve man's every wish, including eating separately from males and even then partaking of inferior food as confirmation of their low caste. Although many Yankees and other intruders exploited Hawaiian women for erotic satisfaction, a goodly number took native wives and treated them in a positive manner, in diametric contrast to their fate in Hawaiian wedlock. This haole esteem for Hawaiian women did not go unnoticed.

On the death of the powerful and despotic Kamehameha I, his son Liholiho, designated Kamehameha II, became king. A malleable, pleasure-seeking man, he was dominated in affairs of state by two royal widows—his mother, Keopuolani, and his father's favorite, Kaahumanu. These island feminists led a move to eradicate what they regarded as anachronistic, demeaning kapus, particularly those that degraded Polynesian women. The symbolic event that marked the beginning of the end of the Hawaiian kapu system occurred just before the missionaries arrived. At a large public feast, the king and leading courtiers sat down to a royal banquet table with the women of the court. Men and women ate the same food simultaneously. The huge audience beheld that no disaster befell the celebrants or the nation for this blatant disavowal of the ancient, kahuna-imposed retrictions.

It was largely through the interceding influence of Keopuolani and Kaahumanu with Kamehameha II that, when the missionaries petitioned him for leave to land and proselyte, the monarch assented to a trial period, which became a permanent license. It is ironic that the Hawaiian leaders in effect exchanged one set of personal restraints, the kapus, for another set even more repressive to personal expression, called blue laws and applied by New England Puritan missionaries. These latter taboos were also claimed to be prescribed by the deity.

Hiram Bingham, physically tough and of strong will and acute intellect, his spirit fueled with the zeal of neo-Puritanism, surfaced as mission leader and principal spokesman, a position he held for over twenty years. On first beholding the archipelago, he perceived none of the natural beauty of the verdant land and its people, but only that it was a heathen territory where Lucifer's forces abided in threatening numbers. His unremitting commitment to cleanse this pagan land he pledged on first beholding it from the deck of the *Thaddeus,* as crewmen fed anchor line into the bay's quiet waters. He gave thanks for receiving a vision of "the altars of the idols falling and the temples of Jehovah rising in their stead" and for the commission "to plant the Rose of Sharon in the vallies and the Tree of Life upon the mountains of idolatrous Owyhee."[7]

Bingham selected Honolulu as the center for the American Board mission, and shortly Christian settlements appeared on Oʻahu and adjacent islands, centering on Congregational churches, first of native architecture with thatched roofs, later of tufa-block construction, each fitted with a spire and cross in the familiar New England mode. Next came schools, staffed largely by missionary wives, "public libraries" in missionary homes, and haole clerical influence alterative to the point of domination.

These intruder clerics "betrayed a concern that the society in which they were working take a shape compatible with their homeland." Their immediate goals were to convert the "pagan" Sandwich Islanders; to stamp out idol worship, intemperance, and native music, songs, dancing, and "heathenish enjoyments." Yankee reformers sought to persuade the natives to shun nakedness and adopt Western dress, the women covering themselves in "Mother Hubbards and coal scuttle bonnets." Additionally it was their intent to inculcate in the Sandwich Islanders a regard for private property and to monitor their advance in the arts of civilization, including the adoption of regular habits, and tilling the earth for profit. Of course Hawaiians had been successful subsistence farmers for centuries.[8]

To faciliate their transformation work, American Board missionaries applied themselves to mastering the Hawaiian language. Bingham led the way; by 1823 he was able to preach eloquently in the "vernacular tongue." His competence in Polynesian had unexpected but immensely important results. The monarch and court officials increasingly were pressed by resident agents of foreign governments, notably those of France, Great Britain, and Russia, for treaties granting rich commercial concessions, payment of claims for alleged damages to property of subjects of those nations, and cessions of portions of the kingdom's territory. Because American Board missionaries appeared disinterested, they were called upon for interpreting service at court in these confrontations and negotiations with foreign agents. This function gradually led to an enlarging dependence on the New England clergymen for counsel and ended in their direct participation in the royal Hawaiian government.

Having mastered the Polynesian language, American Board missionaries, with the assistance of English missionaries from Tahiti, established printing presses and published grammars, spellers, readers, and other textbooks for the mission schools, as well as tracts, scriptures, and songbooks for the mission churches. As native literacy increased, they also published newspapers.

By 1832 missionaries claimed that one-half of the native population could read Polynesian, many could write in the language, and an increasing number were becoming bilingual in English. To meet the enlarging demand for education, American Board missionaries persuaded the Hawaiian government to establish a system of crown-supported but Yankee-managed schools. Missionaries also established Saturday schools for adults. By 1847 thirty-four crown-supported, missionary-managed schools functioned in the islands, with a thousand students in attendance.[9]

Because of all their activities, American Board officials sent out six companies of workers to assist Bingham's original mission. Thus by 1842 the missionary frontier in the Sandwich Islands was staffed by seventy-nine workers in nineteen stations.[10]

Their greatest moment began during 1839, in what came to be called the "Great Revival." A missionary inspector reported that this "Religious awakening spread like wildfire from island to island . . . a vertible National Penticost." Bingham preached to crowds from two to three thousand each week, but Titus Coan, missionary pastor at Hilo on the island of Hawai'i, exceeded all others in attracting the multitude. Described as a "powerful evangelical preacher," he drew an estimated ten thousand at a single service during 1839. Thousands were converted during worship service at several island churches. Coan received five thousand into his Hilo church in a single year, baptizing the penitent with a whisk broom dipped in a pan of sanctified water. The missionary rolls contained the names of twenty thousand converts when the fervor subsided in 1842. Coan's Hilo mission church claimed seven thousand members and was rated the largest Protestant congregation in the world.[11]

Besides conversion, American Board missionaries gave primary attention to native moral rehabilitation. Yankee reformers regarded alcohol and tobacco as twin evils, destructive of native moral fiber and physical vigor. Missionaries blamed native addiction to alcohol and tobacco as a major cause of Polynesian population decline. Thus in every mission station and school, preachers and teachers stressed taking the pledge and joining the Hawaiian Temperance Society. A missionary reporter acknowledged that when the first company of American Board representatives reached the islands, "The river of intemperance was made to run through the land, and, connected with the curse of infamous dissipation, made quick in numbering the unwary people for the grave." But because of this small Christian force, the "idolatry of Hawai'i . . . by faith and prayer, and like the walls of Jericho, crumbled and fell."[12]

Once admitted to the mission church, any Hawaiian who faltered by resorting to alcohol or tobacco faced excommunication. By 1836 the temperance movement was reported a limited success. In particular "the tobacco reformation" was "gaining ground." Mission monitors reported that natives were turning in their pipes and tobacco, and when at each station a supply had accumulated, the pastor in charge conducted a public bonfire, with appropriate praise and exhortation. One missionary observed that "It is no less hard for them to leave it [tobacco] off than for the drunkard to forsake his cup."[13]

Besides studying at adult-education classes on Saturday and attending worship services on Sunday, native communicants returned to their mission station the first Monday of each month to labor on the church farm, tending the cotton, sugarcane, and coffee trees. Some were assigned to bring in bundles of sandalwood and arrowroot. These products and the farm yield were sold, and the proceeds were placed in the missionary fund to support Christian outreach in other parts of the Pacific Basin.[14]

The Hawaiian mission's outreach included establishing sailors' refuges at Sandwich Island ports and sponsoring missionary expeditions to other Pacific Island peoples. American Board missionaries had a threefold interest in seamen whose ships plied Pacific waters. Most were fellow New Englanders. Their abandoned habits and wild orgies when in port debauched many natives. And their spiritual needs could not be ignored. Therefore Bingham's staff directed the construction of chapel retreats, "moral lighthouses," at Honolulu, Lahaina, and Hilo. Each Seamen's Bethel was situated near the port landing, with a sanctuary for seating up to three hundred, and was supplied with newspapers, Bibles, and religious tracts by the local missionary. Yankee clerics working in these retreats claimed that sailors were "thankful they have a true friend in the midst of the ocean." Appeals to the mainland for support led the American Seamen's Friend Society to assign a chaplain to the port of Honolulu. The Reverend Samuel Damon, the second clergyman to hold this appointment, began in 1843 to publish *The Temperance Advocate and Seamen's Friend;* later he shortened the title to *The Friend.* Damon's newspaper, published for forty years, has been recognized as the oldest American newspaper published west of the Rocky Mountains.[15]

During 1842 American Board emissaries began exploring for additional convert territory beyond the Sandwich Islands. After visiting Tahiti and other islands in the London Missionary Society jurisdiction, they recommended to their Boston headquarters that they receive support for a mission on Madison Island in the Marquesas, the tropical paradise where Herman Melville abandoned his whaleship and that provided the setting for *Typee,* an account of his adventures there. Prompt approval led Bingham to dispatch three Hawaiian mission pastors and their wives. At Nuku Hiva's anchorage, which Commodore David Porter had named Massachusetts Bay, his base for preying on British Pacific shipping during the War of 1812, the American Board party founded a mission station. To their disappointment they found the natives uninterested, the London Missionary Society protested this invasion of what they claimed as their territory, and after eight months of living in what they called "the suburbs of Hell," a place "too small to justify . . . maintaining a mission," they returned to Honolulu.[16]

American Board adventurers continued to explore the Pacific Basin for spiritual sites. Several times they came upon heretofore uncharted islands, most of them uninhabited. However, on one expedition, Honolulu mission-based explorers discovered an unknown island on which resided thirty-nine people.[17]

In 1852 American Board officials concluded that the Hawaiian Congregational Church in all of its branches over the Sandwich Island archipelago was soundly established and competent to stand on its own. Its clergy had been training native preachers, teachers, and missionaries. In the year of its elevation to an independent entity, the Hawaiian Congregational Church, in cooperation with the American Board, expanded the American missionary frontier in the Pacific Basin by settling Anglo and Hawaiian missionaries on Kusai and Ponape, in the eastern Carolines. And in 1853 Hawai'i-based missionaries resumed conversion work in the Marquesas, where they were "tolerated by the French," who had established dominion over the archipelago. In addition missionaries from Hawai'i started church stations in the Gilbert and Marshall islands, on Tonga, Sumatra, and in Samoa. These scattered mission settlements were supplied from Honolulu by the *Morning Star*, a sleek schooner built in New England yards and paid for with pennies collected by Sunday school children in stateside churches.[18]

The Sandwich Island–based missionary frontier had some of its most dramatic alterative impact on the Hawaiian royal government. Because of their fluency in Polynesian, American Board missionaries were called upon to serve as government interpreters. Their influence at the Hawaiian court was enhanced by the royal school they maintained for male and female children of ranking kingdom families. Five of their pupils later became monarchs of the kingdom.

Missionaries had a mandate from American Board officials in

Boston to concern themselves exclusively with gospel dissemination and to shun politics and commercial matters, but this proved "impossible to follow absolutely." Native leaders desperately needed advice, direction, even leadership in the face of growing pressure from European imperial nations, particularly France, Russia, and Great Britain, each aggressively competing for Pacific Basin territories. There is no doubt that certain members of the American Board mission regarded this state of affairs as a doubly fortuitous opportunity: "to convert the Hawaiians to a new faith," as well as to "dominate the government and make the islands an outpost of American civilization."[19]

Thus several missionaries with a propensity for politics requested release from the mission to serve in the Hawaiian royal government, beginning in the late 1830s during the reign of King Kamehameha III. The Reverend Richard Armstrong became minister of education, and the Reverend William Richards and Dr. Gerrit Judd (a medical missionary) became the principal advisers to the monarchs. Judd served as de facto prime minister and, with Richards, was the architect of substantive changes in royal government form and function that drastically altered island economy and society.

Richard and Judd modernized the government, changing it from a feudal autocracy to a constitutional monarchy; a responsible representative government replaced the arbitrary power of the monarch. In 1838 under their tutelage the royal court issued a Declaration of Rights, followed a year later by a constitution providing for a bill of rights, a cabinet, a bicameral legislature (lower house of commoner delegates, upper house of nobles), and a supreme court. Judd controlled the treasury and regularized state taxes, income, and expenditures, with the result that the kingdom became solvent and less dependent on foreign bankers for loans. This had become the bane of small, weak governments and provided a common excuse (upon default) for intervention, even absorption, by imperial governments during the nineteenth century. Judd and Richards were ardent Americanists and formulated foreign policy that sought to exclude official French, Russian, and British influence from the government.

One of the most basic changes wrought by Judd and Richards

was that involving land distribution. Land by tradition was regarded as crown property, and it was held by commoners and haoles at the pleasure of the monarch. At the instigation of Judd and Richards, the national assembly adopted the Great Mahele, which directed that small tracts be assigned to commoners in fee-simple and that the royal family give up all rights to the land except the reserved crown estates.

Besides successfully transplanting several familiar American institutions to the islands (sectarian religion, constitutional government, and fee-simple land tenure), the American missionaries also influenced the recently created national assembly to follow the precept that "no law shall be enacted which is at variance with the word of the Lord Jehovah." That deliberative body readily adopted legislation resurrecting the old-style New England Puritan theocracy. This included a code of blue laws of two parts, one for Hawaiian subjects (natives and haoles), the other for visitors (largely crewmen from sojourning whaling, trading, and naval vessels, who regularly ravaged kingdom ports for rum and women).

The code of conduct pertaining to subjects banned the hula, native games, gambling, and other native entertaiments, sloth, sexual misconduct, and demanded abstinence. Judd exulted that the "Temperance laws are now triumphant, and the kingdom is a temperance nation, from the king on the throne down to the little children. All are collected into a 'cold-water army.'" The subjects' code stipulated observance of Sunday as the focus of the week: "The Lord's Day is *taboo;* all worldly busines, amusements, and recreation are forbidden on that day; and whoever shall keep open his shop, warehouse, or work-shop, or who shall do any manner of labor, business, or work, except only works of necessity or charity, or be present at any dancing, public amusement, show or entertainment, or taking part in any game, sport, or play on the Lord's Day, shall be punished by a fine not exceeding ten dollars."[20]

The visitors' section of the code set a ten-dollar fine for coming ashore armed; a two-dollar fine for a seaman found ashore after the 9:30 P.M. curfew, announced by the firing of the second gun at the fort; a fine of from one to five dollars for making noise in the street at night; six dollars for fighting; five dollars for racing on horseback down city streets; six dollars for desecrating the

Sabbath on first offense and double assessment for each repetition; six dollars of drunkenness; ten dollars for lewd, lascivious, or seductive conduct; five dollars for fornication; thirty dollars for adultery; fifty dollars for rape; and hanging, as a murderer, for knowingly and maliciously violating those laws whereby a contagious [venereal] disease is communicated on shore.[21]

Reaction varied to this New England–style Puritanism. Native Hawaiians, previously accustomed to regimentation of their personal lives by kahuna-imposed kapus, for the most part conformed, although their observance of the Christian blue-law code was rated uneven. That there was considerable "backsliding" was evidenced by the frequent convening of ecclesiastical tribunals to consider "excommunicating" faltering native converts.

Some of the strongest protest came from haoles (subjects by marriage or naturalization and nonsubject residents). Their resentment at the repressive conduct code derived from its hectoring interference with personal life, intruding even into the privacy of their households, and its effect on local businesses, notably pubs, brothels, and casinos, devoted to entertaining crewmen ashore from vessels calling at Hawaiian ports. One prominent haole complained:

> The late attempt to prevent . . . drinking wine and spirituous liquors . . . to close the billiard rooms, and to take over the horses of those who should ride on Sunday for innocent recreation, appears to me to be despotic and vexatious and to emanate rather from sectarian enthusiasm, not to say intolerance, than from justice or sound policy. . . . evangelical zeal sometimes carries them [missionaries] to extremes. . . . [their] restrictions on society . . . I conceive ought to be attributed rather to over-righteous opinions peculiar to their sect than to true religion. The natives had formerly numerous games such as running, wrestling, throwing the spear etc., but those have either been prohibited or discontinued . . . by the Missionaries under the pretext of being too nearly allied to idolatry . . . as time ill-spent which ought to be employed in religion.[22]

An American Board inspector concluded that the clerics had gone too far in regimenting the lives of young people by serving as matchmakers. He charged that the primary purpose of the

Wailuku Seminary for girls was "raising up wives" for male students at Lahainaluna Academy. The young men there complained that courting had to be done "mostly thro' teachers," and only in one or two instances had pupils of the two schools married.[23]

Captain Charles Wilkes, commander of the ambitious 1838–42 American maritime exploring expedition, observed the state of missionary-dominated affairs in these islands during a sojourn at Honolulu. It was his considered opinion that the missionaries' practice of "maintaining segregated schools and services of worship for their own offspring" was "a self-defeating measure that smacked of hypocrisy." And the American consular agent at Honolulu denounced the New England divines for "disturbing the minds of these children of Nature with the idea that they are to be eternally damned unless they think and act as they do."[24]

Ranking British visitors found the stern Yankee missionaries unbending fanatics, their system of life guidance "inhuman." One observer from Lord Byron's HMS *Blonde* during the British Pacific expedition of 1825 was distressed that an American with a native wife had "often applied without success, to the missionaries to baptize his children, but they are considered by them to be born out of wedlock," and refuse. Lord Byron offered a magic-lantern show at the palace, but "owing to the religious fanaticism" of the missionaries, "the king was prevented from being present. . . . These missionaries possess . . . what power they please over the credulity of the natives and have already carried their system of religion too far to be upheld."[25]

Sailors' responses to the Christian-saturated milieu took two directions. Some chose the recreation offered by port chapels maintained by representatives from the Sandwich Island missionary frontier, reading newspapers, the Bible, and attending preaching services. Many reacted violently. Enforcement of the blue laws had dried up "the sloughs of intemperance and licentiousness," sources of their accustomed pleasure while ashore. Crewmen from ships of all nations plying the Pacific and rendezvousing in Hawaiian ports joined in rioting, burning, and plundering private and public property and in attacking the source of their desperate denial—missionaries. French sailors in port would drink and "fight till the blood runs from the head to the feet." They "are an abandoned, hopeless class. They drink in iniquity like water and their feet are swift to do evil."[26]

British sailors were notorious for raids on missionary properties to demonstrate their rage at the changing order. During October 1825 a "limey" whaleship anchored at Lahaina. "Instead of the accustomed throng of native females not an individual of the sex appeared." The pleasure-deprived crewmen became enraged, concluded that blame rested on the missionaries, and marched en masse to the local missionary compound, surrounded it, and hurled "horrid oaths and threats" through open windows. Shortly afterward the fired-up demonstrators returned armed with pistols and knives, prepared to rush the missionary compound. However, native converts armed with clubs drove off the intruders. Two years later a British whaling ship anchored at Lahaina sent its crew ashore on liberty. Local missionaries had removed the native girls to the mountains. Denied their expected satisfaction, the crewmen returned to their ship, charged the bow cannon, and fired several rounds into the missionary compound.[27]

American sailors on whaling, trading, and naval vessels were the most numerous in the Pacific Basin, and they were the most persistent in resorting to violence, protesting the missionary elimination of their accustomed pleasures. The most serious outrage perpetrated by Yankee sailors occurred during 1827. Crewmen from the sloop of war USS *Dolphin* panicked the citizens of Honolulu with an extended riot that included burning the city jail, plundering several businesses, and threatening American Board missionaries. Lieutenant Commander John Percival, captain of the *Dolphin,* supported and encouraged his men in their predacious acts. American Board missionaries were incensed at this officer's stance, accustomed as they were to receiving courtesy and support from American naval officers calling at Hawaiian ports. Bingham reported the incident and Percival's dereliction to American Board officials in Boston. Demands for an investigation of the incident reached Washington. A naval board of inquiry conducted an extended hearing, which ended in official censure of Percival.[28]

The American missionary frontier in the Pacific Basin became a source of enlarging concern and intensifying competition from territory-seeking nations, concerned that Yankee missionary domination of Hawaiian society and government was a prelude to absorption by their home government. In addition several sectarian groups in the United States, anxious to enter the Pacific Basin, were concerned over the advantage enjoyed by the Congregational-Presbyterian emissaries based in the strategically situated Sandwich Islands. Methodists and Mormons, especially, determined to challenge the vanguard of the American missionary frontier in the basin.

France, a pioneer in the support of seventeenth- and eighteenth-century exploration of the Pacific Basin, belatedly returned to the region for territorial expansion. Great Britain had maintained a continuing presence from its eastern rimland on the Canadian shore and in the basin's southwestern quadrant. During the 1840s Great Britain and France began partitioning the surviving unclaimed basin territories. French forces occupied the Marquesan and Society archipelagoes, including Tahiti and peripheral islands, and Great Britian extended its final control over New Zealand and adjacent islands. Naval forces of both nations cruised in Hawaiian waters; on one occasion each occupied Hawaiian fortifications and ports and announced annexation under the guise of treaty violations by Hawaiian authorities. However, diplomatic pressure on both France and Great Britain by the United States to respect the island kindgdom's independence caused the home governments to disavow these actions. This caused British and French annexationists to seek more subtle measures for promoting imperial influence. The American missionary frontier's success there was instructive and showed the way.

British ambitions in the Sandwich Islands received an assist from the Hawaiian royal family after the death of Kamehameha III in 1854. British residents in the islands had for some time sought to have an Anglican mission established. The two monarchs who succeeded Kamehameha III, Kamehameha IV and Kamehameha V, had visited England as guests of the British government, frequently attending Anglican worship services. Kamehameha IV came away with the conviction that Anglican "doctrine and ritual" were "more compatible with monarchical government than those of the Congregational and Presbyterian already established in his kingdom." He and Queen Emma had submitted to the vows of this church for their wedding rites, and at their behest, Queen Victoria agreed to be godmother for their infant prince. These manifestations of support led to the formation of an Anglican mission in Hawai'i. American Episcopal bishops from New York and California cooperated, and in 1862 Bishop Thomas Staley and his family arrived from England at Honolulu to found the Anglican church for the kingdom.[29]

This Anglican-Episcopal intrusion aroused the proprietary sensibilities of the American missionary community. They protested loudly to American Board officals in Boston and public officials in Washington. They warned that this invasion by the Church of England meant the "probable extension of British dominion." They also predicted that the increasingly expansive French government would be stimulated "to connect itself more than it has done, with the Roman Catholic mission in these islands."[30]

Wesleyan missionaries from England en route to Samoa also stopped in the Kingdom of Hawai'i during this period. A member of the party commented that while "Queen Emma was a staunch adherent of the English Church" and her husband had translated the prayer book into the Hawaiian language, "the majority of people of Hawai'i . . . find the less ceremonious form of religious worship better adapted to their needs."[31]

No British imperial attempt of consequence followed the erection of the Anglican establishment in the Hawaiian Islands, and the American missionaries maintained their influence. It was the French who persevered in attempts to implant an imperialist wedge in the islands, using religious agents as vanguards. French naval commanders operating in the Central Pacific maintained a combative, threatening stance for several years toward the Hawaiian kingdom, using the exclusion of Roman Catholics as their primary justification.

The nineteenth century, besides being a time of aggressive national expansion, was also an age of bitter, competitive Christian sectarianism and zealous evangelization. Protestant religious bodies carried on intensive rivalry and intersectarian competition, but coalesced in their consummate intolerance of the Roman Catholic church.

Thus American Board missionaries, quite early in the formation of the American missionary frontier in Hawai'i, convinced the monarchs that Roman Catholics were "agents of Satan" and that it was essential for the spiritual peace and well-being of Hawaiian subjects to exclude Roman Catholics from the kingdom.[32]

French naval commanders on Pacific assignment, as representatives of a Catholic nation, regarded this stance as a "national affront" and were determined to counter and exploit it to their country's advantage. During the early 1820s, they began sending Roman Catholic priests ashore in the Hawaiian Islands on missionary reconnaissances. Then in 1826 Pope Leo XII appointed John Alexis Bachelot to be Apostolic Prefect of the Sandwich Islands; Bachelot arrived with a party of priests and mechanics the following year. American Board divines were surprised and shocked by what they regarded as trespass on their private spiritual preserve. When they reported the invasion to Boston headquarters, an American Board official warned Bingham that "We have more to fear in respect to them than in respect to all other foreigners."[33]

Claiming that his subjects regarded "Romanism as a species of idolatry," and to prevent ecclesiastical divisiveness in his kingdom, the native monarch banished the French missionary party; they took refuge in California. In 1831 the court issued a law banning Catholic priests from the kingdom.[34]

Bachelot and his missionary party returned to the Hawaiian Islands in 1837, attempted to come ashore, and were arrested by Hawaiian authorities for violating the Catholic-exclusion statute. Commodore Dupetit Thours, with armed crewmen from his warship, forced Hawaiian authorities to allow the party to land. The Hawaiian court reacted by promulgating a second law "rejecting the Catholic religion." Thereupon Captain M. L. Laplace, in command of a sixty-gun frigate and braced with seven hundred heavily armed troops, stormed the Hawaiian capital and forced a humiliating treaty from royal officials. First it recognized the Roman Catholic religion, assured its toleration in the islands, and guaranteed the freedom of Catholic clergy to establish missions and proselytize for converts. Additionally the pact extended enormous commercial advantages to French goods entering Hawaiian ports, and it established extraterritorial courts to hear offenses involving Frenchmen. By 1842 the Roman Catholic establishment in the Hawaiian Islands was strong enough for its clergy to form a diocese, and the local missionaries reported over two thousand converts.[35]

Next to American Board missionaries, Latter-Day Saints, or Mormons, made the most significant contribution to the force, the vitality, and presence of the American missionary frontier in the Pacific Basin. Although they arrived some twenty-five years after the American Board, they eventually exceeded the latter in missionary territory and diversity of people affected, as well as in sustained mission support over time. Interestingly Mormons founded their prime mission establishment next to American Board operations. Their Hawaiian Island compound became the support center for their far-flung ecclesiastical network.

The Mormon venture in the Pacific Basin began in 1843, when Joseph Smith sent Addison Pratt and four others from Nauvoo, Illinois, on a missionary reconnaissance of the Pacific Basin. Pratt expected first to visit the Sandwich Islands but, unable to obtain transportation to the mid-Pacific at that time, he and his party took passage on an American whaler bound for the Society Island whale fishery. Their first stop was at Tubai Island, 350 miles due south of Tahiti. London Missionary Society agents challenged the newcomers, claiming it to be their territory, but Pratt and associates converted some natives of Tubai before proceeding to Tahiti and from there to the Tuamotu Islands. By 1846 the Mormons had formed ten island-mission settlements; four years later, when they and several native converts met at Putuhara, Anaa, the first Mormon missionary conference in the Pacific, native membership numbered 866. On the eve of the American Civil War, Latter-Day Saints had formed missionary settlements on twenty islands of southern Polynesia, with a membership of two thousand, a foundation for their activity there into modern times.[36]

Mormon leaders, having by this time relocated their sectarian community in Utah, maintained a strong interest in the Hawaiian Islands as a strategic station from which to proselytize the peoples of the central and western Pacific. Therefore Brigham Young selected eight Saints working the placers of the newly discovered California goldfield as the missionary vanguard to Hawai'i. The party sailed from San Francisco in 1850. Landing at Honolulu they surveyed the islands for favorable mission sites and formed the first Mormon settlement at Kealakou. Shortly thereafter four additional stations were established and, encouraged by the native response, the missionaries requested a printing press. They translated the *Book of Mormon* into the local language, printed it, and distributed it to converts. By the late 1850s, Mormon missionaries had established fifty spiritual centers, maintained a number of schools for native youth, and claimed four thousand converts.

American Board representatives and the native Hawaiians under their influence extended a reluctant toleration to the newcomers. However, lurid and salacious tales then circulating in the states reached Hawai'i, the product of public reaction to the Mormon practice of plural marriage (a source of bitter recrimination and even persecution inflicted by non-Mormon neighbors in Missouri and Illinois). These rumors created an undercurrent of suspicion and reduced the effect of Mormon missionary effort during their early years in the Hawaiian kingdom. Island officials responded with restrictions on Mormon activity, including a law that forbade them to perform marriages. Mormons could be wed only before a certified Protestant clergyman.

In spite of private scorn and civic repression, the Mormons established a missionary beachhead in Hawai'i that initially showed promise. They withdrew to Lāna'i, a thinly populated island west of Maui, and prepared to establish a local Zion there. By the mid-1850s they had converted four thousand natives, erected and maintained mission churches and schools, translated the *Book of Mormon* into the native language, received a printing press, and published and distributed their scriptures.

However, this first attempt to develop a strong, ongoing mission presence had petered out by 1857. Crop failures, approaching destitution, growing bigotry from Protestant and Catholic communities on other islands, and, worst of all, the escalating apostasy of converts, caused Mormon leaders to decide to close the Lāna'i Zion. Most mission workers returned to the states; a few remained to maintain the Mormon presence.

In 1861 Walter Murray Gibson, a consummate adventurer, arrived on the scene. During 1859 he appeared in Utah and discussed with Young his plan for relocating Mormons in New Guinea, where, he promised, they would finally be safe from American private and public recrimination; the Mormons had just concluded their "war" with the United States. Young rejected Gibson's plan, but did receive him into the Mormon church and commission him to carry the Mormon gospel to Japan and Malaysia.

Gibson stopped off in Honolulu and decided to settle on Lāna'i, assuming the title "President of the Hawaiian mission." He reportedly callously appropriated mission functions and property to himself. He collected scattered converts to the Lāna'i settlement, had the Lāna'i plantation placed in his name, sold other Mormon properties in the islands, and used the proceeds to purchase livestock, tools, and supplies for the Lāna'i plantation, exploiting converts as laborers.

Gibson sealed his doom with the Mormons when, during 1864, a delegation from Utah arrived on Lāna'i to demand the deeds to property and proceeds they charged he had converted to this personal use. Gibson refused and was excommunicated. But Gibson remained in the islands, inveigled himself into high court circles, and received several lofty and lucrative appointments, including that of prime minister from 1882 to 1887.

Gibson's alleged larcenous handling of mission affairs and the Mormon exodus to Utah damaged the cause of that sect in Hawai'i. However, by 1865 representatives from Utah were back in the archipelago in strength. They purchased Laie Plantation, a six-thousand-acre property situated on the north side of O'ahu. It became the Zion of the Pacific Basin, the staging ground for Latter-Day Saint missions to New Zealand, Australia, Samoa, Tonga, China, and, in recent times, Japan and Taiwan.

Several other religious denominations joined the American missionary frontier in the Pacific Basin. While each functioned in a more limited territory than that served by the American Board and Mormon evangelists, they accomplished similar if more limited successes for the American westward advance. One area where the missionary frontier played an indisputable role in assuring territorial absorption by the home government was the basin's northeastern rimland, comprising Oregon, Washington, and the immediate hinterlands. Although held jointly by Great Britain and the United States by virtue of a series of treaties begining in 1818, Hudson Bay fur brigades from Fort Vancouver on the Columbia

River so dominated the region as to exclude the Yankee continental fur frontier, thus negating the expansionist potential it had provided in other parts.

It was a request for spiritual attention delivered to Saint Louis in 1831 by a party of Northwest Coast Indians that provoked the attention of three denominations there: Methodist, Presbyterian, and Roman Catholic. The first body to respond with a definite plan for establishing missions in the new territory was a consortium of Methodist congregations in New England and New York. The Methodist mission board appointed Jason Lee to lead the Oregon mission and carry the gospel to the Northwest tribes. He and a small party of workers arrived on the Columbia during 1834. Hudson's Bay Company officials welcomed the Methodists, relieved that they were no particular threat to their domination of the rich fur trade of the region, and pleased that they could be expected to minister to the spiritual needs of post staff and to teach their children. Lee's first mission stations were on the upper Willamette River, including one at French Point. While the Methodists did establish schools, teach Indian children, and attempt to convert their parents, they also imported herds of cattle and horses from California ranches, opened substantial fields, planted orchards, and demonstrated the fertility of the lands. Jason Lee has been called an expansionist, a missionary with a "colonizer's heart and pioneer's shrewdness," intent upon importing New England values and that region's "superior brands of American culture to the Pacific." It is claimed that he conceived his true mission to be providing "New England farmers a foretaste of Heaven," by attracting them to Oregon.[37]

The steadily growing mission staffs spent more and more time opening farms and developing livestock herds for their personal benefit, to the neglect of the Indians. They corresponded with families and sponsoring church congregations in the East, their letters replete with superlatives describing the bounty of this part of the Pacific Basin. Often these letters were shared with newspaper and magazine editors, who published them for a wider constituency. Missionaries also regularly returned to the United States to raise funds to support their work in the Oregon Country and to recruit additional mission workers; these junkets served as promotional campaigns. From the Mississippi Valley to the Atlantic seaboard, in churches and public buildings at every stop on the missionary itinerary, attentive audiences listened to appeals for funds to support missions in the Oregon Country, each address laced with vivid descriptions of the wonders and promise of the new land. Jason Lee exposed the expansionist dimension of the missionary frontier in 1838 when, in a fund-raising tour in the eastern United States, he recruited a party of fifty men, women, and children, certainly more persons than were needed for the mission staff in the new country.

The American Board also assigned missionaries to this area. Workers from the Hawai'i mission had visited the Northwest Coast on several occasions and expressed a strong missionary interest in the region. American Board officials assigned Marcus Whitman, Samuel Parker, and three workers to the territory. During the spring of 1835, this missionary party, largely Presbyterian, began the overland trek to the juncture of the Snake and Columbia rivers, where they established a station. Waiilatpu Mission was indeed the center for some conversion work among resident Native Americans. But of greater importance, it also became a functioning enclave of American presence near the Pacific Basin's eastern rimland.

Roman Catholic missionaries also penetrated this region, coming from Canada and Saint Louis. Françoise Blanchet and Modeste Demers founded missions at Cowlitz on Puget Sound and at Misqually, midway between the sound and the Columbia River. The premier cleric representing the Catholic contribution to the American missionary frontier in the Northwest was Father Pierre Jean de Smet. By 1842 he had established the most successful Christian mission in the region. The Roman Catholics far exceeded competing Protestant missions in sustained commitment, service, and results. More than to any other reason, this fact is attributable to the Catholics' single-mindedness in their charge; the Protestants were torn by mixed interests.

California, the southernmost segment of the Pacific Basin's eastern rimland receiving intensive American expansionist attention, was a less-productive environment for the American missionary frontier than most other populated territories. A former Spanish and Mexican province, it bore a heavy Roman Catholic imprint. Sustained pressure from padres in the chain of Franciscan missions extending from San Diego to San Francisco had converted large numbers of Native Americans, and the California Hispanic population retained its religious affiliation even following the American conquest. Other American frontiers (fur, mercantile, and mining) had rather thoroughly Americanized much of California before the conquest. Thus there was little left for the American missionary frontier to contribute in a purely expanionist role; its function became largely to minister to the thousands of immigrants, most of them Americans, streaming westward.

During 1847 Methodist clergy from the Oregon mission ventured to San Francisco and formed a small Sunday school. Chester Lyman, an observer for the American Board, reported that a Methodist prayer meeting was "attended by the few Christians here. . . . the whole town has been one scene of uproar and confused dissipation, and gambling. The Sabbath is said to be usually a time of revelry."[38]

In addition to the Methodist clergy, there were Presbyterians, Episcopalians, Congregationalists, Disciples of Christ, Society of Friends, and Mormons. The religious body carrying out the most proselyting in the new territory was the Latter-Day Saints. Their activity provoked envy and bitter sectarian competition, interfaith exclusionism, and bigotry. Communicants of other faiths scorned the Mormons, even persecuted them. Lyman found "a strong prejudice . . . exists on the part of Californians" against the Mormons. A woman "complained against a man that he had struck her boy & called him *Mormon* and she wished the culprit hauled up and punished. The striking part she said she cared nothing about, but to have her son called a Mormon was more than she could put up with."[39]

On the Pacific Basin's northern rim, native peoples of Alaska and the Aleutians for some time had received the attention of Russian Orthodox missionaries. Following the purchase of this huge area by the United States in 1867, the American missionary frontier, comprising Presbyterian, Baptist, Roman Catholic, Methodist, Moravian, Society of Friends, and Lutheran denominations, ventured north. Presbyterian and Russian Orthodox missionaries achieved the greatest success among the natives with their Presbyterian accomplishments largely attributable to their principal agent in Alaska, Sheldon Jackson. For years he worked tirelessly promoting Alaskan and Aleut welfare before the American public and committees of Congress. Through missionary influence reindeer from Siberia were introduced into Alaska to sustain Arctic peoples who faced starvation because of the slaughter of whales, walrus, and caribou by commercial hunters.

Added to the American missionary frontier's predominant Protestantism, splintered sectarianism, passionate exclusionism, and intense competitiveness was an irrepressible momentum, a vigorous mobility by which it swept westward across the Pacific Basin from its continental and Hawaiian Island moorings, reaching the Asian rimland and adjacent islands during 1829. First to arrive and form the American missionary frontier in the west were American Board representatives. They joined Roman Catholic missionaries, with their record of uneven conversion success extending over six hundred years, and recently arrived British missionaries, to compete for converts among Confucionist, Taoist, Buddhist, Shintoist, and Islamic adherents.

British missionaries arrived in China during 1807. East India Company officials at Canton, the only place in China aliens were permitted, anxious over the church's stance on the rich opium trade and regarding missionaries as "pernicious distractions" to commerce, refused them passage on company ships and denied them residence in the Cantonese compound. Thus British missionaries reached China aboard American ships and for several years resided in the American compound at Canton. One of the early arrivals, Robert Morrison, mastered the Chinese language and compiled an English-Mandarin dictionary, useful both to religious and commercial interests. His linguistic success served as a foundation for American missionary work on the Asian coast.

Among the first American Board missionaries to reach China were Elijah Bridgman, David Abeel, the medical doctor Peter Parker, and Samuel Wells Williams. Denied access to the interior, they preached at Canton and translated, published, and clandestinely distributed to interior settlements religious tracts and scriptures. American Board missionaries also established a center at Singapore, where the Chinese interdict did not apply.

This pioneer missionary activity stirred considerable interest and broadened support in the states. Publications by missionaries in the field enhanced this interest. In 1832 Bridgman began publishing a sinological journal *The Chinese Repository*. In 1848 Williams published his two-volume study of China, *The Middle Kingdom.* Statewide interest in the Asian rimland was manifested in 1843, when the Massachusetts General Court incorporated the American Oriental Society, its purpose to "cultivate learning" in the Asiatic languages, assist in translating the scriptures, and aid in the transaction of commerce.[40]

In addition to preaching, publishing, and distributing religious literature, American Board representatives in the Far East established schools, churches, and hospitals. Dr. Parker's indefatigable work in founding medical centers and treating Chinese patients won more initial support for the missionary frontier's work than did the preachers. By midcentury the American missionary frontier in Asia was enhanced by the arrival of Baptist, Methodist, Episcopal, Dutch Reformed, and Mormon missionaries.[41]

The several military actions taken by British and French forces against China between 1839 and 1900, primarily to redress grievances (the degraded status assigned Westerners by the emperor's court, the quarantine of Westerners at Canton, missionary massacres, and peremptory restrictions on commerce), each conflict resulting in Chinese defeat, yielded pacts to which the United States was a party, granting Western demands and including clauses extending tolerance for Christians and permitting increased activity for the American missionary frontier over an ever-expanding portion of China. These prerogatives came about largely because of the influence of churchmen on the treaties. Missionaries were almost the only Westerners with a command of the Chinese language, and they were called upon to participate in the diplomatic negotiations concluding these conflicts, translating the proceedings, and drafting the treaties. Certainly they could be expected to work for the inclusion of clauses favorable to their cause. As one instance Bridgman, Parker, and Williams assisted Caleb Cushing in drafting the 1844 Treaty of Wanghia; it included a provision permitting Christians to work and to publish and distribute books beyond Canton.

At first only port cities were opened to them, but by subsequent treaties, Chinese officials removed the ban on travel and work in the interior. Shanghai became the center for evangelizing China. Missionary-frontier facilities distributed across China included compounds, each with a church, school, library, and often a hospital. Eventually mission-supported colleges made their appearance. In addition a few promising students studied in stateside institutions of higher education.

Periodic reactionary outbursts, at times from the imperial court, at others from the provinces, led to the repression of Christian activity and massacres of missionaries and converts. Each incident was taken up by the intruding Western nations as a cause for redress resulting in punitive expeditions, Chinese defeats, and further weakening of the Middle Kingdom.

Ironically the missionary frontier, while making only modest and certainly uneven progress in Christian conversion, became the prime source of Chinese nationalism. The new learning brought to China by the several, largely American, missionary establishments, stirred revolutionary movements by Chinese to free themselves from their imperialist oppressors. "Chinese reformists and revolutionists . . . were the products of the mission schools, where they were exposed to concepts which to a great extent were antagonistic to traditional Chinese concepts of government and social organization." This influence continued into the twentieth century, contributing to the formation of the Chinese Republic and other cataclysmic sociopolitical changes.[42]

From its base in China, the American missionary frontier proceeded onto the island of Formosa. After the opening of Japan in 1853–54 by Perry's naval squadron, leaders of Japan also reluctantly, slowly, permitted the formation of an American missionary frontier there. As in the case of China, its influence was due less to pervasive religious conversion and more to the introduction of Western knowledge and ideas through missionary-supported schools, books, and role models. This unintentional cultural infusion precipitated the transformation of Japan. Later in the nineteenth century, American missionaries began entering the hermit kingdom of Korea in the 1870s.

The American missionary frontier was the most complex, enduring, and alterative of all the entities serving the cause of Yankee expansion across the Pacific Basin. Granted its high, otherworldly motives, it was no less imperialistic than the other frontiers. In some parts of the basin, as in Hawai'i, its work resulted in cultural imperialism as well as in preparing the archipelago for absorption by the United States. In many other parts, including China, the result was cultural imperialism—pervasive societal and institutional change. Education, rather than Christian conversion, became the missionary frontier's most widely accepted offering. Certainly the sectarian clerics were prime carriers of Anglo-American civilization. Knowledge of science, technology, political thought, and general Western culture was more esteemed by many peoples, particularly those on the Pacific Basin's western rim, than were Christian salvation, theology, and doctrine. It has been observed that Western education transcended "traditional values" on Asia's rimland; protégés of the mission compounds came to advocate "new ones based on exposure to new ideas."[43]

Missionaries often became permanent Pacific Basin residents, seeding a strategic American presence. In Hawai'i most missionaries spent their lives in the archipelago, rearing their families there. Missionary children became business, social, and political leaders of the kingdom and were principal founders of the republic. The Judd family illustrates this process. Dr. Gerrit P. Judd, American Board medical missionary to the Hawaiian kingdom, subsequently held multiple cabinet positions in the native government. His son, Charles, established large business interests and served as legislator, chamberlain, king's secretary, and agent for crown lands. Another son, Albert, graduated from Yale, studied law at Harvard, and returned to the islands, where he developed extensive business interests, entered public life, and served as the kingdom's chief justice.

There exists a wealth of evidence of the missionary frontier's role as an alterative force in basin society and institutions. In the Kingdom of Hawai'i this influence was virtually complete. American Board partisans drastically altered the social, economic, and political landscape there by establishing a New England social order. The missionaries altered government, changed property concepts and the land-tenure system, restructured social institutions, and abolished native religion, customs, and amusements, including dancing, games, and festivals.

Like the Jesuits in the Roman Catholic universe, mission clerics representing several Protestant denominations in the basin were consummate politicians and expansionists as well. They were imbued with what has been called "Protestant manifest destiny." Applied to Hawai'i in 1851, one Protestant spokesman wrote:

> Certain events of Providence, and the fact that the Hawaiian Islands are already a virtual colony of the United States, a missionary offshoot from the stock of New England . . . give a strong probability to what might otherwise seem but a presumption, namely, that the lapse of a few years will find the Heart of the Pacific a twin heart with the Great American Republic, organized under the same laws, and beating with the same Anglo-Saxon blood that shall animate the united millions of all North America between the Atlantic and Pacific.[44]

Inevitably it seemed, missionary frontier workers in remote places found it more efficient in pursuing their conversion goals to "take charge." United States naval officers on duty in the Pacific observed that the American Board missionaries' influence was overpowering in Hawai'i and so strong on several more westerly islands that virtually all natives rendered "voluntary submission" to their directions.

Certainly every American frontier functioning in the Pacific Basin served the national interest, but the missionary frontier exceeded all others in this regard. Protestant missionaries there regarded it as their sanctified mission to convert and transform pagans and make their land "an outpost of American civilization." There is compelling evidence that in many areas they were immensely successful, and it cannot be denied that their achievements as Christian imperialists were due in no small measure to the bracing effect of the supportive American military frontier.

U.S. Frigate *Essex* with her prizes lying in the Harbor of Nuku Hiva, Marquesas Ids. Watercolor sketch by George Ropes, 1816 (M6566). (Courtesy Peabody & Essex Museum/Peabody Museum Collection, photo by Mark Sexton, neg. no. 12204.)

Capture of the U.S. Frigate *Essex* in Valparaíso Harbor by HMS *Phoebe* and *Cherub*. Oil by George Ropes (M455). (Courtesy Peabody & Essex Museum/Peabody Museum Collection, photo by Mark Sexton, neg. no. 11763.)

Portrait of Commander Charles Wilkes, U.S.N. In Wilkes, *Exploring Expedition,* vol. 1 frontispiece. (Courtesy Alaska and Polar Regions Department, Rasmuson Library, University of Alaska Fairbanks, acc.# A1693.)

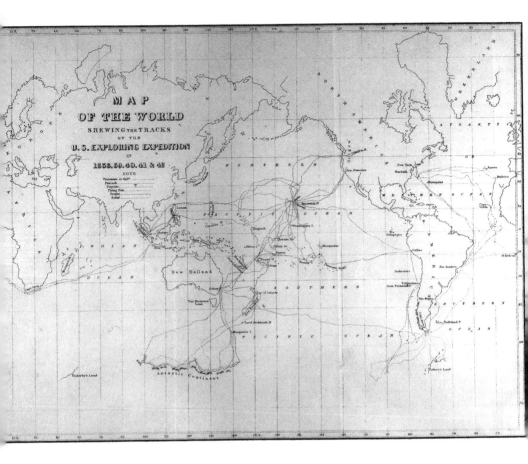

A general map of the Wilkes expedition. In Wilkes, *Exploring Expedition,* vol. 1 prior to the Table of Contents. (Courtesy Alaska and Polar Regions Department, Rasmuson Library, University of Alaska Fairbanks, acc.# A1693.)

A view of the Antarctic continent. In Wilkes, *Exploring Expedition*, vol. 2 prior to page 325.

West Crater "Kaluea Pele" from the "Black Ledge." Wilkes Expedition. Oil painting by Titian Ramsey Peale, 22 November 1840. (Courtesy Department Library Services, American Museum of Natural History, photo by Boltin, neg. no. 323781.)

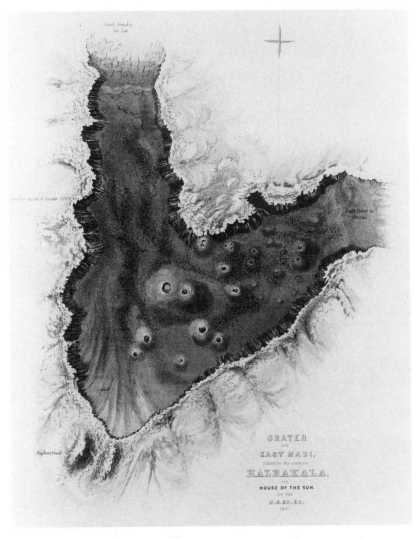

A map of Haleakala volcano. In Wilkes, *Exploring Expedition*, vol. 4 prior to page 255.

Camp on Pendulum Peak, Hawai'i. In Wilkes, *Exploring Expedition,* vol. 4 prior to page 145.

A postcard view of Sitka after the American purchase of Alaska in 1867.
(Courtesy Hamlin Collection, Alaska and Polar Regions Department, Rasmuson
Library, University of Alaska Fairbanks.)

"Perry in Japan" by Gessan Ogata. (Courtesy U.S. Naval Academy Museum, cat. no. 50.12.)

Manila. In Wilkes, *Exploring Expedition*, vol. 5 prior to page 275.

Believed to be one inspiration for Melville's *Moby Dick*, "The Loss of the Essex" depicts a wounded and vengeful sperm whale's successful attack on the *Essex* on 20 November 1820. (Courtesy Hart Nautical Collections/The MIT Museum, Forbes WB 797.2.)

Jack London aboard the *Snark*, Apia, Samoa, 1908. (Courtesy The Huntington Library, JLP Large Album 15 Number 13165.)

A view of Glacier Bay illustrative of the Northern Literary Frontier of John Muir.
Photograph by John S. Whitehead.

Pu'uhonua o Hōnaunau: Place of Refuge of Hōnaunau. This ancient Hawaiian temple on the island of Hawai'i was featured in the writings of Mark Twain. Photograph by John S. Whitehead.

309

Flag raising ceremony at the Normal School in Honolulu performed by students on the last day of the existence of the Republic of Hawai'i, 13 June 1900. (Courtesy State Archives, Hawai'i.)

A postcard advertising the Alaska-Yukon-Pacific Exposition held in Seattle 1909.
(Courtesy Charles Bunnell Collection, Alaska and Polar Regions Department, Rasmuson
Library, University of Alaska Fairbanks.)

The Arizona Memorial, Pearl Harbor, Hawai'i, 1970. Photograph by
John S. Whitehead.

CHAPTER FOURTEEN

The Military Frontier

The nineteenth-century American military establishment, consisting of an army and a navy, was an essential element in the nationalizing currents, and served the additional role of an expansion entity in and of itself. The army dominated the continental conquest; soldiers established an American presence in western lands ahead of permanent agricultural settlement. They constructed forts at strategic locations in the forests, on the prairies, plains, and deserts, and in the mountains; these tiny martial settlements often served as vanguard urban nuclei in the wilds of the West. Troopers hewed roads and established the first communication system across the continent. They fought Indians and drove them from lands coveted by settlers, explored and mapped remote portions of western America, and provided the first law and order for the region. Often army officers served as governors of newly formed territories; as paradiplomats they frequently conducted councils with powerful Indian nations and negotiated treaties with tribal leaders. And the military frontier solidified the American presence in forward regions, since troopers, at the expiration of their enlistments, frequently chose to remain in the region they had recently tamed, to take up enlistment land bounties and join the farmer's frontier.

The military frontier also played a strategic role in the American occupation of the Pacific Basin, where the navy dominated. At the beginning of the nineteenth century, when it first entered the region, the American navy consisted of officers and crewmen (including a complement of marines on most ships) manning several types of wooden-hulled sailing vessels: the ship of the line (dreadnaught of that maritime age), the frigate (contemporary cruiser), and several smaller crafts, including the sloop of war and the schooner.[1]

The navy's mission on the sea was similar to that of the army on land. As the pelagic arm of the military frontier, it guarded and aided the expanding national interest in the Pacific Basin. Its ships protected Yankee trading and whaling fleets from raids by pirates and predacious islanders. Crewmen explored the far reaches of the Pacific, mapping and charting the oceanic landscape, occasionally discovering an unclaimed island and in one case a subcontinent. Naval officers served as paradiplomats, negotiating treaties with heads of state of Pacific Basin nations. And with support from the American army, the navy applied military force on occasion to carve territories out of the Pacific Basin for absorption by the nation. Emulating the troopers' practice on the continent, sailors, at the conclusion of enlistments, occasionally chose to settle Pacific Basin locations, additionally strengthening the American presence there.

Interestingly the earliest activity by the military frontier in the Pacific Basin was an army exercise—the Lewis and Clark expedition. This column of explorers led by Meriwether Lewis and William Clark proceeded from Saint Louis in 1804 by way of the Missouri River to the northern Rocky Mountains, thence west into the Columbia River drainage, and on to the Pacific shore. The momentary presence of this official party on the Pacific Basin's eastern rim provided the beginning of an enlarging American claim to the region, settled by treaty with Great Britain in 1846, by which the United States acquired all of the Northwest Territory to the forty-ninth parallel, the present boundary separating the United States and Canada.

The frigates *Congress* and *Essex* were the first Yankee naval vessels assigned duty in the Pacific Basin. During 1800 the *Congress* ranged through the Sunda Strait, between Sumatra and Java, guarding American commerce from French privateers, while the *Essex* escorted a convoy of American merchantmen to home port by way of the Cape of Good Hope.

American naval activity in the Pacific Basin quickened during the War of 1812. The Yankee sloop of war *Peacock* captured four British merchantmen near Batavia, but the most successful sortie carried out by American naval forces in the Pacific Basin during that conflict was accomplished by crewmen aboard the frigate *Essex,* commanded by David Porter. This combative captain from Boston navigated the *Essex* into South Pacific waters during 1813, after a punishing passage around Cape Horn. Porter's quarry were British whalers and merchantmen fitted with heavy armament and authorized with letters of marque to halt and seize Yankee ships plying Pacific waters.

Chilean revolutionaries having recently overthrown the Spanish colonial government in that South American province, Porter and his crew were hospitably received at Valparaíso, Chile's principal port. Shortly thereafter with rested crew and refitted ship, Porter ventured on a hunt beyond the Galápagos Islands. For a year the *Essex* achieved an unbelievable record of success; Porter's crewmen captured twenty-four British vessels, sixteen of them whalers, virtually destroying the British whaling fleet in the Pacific.[2]

Porter regaled his friend Washington Irving with a report of his successes: "It occasioned great uneasiness in Great Britain. The merchants who had any property afloat in this quarter trembled with apprehension for its fate; the underwriters groaned at the catalog of captures, while the pride of the nation was sorely incensed at beholding a single frigate lording it over the Pacific, in saucy defiance of their thousand ships."[3]

Porter provisioned his crew with foodstuffs plundered from the commissaries of captured vessels, including giant tortoises from the Galápagos, which the crew rated as "delicious." He also maintained the *Essex* magazines with appropriated powder and shot, and kept his ship in good repair with the cordage, canvas, tar, and paint taken from captive vessels. Several of the seized ships he convoyed to Peruvian harbors, sold as prizes, and paid his crew from the proceeds. And he increased American naval strength in the Pacific by converting three of the captive vessels into warships manned by detachments from the *Essex* roster. One converted auxiliary raider, the *Georgiana,* captured three British whalers. The British whaler *Atlantic* he renamed *Essex Junior* and assigned it escort duty with the *Essex.* The *Hammond,* a British trader fitted out as a marque vessel, he designated an auxiliary raider under the command of Marine Lieutenant John M. Gamble.

During October 1813 Porter led his nondescript squadron into a sparkling anchorage on the island of Nuku Hiva in the Marquesas archipelago to refit, careen, and scrape off the barnacles, caulk, and paint all the hulls. Porter in council with island chiefs concluded a treaty annexing Nuku Hiva to the United States. The Bostonian had crewmen erect a fortification, which he dubbed Fort Madison, raised the American flag over it, renamed the tropical paradise Madison Island, and designated the commodious anchorage Massachusetts Bay. Porter claimed he was simply re-affirming the right of discovery for his nation established by Joseph Ingraham in 1791.[4]

Porter prepared to return to his British shipping hunt during December of 1813. He left Lieutenant Gamble at Nuku Hiva, under orders to use the converted raider *Hammond* as convoy to deliver four prize-ships laden with whale oil to United States ports. Before Gamble could carry out this mission, however, the Nuku Hiva islanders revolted, making it impossible for him to provision his ships there. He concluded to run the *Hammond* to the Sandwich Islands for a cargo of foodstuffs; there the *Hammond* was designated in the Kingdom of Hawai'i's maritime records as the first American warship to anchor at Honolulu. Hardly seaborne again, the Americanized *Hammond* and crew were captured by the British sloop of war *Cherub*.[5]

Captain Porter's quest for British ships led him to the South American coast during the early months of 1814. No sooner had he entered Valparaíso harbor for wood, water, and foodstuffs, than his ship was blockaded by two British warships, the frigate *Phoebe* and the sloop of war *Cherub*. On 28 March 1814 Porter decided to fight his way to freedom. As the *Essex* sped into the blockade line, a violent storm swept away the ship's main topmast, virtually immobilizing it. The British warships closed in, pouring a devastating barrage into the crippled Yankee vessel. Porter's gunners answered with furious defense, bloodying the decks of the attacking ships, but the contest was uneven; the *Essex* was destroyed.[6]

Several surviving crewmen from the *Essex* joined the Chilean republican army; some returned with Porter under parole in the *Essex Junior* to the United States. The *Essex* guns had been silenced, but its daring sally created a legacy for the nascent Yankee military frontier in those parts. And the heroes' welcome accorded Porter and his reduced crew on arrival in the states was matched by the reluctant acknowledgment of their success from British sources: Porter and crew had "annihilated our commerce in the South Seas" and had "harmed the British Empire more than all the rest of the American Navy."[7]

The national government built on this legacy by gradually expanding its naval forces in the Pacific Basin, thus creating what became a two-ocean navy. This was in keeping with America's role as one of the world's leading maritime nations, a position it maintained until around 1861. Enterprises with growing interests in the Pacific Basin (bankers, shipbuilders, exporters, importers, shippers, whalers, and traders, as well as an increasing number of carriers engaged in mail and passenger transport) pressed the national government to protect their mercantile fleets from threats of piracy and depredations by island raiders, and to assist in collecting debts by "showing the flag." And there was the recurring request that the American navy intensively explore and chart this vast water hemisphere and publish accurate navigational guides to reduce maritime losses. Appeals from these interests led to the formation of the military frontier in the Pacific Basin, largely by the navy.

Several additional factors influenced the entry of the navy-dominated military frontier into the basin. One was the naval officer corps's interest in land there to construct ship-repair and supply bases to sustain their fleets, at times operating twenty thousand miles from home stations on the Atlantic. Throughout the nineteenth century, navy men were irrepressible advocates for enlarging the American presence in the Pacific Basin.

Yet another persuasive factor influencing the formation of the navy-dominated military frontier was the turmoil in Latin America. All along the basin's eastern face, from San Francisco to Valparaíso, the quest for independence threatened Spanish dominion. American exporters profited handsomely by supplying arms to Latin rebels, but they risked retaliatory seizure of ships by Spanish naval forces, confiscation of cargoes, and in some instances execution of crewmen. Thus arms traders joined the community of Yankee commercial interests demanding military protection.

Officials in Washington responded during 1816, announcing plans for two naval stations to serve as support bases for warships assigned duty in Pacific waters, one to be situated on the South American coast, the other on the western rimland, in Chinese waters. However, before these stations became operational, the navy was assigned its first postwar mission in the Pacific Basin.

During the War of 1812, a British warship entered the Columbia River, its crewmen raised the British flag over Astoria (the former American Fur Company compound recently purchased by the Northwest Company), and occupied it as an exclusive possession of Great Britain. The Treaty of Ghent, which concluded that conflict, provided the status quo ante bellum; in subsequent interpretation, confirmed by United States–British conventions, this came to mean joint occupation and use of the Oregon Country, the American claim based on Robert Gray's discovery of the Columbia in 1792, the Lewis and Clark expedition to the Northwest Coast in 1804–6, and the establishment of Astoria there by the American Fur Company in 1811. Captain James Biddle, commanding the sloop of war *Ontario,* was ordered during 1817 to proceed to the Northwest Coast to reassert American interest in the Columbia River region.

In the course of the *Ontario*'s cruise, Biddle and his crew performed several actions in addition to their primary assignment, reflective of the varied duties and functions the navy-dominated military frontier would perform in the future. First in the troubled waters off the Chilean coast, a Spanish naval force had formed a blockade of that insurgent colony's ports, seized American ships, confiscated cargoes, and imprisoned crewmen. Biddle forced the Spaniards to release the Americans and restore their ships and cargoes. Second several Yankees had been impressed into the rebel Chilean army; Biddle negotiated their release. Thereupon the *Ontario* sailed up the coast to the Columbia, crossed the deadly bar, and explored the estuary on both its north and south banks. On 18 August 1818 Biddle raised his nation's flag and ceremonially reasserted American proprietorship. His primary mission accomplished, he set the *Ontario* on a southward course, stopping at Monterey for provisions (the first American warship in a Spanish California port), before proceeding to Peruvian and Chilean waters to conclude his intercession between insurgent and Spanish colonial officials concerning American citizens and interest. Thereupon he sailed for home port via Cape Horn.[8]

Shortly after the Biddle mission, the secretary of the navy ordered Captain John Downes to establish the Pacific Station; his ship was the frigate *Macedonian,* a British Royal Navy vessel captured by Yankee gunners during the War of 1812. Downes and his crew reached Valparaíso in 1818 and formed the Pacific Station, the function of which was to support naval craft protecting American interests in the Pacific Basin, marking the beginning of the military frontier there.

Valparaíso and Callao were the oldest and best-developed ports on the Pacific's eastern rim. Officials there, for the most part, welcomed the Yankees. Income from harbor, docking, and ship-repair fees and sale of foodstuffs replenished public and private coffers depleted by the wars of independence. Downes designated Valparaíso the Pacific Stations's primary port. However, as the contest for Peru abated with the rebel triumph, Downes's successors often based the Pacific Station at Callao, Peru's principal port.

American naval commanders faced many problems in maintaining the station, the principal ones being supply and communications. It was expected that ships assigned to the Pacific Station would be out from home port for a three-year cruise, and the Navy Department enlisted crewmen for that period. The Board of Navy Commissioners and the secretary of the navy sent out two supply ships each year to sustain this Pacific outpost. Supply officers also purchased fresh provisions from local sources, paying for them by drawing sight drafts on international banking houses, including Baring Brothers, the Navy Department's London banker. Later Navy Department officials sent out condemned merchant vessels, which were anchored permanently in the Valparaíso and Callao harbors for use as warehouses.[9]

Messages to and from ships on the Pacific Station required, in the early years, up to six months to reach addresses at Washington, D.C. headquarters and at the navy yards at Norfolk, New Orleans, Philadelphia, New York, and Charlestown (in Boston Harbor). Resourceful officers reduced the time in transit by one-half by using a swift dispatch schooner from New Orleans to Chagres (on the

Isthmus of Panama), crossing the isthmus by mounted courier, then sending a schooner to Valparaíso.[10]

The number of ships assigned to the Pacific Station, the first outpost for the American military frontier in the Pacific Basin, was never large. The secretary of the navy and the Board of Navy Commissioners were required to maintain a small national fleet of ships of the line, frigates, sloops of war, and schooners at several points of Yankee interest. Besides the Pacific Station and the soon-to-be formed East India, Asiatic, or China Station, there were the Home or Atlantic Station, the Mediterranean Station, the African Station, the West Indies and Caribbean Station, the Brazil Station, and Indian Ocean Station. Gradually the single-ship station on the Pacific's eastern edge was expanded to squadron strength (three to five warships).

Downes and the *Macedonian* were succeeded by Captain Charles G. Ridgely and the *Constellation* in 1821. Ridgely repeatedly reminded the secretary of the navy of the vast pelagic territory assigned the station and appealed for additional ships to assure more effective fulfillment of his mission. The following year the secretary responded by assigning the ship of the line *Franklin,* commanded by Captain Charles S. Stewart, and the schooner *Dolphin* to the Pacific Station. Stewart purchased three unassembled small schooners stowed on the deck of an American merchant ship trading at Valparaíso, had his carpenters assemble them, manned them with crewmen from the *Franklin* and *Dolphin,* and placed them on patrol and dispatch duty. Thus the Pacific Station supported a squadron of five ships. Commodore Isaac Hull, commanding the frigate *United States,* reached the Pacific Station in 1824 with the sloop of war *Peacock.* The *Franklin* returned to home port, but the *Dolphin* remained at Valparaíso. For several years the strength of the Pacific Station ranged from three to five warships, often including a ship of the line or one or two frigates, two sloops of war, and a schooner or two. Naval officers there rated the sloop of war ideal for duty at the Pacific Station; its shallow draft could negotiate the most uncertain harbor waters, it "possessed respectable batteries," was manned by a small crew, and could operate effectively far from the station.

In the early years, the territory assigned to the Pacific Station and the East India Station were only vaguely defined. Finally in 1838 the Board of Navy Commissioners, in response to the nation's growing interest in Mexico, California, and the Oregon Country, on the one hand, and Asia, on the other, designated the territory of the Pacific Station to extend from the Arctic to Antarctic along the Pacific's eastern rim and west to one hundred eighty degrees, with the East India Station's territory to extend from the coast of Asia and islands east to one hundred eighty degrees.

The East India Station, created to support rapidly enlarging Yankee commerce in that quarter, evolved at a more hesitant pace than its counterpart on the Pacific Basin's eastern rim. The first United States warship to reach China was the *Congress,* in 1819, with Captain J. D. Henley commanding; co-hong officials ordered Henley to raise anchor and depart at once. He proceeded to Manila, where the Spaniards extended him and crew a cordial reception. Between 1830 and 1832 the USS *Vincennes, Potomac, Peacock,* and *Boxer* attempted to anchor in waters off Canton. In each case co-hong officials issued the peremptory order to depart, with the warning that failure to comply would result in suspension of trade with Americans. Naval commanders found this "arbitrary treatment" insulting.

While American businessmen at Canton desired the presence of their nation's warships to assure the protection of their lives and property in this exotic land (where at best trade was conducted on a complicated, even aberrational basis by the tyrannical co-hong), they dared not encourage it. They cautioned naval officers attempting to establish the East India Station that "Only if the greatest care was observed . . . could visits of American naval vessels prove of any benefit," because "There was always the risk that if too bold a course were followed, the Chinese would retaliate by cutting off all trade." Thus when the *Potomac* and *Peacock* reached Canton, Chinese officials directed the captains to "unfurl your sails and return home; they will not be permitted to delay and loiter about, and the day of their departure must be made known. Hasten, hasten!" American businessmen at Canton apparently were so anxious that "nothing should be allowed to interfere with the trade that actually existed" that "they were willing to make almost any concession to remain in the good graces of Chinese officialdom, and their caution made them look with serious misgivings upon the visits of United States naval vessels in Chinese waters." Therefore American naval officers established depots at nearby Portuguese Macao and adjacent islands to support their ships on the Asiatic Station, and for the time being they maintained that distance from Canton required by the co-hong as a condition of continuing business relations with Yankee traders.[11]

The navy's mission in the Pacific Basin, supported by the Pacific and East India stations, varied according to the American interests needing protection. And it expanded progressively throughout the nineteenth century, as Yankee activity expanded there. Its primary functions included maintaining security for business, missionary, and other American enterprises in the Pacific Basin; exploring the waters, islands, and rimland; mapping the landed areas and charting the waters to provide more complete and accurate navigational guides; and paradiplomatic and political missions in the name of the United States government. Secondary functions were transporting nonmilitary officials, including consuls, to duty stations; supplying necessary hands for civilian vessels short of crewmen, due to desertion or epidemic; and conducting agricultural and military surveys.

In addition the navy stood ready to resort to combat in the face of expansionist ventures by competing imperial nations in those territories where the United States regarded its interests as paramount. By fulfilling these functions, the military frontier established an essential American presence and served as a primary agency for nurturing the flow of American political, economic, and cultural influence throughout the basin.

Ships assigned to the Pacific and Asiatic stations for the most part operated in their respective jurisdictions, although occasionally Navy Department orders directed them to range beyond the prescribed limits. Now and then a squadron formed at the home station entered the Pacific Basin on special assignment, as in the case of the Wilkes expedition. For the most part, however, maritime missions were carried out by the local squadron in its designated territory.

The range of duties officers and crew might carry out on a

single cruise is illustrated by those performed by men aboard the *Dolphin* and *Peacock* between 1825 and 1827. The *Dolphin*, commanded by Captain "Mad" Jack Percival, was ordered to the Mulgrave Islands to search for the whaleship *Globe;* its crew had reportedly mutinied and killed the ship's officers. *Dolphin* crewmen found that islanders had slain all the mutineers except two; officers negotiated their release and placed them in irons for ultimate trial in admiralty court. Thereupon the *Dolphin* proceeded to the Kingdom of Hawai'i. Just before the ship docked at Honolulu, missionaries spirited most of the local native women to mountain hideaways. Percival's sailors ran amuck, looting and burning shops near the port and threatening the resident missionaries. American consuls repeatedly reported that wherever American warships anchored in the basin (Papeete, Apia, Valparaíso, Callao, Lahaina, or Honolulu), each sailor regarded himself a law unto himself, and "defied local law and authority." Percival approved the predacious actions of his sailors. After his sailors had calmed down, he turned them to repairing damaged whaler and trader ships in port and salvaging cargo and specie from a wrecked merchantman.[12]

In 1826 the *Peacock*, commanded by Thomas ap Catesby Jones, cruised first to the Marquesas, and then to Tahiti, where Jones concluded a treaty with officials of the native government, guaranteeing fair treatment of American nationals and their property while in that kingdom's territory. Next Jones turned the *Peacock* on a course to Hawai'i, docking at Honolulu; there he sought to collect debts owed American traders by several chiefs and members of the royal family. He also concluded a treaty with the monarch assuring the protection of Americans in the island kingdom and containing a most-favored-nation clause, which meant that any benefit or advantage granted other nations would automatically extend to the United States. This pact was never ratified by the United States Senate, but the Hawaiian royal government accepted it as binding. From Hawai'i Jones sailed to the basin's eastern rim, visiting California and Mexican ports before returning to his station at Valparaíso.[13]

The navy acted as a maritime police force and suppressed lawlessness in the Pacific Basin much as the army performed that function on the continent. Officers and crewmen aboard ships of the Pacific and East India stations suppressed piracy, watched for filibusters, forced native islanders to pay debts due Yankee traders, rescued traders and missionaries, punished islanders for killing captives, searched outlaw ships suspected of engaging in "black-birding," and hunted mutineers and deserters from American ships and delivered them to American authorities for trial.[14]

A major operation against pirates was carried out by the frigate *Potomac,* commanded by Captain John Downes, en route to his second assignment at the Pacific Station. On the voyage out, via the Cape of Good Hope, Downes was directed to investigate charges that Malaysian pirates based on Sumatra had attacked the American merchantman *Friendship* from Salem, Massachusetts. Downes reached Sumatra during February 1832. He anchored off the settlement of Quallah-Batto, reported to be the brigands' headquarters. He sent heavily armed parties ashore under cover of night; they captured the fortification and spiked its guns. At daybreak the *Potomac*'s heavy guns leveled the pirate sanctuary.[15]

From the days of Philip Nolan and Aaron Burr, restless, inordinately ambitious American adventurers, called filibusters, had ranged over the Southwest into Mexico and Central America, even casting covetous eyes on the Kingdom of Hawai'i. Tennessean William Walker, the most daring and irrepressible of these American adventurers, during 1853 led an expedition from San Francisco into the Gulf of California and established himself as president of the Republic of Lower California. Thereupon Walker led his small army onto the mainland and proclaimed the Republic of Sonora. These political enterprises failed, causing Walker to return to San Francisco. In 1854 he led an invasion of Nicaragua, installed himself as head of state, and presided until 1860, when Nicaraguans rose up, replaced the alien government, and executed Walker.[16]

Pacific Station naval forces sought to curb filibustering in their territory and succeeded in breaking up several expeditions bound for Mexico, Central America, and the Pacific islands. The navy's most notable success was against private political venturing in the Kingdom of Hawai'i. During the early 1850s, frequent reports reached the royal court of planned incursions into the kingdom from California. One warning, which led to the formation of a special security force to guard the royal family, eloquently admitted that American "eagles in the westward flight" were seeking "a resting place" and several "young eaglets are trimming their wings for a flight to the Sandwich Islands. . . . They take their arms with them, with the design of forcibly abolishing the monarchy, and establishing a republic." The presence of the special security force, braced by the USS *Vandalia*, which spent the winter in port at Honolulu, gave pause to the adventurers, and the threat passed.[17]

Armed sailors and marines regularly stormed the beaches of remote Pacific islands to rescue American, British, and French missionaries held captive by islanders. Fijians more than other native peoples received retaliatory attention from ship-based land parties, ordered ashore to collect debts due American traders and to punish natives for property theft and killings. The retaliatory cruise of the sloop of war *John Adams,* commanded by Edward B. Boutwell, to the Fiji Islands in 1855 included shelling and burning five villages and forcing a treaty from Thokambau, "King of Feejee," pledging protection by his government of Americans and their property. Postinvasion reports concluded that the "visit of this ship to the Feejee Islands, has resulted in reestablishing order and restoring confidence of American residents there." Ships of the Pacific Squadron, the *Active, John Hancock,* and *Decatur,* also participated in suppressing an Indian uprising on the Northwest Coast during 1855. War parties held Seattle under seige until scathing fire from the *Decatur*'s heavy deck guns drove off the attackers.[18]

American naval officers on Pacific duty also sought to suppress blackbirding. Yankee skippers cooperated with British naval officers to interdict this human traffic, but achieved only limited success, due largely to the vast expanse over which they were required to maintain their surveillance.

One enduring contribution of this military frontier was conducting explorations and surveys. Assignments ranged from examining islands and rimlands for possible anchorages and naval-station sites to mapping and charting the waters and landed areas, collecting botanical, biological, and ethnological specimens, and conducting agricultural surveys. Thus commanders at the China and Pacific stations were ordered to gather information on Pacific

Basin agriculture, particularly sugarcane culture. Expanding American interest in California led officials in Washington during 1841 to order Commodore Thomas ap Catesby Jones to "examine bays and harbors in the interest of commerce and science." And Lieutenant I. W. Curtis, a marine officer aboard the frigate *Constitution*, at anchor in the harbor at Honolulu, was asked by Dr. Gerrit P. Judd, royal minister of foreign affairs, "to survey the Honolulu region with a view toward planning against foreign aggression"; during the 1840s the Kingdom of Hawai'i faced repeated threats of annexation by French and British naval forces.[19]

Certainly the cruise of each Yankee Pacific navy vessel was in a sense an exploring expedition, because in the Pacific's vastness, navigators could still find undiscovered or unmarked islands, atolls, and reefs, or observe some previously undisclosed natural or human phenomenon. Both the land-based and the water-based military frontiers carried out extensive explorations, and each conducted one reconnaissance that exceeded all others in scope and results. For the army it was the Lewis and Clark expedition, 1804–6; for the navy it was the United States Exploring Expedition, 1838–42. Both immeasurably served national purpose and generated a published body of useful information.

Federal officials authorized the United States Exploring Expedition during 1838, placing Lieutenant Charles Wilkes in charge. A forty-year-old officer with twenty years of naval experience, at the time he was in charge of the Depot of Charts and Instruments (forerunner of the Naval Observatory and the Hydrographic Office). Wilkes has been characterized as a meticulous, hard-driving naval scientist.[20]

Rather than assigning the mission to the squadron at either the China or Pacific stations, naval authorities formed the expedition at the Hampton Roads Station. It consisted of six ships led by two sloops of war, the *Vincennes* (Wilkes's flagship) and the *Peacock*. The civilian complement included a botanist, a conchologist, a mineralogist, a philologist, and artists and naturalists. The charge for the expedition was "not for conquest, but for discovery. Its projects are all peaceful; they extend the empire of commerce and science; to diminish the hazards of the ocean, and to point out to future navigators a course by which they may avoid dangers and find safety."[21]

The fleet sailed from Hampton Roads on 18 August 1838. Near Valparaíso Wilkes lost the tender *Sea Gull* in a gale. From Valparaíso he turned his ships west, exploring, surveying, mapping, and charting the South Sea islands from Tahiti to Tonga, including the Navigator (Samoan) and Fiji archipelagoes. Wilkes negotiated several treaties with island heads of state, stipulating protection for Americans and their property, appointing United States consuls from American communities, and in the case of Samoa, selecting a British subject for this post. At Upola, a Samoan named Tuvai had killed Edward Cavanaugh, an American citizen. Wilkes conducted an ad hoc court, determined Suvai's guilt, and respecting the local law banning execution as punishment, ordered the defendant exiled from his home island. While in Samoan waters Wilkes examined the spacious harbor of Pago Pago on the island of Tutuila and, as a pioneer navy expansionist, reported most favorably on its value to American shipping and national-security interests in the South Pacific. Thereafter American naval vessels increasingly called there.[22]

Wilkes continued on to New Zealand and Australia, pausing in Sydney Harbor before sailing into south polar latitudes, examining the Antarctic's icy landscape at great risk to ships and crews. He maintained a course along the rim of a frozen mass that he concluded was a continent, subsequently designated on maps as Wilkes Land. Returning to Australian waters, Wilkes came upon an uncharted island he named Hull Island, after Commodore Isaac Hull.

Searching for milder climes to rest his worn-down crews and restore his battered vessels, Wilkes continued to the Kingdom of Hawai'i. There crewmen and scientists mapped and charted the archipelago and environs and established an observatory on towering Mauna Loa to study the lava flow and make meteorological observations.

Crews restored and ships repaired, Wilkes moved the expedition to the Northwest Coast and explored coastal waters north and south of the Columbia. Thereupon he followed a path westward for more island reconnaissance, before returning to the Northwest Coast for a more thorough examination of the area, concentrating on the Columbia River. The only expedition vessel that failed to breach the river's deadly mouth was the *Peacock;* it foundered on the bar and sank, although sailors from the other ships rescued the *Peacock*'s crew. Wilkes sent one party up the Columbia past The Dalles, another south along the coast to Yerba Buena on San Francisco Bay, while a third surveyed the Sacramento River and San Francisco Bay.[23]

Wilkes collected his ships in the Mexican California ports and proceeded to Honolulu, thence west toward the China Sea, anchored briefly at Manila and Singapore, then set a course across the Indian Ocean for the Cape of Good Hope and the Atlantic Ocean, arriving in New York Harbor on 10 June 1842. The United States Exploring Expedition had been at sea for three years, ten months, and twenty-one days. Wilkes had unwaveringly held the highest expectations of himself and expedition members; he pushed his crew and civilian complement for ever-increasing productivity. His officers and crew rated Wilkes as "gifted but stiff-necked and endlessly demanding," with "a passion for precision." Their accumulated rage at what they regarded as martinet management of the expedition led them to press for a court martial on charges largely of harsh discipline and excessive punishment inflicted on errant crewmen. The naval tribunal acquitted Wilkes of all charges except that of excessive punishment, for which he received a public reprimand.[24]

The rich legacy of this exercise in the Pacific Basin yielded sustained benefit for the nation. The maps, charts, and hydrographic studies produced by expedition members have immense contemporary value. The plant, animal, and artifact collections were so vast that display and storage needs led to the formation of the Smithsonian Institution as a museum in 1857. Wilkes directed his ships on this exploratory enterprise across the Pacific three times, logging nearly ninety thousand nautical miles. Oceanographers rate this Pacific Basin reconnaissance as "one of the greatest peacetime accomplishments of the United States Navy."[25]

Although no other survey exceeded that of the Wilkes expedition in scope and value to the nation and to science, exploring continued as part of the navy's mission in the Pacific Basin for the remainder of the nineteenth century. During the 1850s several naval squadrons explored the waters of the central, western, and northern Pacific to supplement the work of the Wilkes expedition, charting routes for steamship mail and passenger lines, for telegraphic communications via Bering Strait (the trans-Pacific cable), and coordinating the search with private shipping interests for guano-bearing islands.

Commodore Cadwallader Ringgold was placed in command of the second Pacific expedition. From his Atlantic home port he sailed via the Cape of Good Hope to Australia and the Coral Sea, his crewmen charting the waters adjacent to the Santa Cruz, Caroline, and Ladrone archipelagoes. Captain John Rodgers was detached from the squadron with three ships, with orders to explore North Pacific waters into Bering Strait. The second Pacific reconnaissance produced "many important observations, barometrical, thermometrical, and geographical," to be forwarded promptly "to the Navy Department in Washington, and published as speedily as possible, for the benefit of our valuable and growing commerce with Australia, the East Indies, and California."[26]

Officers, crew, and ships of the Pacific Squadron spent considerable time during the 1850s casting over central Pacific waters for guano-bearing islands. Captain John Mervine and other skippers found several islands, claiming them in the name of the United States and following up private discoveries by taking possession of them in the name of the United States.[27]

One of the most important postwar surveys carried out by the military in the Pacific Basin, because of its diplomatic and territorial implications for the United States, centered on the harbor at Honolulu, rated by mariners the finest in the Pacific. Several nations coveted this anchorage. Americans, civilian and military, had for some time advocated some form of American control for national-security and commercial enhancement in the Pacific.

Marine Lieutenant I. W. Curtis, after completing a security survey of the Honolulu harbor for the Hawaiian royal government during the 1840s, recommended that the United States appropriate and develop Pearl Harbor as a "fortified base." His was one of many voices urging a response by the federal government to thwart the prospect of similar action by competitor imperialist nations. Finally during 1873 federal officials answered these appeals by ordering Admiral A. M. Pennock, commanding the Pacific Squadron, to transport aboard his flagship *California* to the Kingdom of Hawai'i two army officers, General John M. Schofield, Commander, Military Division of the Pacific, and General B. S. Alexander, Corps of Army Engineers. Ostensibly on vacation in the islands, these men were on assignment to ascertain "the defensive facilities" and "collect all information that would be of service to the country in the event of war with a powerful maritime nation." They prepared a report emphasizing the value of Pearl Harbor to the national interest, adding that it could be improved by "cutting through the coral reef that forms a bar outside the entrance channel," and building docks and shops.[28]

The China or Asiatic Station, like its eastern counterpart, supported exploratory, survey, and mapping expeditions, as well as diplomatic, rescue, and punitive missions. But for many years its role was secondary compared to that of the Pacific Station. This was due largely to the unyielding stance of Chinese officials, who refused access to warships of any nation to the Whampoa estuary and Canton anchorage, the only port of the empire where the Chinese permitted commercial vessels to dock. Thus denied a viable mainland support base, Asiatic Squadron officers and crewmen searched offshore islands, Formosa, and the Bonin archipelago for suitable station sites.[29]

After 1842 this station in a real sense came into its own, because of two spectacular occurrences in these far-western waters. One was a bold initiative by American naval officers in the wake of the Chinese military defeat of 1842. The second was the opening of Japan to the West (1853–54), in which the Asiatic Squadron played a vital support role.

During the first Opium War, 1839–42, while invading British naval and army units were smashing Chinese defense forces, Commodore Lawrence Kearny, in command of the Asiatic Squadron, kept his flagship, the frigate *Constitution*, and other vessels under his charge positioned near Canton to maintain a protective presence, guarding American residents in the trader community. But Kearny also made it clear to Yankee businessmen that he would not "countenance" their involvement in the opium trade "under the protection of the American flag."[30]

As British and Chinese officials negotiated the 1842 Treaty of Nanking, which concluded this conflict, Kearny learned that the pact would establish diplomatic relations between the two countries and open several ports to British subjects. He contacted Chinese High Commissioner Kiying, who assured Kearny that American interests would receive due attention. As a paradiplomatic officer of the United States, Kearny rushed the contents of the Treaty of Nanking to the United States by naval courier. This led to Caleb Cushing's mission to China. A naval squadron consisting of four ships and including the steam-powered frigate *Missouri* transported Cushing to China. His negotiations with Chinese officials concluded in the 1844 Treaty of Wanghia, which reiterated the substance of the Treaty of Nanking, confirming that China was opened to the West, establishing diplomatic relations with the United States, and pledging access to several ports in addition to Canton. By this pact and subsequent agreements between Chinese and American officials, the navy finally was able to embed itself in the Chinese mainland, with access to several station sites.[31]

The expanding American commercial and missionary community dispersed about China following the Cushing mission increased the function and range of the Asiatic Station. For the remainder of the century, Chinese political stability declined and regional chaos and insurrectionary outbreaks occurred with greater frequency, inevitably imperiling American interests there. Repeatedly mission-station directors, traders, and naval officers warned that "China is in a most unsettled condition."

Asiatic Squadron ships continued to patrol the China Sea and approaches to the newly opened ports, to thwart brigandage on American shipping by ubiquitous Asian corsairs. And to protect American citizens in China's interior, Yankee commanders turned to small, steam-powered river craft, for easier access to points on China's great rivers.

Great Britain and France, joined by Germany after 1856, maintained a punishing military stance toward China in partitioning that decaying nation's long coast into "spheres of influence." The United States followed a course of neutrality; its ships stood back and only observed the repeated naval and army assaults by forces representing intruding European nations. However, two exceptions to this pose of neutrality occurred around midcentury. The first grew out of the so-called Arrow War, the conflict precipitated by Chinese officials at Canton forcibly removing a crewman of Chinese nationality from the British ship *Arrow*. British naval officers in that sector considered the act an "insult to the British flag," and demanded that Chinese officials make amends; when they refused, royal gunners shelled the port. Ships of the American Asiatic Squadron lay close by, watching over American interests but maintaining neutrality, until Chinese shore batteries fired on an American ship. Commodore James Armstrong, in command of the Yankee flotilla, answered by bombarding Canton's outer forts. The shelling so devastated coastal defenses that Chinese officials asked for quarter and apologized for firing on the American flag. The other occasion grew out of one of the many punitive actions against Chinese coastal towns by British and French naval craft. Coincidentally the American frigate *Powhatan* hovered close by, transporting an American commissioner observing the conditions of Americans residing in China. On one British thrust, the advance was stalled by coastal batteries wounding gun crews on the assault vessel; *Powhatan* crewmen boarded the British vessel and "helped serve the guns."[32]

Perhaps the most dramatic role of the navy-dominated military frontier in the Pacific Basin, other than the sensational Yankee victory over the Spanish fleet in the Battle of Manila Bay, was its opening of Japan to the West. From a stance of receptivity to traders and missionaries in the sixteenth and seventeenth centuries, Japan, dominated by the military-based shogunate, came to exclude all aliens except a community of Dutch traders, who were permitted to reside and do business with Japenese subjects on the tiny island of Deshima, in Nagasaki harbor. As Yankee frontiers in the Pacific Basin increased in vigor and range of activity in the early nineteenth century, Japan's exclusionist stance created increasing difficulty and concern for Americans and their government. Token contact occurred periodically until 1853, but only at the reluctant sufferance of the Japanese.

American ships (whalers, merchantmen, and warships) made

repeated attempts to call at Japanese ports. First came Yankee skipper John Kendrick; in 1791 he piloted the *Lady Washington* and *Grace* into Japanese waters on a trading venture, but was rebuffed. The Napoleonic Wars in Europe limitedly opened Japan to American merchantmen willing to practice deceit. When French armies occupied Holland in the 1790s, Great Britain turned the royal navy to sweeping Dutch ships from the seas. Dutch East India Company officials thereupon chartered American ships to supply their trading center at Deshima. Thus from 1797 to 1808, when this arrangement ended, eight American ships under Dutch charter, flying the flag of their nation at sea to avoid British seizure, would raise the Dutch flag on entering Japanese waters and prospered enormously.

The discovery of a bonanza whale-hunting territory near Japan in 1821 attracted many vessels of the Yankee hunter fleet. Storms over these waters wrecked several ships and cast surviving seamen on the Japanese home islands. Reports reached American officials through Dutch traders at Deshima of imprisonment and ill-treatment of these castaways by shogunate officials, who regarded the Americans as spies.

Repeated attempts by United States officials and private interests to recover the captives were to no avail. In 1837 the *Morrison*, with a complement of missionaries, traders, and seven Japanese crewmen rescued from shipwreck, sailed into Yedo (Tokyo) Bay. Fire from shore batteries drove the *Morrison* off and caused the ship's captain to abandon the contact attempt. Nine years later Commodore James Biddle, commanding two warships, entered Tokyo Bay and attempted to open negotiations with the Japanese for recovery of Americans held in island prisons. The shogun ordered him away, with the warning "never again to appear on the Japanese coast." Naval commanders ignored this warning and increased their pressure on adamant Japanese officials through periodic confrontations. In 1849 Commodore James Glynn anchored the *Preble* off Nagasaki, to negotiate the recovery of Yankee seamen. His tenacity in the face of repeated warnings to retire led finally to the delivery of fourteen captives. Subsequently the commodore recommended to the president that because the Japanese islands contained anchorages ideal for coaling stations to supply trans-Pacific steamships, "strong diplomatic measures be taken to get the ports open."[33]

High officials in the government at Washington concluded that the time had come to act on Glynn's recommendation. Commodore Matthew C. Perry was appointed to command the mission to Japan, for the purpose of establishing some form of relationship with the island kingdom. Perry proceeded from Norfolk on 24 November 1852, aboard the steam side-wheeler *Mississippi*. Stopping at Hong Kong, Perry added three ships from the East India Squadron to his command and then proceeded to Shanghai, where the steam-powered *Susquehanna* joined them. Perry explored the coast of Okinawa and the Bonin Islands, searching for coaling-station sites to sustain the enlarging commercial and naval fleets powered by steam, then proceeded into Japanese waters with two steam frigates and two sloops of war. As he prepared to anchor near Tokyo Bay, shogunate officials mobilized coastal defenses and warned the Americans to weigh anchor and depart. Perry refused, announcing that he carried a letter from his head of state to the Japanese head of state and was determined to deliver it. Furthermore he would communicate only with high officials. Thereupon port officials ordered him to move the flotilla to Nagasaki. Perry again refused and warned that unless he received proper treatment, he would march on Tokyo and deliver the president's letter to the emperor in person. When Japanese officials finally assented to accept the letter, Perry sent ashore a column of marching sailors and marines, resplendent in full dress uniform with navy band providing accompaniment and cadence, to deliver the president's letter. He informed his reluctant hosts that he would return in the spring; on 17 July 1853 the American squadron sailed for Hong Kong.[34]

Perry returned in February 1854 and on 8 March began negotiations with shogunate officials. His preliminary pageantry included a twenty-one-gun salute to the emperor, seventeen-gun salutes to lesser officials, marching columns of sailors and marines led by massed naval bands, and huge gift exchanges. On the last day of March, American and Japanese officials signed the Treaty of Kanagawa, Nippon's first pact with the West. It committed the Japanese government to "open" the island kingdom, in that American vessels were to be received at the ports of Shimoda and Hakadote for repair, restoration of crews, and access to supplies. Government officials pledged humane treatment and repatriation for ship-wrecked seamen, consented to the establishment of an American consulate, and accepted a most-favored-nation clause. Although the Treaty of Kanagawa contained no commercial-relations clause, trade was to be established by subsequent commercial agreements. Samuel Wells Williams, the esteemed author, missionary, and lin-guist, served as interpreter for the American expedition and for the diplomatic negotiations leading to the Treaty of Kanagawa. This marked the coalescence of two Yankee frontiers, the mis-sionary and military, to advance the national interest in the Pacific Basin.[35]

The nineteenth century was a violent time in the Pacific Basin, and the American military frontier, primarily the navy but twice joined by the army, was a participant on seven occasions—four declared wars and three near wars. The first conflict to engage the American navy was the extension of the War of 1812 there, cen-tering on the exploits of the recklessly successful Captain David Porter and the *Essex*.

The Pacific-based military frontier's most serious near war grew out of the determination of the United States to protect the independence of the Kingdom of Hawai'i. Great Britain and France were notoriously predatory in the Pacific Basin during the 1830s and 1840s; the former had annexed New Zealand, the latter the Marquesas archipelago, and naval forces of both nations lurked ominously in the waters of Hawai'i, making threatening gestures toward the royal government. Representatives of these nations resented Yankee influence in that archipelago through American missionary and business communities and the high positions sev-eral of its citizens held in the royal government. British and French agents in the Pacific warned that unless their governments acted promptly, the United States would absorb the island kingdom. Of the two the French were the more haughty and combative, peri-odically bullying the weak royal government. British actions, with one notable exception, were restrained but no less committed to imperial goals.

France used missionaries to open a wedge for its planned take-over of the kingdom; regularly naval forces landed parties of Catholic missionaries (Congregation of the Sacred Heart of Jesus and Mary). But Hawaiian officials banished each missionary party, which then took refuge in the missions of Mexican California. Claiming insult to its national honor and demanding damages, French naval officers periodically invaded the islands with token forces to intimidate the Hawaiians and to "inculcate on its rulers a salutary lesson in respect for France." Pacific Squadron ships were on more or less permanent duty in Hawaiian waters during the 1830s and 1840s, to discourage French and British actions that might lead to annexation by either nation. Commodore Downes, of the frigate *Constitution,* initiated this extended surveillance in 1832; at the same time, he expressed disapproval of the Hawaiian government's persecution and expulsion of Catholics, pointing out that this was "contrary to the practice of enlightened governments."[36]

British naval forces, commanded by Lord George Paulet, were the first to make an annexation move. During 1842 armed crewmen from Paulet's squadron marched on the royal palace, forced the king to cede the kingdom to Great Britain, hauled down the Hawaiian flag, raised the British flag, and saluted it with twenty-one-gun volleys from ships in the harbor, while a navy band played "God Save the Queen." For five months the Hawaiian archipelago was ruled by a commission of British subjects appointed by Paulet. Commodore Lawrence Kearny, commander of the East India Squadron, protested this cession of the kingdom to Great Britain, from the frigate *Constellation,* anchored in Honolulu harbor. When native leaders visited the *Constellation,* Kearny's crewmen raised the Kingdom of Hawai'i flag on the ship's foremast and "saluted it in good style." It was reported that this incident so enraged Paulet that he warned the Hawaiian monarch not to permit "himself to be saluted in this manner again under any [other] flag than the British Union Jack."[37]

Because of reports by American naval commanders on duty in the Pacific, official American protests were submitted to the British government. President Tyler supported the stance of the navy in Hawaiian waters by declaring that American interests in the islands were paramount and that the United States would oppose the attempt of any nation to appropriate the island kingdom. In effect Tyler extended the Monroe Doctrine to Hawai'i. During July of 1843 British Admiral Richard Thomas reached Honolulu aboard the frigate *Dublin,* restored the Hawaiian flag, and withdrew the British claim of annexation made by Lord Paulet. And on 28 November 1843, French and British officials acknowledged the independence of the Kindgdom of Hawai'i.[38]

But French naval forces continued to harass the Hawaiians, particularly during 1849–50. French consuls lodged petty protests about such matters as the duty charged on French wines and demanded that documents of state, by law required to be in Hawaiian and English, also be published in French, claiming the law favored the Americans and British. They also urged the king to dismiss his ministers of finance and foreign relations. Royal officials found this attempted interference tiresome and charged that the French "welcome every opportunity to elevate small difficulties into diplomatic issues." Braced by the presence of supportive Yankee naval forces in Hawaiian waters, Kamehameha III and his ministers maintained a posture of indifference to French critics.[39]

A second near war confronted the United States when the nation was engaged in the Civil War. France defied the Monroe Doctrine's interdict against foreign ventures in the Western Hemisphere in 1863, when the Emperor Napoleon III of France sent an army to Mexico to install his puppet, Maxmilian of Austria, as emperor. And Queen Isabella II of Spain sent a naval force to the Pacific to recover these former colonies situated on the Pacific's eastern rim. In 1866–67 the United States was in a position to respond to these challenges and its restored military frontier in the Pacific Basin confronted the interlopers, which resulted in the withdrawal of both. During Spain's attempted reconquest, Iberian naval forces cruised off the Chilean and Peruvian coasts, threatening invasions at several points. Chile and Peru declared war on Spain and maintained defensive readiness. Then during 1866 Commodore John Rodgers led a squadron to the troubled zone, pressed the Spaniards to pull back, and sought to mediate the conflict. International diplomatic pressure on Spain led officials in Madrid to "get decently and finally out of the eastern Pacific forever."[40]

The third near war grew out of the navy's assignment to protect the nation's growing interest in Samoa, also called the Navigator

Islands. Excellent anchorages and abundant food supplies there made the islands a popular stop for American whaling and trading fleets. During the United States Exploring Expedition sojourn in Samoan waters, Wilkes concluded a treaty with island chiefs pledging native-government protection of American residents. And he appointed a consul to promote the interests of his nation in the archipelago. Wilkes wrote most favorably of the island of Tutuila and its excellent harbor at Pago Pago. Thereafter American naval vessels on South Pacific assignment routinely called there. In 1872 Commander Richard Meade reached Samoa aboard the *Narragansett*. He negotiated a treaty with Samoan chiefs granting the United States permission to establish a coaling station and naval base at Pago Pago, which the United States Senate failed to ratify. However, six years later the Senate did approve a pact of amity and commerce with Samoa; the agreement included American use of Pago Pago, but not on an exclusive basis. Thereafter the intensification of British and German interests in Samoa and the occupation of these several islands of the archipelago by their nationals led to a serious challenge of the American position there. During March of 1889 seven American, German, and British warships confronted one another in Apia harbor on the Samoan island of Upolu; a major naval battle was averted only by the advent of a hurricane, which destroyed six of the seven warships. This encounter led to a tripartite division of the archipelago, the United States receiving a group of islands that came to be called Eastern Samoa, centering on the island of Tutuila and Pago Pago. Naval officers were assigned the task of governing this American acquisition.[41]

The second actual war in the Pacific Basin involving this military frontier was the Mexican War, 1846–48. American interest in California, fed by the expansive rhetoric of Manifest Destiny, had become a national obsession by the 1840s. However, there existed a very real prospect of preemptive seizure of this northern Mexican province by a European power. The Russian-American Company had recently withdrawn from Ft. Ross in northern California, and Imperial Russia was no longer regarded as a competitor, but Great Britain and France, successful in their Pacific island seizures and each competing for dominion over the Kingdom of Hawai'i, were making threatening moves toward California.

This jeopardized American government schemes for acquiring California, causing officials to order naval commanders in the Pacific to be vigilant for any move on California by either France or Great Britain and to be prepared to take steps to establish "prior claim" for the United States there. During 1842 Commodore Thomas ap Catesby Jones, commanding the Pacific Squadron, learned that a French flotilla had sailed from Valparaíso and was rumored to be bound for the North Pacific, to occupy California ports. Intelligence also revealed that American relations with Mexico had deteriorated and that Mexico was preparing to cede California to Great Britain. Jones rushed his squadron to Monterey, where crewmen occupied the capital of Mexican California and raised the American flag. Shortly thereafter Jones learned that he had acted prematurely. He apologized to Mexican officials and restored the capital to them, but before returning to Callao, he hovered off Monterey for a month to guard against Mexican reprisals against Americans residing there.[42]

Relations between Mexico and the United States worsened, provocative incidents fed the militaristic propensity of both nations, and finally, on 13 May 1846, the United States Congress declared war on Mexico. President James Polk directed Commodore John D. Sloat, commander of the Pacific Squadron, to seize California ports. On 7 July Sloat began the conquest of coastal towns; parties of marines and sailors took Monterey without firing a shot. But ill health forced Sloat to tender command of naval operations along the California coast to Commodore Robert F. Stockton. Stockton's ships and crew linked with and supported the march of a 150-man column, part regulars, part American settlers, commanded by Colonel John C. Frémont. This coordinated land-and-sea campaign resulted in the near-bloodless capture of California towns from San Francisco to San Diego. Naval forces also relieved two American army units trapped by Mexican defenders. A column of one hundred dragoons, commanded by General Stephen Watts Kearny, marching from the Río Grande to the Pacific, was surrounded by a Mexican army in the mountains east of San Diego. Stockton, in control of the port of San Diego, sent a column of marines to drive off the Mexicans and rescue General Kearny and the surviving dragoons. The second rescue mission assigned to

Stockton's marines and sailors was directed at Los Angeles, where the local population contested the small American occupation force and threatened to annihilate it. Stockton's crewmen relieved the beleaguered defenders and restored American rule to the village.[43]

Two American armies in Mexico defeated General Santa Anna's troops and forced a surrender, culminating in the 1848 Treaty of Guadalupe Hidalgo. By its terms Mexico ceded to the United States a vast southwestern territory including California. And an agreement with Great Britian two years earlier acknowledged American title to the territory between forty-two degrees and forty-nine degrees north. These two pacts provided the nation with a face on the Pacific from Puget Sound to San Diego, and brought many changes to the military frontier in the Pacific Basin, including access to several home ports, notably the splendid anchorage at San Francisco. The Pacific Squadron moved its station there from the ports of Callao and Valparaíso, which had sustained it during the formative years. In addition the military frontier provided the government for California until 1850, with army officers occupying the principal positions, naval officers serving in support positions.[44]

During the period 1861–65, for a third time the military frontier in the Pacific Basin became involved in a war, as a peripheral phase of the American Civil War. Naval commanders at the Pacific Squadron's station in San Francisco Bay at the beginning of hostilities received orders from Secretary of the Navy Gideon Welles, via the new transcontinental telegraph, to prevent secessionists from establishing a stronghold in Lower California or elsewhere on the Pacific coast. For most of the war, this fleet of six vessels patrolled the Pacific's eastern rim in compliance with Welles's order.[45]

However, during 1864 the commanders of the *Suwanee* and the *Saranac* were directed to move their vessels into the Pacific's shipping lanes and seek out the *Shenandoah,* commanded by Confederate Lieutenant James Waddell. This raider, constructed in British shipyards, sailed from a port near London during the summer of 1864, bound for the Pacific. In less than a year of action, the *Shenandoah*'s gunners destroyed thirty-eight ships of the American whaling and trading fleets. Waddell eluded Union warships and soon after the close of the Civil War berthed the *Shenandoah* in the Mersey River, England.[46]

The close of the Civil War marked a shift in direction of national interest. From its earliest days, the United States had occupied a position of leadership among the world's seafaring nations and had maintained an extracontinental commitment that included sustained support for maritime industries of the sea with the navy as a protective military arm. After 1865 the interest and energy of the nation's business and political leaders were deflected to interior concerns; much of the capital that had sustained shipbuilding, commerce, whaling, and other maritime enterprises was applied to transportation, mining, lumbering, and other industries being developed in the trans-Missouri West. This diversion of American interest from the Pacific Basin to the continent slowed the momentum of the Americanizing expansion entities at work there. Certainly this included the military frontier. For the remainder of the nineteenth century, excepting the momentary resurgence of Manifest Destiny during the 1890s, the navy-dominated military frontier, although it continued to function in the Pacific Basin, was considerably less significant than it had been before 1865.

The character of this oceanic military frontier slowly changed in the postwar period, due to the application of improvements in marine technology made possible by appropriations supplied by a reluctant Congress. One was the gradual adoption of steam-powered naval vessels, which totally replaced wind-powered warships by the 1880s. Commodore Robert Stockton had been a pioneer advocate of the change. In 1841 he served as adviser for construction of the first steam-powered warship, the *Princeton*. During the 1850s several naval craft, including the *Wabash, Pawnee,* and *Mississippi,* had been equipped with steam engines and boilers below decks and a "full outfit" of masts and sails above. However, ships' hulls were made of oak as late as the 1870s, and ordnance was archaic. Naval commanders complained of "modern armor-belted ships flying the flags of fifth-rate powers whose modern breech-loading cannon could range" American ships with "cast-iron smoothbores and in a matter of minutes reduce . . . their white oak hulls to rubble." Finally in 1884 the *Dolphin* became the first of a group of steel-hulled cruisers, with Commodore George Dewey in command.[47]

Conversion of the American navy to steam power required a constant and reliable supply of coal. The first coal for naval vessels in the Pacific came from the United States, transported in vessels (colliers) that eventually specialized in this function, stockpiling coal at scattered bases and servicing ships afloat. The capacity of these coal-bearing ships gradually was increased from less than two hundred tons to two thousand tons. Naval supply officers stored vast quantities of coal at Mare Island in San Francisco Bay, to service the Pacific fleet. Eventually they also purchased some coal from English and Australian mines.

This shift in power source strengthened the position of political, business, and naval leaders who advocated territorial expansion in the Pacific Basin. A companion need for coaling stations was shared by American mail and passenger steamers traveling from the United States to Australia, China, and other points in the basin. In these times the navy continued its historic function of mapping and charting, adding to its mission the search for locations suitable for coaling stations. And there was the additional assignment of surveying a path for laying the projected Pacific cable to match the Atlantic communications facility linking Europe with the eastern United States, completed in 1866. The Pacific's vastness made necessary the careful selection of island relay stations for the cable system.

The quest for coaling and relay stations began in earnest in 1867. Admiral William Reynolds, in command of the *Lackawanna* at Honolulu, received orders to survey and take possession of a reportedly unclaimed tiny land extrusion called Brook's Island, situated at a point estimated to be halfway between the Hawaiian archipelago and Japan. Reynolds's navigator guided the *Lackawanna* to Brook's Island; Reynolds and most of the crew went ashore and raised the Stars and Stripes on the highest point of land, his gunners fired a salute, and the admiral took possession of the tiny terrestrial speck in the name of the United States, designating it Midway Island. Then "a seine was hauled, a large number of fish caught, and the day spent picnicing." Midway was improved with shore installations and became a strategic haven for ships of the American navy and Pacific Steamship Company.[48]

By approving the 1878 and 1889 Samoan treaties, congressmen added Tutuila to the expanding chain of Pacific Basin stations for the military frontier. And increasingly Yankee naval vessels spent time in Hawaiian waters, as the American interest continued to grow there. On several occasions navy and army officers surveyed island harbors and made the strongest recommendation for American control of Pearl Harbor as a military station. After several rebuffs by the United States Senate, American negotiators concluded a pact, which the Senate ratified in 1887, giving the United States exclusive rights to develop Pearl Harbor.[49]

Thus in spite of the reduced momentum of the American effort in the Pacific Basin between the close of the Civil War and the resurgence of Manifest Destiny, in the late 1890s, naval officers as agents of the military frontier there continued during most of these years to function both as paradiplomats and political administrators of Pacific territories reluctantly annexed by their host government. Their role in treaty negotiations varied from that of direct participants, as in the case of the several Samoan pacts, to that of joint participants or advisers to State Department officials in concluding the Hawaiian treaty of 1887. A conspicuously successful negotiator in this period was Admiral Robert Wilson Shufeldt, no less committed to extending American influence to the far corners of the Pacific Basin than were Captain David Porter, Lieutenant Charles Wilkes, Commodore Matthew Perry, or Admiral Alfred Mahan. Shufeldt passionately desired to make the Pacific an "American sea." In his vision of it, "the Pacific was the ocean bride of America . . . Japan and China were the bridesmaids." He worked assiduously to convince officials in the Department of the Navy and Congress of "the importance of the navy as a pioneer of commerce." And he declared that the merchant marine and navy were "joint apostles for the greatness of the United States." His greatest coup was negotiating a treaty providing for the opening of Korea during the 1880s, with long-term results much like those of the opening of Japan.[50]

Pacific naval officers had served in the California military government in the immediate postconquest period, and they were fully in charge of the colonial government the United States installed in its portion of the Samoan archipelago, following the partitioning in 1889. After the United States purchased Alaska in 1867, army officers governed that North Pacific possession until the army's withdrawal, in the late 1870s. For a period the navy administered Alaska, until a civil government was authorized. And following the Spanish-American War, at the close of the nineteenth century, naval officers performed limited political functions in the Philippine archipelago and were assigned full responsibility for governing the island of Guam.

Throughout the nineteenth century, naval officers produced a corpus of expansionist rhetoric rationalizing their nation's advance across the Pacific. Their memoirs, articles, essays, and books were dominated by Porter's *Journal of a Cruise Made to the Pacific Ocean . . . in the U. S. Frigate "Essex,"* Wilkes's *Narrative of the United States Exploring Expedition,* Perry's *Narrative of the Expedition of an American Squadron to the China Seas and Japan,* Shufeldt's *The Relation of the Navy to the Commerce of the United States,* and Mahan's *The Interest of America in Sea Power, Present and Future.* They urged the reading public and national business and political leaders to maintain the supremacy of the United States in the Pacific Basin by supporting an adequate military presence there and supplying the necessary resources (vessels, manpower, and strategic land bases). Their writings fed the national appetite for collective, if vicarious, adventure; provided essential conscience balm for citizens with qualms about territorial expansion (via force if required); and contributed to the resurgence of Manifest Destiny.

The military frontier closed its century in the Pacific Basin with a rattling, smashing rally. Yankee warships in Hawaiian waters supported the American-haole-dominated annexationist movement during the 1890s. In mid-January 1893, 150 armed crewmen for the USS *Boston* marched on the royal palace in Honolulu to brace the republican force that forced Queen Lili'uokalani to abdicate. Insurgent leaders raised the American flag, declared Hawai'i a protectorate of the United States, and asked for annexation. Presidential reluctance to ratify this joint action by elements of the military frontier and the dominant American haoles resulted in the creation of an independent Republic of Hawai'i (much like the Republic of Texas) that governed the islands until by joint resolution in July 1898, the former island kingdom was annexed to the United States.[51]

American provocation with Spain, largely over events occurring in the Caribbean, precipitated the Spanish-American War of 1898. This involved the Yankee military frontier in the Pacific Basin in its fourth war of the century. Admiral George Dewey, commander of the Asiatic Fleet, learned of the American declaration of war on Spain at Hong Kong. Battle ready, he directed his warships at Spanish territories in the western Pacific. His principal quarry was the Spanish fleet operating from the ancient colonial base of Cavite, in Manila Bay. Dewey's scout vessels found the enemy warships anchored there; the admiral's impetuous thrust and the deadly work of his gunners made short work of the Spanish fleet. Subsequent negotiations between diplomats from the United States and the vanquished Spain resulted in the cession of the Philippines and Guam to the United States. One final expansionist gasp came from the American military frontier before it concluded a century of advance and support of the national interest in the Pacific Basin. During 1899 Commander E. D. Taussig, from the navy gunboat *Bennington,* claimed a remote unclaimed island for the United States—Wake Island.[52]

The military frontier performed those functions common to all American expansion entities, by advancing Yankee economic, cultural, and territorial dominion. It established an American presence in remote regions. It populated those regions, in that retiring naval crewmen often elected to settle in California, the Kingdom of Hawai'i, or Samoa. And when required, this navy-dominated military frontier strengthened American proprietary interests in those distant places, on several occasions resorting to military action to protect them. Its officers also served the nation there in diplomatic and political capacities. And several composed and published eloquent appeals for public support for Pacific expansionism. In addition this military frontier, as an agency of the federal government, articulated with other frontiers to mobilize those nationalizing currents essential for drawing substantial segments of the basin into the national embrace.[53]

Nationalizing Currents and Yankee Frontiers

Intruder nations have used the Pacific Basin for nearly five hundred years as a stage for acting out their imperialist dramas. First came the Spaniards; from 1500 to 1700 they labored to transform it into a Mare Iberium. Colonial partisans of Portugal and Holland nibbled at the western margins of Spain's preserve, but at no time did they pose serious threats to its vast interior. The eighteenth century was Great Britain's era; Englishmen erected what is called the Second British Empire, most of it situated in the Pacific Basin.

The infant United States entered the contest for a share of the bounty in 1784, when the vanguard of its mercantile fleet, the *Empress of China*, anchored in the Pearl River off Canton. It dominated the Pacific Basin during the nineteenth and much of the twentieth century, but not without periodic and at times serious challenge.

Imperial Russian agents from Aleutian and coastal Northwest fur-trade settlements attempted territorial access to the Hawaiian Islands and northern California, before finally retreating. France, consistently assertive in its attempt to build an empire in the Pacific, on several occasions sent naval expeditions from its Society and Marquesas island possessions to menace the Kingdom of Hawai'i and Mexican California. And royal marines from Great Britain's Pacific squadron actually briefly occupied and annexed the Kingdom of Hawai'i to the British Empire.

In the twentieth century, American supremacy in the Pacific Basin has been challenged by locally based rivals. Since 1900 Japan increasingly has competed for first place in the region. Nationalistic assertions of the now autonomous Australia and New Zealand must also be accommodated in United States Pacific policy. And beginning in 1980, a renascent China has faced eastward, indicating a determination to assert itself in Pacific Basin affairs.

In this five-hundred-year period of imperialist adventuring in the Pacific Basin, each intruder nation has followed a scenario of maritime questing for colonial sites in the islands and on the rimland and bringing to bear varying degrees of economic, diplomatic, cultural, and political hegemony. One of the most unique and successful was the expansion formula applied by the United States, consisting of a combination of private and public initiatives, expansion entities formed by clusters of socioeconomic and cultural (largely religious) partisans supported by nationalizing currents.

The irrepressible progression of the American nation from the upper Ohio Valley into the Pacific Basin during the nineteenth century is one of the most intriguing phenomena of recent history. Anglo-American civilization, planted at Jamestown in 1607, required over 150 years to achieve the maturity, strength, and know-how required to sustain itself in the western hinterlands. Then with incredible velocity and sustained momentum, it swept from its seaboard nursery, over the Appalachian barrier, and into the continental interior. By the 1840s Yankee frontiersmen had reached the western shore, then occupied the interstitial lands, and at the same time were transmitting their personal and national interests into the Pacific Basin, by means of the same expansion formula they had tested on the continent.

The vanguard of this expansion formula, the antecedent frontiers, have been presented. There remains to be examined the supporting component of the Yankee expansion formula—nationalizing currents. These were integrating impulses sent out by the national government to protect its adventuring citizens and nourish their interests. In so doing it advanced the national interest. Nationalizing currents gave official character to private actions and legitimated trespass and territorial appropriation. What evolved from the natural combination of these forces was a symbiotic, mutually reciprocal relationship between frontiersmen and their government, the frontiersmen serving as agents, their government serving as patron, to generate essential nationalizing currents that bound the West and eventually much of the Pacific Basin to the nation.

In the period from 1800 to 1828, these currents were refined and regularized. The national government responded to the demands coming from the continental West by acquiring territory, reducing the Indian menace, and adopting laws tailored to western needs. As citizens of territories and states in the federal system, frontiersmen voiced their needs through the ballot, through representatives they elected to advance their interests in Congress, and by petitions for remedy or support of demands to leaders in Washington.

Yankee adventurers carried these same expectations of support from their government into the Pacific Basin and sought the same supportive application of nationalizing currents. The response by their home government was often reluctant, uneven, and never as prompt as in the case of response to the more immediate continental frontier demands. However, the linkage more often than not was eventually established.

The pace of federal response to Pacific Basin–frontier demands during the nineteenth century divides into two periods: 1800–61 and 1866–1900. In both periods because of remoteness, slowness of communication, and noncontiguity with the continental United States (except for the basin's eastern rimland), the rate of federal response was slower than that accorded demands from continental frontiers. But the pioneers in the basin expected the same support their continental counterparts received.

Salient characteristics of the federal response to Pacific Basin demands include a general willingness to support demands more readily in the early than in the later period. This was largely due to generational changes in the national economy. Agrarian and maritime interests dominated the American economy before the Civil War, although each year before 1861 the nation's industrial capability. increased. Much American capital in the period from 1800 to 1861 was drawn to maritime enterprises in which the United States was a world leader: shipbuilding, marine fisheries, commerce (export and import), performing the carrying trade for nations with limited merchant fleets, and whaling.

In addition during the antebellum age American Protestantism, a prime carrier of the American expansion ethic, maintained a strong missionary commitment. Sectarian spokesmen covertly and overtly supported the adoption of those nationalizing currents that enhanced the missionary frontier advance in the Pacific Basin.

However, even during the antebellum period, when petitions for aid were more readily accommodated, deterrents occasionally intruded to arrest the formation of nationalizing currents.

Yankee frontiersmen, by their swift westward advance both on land and sea, regularly created confrontations for their home government, committing it to a policy of remedying frontier problems or filling western needs, including territorial absorption, more often than not before national leaders were ready to respond. Recurring, bitter, divisive issues (western extension of slavery, the punitive impact of protective tariffs on the South, intense competitive striving between emergent eastern industrial interests and entrenched maritime interests for limited capital resources) forced national leaders, even those generally supportive of expansion opportunities, occasionally to devise ideology and policy, in the interest of sectional and partisan peace, that cooled the heat of expansionism.

One ploy conceived by national compromisers during the 1820s, primarily to guard the painfully constructed Missouri Compromise, was the propagation of the doctrine of "National Completeness." It assured the nation's citizens, predominantly agrarian at the time, that situated between the Appalachians and the western border of Missouri they had access to all the land they conceivably would ever require. Thus any American territory beyond Missouri they classed as surplus, a special national province to be used as a military buffer and a settlement zone for colonizing Indians from tribal territories situated east of the Mississippi River.

At best these attempts to curb the westward surge of the American nation for the sake of sectional and special economic interests and partisan peace had only an occasional and temporary restraining effect on the continental frontiers. But each deterrent application also inevitably reached out to impede Pacific Basin frontier formation as well, because it diminished or for a time halted the essential nationalizing support there.

While the confrontational action of Yankee frontiers before 1861 quite often activated nationalizing currents, additional elements were required to achieve the desired response from the national government. These included strong-willed, single-minded individuals with expansive vision, an intense sense of mission for self and nation, and the gift of eloquence and/or literary talent to propagate their extraterritorial goals. Through their public appearances in the eastern United States and through their writings, they worked at overcoming the timidity of the fainthearted, bracing the hesitant and uncommitted, and supplying the rhetorical justification for their nation to fulfill what they conceived to be its mission in the Pacific Basin. They also challenged those deterrents to national expansion that periodically threatened their frontier-created goals.

Advocates began a sustained campaign to draw private and public attention to the promise of national destiny in the Pacific Basin soon after the *Empress of China* reached Canton in 1784. Leading private spokesmen included John Ledyard, Samuel Shaw, John Kendrick, William Shaler, Richard Henry Dana, Hall J. Kelley, Thomas Jefferson Farnham, Thomas O. Larkin, and George Washington Bates.

John Ledyard, an American colonial, had served aboard Captain James Cook's third Pacific expedition in search of the Northwest Passage. Subsequently Ledyard published his *Journal of Captain Cook's Last Voyage to the Pacific Ocean* (1783). He stressed the opportunity for personal fortune in the sea-otter trade on the Northwest Coast in the first treatise on this subject published by an American; it served as a lure for the formation of the Yankee maritime fur-trade frontier there. Ledyard's additional influence in creating an engaging American interest in the Pacific Basin came from a meeting in Paris with American Minister to France Thomas Jefferson. Jefferson added Ledyard's enthusiastic report on the Northwest Coast to his enlarging range of interests; it influenced him as president to support the Lewis and Clark expedition to the Pacific, in 1804.

Major Samuel Shaw, supercargo for the *Empress of China* on its Pacific voyage in 1784, came away from Canton an enthusiastic advocate of commercial expansion to the Pacific Basin's western rimland. He shared this attitude with John Jay, the Confederation government's secretary for the department of foreign affairs, and he composed a message for the American people on trading op-

portunities in the Orient in *The Journal of Major Samuel Shaw.*
Shaw was subsequently appointed consul of the United States at
Canton.

John Kendrick and Robert Gray were pioneer American adventurers in the Pacific Basin, arriving on the Northwest Coast
during 1787 in command of the *Columbia* and *Lady Washington*
to establish the American fur-trade frontier there. While crewmen
filled the holds of their ships with sea-otter pelts for the Canton
market, Kendrick negotiated land-transfer agreements with local
Indian leaders, his intent to establish American settlements on the
Northwest Coast. He was reported to have sent these documents
to Philadelphia for offical filing.

After 1800 the flow of Yankee entrepreneurs into the Pacific
Basin increased substantially. William Shaler, pioneer maritime
merchant and expansionist, was particularly drawn to Spanish
California, where he conducted a profitable, if clandestine, commerce with the isolated mission and lay settlements. In 1808 Shaler
published the *Journal of a Voyage Between China and the Northwest Coast of America Made in 1804,* a commercial report on the
rich maritime trade opportunities there and an appeal for Yankee
appropriation of Spanish California as the advance station to support further American expansion. He assured federal officials that
"the conquest of this country should be absolutely nothing; it
would fall without an effort to the most inconsiderable force."

A well-received, widely read book detailing an adventure in
the Pacific Basin and calling attention to opportunities there came
from the pen of Richard Henry Dana in 1840: *Two Years Before
the Mast.* A crewman aboard a New England trader vessel collecting California cowhides, Dana exulted over the excessive bounty
of this land, "blessed with climate, than there can be no better in
the world. . . . In the hands of an enterprising people, what a
country this might be."

About the same time, another young New Englander, Hall J.
Kelley, was introduced to the Pacific Basin's eastern rimland and
became convinced that it was the seat of American destiny. He
explored the Mexican coast north to San Diego and from there
to the Columbia River region, which he designated the "Pacific
Eden." Kelley became an authority on the subject of the basin's

eastern littoral and worked assiduously for the cause of American occupation of Oregon. He lectured to audiences across New England on the promise of the Oregon Country and stressed the threat of the "iniquitous Hudson's Bay Company" and British power on the Northwest Coast. To strengthen the American position there, Kelley formed the American Society for Encouraging the Settlement of the Oregon Territory and published a pamphlet entitled *A Geographical Sketch of That Part of North America Called Oregon* (1831). And he told listeners and readers that "the time is near at hand, and advancing in the ordinary course of providence, when the Oregon country shall be occupied by enlightened people."

Thomas Jefferson Farnham, a lawyer from Illinois, explored the Northwest Coast, California, and the Kingdom of Hawai'i and wrote two books: *Travels in the Great Western Prairies* and *Life, Adventures and Travels in California.* Concerning California he commented that "no country in the world possesses so fine a climate coupled with so productive a soil. . . . But its miserable people live unconscious of these things. . . . they sleep, and smoke and hum some tune of Castilian laziness, while surrounding Nature is thus inviting them to the noblest rewards of honorable toil."

No advocate of American advance to the Pacific was more devoted than Thomas O. Larkin. Entrenched at Monterey, the capital of Mexican California, he served his nation as United States consul, himself as businessman, and the cause of American expansion as correspondent for several East Coast newspapers, including the New York *Sun,* New York *Herald,* and the *Journal of Commerce.* His journalistic reports from Monterey contained glowing promotional accounts of the opportunities for American enterprise in the Pacific Basin.

Perhaps the most persuasive publication urging American expansion into the Pacific Basin was drafted by George Washington Bates: *Sandwich Island Notes: By a Haole* (1854). Writing after a reconnaissance of the Pacific Basin, he concluded that

> the commerce of the United States is yet in its infancy. It will not be long before such a mighty tide of wealth will roll between California and the Orient as shall render the Pacific the "highway of nations" on

353

a grander scale than the Atlantic is now. California will sit as empress over the Pacific. She will be the great outlet through which America shall send her arts, sciences, Christianity, and civil liberty to the remotest regions of the earth, teaching mankind their universality and unity.

Bates strongly pressed American leaders to proceed with the annexation of the Kingdom of Hawai'i. He pointed out, in his 1854 *Sandwich Island Notes,* that this archipelago was of "vast importance" to the nation; "Less than a century has witnessed the birth and growth of an empire, and brought these fair islands in the once desert waste of the Pacific to be the station and harbor of thronging ships." The lands where formerly the "naked savage roamed amid cocoa-nut groves, and over the slopes of fertile mountains, are inhabited by Americans, and are necessary for American commerce." Bates observed firsthand that the "commercial importance" of Honolulu was increasing daily, and he predicted that "in a short time it will rank only second to San Francisco among the towns of the Pacific." He concluded that "Annexation to the United States would be of definite benefit" for the "protection of American interests already firmly established there." And "once possessed by our government," from these islands "would radiate the blessings and advantages of American civilization over the whole of Polynesian." Above all else, Bates stressed that the nation that controlled the Kingdom of Hawai'i would become master of the Pacific Basin.

These advocates of expanding American hegemony in the Pacific Basin, which would require the application of nationalizing currents by their home government, were on-the-spot observers. But they were joined by supportive voices at home: maritime interests (shipping, import-and-export firms, shipbuilders, whalers), bankers, manufacturers, missionary groups, and other committed institutions and individuals. Most important in this growing coterie of promoters were newspaper editors and journalists, who took up the cry for fulfilling the American mission in that water hemisphere. Several became publicists for the cause, composing the litany of expansion, eloquent rhetoric justifying the American continental and oceanic thrust.

Their collective urging for government support of Yankee economic institutional and cultural, even territorial, imperialism in the Pacific Basin was transmitted through a host of newspapers: on the Atlantic Coast by the Boston *Advocate,* Boston *Evening Mercantile Journal,* Boston *Christian Watchman,* Boston *Patriot,* Boston *Daily Advertiser,* Boston *American Traveler,* Boston *Post,* Boston *Commonwealth,* New Bedford *Mercury,* New Bedford *Whaleman's Shipping List,* New Bedford *Whaleman,* Salem *Gazette,* Fall River *News,* New York *Sailor's Magazine and Naval Journal,* New York *Sun,* New York *Herald,* New York *Journal of Commerce,* and Washington, D.C., *Daily National Intelligencer;* on the Pacific coast by the San Francisco *Alta California;* and in the Kingdom of Hawai'i by the *Honolulu Friend.*

Editors devoted space in these publications to news and commentary about native peoples, cultures, resources, American interests and prospects, and the escalating threat posed by competing imperial nations.

Widely read magazines containing much the same material included the *Niles' Weekly Register,* the *Democratic Review,* and the *Missionary Herald,* an American Board periodical reporting its far-ranging spiritual outreach and the American Christian opportunity for the "great triumph of . . . Christianity in the conversion of Pacific Islanders and Asians." The *Democratic Review,* founded in 1837, must rate as the most ardent of all publications for the cause of American expansion. Its editor John L. O'Sullivan coined the phrase "Manifest Destiny," which galvanized the American nation during the 1840s. He assured readers that much of the world was eager to receive "the blessings of American principles."

Frontiersmen as provocateurs and journalists as ardent spokesmen for American prospects in the Pacific Basin were essential agents in activating nationalizing currents. But Yankee daring and advocacy were of no consequence without national adoption of the causes they promoted.

Public response to appeals from the frontiers was considerably greater during the period before 1861 than after 1865. Most presidents and many congressmen in the first half of the nineteenth century, expansionists themselves, associated these vanguards with the national interest and sought to meet their demands; they often extended themselves to overcome partisan objections to activating nationalizing currents. Notable among supportive presidents before 1861 were Thomas Jefferson, James Monroe, John Quincy Adams, Andrew Jackson, John Tyler, and James K. Polk.

John Ledyard's writings and counsel introduced Jefferson to the American promise in the Pacific that became his enduring interest. Jefferson asked the scientist Andre Michaux, in the course of his planned western scientific reconnaissance, to watch for continental routes between the Mississippi Valley and the Pacific. He entertained the German scientist Alexander von Humboldt in the nation's capital and received a briefing on his Pacific explorations, including those of South Sea waters and the current bearing his name. They exchanged letters, maps, and books on the subjects of Pacific exploration, routes, and resources. And of course he commissioned several transcontinental expeditions to probe the continent's interior for approaches to the western shore: the southwestern expeditions led by Captain Richard Sparks and Zebulon Montgomery Pike; and the northwestern expedition led by Meriwether Lewis and William Clark. Certainly Jefferson's support of the Louisiana Purchase Treaty, which gained for the United States the vast continental interior, provided the nation with a huge leap toward the Pacific. However, the president regarded it as essential to limit the territorial dominion of the United States, in order to prevent the "ruinous diffusion" of its population. Therefore he favored a division of the trans-Missouri West by the creation of a separate nation in the lands between the eventual western boundary of the Louisiana acquisition and the Pacific shore. That new republic, the political child of its Yankee parent, would supply his fellow citizens with a land bridge to Pacific ports for access to the commerce of the Pacific Basin.

James Monroe, secretary of state during the Madison administration and then president, was responsive to American adventurers in far-off places and sought to guard their and the nation's interests in the westward movement. As secretary of state, he pressed for the restoration of American dominion on the Columbia River; as president he and Secretary of State John Quincy Adams drafted and promulgated the so-called Monroe Doctrine, which closed the Western Hemisphere to European, particularly British and Russian, imperialism. This became a valuable support stance for Amer ican interests facing the Pacific Basin, as he noted in his eighth annual message, delivered during December 1824, in which he called for the establishment of a military post at the mouth of the Columbia River to service and protect military ships and commercial vessels.

John Quincy Adams, both as secretary of state and as president, was a constant advocate of the expanding American mission on the continent and in the Pacific Basin, and personally fashioned several significant policies that served the several frontiers there immensely. In conceiving the Monroe Doctrine, he materially contributed to easing the application of nationalizing currents to the continent and beyond. Adams was the primary force in concluding substantive pacts serving the advancing Pacific Basin frontiers in this period. He influenced negotiations with Great Britain during 1818 that resulted in a convention that set the boundary separating the United States and Canada, from the western Great Lakes to the crest of the Rocky Mountains, to be along the forty-ninth parallel and that established joint occupation of the region westward to the Pacific, which reenforced the American claim to the Northwest Coast portion of the Pacific Basin. The next year Adams and Spanish minister Luis de Onís concluded the "Continental Treaty," which included a renunciation by Spain of claim to the territory north of forty-two degrees, which terminated that nation's long-standing presumptive dominion over the Pacific coast above California. Adams also directed events that led to negotiations in 1824 whereby Russian officials accepted fifty-four degrees forty minutes north as the southern extension of Russian America; the following year British and Russian agents signed a treaty containing a similar clause. This Russian-American pact also marked another extension of federal activity, the beginning of American regulation of trade in the Pacific Basin, in that the signatories agreed to ban the sale of arms, ammunition, and liquor in Northwest Coast commerce. Yankees were also granted trading rights with the native peoples of that territory at Sitka and other posts in Russian territory and the use of any Russian port in the North Pacific. In settling questions of boundaries and territorial tenure on the continent and in the Pacific Basin Adams ranks with James K. Polk as the consummate Yankee expansionist.

Andrew Jackson, with all his partisan, sectional, and Indian concerns, was additionally an expansionist and supporter of nationalizing currents. However, by the time of his presidency, sectional and partisan issues were corroding the support process and forcing a less activist response to the demands of frontiersmen. Thus he was never able to preside over his heart's ultimate desire, the reception of the Republic of Texas into the American Union, which would have advanced the American territorial bridge toward the Pacific. However, he was able to serve the cause of expansionism in less dramatic ways, including the appointment of consuls to several Pacific Basin island kingdoms. He added to official knowledge of the Columbia River region under joint occupation, following the British–United States convention of 1818 (renewed in 1828), by sending Confidential Agent William Slacum to survey British activities there. And he commissioned John Charles Frémont to undertake one of his several transcontinental explorations to map additional American territories west of Missouri. In addition Jackson supported the navy's undertaking of a comprehensive reconnaissance of Pacific waters, which eventually led to the United States Exploring Expedition.

Another chief executive most supportive of American expansion was John Tyler, whose accomplishments are unfortunately obscured by the heavy shadow of the hugely expansionist James K. Polk. Tyler courageously pressed for the annexation of the Republic of Texas, stressing to Congress and the public the threat of British designs on it. Succeeding in this effort on the eve of his departure from the White House, he thus added to the land connection toward the Pacific shore. Tyler was enduringly and intensely interested in his nation's place in the Pacific Basin. He regarded it as essential to protect the expanding American interest there in commerce and whaling, which drew his attention to the value of California and the Kingdom of Hawai'i for the nation's future. Thus he pressed American Minister to Mexico Waddy Thompson to use every effort to acquire California by purchase from Mexico; its anchorages would supply the strategic commercial and military stations needed for ready access to the water hemisphere. And to support the growing American establishment in Hawai'i, in the face of threatening British, French, and Russian pressure, Tyler in 1842 issued a policy statement that no nation should seek exclusive commercial or colonial privileges there. He added that American interests were paramount and that the United States would oppose the attempt of any nation to appropriate the island kingdom. In effect the president extended the Monroe Doctrine to Hawai'i.

James K. Polk was elected in 1844, on an expansionist platform, which enabled him to lead the nation in activating essential nationalizing currents to serve both continental and maritime frontiers. From 1845 to 1849, he followed a feverish course of national growth and power. Oregon and California he regarded as essential for fulfilling this commission, and he was determined to acquire them. Polk followed "Manifest Destiny" imperatives and left to others the task of deciding the morality of his policy. His unrelenting obsession carried the boundaries of the United States to the Pacific and opened the door to an expanding American empire.

The sharing of national power and authority through the separation-of-powers principle required that to succeed in their expansionist designs, committed chief executives required the support of men in the legislative branch for policy formulation, passing legislation, treaty ratification, and appropriations to fund westering enterprises. Throughout the first half of the nineteenth century, representatives and senators surfaced to join presidents and often succeeded in turning back opposition to expansion.

John Floyd, congressman from Virginia, was a pioneer in this regard. Throughout the 1820s he urged increasing public support for Yankee frontiers forming on the continent and in the Pacific. He introduced in the House, during 1819, a resolution calling for the appointment of a select committee to consider the question of the United States occupying the Columbia River region. Members approved Floyd's motion, and the Speaker appointed him chairman of the select committee. The committee report submitted the following year advocated that the United States establish a position of strength on the Northwest Coast, to provide "this country the advantage of all its resources, which otherwise must be lost forever." Members of Congress at the time were so absorbed by the vexing problem of the Missouri question and the extension of slavery that they gave short shrift to Floyd's appeal. However, throughout the 1820s the Virginia congressman persisted as an advocate of the cause of Yankee expansion to the Northwest Coast, stressing the competitive threat of British and Russian imperial interests there.

During the 1830s United States Senators Lewis F. Linn and Thomas Hart Benton succeeded Floyd as voices in the Congress urging the adoption of nationalizing currents to support the advancing continental and oceanic frontiers. Linn concentrated his attention on American occupation of the Northwest Coast. He challenged those who argued for "national completeness," claiming that setting the limits of American settlement on the western border of Missouri was unrealistic and would suffocate the pioneers' instinctive expansionist spirit. And he scorned the oft-advanced argument in the halls of Congress that the western mountains formed a fixed national boundary. Senator Benton warned that "national completeness" was public folly; America's destiny, he urged, was to extend to the Pacific shore and beyond. By 1840 he had developed his doctrine of a Yankee commercial highway to China and India, with the territory between Missouri and the Pacific shore to serve as a transcontinental causeway for accommodating the railroad, which would link Atlantic entrepôts with Pacific ports.

William H. Seward of New York succeeded Linn and Benton as the primary advocate in the Senate for an ever-enlarging American presence in the Pacific Basin and of the western frontiers in general. During the 1850s when "Manifest Destiny" had nearly spent itself, that ideology remained paramount for him. Seward continued Benton's cause of expanding American commercial activity in the Far East and supported the transcontinental railway to bind the East and West into a powerful functioning entity, as well as to provide a link with the Orient. Seward maintained an abiding interest in China and Japan; he had deep respect for the energy and diligence of their peoples. As early as 1852, he urged the acquisition of Hawai'i, and following the discovery of gold in California, he exulted in its potential for great national wealth. And he presciently declared that "the Pacific Ocean, its shores, its islands, and the vast regions beyond, will become the chief theater in the world of the great hereafter." Seward is rated a worthy successor to expansionist John Quincy Adams.

Officers assigned to the maritime military frontier also contributed to the activation of nationalizing currents in the Pacific Basin. Duty on Pacific waters was said to stir their "empire building instincts." They observed firsthand the needs of Yankee frontiersmen there and the prospects for enlarging national dominion, influence, and power; by their energetic, even aggressive actions, they confirmed the ancient imperialist maxim that "the flag follows the commerce." Their reports and recommendations to the president and cabinet officers influenced presidential initiatives to respond to frontiersmen's needs with nationalizing currents. Their exploring, charting, mapping, law enforcement, paradiplomacy, and military operations were substantive applications of nationalizing currents.

Whalers, traders, missionaries, miners, and other Yankee frontier groups appealed to their government for several types of support. These included treaties with nations and island kingdoms to guard and enlarge their interests, naval patrols to protect them from natives and competing imperialists, tariff benefits for their products in the American market, resident consuls to adjudicate issues of personal and property rights, ratification of rights to territorial beachheads they had established, and government-sponsored expeditions to chart and map this immense territory. During the first half of the nineteenth century, the most significant and supportive official responses by federal officials, from the president on down through the cabinet and into the Congress, as well as by consuls, envoys, and naval officers acting in a paradiplomatic capacity, were treaties.

Two treaties concluded during the 1840s by American officials answered an appeal from Yankee enclaves in the eastern Pacific and also completed the extension of United States dominion from Puget Sound to San Diego. In 1846 British and American diplomats concluded the Oregon Treaty, which stipulated that the international boundary along the forty-ninth parallel be extended from the Rocky Mountains to the Pacific, ending joint occupation of that vast region and assigning to the United States all territory south of that line. Two years later, by the Treaty of Guadalupe Hidalgo, Mexico ceded to the United States its northern frontier provinces of New Mexico and California. Thereby the United States finally obtained a land connection between Mississippi Valley settlements and ports on the Pacific.

Other treaties concluded during the antebellum period that enhanced American presence in the Pacific Basin and consolidated territorial, commercial, and cultural gains there included a pact with Siam, negotiated by Edmund Roberts in 1833. Lieutenant Charles Wilkes elicited treaties from several Samoan chiefs during 1838, providing for American use of harbors, access to local supplies of water, wood, and provisions for American merchant, whaler, and naval ships, and reception of resident United States consuls. Commodore Matthew C. Perry negotiated the Treaty of Kanagawa with Japanese leaders in 1854, which provided for the opening of Japanese ports to American ships, followed by more comprehensive pacts concluded by Townsend Harris concerning trade, extraterritoriality, and most-favored-nation status. Even before Perry's success, American officials had begun the progressive diplomatic dismantling of Chinese diplomatic and mercantile barriers beyond Canton. During 1844 Commodore Lawrence Kearny and Commissioner Caleb Cushing produced the Treaty of Wanghia, which marked the beginning of what became a pervasive extension of American diplomatic, commercial, and cultural influence throughout China.

In the period before 1861, the federal government transmitted several additional types of nationalizing currents into the Pacific Basin. These took the form of legislation to fund oceanic explorations and navigational improvements, to establish an official American presence there in the form of resident consuls and wide-ranging naval patrols, to provide subsidies for mail carriage and shipbuilding, and to permit favored treatment in the American market of the products gathered from the basin.

Federally sponsored shipping aids included port improvements in harbors from Puget Sound to San Diego, and lighthouses, habor pilots, and drydock installations, first at San Francisco and later at Honolulu. Drydocks made unnecessary the ancient practice of careening a vessel on the beach at low tide to repair hull damage.

Federal officials also subsidized the work of oceanographers, published their works, and disseminated them to the navy and merchant marine. Nathaniel Bowditch and Matthew Fontaine Maury were America's pioneer navigational authorities. Bowditch, a New England astronomer, mathematician, and mariner, published *The Practical Navigator* in 1801, in which he corrected a reported eight thousand errors he found in navigational manuals in use at the time. His work became the standard treatise on navigation and was adopted by the United States Hydrographic Office; it was in use on all naval and merchant ships of the United States, and was translated into at least twelve languages. Maury, a naval officer and oceanographer, made several Pacific cruises before he published *Physical Geography of the Sea* (1855), the first modern textbook on oceanography. His studies of oceanic currents and winds, rendered on charts, brought him international recognition. Subsequently he was appointed head of the United States Naval Observatory and Hydrographic Office. His system for recording oceanographic data was adopted for use by naval and merchant vessels around the world. The research of Bowditch and Maury was of inestimable value to Yankee naval, whaler, and trader-vessel officers ranging the wide Pacific.

The secretary of state supported Pacific mariners by issuing each captain credentials printed in English, Dutch, Spanish, Portuguese, and French, and bearing the great seal of the United States. The documents declared the bearer to be engaged in legitimate business, with the approval of the American government.

Congress appropriated funds supporting several official, wide-ranging expeditions to the Pacific Basin. As noted earlier, the most significant of the antebellum Pacific reconnaissances was the four-year United States Exploring Expedition, commanded by Lieutenant Charles Wilkes. Wilkes directed his crewmen in pervasive astronomical, geological, flora, fauna, and ethnic researches, charting and mapping much of the basin and discovering a continent. As a carrier of nationalizing currents, Wilkes negotiated amity and trade treaties with island chiefs, appointed consuls in several settlements, and established extraterritorial courts for the application of American law to his countrymen held locally for trial.

Consuls were the principal resident officials who established legal American presence at several points in the Pacific Basin during the antebellum period. The first Yankee consul was assigned to the Chinese port of Canton, soon after the advent of the *Empress of China*. As American interests in the Pacific Basin expanded, the United States government designated consular stations at Papeete, Concepción, San Diego, Honolulu, Monterey, Valparaíso, Callao, Bay of Islands (New Zealand), and Batavia (Java). The consul's functions included protection of American rights and property, holding deserters in local jails for restoration to ships' crews, lodging claims for damages against local governments, settling claims for destruction to local property due to American seamen on shore leave, advising his government of the state of political affairs and conditions in his jurisdiction, and serving as judge in the local extraterritorial court.

One nationalizing current persistently sought by partisans of the Yankee maritime frontiers was American annexation of certain Pacific Basin territories. Naval observers such as Charles Wilkes and Matthew Perry repeatedly urged national leaders to extend American dominion to Formosa and islands in the Navigator, Bonin, Marquesa, and Hawaiian archipelagoes, in order to re-enforce the increasing Yankee presence in the Pacific Basin. Officials in Washington, D.C., gave support to the Kingdom of Hawai'i as an extracontinental acquisition. President John Tyler took the first step in this direction by extending the Monroe Doctrine to the archipelago and declaring the primacy of United States interests there. Congress made the most serious antebellum gesture for annexation during 1852, with members of both houses offering resolutions of support for absorbing the Hawaiian kingdom. This move was influenced by the recent acquisition of California and a large portion of the Northwest Coast, congressional rationale being that the Hawaiian Islands were required to protect this new territory and to assure the preeminence of American commerce with Asia.

A most convincing manifestation of national support to adventurers in the Pacific Basin came from actions by the maritime military frontier. Naval craft patrolled Pacific waters, ships' batteries charged and ready. Gunnery officers ordered crewmen to shell island villages harboring natives in arrears to American traders, and heavily armed marines regularly stormed beaches to rescue missionaries consigned to cannibal feasts. Naval commanders were ever vigilant for intrusions by British, French, Russian, and Spanish expeditions bent on threatening their nation's enlarging interest in the Pacific Basin. American naval forces were largely responsible for opening China to Yankee traders and missionaries beyond the confines of the commercial compound at Canton after 1840, and for opening Japan after 1854. In addition the navy waged successful combat on Pacific waters against Great Britain during the War of 1812 and against Mexico during the 1846–48 Mexican War.

But the 1860s marked the beginning of a change in national attitude toward America's role in the Pacific Basin. Subduing the Confederacy and imposing Reconstruction on the vanquished states absorbed the Union's energy from 1861 until the mid-1870s. At the same time, an aggressive preoccupation was growing with national territory situated between Missouri and the Pacific shore. This near obsessive civic fascination with the continental West produced bonanza successes in mining, lumbering, ranching, and farming. In addition pervasive applications of communication and transportation (railroad) technology integrated this vast colonial preserve into national life. Collateral responses included demographic expansion, urbanization, and state making, so that by 1900 Congress had admitted all but four of the contiguous trans-Mississippi territories to the Union (the exceptions were New Mexico, Arizona, Oklahoma, and Indian Territory).

These developments caused the Yankee maritime frontiers to suffer a corresponding decline in support. No longer did Pacific Basin adventurers enjoy easy access to American capital to fund their shipbuilding, fleet maintenance, mercantile, whaling, and other enterprises, as eastern financiers increasingly applied their capital to developing the adjacent continent. In this postbellum age, maritime frontiers persisted, but their pace of expansion lessened. And when after 1861 they did occasionally catch the public fancy, they were confronted with increasingly powerful deterrents at home, where the shift in private and public interest and support from maritime to land-based development also generated a restrictive, continental-bound mentality and a strong isolationist stance. The purchase of Alaska in 1867 was widely derided by the public as Secretary of State William Seward's folly.

In addition to capital deprivation and diminishing national support, these oceanic vanguards of American expansion were also challenged by technological change. Yankees lagged in applying marine technological innovations. Sails of American civil and naval craft had whitened the Pacific during the first sixty years of the nineteenth century. Soon after 1830 American shipbuilders produced the majestic clipper, a sailing craft that immediately revolutionized ocean transportation. These incomparable "greyhounds of the sea" became paramount in the carrying trade; Yankee clippers almost exclusively made up the "tea fleet" supplying Great Britain. With favorable winds the clipper raced from Boston to San Francisco in ninety days, halving the time spent by traditional sailing vessels. However, contemporaneous with the introduction of the clipper ship came the application of steam power to maritime craft. Shipping interests in Great Britain, France, Holland, and other maritime nations promptly adopted this mode for powering their fleets. American shippers, mesmerized by the indisputable grace of line and time advantage of the clipper, failed to respond before 1861 to the steam imperative except for limited Atlantic, Gulf, and Pacific-coast mail and passenger service. After the Civil War, when American shippers returned to the Pacific Basin, they faced a disadvantage competing with steam-powered British, Dutch, and French fleets, so that for the remainder of the century they were unable to recover their favored antebellum carrying-trade status.

Yankees after 1865 also faced enhanced competition. Accelerated expansionist activity by Great Britain and France nearly completed imperialist appropriation of the insular Pacific. Great Britain had absorbed the Fiji Island kingdom, a large segment of New Guinea, the Solomons, and islands in the Samoan archipelago. France had occupied New Caledonia and, with Great Britain, shared dominion over the New Hebrides. This accelerated activity produced a decline in the margin of Yankee trade dominance in island and Asian mainland ports from perhaps 20 percent to 10 percent or less of the nation's volume of international commerce. American preeminence in the Pacific Basin was additionally diminished by the arrival of Germany, which attempted to appropriate holdings and challenge entrenched imperialist tenants. And the seed had been planted for the rise in Asia of a serious rival to the United States and all other intruders. By 1890, through conquest and trade, Japanese expansionists were prepared to establish their nation's place in the basin.

Before the late 1880s, the United States had followed a different practice in achieving its preeminent position in the Pacific. Yankee adventurers had implanted themselves on islands and rimland throughout the basin, applying intensive economic and cultural pressure at each point. However, their national government failed to take the additional step of absorption, except to complete its contiguous territory between Canada and Mexico and to annex certain guano-bearing atolls. In the Kingdom of Hawai'i, where its missionary, trader, agrarian, and military frontiers had established overriding personal and public interests, a state of quasi-absorption existed through the application of the Monroe Doctrine by President Tyler. But having gained most-favored-nation status from various island and mainland nations, along with concessions for its aggressive missionary frontier, the United States had enabled its citizens' frontier enterprises to prosper without the necessity of annexing additional territory. Thus the nation avoided those problems endemic in managing a colonial empire. Certainly its frontier partisans, their competitive sensibilities stirred by the progressive seizure of islands and mainland territories by competing imperial nations, urged annexation. But the United States government consistently refused to meet this request, content to rely on economic and cultural imperialism as the foundation of its power in the Pacific Basin.

Another factor that limited the force of Pacific Basin frontiers and diminished the response of nationalizing currents after 1861 was the reduction in the number of Pacific Basin advocates, both public and private. Many changed their focus and interest, joining the rush to participate in the continental development which so absorbed postbellum America. And there were those who believed that their nation, having acquired a commanding stretch of the eastern Pacific Basin, from Puget Sound to San Diego, had achieved enough territorial goals. Now it was time to attend to the thorough Americanization of this vast continental heartland, connected in 1869 by a transcontinental railroad to ports on the Pacific Basin.

Notwithstanding slackened support and enlarging deterrents, several Yankee frontiers (mercantile, missionary, mining, agrarian, and military) continued to function in the Pacific Basin after 1861, and occasionally each received at least limited support from the government. Spokesmen for the military frontier stressed the increasing need for improved maritime communications and additional, dispersed sites for stations and bases, both crucial. Already the navy included several steam-powered vessels in its Pacific fleet; naval policy called for total conversion to steam as appropriations permitted.

During 1866 private interests with charters and subsidies from the national government to support mail and passenger service on trans-Pacific steamships also pressed for the selection of coaling stations at intermediate locations between San Francisco, Australia, and the basin's western rimland. Cable communication officials joined them and naval spokesmen in the appeal for support for their enterprises. Technicians completed the Atlantic cable during 1866, connecting European and Atlantic coastal cities. Two moves were also made early in the postbellum period to establish rapid communication across the Pacific Basin. Naval expeditions occupied Midway and Wake islands, each designated a coaling station and cable-relay point. And field-workers for the Western Union Telegraph expedition surveyed a proposed line across Alaska with a cable connection under Bering Strait to Siberia. After two years of uncommon hardship and difficulties in determining a suitable route, as well as following the successful laying of Cyrus Field's Atlantic cable, this venture was abandoned.

Transportation-industry managers had used oceangoing, steam-powered vessels only to a limited extent for mail and passenger service until 1867. During the antebellum period, they restricted steam vessels, except on inland waterways, to passage from Atlantic and Gulf ports to the Isthmus of Panama. Passengers and mail moved to the Pacific side of the isthmus in dugouts and on muleback until the mid-1850s, when a railway connected the two sides. Coastal steamers carried passengers and mail from the Pacific side of the isthmus to San Diego and San Francisco. In addition Yankees used steamers during this time on the rivers of China, to penetrate interior trader territories, and for coastal shipping on the basin's eastern rimland. In 1865 Congress chartered the American Mail Steamship Company with a subsidy of five hundred thousand dollars in 1865; two years later ships of this line provided mail and passenger service between San Francisco and Honolulu. Shortly thereafter American steamers ventued to Australia, New Zealand, and China, which led to demands for coaling stations at Pago Pago, on the island of Tutuila in Samoa, and other remote archipelagoes.

American naval spokesmen had urged their government to secure the anchorage at Pago Pago, both as a coaling station and as a general-purpose naval base. A treaty with Samoan chiefs in 1879 granted Yankees the use of Pago Pago as a coaling station. Competition for dominion over the Samoan archipelago, involving Great Britain, Germany, and the United States, culminated during 1889 in a tripartite division of these islands; Americans were confirmed in their choice of Tutuila. Ten years later Great Britain withdrew from the arrangement, leaving Germany holding the western islands, the United States the eastern islands. A year later Samoan leaders ceded Tutuila and adjacent islands to the United States. Not until 1929 did Congress formally accept this grant, although during the intervening years United States authority was maintained by naval officers.

Another instance during this period of a limited response to strengthen American transportation and communications in the Pacific Basin was the support of surveys to plot possible Isthmus of Panama canal routes. Interest in this enterprise quickened after the completion of the Suez Canal in 1869.

Rather general postbellum public and private indifference substantially reduced the flow of nationalizing currents to the expectant frontiers there, particularly those that would require the acquisition of territory. A surprising exception occurred in 1867. Secretary of State William Seward learned that Russian-American Company managers and imperial court officials were ready to dispose of their northern colony, and during 1867 he concluded a treaty providing for the transfer of Russian America to the United

States in return for the payment of $7,200,000. The treaty also changed the name of the northern territory to Alaska. His position was that by this negotiation his nation acquired "an outpost to control the North Pacific and upper latitude trade routes to China and Japan" that would overcome the British advantage due to West Coast Canadian ports. This action added almost six hundred thousand square miles to the country's land area, a territory one-fifth the size of the contiguous continental United States.

In this period of uneven national response to American interests in the Pacific Basin, the military frontier played a double role; besides being an identifiable frontier, as it had been from its advent in the Pacific early in the century, it also provided certain essential nationalizing currents. From its scattered stations and cruising warships, the Pacific fleet provided a continuing military presence. Naval forces occupied Pago Pago, establishing a strong position there. Besides continuing the survey and mapping of the basin's waters, islands, and rimland and preparing navigational charts, wide-ranging naval patrols still forced the payment of delinquent islanders' debts to American traders, rescued missionaries, and patrolled the Chinese coast and rivers, guarding mission stations and thwarting pirate attacks on American shipping. Naval commanders continued to watch for blackbirding ships, negotiated treaties for their government with Korean officials, and served as the government of American Samoa and, at times, Alaska.

The agrarian, maritime, trading, mining, and missionary frontiers functioning in the Pacific Basin also occasionally received national attention during the period 1866–90. Americans controlled most of the Kingdom of Hawai'i's arable land and exercised a pervasive influence over its royal government. Increasingly these agrarian pioneers followed a monocrop strategy of sugarcane produced on large plantations worked by Chinese, Japanese, Portuguese, and Filipino contract laborers. The planters, dependent on the American mainland for marketing their product, sought through negotiations with Hawaiian court officials a reciprocity treaty granting favored tariff treatment there. Several times after 1866 the Hawaiian reciprocity treaty came up for consideration by the United States Senate, but sustained opposition from mainland sugar growers and refiners repeatedly dashed the pact. In 1876 the Senate finally ratified the reciprocity treaty.

In this period the mining frontier slowly entered newly acquired Alaska, testing modest placers in streams draining the southeastern panhandle. Each year saw an increased civil government. The final burst of the Yankee mining frontier, a massive demographic stampede to the riches of the Klondike, occurred late in the century, a flamboyant accompaniment to renascent Manifest Destiny.

The missionary frontier fared better than other expansion entities in the Pacific Basin during this period, largely because of the increased interest of home denominations in foreign missions, reflected in increased funding and more workers to staff mission churches, schools, and clinics. Presbyterian, Mormon, Baptist, Methodist, Disciples of Christ, Episcopal, Seventh Day Adventist, and American-supported Roman Catholic missionaries scattered over a widening territory of islands and rimland in their quest for so-called "heathens." Presbyterian workers in Alaska were met by Russian Orthodox clergy, who stayed on after the Russian-American Company exodus. Missionaries enlarged their outreach in China by treaty stipulation permitting additional compounds in the interior. They attended treaty negotiations between American and Chinese officials as interpreters, which placed them in the position to have their plans included in treaty texts. Many Chinese youth, content with ancient Confucianist, Taoist, and Buddhist teachings, but seeking alternatives to anachronistic traditional secular education, enrolled at the mission schools because the curriculum included, besides biblical and sectarian subjects, instruction in Western political philosophy and science. Japanese officials overtly opposed missionaries, and at one time the imperial government promulgated an order banning the practice of Christianity. Many missionaries working the islands and western rim of the basin were intensely evangelical and advocated the extension of American dominion to these lands.

The nineteenth century was the pioneer period for Yankee frontiers in the Pacific Basin. Their energetic collective performance had established an enduring American presence and a potentially overpowering dominion. Until 1861 these frontiers flourished, in part because of generally sustained support from their national government. The vitality of their economic and cultural imperialist efforts declined during the postbellum age, largely due to the diversion of national interest to the consummation of continental development. As the nineteenth century reached its final decade, and the Pacific Basin frontiers came to the end of their pioneer epoch, however, there occurred at home a renaissance of public and private interest in extracontinental matters. This phenomenon, in its mature form taking on many of the attributes of the chauvinistic 1840s' Manifest Destiny, was a synthesis of diverse intellectual streams: Social Darwinism, Christian imperialism, Anglo-Saxon genetic and institutional superiority, and Kipling lyrics. These were compounded by national economic imperatives.

Charles Darwin and Herbert Spencer transformed contemporary concepts of humans and nature by their writings and lectures on the revolutionary doctrines of natural selection and the survival of the fittest. Intellectuals appropriated these scientific theories and by analogy applied them to humankind, society, and institutions, yielding revolutionary challenges to established views in a body of doctrine called Social Darwinism.

Four men between 1885 and 1890 loom as preeminent propagators of Social Darwinism and as the most responsible for the renewal of public and private interest in and support of Yankee frontiers in the Pacific Basin. John Fiske, a leading New England intellectual, writer, and lecturer, was strongly influenced by Darwinian thought, which he skillfully melded into a resurrected Manifest Destiny. His *American Political Ideas* (1885) contained an essay that nicely supported the goals of Pacific Basin frontiers. It assured Americans, as an Anglo-Saxon people, of their imperial destiny to go forth into the Pacific, among other regions, and transform the unenlightened and unworthy, if they could endure the Darwinian test of "survival of the fit."

Josian Strong, a Congregational minister and writer and also a proponent of Social Darwinism, added Christian imperialism to his doctrine of national mission. In *Our Country* (1885) he counseled Americans that they were a chosen people, with the demanding duty of fulfilling a cosmic destiny. He stressed that American institutions were superior and destined to be disseminated throughout the world. In this book, in other writings, and from the pulpit he thundered the call to fellow citizens to fulfill their destiny, do their duty, and be blessed in the "Imperialism of righteousness."

A third populizer of Social Darwinism as a rationale for national expansion was John W. Burgess, a Columbia University professor of political science. He wrote in *Comparative Constitutional Law* that of the world's races, only Teutons (including Americans) "had talent for the highest order." They were called to carry their illuminating institutions to the outer world, dark and barbarous, to transform the unfortunate and deprived with the illuminating force of American ways, and to assume colonial sovereignty over them.

Yet another potent generator of support for the cause of resuscitating Yankee imperialism came from the pen of the combative Englishman Rudyard Kipling. In 1889 he published a poem entitled "The White Man's Burden," which became the credo of late-nineteenth-century chauvinists:

> Take up the White Man's burden
> Send forth the best ye breed
> Go bind your sons to exile
> To serve your captive's need; . . .

This expansionist rhetoric attracted many powerful disciples. Admiral Alfred Thayer Mahan, a pioneer advocate of Pacific expansion for naval stations and coaling bases, added the essence of Social Darwinism to his writings and lectures during the 1890s. And he appropriated another concept of science—life stages of an organism and the inevitability of its progression from birth to youth, maturity, old age, and death. In his analogy of the life of the nation, it progressed from infancy on the Atlantic seaboard to youth in the Mississippi Valley and incipient maturity on the Pacific shore. He and his followers observed that the nation following the Civil War had turned its attention "inward" to continental development; as fulfillment of the maturity stage, it was time the nation returned "to the sea." Continuing the organic image, Mahan warned that failure to accomplish the essentials of territorial absorption in the Pacific Basin would "stunt" national growth in competition with European nations.

Influential Americans were drawn to these rhetorical challenges. They included William Allen White, Brooks Adams, and Henry Adams. White, editor of the Emporia, Kansas *Gazette*, foresaw a resurgence of American Manifest Destiny in the Pacific. Brooks Adams and Henry Adams both joined in urging their fellow citizens to establish "superior" Anglo-Saxon civilization and religion in the Pacific Basin. And they pointed to the danger facing struggling American interests in the face of aggressive Germany, perennially threatening Great Britain and France, as well as the upstart Japan.

The new doctrine and its warm support by men of wealth, influence, and power did not go unnoticed by politicians. Prime formulators of American international policy during the late 1890s were Theodore Roosevelt, Henry Cabot Lodge, O. H. Platt, and Albert Beveridge. Their advocacy of American extraterritorial extension bore the imprint of Social Darwinism and the teachings of Fiske, Strong, and Burgess.

Several domestic conditions surfacing during the 1890s further enhanced the appeal of expansionism. One concerned the "frontier," which to most nineteenth-century Americans meant wilderness territory in the continental West between the Mississippi Valley and the Pacific shore, an "unpopulated," naturally rich region where an individual could by initiative and hard work exploit its bounty and achieve material success. The public at that time had not accepted the Pacific Basin as constituting a "frontier" in this sense. In 1890 the United States superintendent of the census announced that because Americans had so completely populated the West to the Pacific shore, the "frontier" no longer existed. The force and near sacredness of the frontier to nineteenth-century Americans is incalculable; it was fortuitous that at this juncture, when this long-standing source of hope and opportunity of the individual had ceased to exist, there was a new frontier beyond the western shore—the Pacific Basin.

Another condition that aided the cause for resuscitating American expansion into the Pacific Basin was the economy. It had undergone phenomenal expansion since 1866. Factories produced textiles, leather and metal goods, and machinery at a rate its domestic consumer community could not absorb. Periodic depressions plagued industry. Industrial competition and market restrictions limited American access to European markets. Therefore businessmen looked to the Pacific Basin, and particularly the millions on its western rim, as a market solution.

Specific expansionist goals began to materialize soon after 1890. Yankee imperialists gave much attention to the Kingdom of Hawai'i. During 1893 resident Yankees, following the Texas model, took the extreme step of leading a successful revolt, forcing out the Hawaiian monarch Queen Lili'uokalani, forming a constitutional republic, and asking for annexation to the United States. They were rebuffed by the Democratic administration of Grover Cleveland (1893–1897), who became convinced that the United States had intervened illegally with the support of American naval forces to topple the monarchy. But in 1898 the Republican administration of William McKinley granted the request of the annexationists. Again as in the case of Texas, annexation was achieved by a joint resolution of Congress.

But there were counterarguments to expansion. One repeated the claim of "national completeness": that the nation already had sufficient territory within its continental limits to meet all foreseeable land needs of its citizens. Accompanying this claim was an articulate isolationist trend. Interestingly the major political parties had switched positions on support of territorial expansion. The Democratic party, ardent protagonist of Manifest Destiny in the antebellum age, increasingly took on an isolationist stance in the latter part of the century, and the Republican party, pre–Civil War opponent of expansion, became the supporter of reconstituted Manifest Destiny.

Isolationists also pointed to distance as a compelling reason for avoiding imperial commitment. They claimed that Hawai'i, situated nearly twenty-five hundred miles west of San Francisco, would weaken American defenses. Annexation was "national folly."

Several continental agricultural interests, including sugar, tobacco, and cotton producers, regarded Pacific Basin enterprises as threateningly competitive, and their spokesmen opposed any form of territorial extension there. Those sensitive to domestic racial problems opposed the extension of American dominion into the Pacific because of its diverse peoples and cultures, fearing that such expansion would only exacerbate domestic racial problems. Outright racists expressed alarm over the prospect of the Japanese "Yellow Peril" and any imperial policy that might lead to further Asian immigration to America.

Organized labor, through the Knights of Labor and the American Federation of Labor (AFL), also opposed the annexation of Hawai'i and other parts of the Pacific Basin. Leaders claimed that annexation would result in increased competition for employment and lower wages for American workers. AFL president Samuel Gompers warned that absorption of Pacific territories would lead to a weakening of the American labor force.

By 1898 adventuring in the Pacific Basin had become a national passion. In June of that year the Boston banker Gamaliel Bradford convened a meeting to counter it, which led to the formation of the Anti-Imperialist League, a national organization committed to uniting those opposed to expansion. Chapters of the league in major cities mounted a nationwide program to combat expansionism. Through newspaper and periodical articles, speeches, and support of candidates and issues opposed to territorial extension, the league concentrated on the theme that imperialism was un-American, that it was "unbecoming of a democratic nation" to thrust itself on colonial peoples, and that there was no demonstrated economic or other need for Pacific Basin territories. League power was manifested in elections, where isolationist candidates won seats in legislatures and Congress, and in the diversion of public-policy formulation away from a certain expansionist course.

The year 1898 was a time of fruition for many of the expansionists' colonial goals. A quick victory in the war with Spain brought to the United States increased prestige in the Pacific Basin and an increment of extracontinental territory—the island of Guam and the Philippine archipelago. American naval forces also occupied tiny Wake Island. And in the same year, striking while the iron of victory still glowed, imperialists were successful in gaining the annexation of Hawai'i.

It was fitting that the American pioneer century in the Pacific Basin closed with such an enhancement of frontier goals. But except for annexing the eastern rimland territories of California, Oregon, and Washington; acquiring Alaska; and absorbing guano-bearing atolls and Midway Island, the national government had denied expansion entities' regular appeals for the absorption of additional Pacific territory. Only in the closing years of the century did the United States add territorial expansion to its economic and cultural imperialism, completing the Americanization trilogy long sought by Yankee frontier advocates.

America's heady successes in the Pacific Basin in the 1890s confirmed the international maturation of the nation. As the twentieth century opened, one official observed that the United States finally had to face the problem it had so long avoided, that of managing a colonial empire. It became necessarily committed to an increasingly complicated set of policies, enlarged responsibilities, and ever-escalating involvement in the Pacific Basin, extending well into the twentieth century.

Before concluding with an analysis of the inheritance bequeathed by Pacific Basin frontiers, it would be well to examine one last frontier that has maintained a powerful survival to the present day—the literary frontier. It, no less than the mining, maritime trader, missionary, military, and agrarian frontiers, drew Yankees and their culture into the Pacific Basin, enhancing its Americanization.

CHAPTER SIXTEEN

Writers as Pioneers

John S. Whitehead

While America's nationalizing interest in the Pacific waxed and waned in the nineteenth century, reaching a final climax in 1898, national imagination and passion for the Pacific as a literary frontier remained strong throughout that century and advanced vigorously into the twentieth century. While anti-imperialist political sentiments limited further territorial acquisitions after 1898, the literary muse of the Pacific, with its hedonistic themes of physical beauty, leisure, and sexual freedom, maintained a firm hold on the American mind and continued to draw Americans into the South Seas. While the maritime, whaling, and missionary frontiers had lost much of their vigor by 1898, the literary frontier remained vital. It was the most lasting link to the Pacific, as the nation's continental economic and political interests displaced the older maritime and commercial links to the Far East. The literary frontier was in many ways the most lasting and significant of all the Pacific Basin frontiers.

In the nineteenth century, the lure of paradise in literature emerged as a constant foil and escape from the increasing commercialization and industrialization of America. While it served as an escape, this frontier also functioned as an extension of the American mainland, reflecting the tensions and anxieties of American society at any given time as much as it did life in paradise. At times the description of hedonism motivated missionaries and other would-be civilizing agents to head for the Pacific. More often the literature decried the spoliation rather than the salvation of paradise due to the encroachments of both Americans and Europeans.[1]

An informal American literary tradition proclaiming the discovery of paradise began with the writings and letters of American sailors and explorers in the late eighteenth and early nineteenth centuries. Its espousal by professional men of letters blossomed with the writings of Herman Melville in the 1840s. Mark Twain advanced the tradition in the 1860s and was joined in the later decades of the century by Charles Warren Stoddard and Henry Adams, who turned his historical muse to the Pacific after writing the history of the United States.

As the twentieth century dawned, Jack London kept the tradition alive with tales of paradise and of a darker, threatening side of the Pacific in such locations as the Solomon Islands, where Americans would later experience death and hardship during the Second World War. London was followed by other American writers after World War I. Two American pilots who had served in the war, Charles Nordhoff and James Norman Hall, moved to Tahiti in the 1920s, where they rediscoverd the 1792 South Seas journal of Captain William Bligh and transformed it into their *Bounty Trilogy,* published in the 1930s. After World War II, James Michener kept the genre thriving, first with his 1947 *Tales of the South Pacific,* and later with *Hawaii,* in 1959, the first of his mammoth historical novels. As much as any other influence, the literary frontier maintained American interest in the Pacific and helped lead to the eventual Americanization of Hawai'i and its admission as the nation's fiftieth state in 1959, certainly the most lasting symbol of American presence in the Pacific.[2]

The Pacific as a literary setting was not a Yankee invention; Americans blended and adapted the theme of paradise first proclaimed by European explorers and writers. As was the case in other Pacific frontiers, Americans eventually came to dominate the literary frontier. Although accounts of the Pacific date to the sixteenth-century journals of Ferdinand Magellan, Sir Richard Hawkins, and other explorers, the first literary embodiment of the South Seas appeared in 1719, with the publication of Daniel Defoe's *The Life and Strange Surprizing Adventures of Robinson Crusoe.* But Defoe's saga did not proclaim the paradise that would make the Pacific famous. That image surfaced in the latter half of the eighteenth century, shortly after Jean Jacques Rousseau's vision of the noble savage sent Europeans questing for the land these idyllic primitives inhabited.

Rousseau announced his vision in his 1754–55 "Discourse of Inequality." Little more than a decade later, the longed-for paradise was found, when the English captain Samuel Wallis discovered the island of Tahiti in June 1767. Eight months later the French explorer Louis Antoine de Bougainville followed Wallis there and proclaimed paradise to the world in his *A Voyage Round the World*, published in 1772. So enchanted was Bougainville with his discovery that he also called Tahiti "The New Cytherea," after the island where Aphrodite rose from the sea. Bougainville and his crew were first impressed with the physical beauty of the land; but what truly overwhelmed the Frenchman was the immediate invasion of his ships by Tahitian women, accompanied by their fathers and brothers, who immediately offered the sexual pleasures of their sisters and daughters to the Europeans. Bougainville described the sight of a young girl who came on board and "carelessly dropped the cloth, which covered her." According to the captain the girl "appeared to the eyes of all beholders, such as Venus showed herself to the Phrygian shepherd, having, indeed, the celestial form of that goddess. Both sailors and soldiers endeavored to come to the hatchway."[3]

Sexual pleasure was not the only allure of Tahiti. Daily life on the island seemed free of so many of the strains and constraints of Western civilization. Stealing and theft, according to Bougainville, were not common among the Tahitians, though a curiosity about European goods sometimes caused items from the ships to disappear. "Nothing is shut up in their houses," the captain explained, "every piece of furniture lies on the ground, or is hung up, without being under locks or under any person's care." As Bougainville described a walk through the island, the theme of Eden emerged over and over again:

> We crossed a turf, covered with fine fruit trees, and intersected by little rivulets, which keep up a pleasant coolness in the air . . . A numerous people there enjoy the blessings which nature showers liberally down upon them. We found companies of men and women sitting under the shade of their fruit trees: they all greeted us with signs of friendship: those who met us upon the road stood aside to let us pass by; everywhere we found hospitality, ease, innocent joy, and every appearance of happiness amongst them.[4]

Rousseau's world was alive.

Bougainville's paradise reached a receptive audience in Europe, where exotic travel literature was popular. His findings were quickly confirmed by others. In 1769 Captain James Cook arrived in Tahiti, on the first of his three Pacific voyages. The officers' journals and logs of this voyage, along with the records of Wallis's earlier Tahitian discovery, were edited and given a narrative form in 1773 by the widely read English writer John Hawkesworth. Some Protestant readers in England, particularly those under the Methodist influence of John Wesley, saw the sexual freedom that so attracted Bougainville as unacceptable promiscuity and concluded that Tahiti was in need of the restraining force of western civilization. Whatever the reaction, Hawkesworth's narrative and the ensuing volumes on Cook's subsequent voyages were best-sellers that brought substantial monetary return to the authors and publishers. Even before the commercial opportunities of fur trading and whaling became evident, literature about the South Seas paradise was one of the most profitable products brought back from the Pacific.[5]

Cook's third voyage (1776–79), in which he discovered Hawai'i, or the Sandwich Islands (as he named them), provided the opportunity for Yankee entrance into the literary frontier. John Ledyard, an American sailor serving on Cook's ship, the *Resolution*, capitalized on the four-year lag between the final return of Cook's ship in 1780 and the publication of the official account. In 1783 Ledyard's *Journal of Captain Cook's Last Voyage to the Pacific Ocean* appeared in Hartford, Connecticut. The American marine's primary goal was to publicize the sea-otter pelts he discovered in Nootka Sound, which fetched such a high price in Canton and Macao. Although Ledyard's commercial rhetoric was less idyllic than Bougainville's, the American portrayed his stay in Hawai'i in positive tones, despite the death of Cook there. American readers gained the sense of a hospitable island with friendly inhabitants. Cook's demise resulted as much from the vices of the Westerners as from any native treachery; Americans reading Ledyard would find little cause to avoid Hawai'i as a station on the way to the fur markets of China.[6]

Ledyard was followed by other American sailors and merchants in the late eighteenth and early nineteenth centuries, such as Samuel Shaw and William Shaler, who published accounts extolling the commercial opportunities of the Pacific. In addition an informal literature that particularly emphasized the lures of leisure, idleness, and sex emerged in the diaries and letters of less-tutored sailors who voyaged to the South Seas. The literary historian Terry Hammons notes that while this early "beachcomber" image was rarely published, it entered American folklore through the oral tradition "countless times in taverns, boarding-houses, and brigs up and down the coasts of the United States."[7]

One exception to the commercial, hedonistic literature of the Pacific in the early nineteenth century was John R. Jewitt's gory *Narrative of the Adventures and Sufferings of John R. Jewitt Only Survivor of the Ship "Boston."* This saga of Jewitt's nearly three-year captivity (1803–5) by the Nootka Indians under the leadership of Chief Maquina detailed the murder and beheading of some twenty-five of his shipmates in the Northwest fur trade. Jewitt escaped this fate only by convincing Maquina that he would be valuable in dealing with other American ships that came to Nootka Sound, one of which eventually rescued him when Jewitt betrayed Maquina to its captain. Despite Jewitt's attempt to highlight the savagery of the Nootka and the Northwest Coast, his widely read narrative, first published in 1815 and reprinted several times throughout the nineteenth century, failed to dull the commercial and hedonistic lures of the Pacific. The accounts of Ledyard and the yarns of the beachcombers prevailed, to fix the Pacific Basin, particularly Hawai'i and the South Seas, in the American imagination as an earthly embodiment of paradise.[8]

The hedonistic tone of the informal beachcomber tradition advanced to the status of best-seller and pacesetter for the emerging American romantic literary tradition with the publication of Herman Melville's *Typee* in 1846, followed by *Omoo* the next year. Melville did not go to the Pacific as a professional writer or as a gentleman looking for escape. His westward quest was motivated by a young man's basic economic needs. Melville was a New Yorker born in 1819 of socially respectable parents who later encountered financial difficulties. He thus reached his teens as a healthy young man who had to support himself. Going to sea presented employment opportunity, and he first signed on as a seaman in 1839 on a vessel going to England. Industrial Europe was not to his liking, and he returned home after four months. The American Midwest, where he worked briefly for an uncle in 1840, held as little attraction for him as England; the young adventurer was soon lured to the Pacific by the whaling frontier.[9]

Melville likely knew about the Pacific from members of his family who had sailed there and from reading the abundant travelogues of the early 1800s. Late in 1840 he signed on the whaling vessel *Acushnet* for the South Seas. Over the next four years, Melville became steeped in the sailor-beachcomber tradition. After eighteen months on the whaler, he deserted the *Acushnet* at the island of Nuku Hiva in the Marquesas, the setting for *Typee*. For several weeks in the summer of 1842 Melville explored the inner Typee valley of the island and enjoyed the company of a sumptuous Polynesian woman named Fayaway. Later the same year he went to Tahiti, the locale for *Omoo*, and finally to Hawai'i in 1843.

Melville experienced the Pacific Basin as a sailor and did no writing or note-taking on his travels; only after his return to Boston in 1844 did he turn from sailor to author. In *Typee* and *Omoo* Melville drew on the travelogue tradition of earlier years, to produce an amazingly accurate portrait of the Pacific frontier he encountered. But he also fictionalized his account with plot and character development, thus crossing into a literary tradition that left the commercial and scientific chronicles of Ledyard and others far behind.

Melville brought Bougainville's hedonistic view of the Pacific alive to American readers, but with one major difference. Bougainville found paradise in its untouched form. Melville chronicled paradise *and* the effects that the successive Pacific Basin trading, whaling, and missionary frontiers wrought upon it.

Even though western culture was altering the South Seas by the time of Melville's arrival, paradise was still there in its geographic and human forms. The *Acushnet* was greeted by swimming women at Nuku Hiva so beautiful that no sailor could avoid temptation. The tantalizing lure of sex was so inviting that Melville also had to restrain himself. "The varied dances of the Marquesan girls are beautiful in the extreme," he wrote, "but there is an

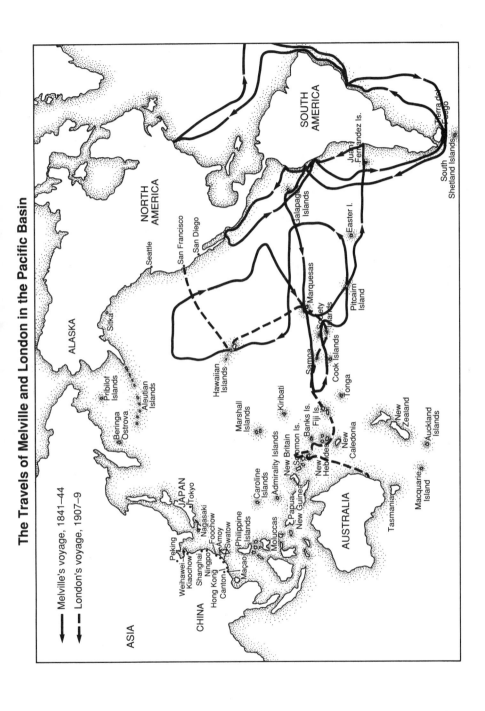

The Travels of Melville and London in the Pacific Basin

Melville's voyage, 1841–44
London's voyage, 1907–9

abandoned voluptuousness in their character which I dare not attempt to describe."[10]

The beauty of the land and people was matched with an idleness and indolence that attracted Melville, at least for a while. "One tranquil day of ease and happiness follows another in quiet succession; and with these unsophisticated savages the history of a day is the history of a life," explained the Yankee. As Melville continued his idyll in the Typee valley, he became elated at some of the things he did not find on the island. In particular, happiness abounded in the South Seas because of an absence of commerce, finance, and poverty. On Typee there were "no beggars; no debtors' prisons; no proud and hard-hearted nabobs in Typee; or, to sum up all in one word—no Money! 'That root of all evil' was not to be found in the valley." Melville's picture of a noncommercial paradise was in many ways a counterimage of the midnineteenth-century America from which he had come and of the Pacific extension of American commerce he had just deserted—the whaleship![11]

Melville was well aware that sailors like himself were not the only Pacific pioneers who had invaded paradise. English missionaries had arrived in Tahiti in 1797; Americans established their Hawaiian beachhead in 1820. With rare exception Melville despised the missionaries and found them spoiling paradise even more than their commercial and whaling counterparts. He emphasized that he had no complaint with the "cause of missions in the abstract," but found their earthly manifestation "evil." He explained in the latter part of *Typee* that natives under missionary influence in Hawai'i "had been civilised into draught horses, and evangelised into beasts of burden ... They have been literally broken into the traces, and are harnessed to the vehicles of their spiritual instructors like so many dumb brutes!"[12]

He continued his attack on missionaries in *Omoo,* almost to the level of an official inquiry, and set a trend that would be copied by other writers who followed him. One may well wonder if Melville was reacting to the missionary imprint on the Polynesians or to the frustration of fleeing Puritanism in America only to arrive in paradise and find his more righteous brothers there ahead of him. He so disliked the Purtian blue laws in Honolulu that he failed to use Hawai'i as the principal locale for any of his novels, although he actually remained there longer than on Nuku Hiva or Tahiti.

Melville usually attributed the presence of vice in paradise to western missionaries and merchants, but there were certain indigenous aspects of Polynesia that also repelled him. In *Typee* he vividly described his panicked flight from a native tatooer who, he feared, would embellish his face to the point that the Yankee would "be disfigured in such a manner as never more to have the face to return to my countrymen." The novel in fact ends with Melville's flight from the island to escape cannibals.[13]

Typee and *Omoo* were so successful that Melville extended his tales of the Pacific with the publication of *Mardi* in 1849. In 1851 he published his masterpiece, *Moby Dick*. Although literary critics emphasize the novel's allegorical importance in defining the nature of good and evil, *Moby Dick* is nonetheless a novel about the nineteenth-century Pacific whaling frontier. It is based on the historic incident of a whale attack on the American frigate *Essex* in 1820 and provides as detailed and accurate an account of the seaborne aspects of whaling as *Typee* and *Omoo* do of the hedonistic islands the whalers sought.

Herman Melville certainly stands as one of America's foremost Pacific pioneers and frontiersmen. Melville was to the western Pacific what Lewis and Clark were to the eastern shore. Like that of these other pioneers, Melville's work had nationalizing consequences. Melville observed as a participant and recorded as a writer the Pacific frontier at the moment when the impact of American commerce and religion on the native peoples of that Rousseauean paradise was at its historic height. Melville's literary genius preserved this image, which would have been lost if paradise had been relegated solely to the travelogues and informal sailor narratives of the past. His Pacific novels also served as a powerful antidote to competing missionary volumes, such as Hiram Bingham's *A Residence of Twenty Years in the Sandwich Islands,* first published in 1847. Bingham's portrait of the heathenism and moral depravity of the native Hawaiians, not to mention his dull prose style, were no match for Melville in creating the image of Polynesia that would be firmly imprinted on the American mind.

Melville's works, along with those of Nathaniel Hawthorne,

Edgar Allan Poe, and Henry David Thoreau, have been viewed by historians and literary critics as forming the base for the American literary tradition that emerged prior to the Civil War. That literary tradition in Melville's hands had an even greater pragmatic significance. In giving the Pacific a literary form at this early stage of American development, Melville had as strong an effect in nationalizing that region as the merchants and ship owners who petitioned the federal government for aid and support. Melville permanently fixed the Pacific in the national consciousness not merely as an exotic land where the odd American wanderer washed ashore, but as a place where Americans of many callings were substantially engaged. Long after the whaling frontier vanished, Melville's literary Pacific remained alive in the national mind. In the years after the Civil War, this literary frontier survived as the most vibrant and resilient of the Pacific frontiers, drawing writer after writer to the ocean and shores that had once lured the young New York sailor. Without Melville, American nationalizing currents might well have reached their limit on the eastern Pacific shores of California and Oregon in the 1840s.

The eastern shore had indeed felt the nationalizing impact of the writer as pioneer a few years before Melville announced his vision of paradise. The publication of Washington Irving's *Astoria* in 1836 (and several subsequent editions) and Richard Henry Dana's *Two Years Before the Mast* in 1840 provided many Americans with their first knowledge of the eastern Pacific since the conclusion of the War of 1812.

Unlike Melville, Washington Irving was not a direct participant in the Pacific frontier. Europe attracted this New Yorker's interest, and by 1832 his books on Christopher Columbus, European travels, and the Alhambra had achieved popular and critical acclaim. It was this literary reputation that prompted another New Yorker, John Jacob Astor, to commission Irving in 1834 to write an account of Astoria, his ill-fated fur-trading colony at the mouth of the Columbia River. Irving, who had been as far west as the Indian Territory, had no intention of going to the Pacific. Instead he relied on Astor's records, previous narratives such as Gabriel Franchère's *Relation d'un voyage a la côte du nord-ouest de l'Amérique septentrionale* (1820) and interviews with Astoria survivors.[14]

Irving included in his narrative an overland trek to the Pacific coast as well as a seaborne voyage to Hawai'i, complete with a description of premissionary island life. *Astoria* was clearly written with the political intent to revive American interest in Oregon and the Pacific trade. Irving lamented America's lost chance to reestablish a commercial empire at Astoria after the War of 1812 and blamed the national government for its failure to gain full possession of Oregon. "Bills have repeatedly been brought into Congress for the purpose," explained Irving on the final pages of the book, "but without success, and our rightful possessions on that coast, as well as our trade on the Pacific, have no rallying point protected by the national flag and by a military force." He feared that American settlers headed for Oregon might one day precipitate a war between England and the United States if the issue of joint occupation were not settled. *Astoria* indeed succeeded in awakening American interest in Oregon, and its author proved an able prognosticator of the tensions that would arise over the next decade. Irving was obviously pleased with the Oregon Treaty of 1846 and proudly noted in the book's second edition published in 1849 "the question of dominion over the vast territory beyond the Rocky Mountains . . . has been finally settled in a spirit of mutual concession."[15]

Astoria gained wide readership, but it was not the literary precursor of the hedonistic novels of Melville and his followers. Nonetheless it had important consequences in paving the way for that frontier. As the country's leading man of letters in the 1830s, Irving established the Pacific for American readers as a locale worthy of the nation's best literary effort. His use of historical records provided a precedent for accuracy that would influence future books on the Pacific, including the hedonistic literature that followed. Irving's description of premissionary Hawai'i in 1810, though not phrased in the prose of Bougainville, clearly depicted the islands as a physically beautiful land with an agreeable, friendly people who were acceptable commercial partners and in no particular need of salvation. Irving prepared American audiences for Melville's view of the islands, rather than that of the Reverend Hiram Bingham.

The American public echoed its favorable response to *Astoria* and the Pacific four years later, with its reception of Richard Henry Dana's *Two Years Before the Mast*. Like Melville, Dana was a participant in the Pacific frontier. In 1834 he signed on with the brig *Pilgrim*, bound for the hide-and-tallow trade of the California coast. But there were significant differences in the two men. Dana was not an energetic young man in search of a livelihood; he was a sickly young Boston Brahmin seeking the restoration of his health. In this persona he was part participant in the sailing life and part observer of a social class beneath him. The hearty beachcomber present in Melville was muted in Dana.

During his Pacific sojourn, Dana took notes and kept a journal, which he unfortunately lost. Nonetheless upon his return to Boston in 1836, he resumed his plan to write a reformist account of life at sea from the perspective of the sailor "before the mast." His goal was to distance himself from romantic novels about the sea, which rarely viewed life below the deck. *Two Years Before the Mast* did portray the hardships of the common sailor, but it was Dana's picture of California in the 1830s, the first many Americans had read, that had the most lasting effect on the nation.

Dana, like Irving, employed a descriptive style that was more commercial than romantic. He depicted the eastern Pacific coast as a garden of natural beauty and grandeur, awaiting only the arrival of an "enterprising" people to develop its commercial potential. While Dana emphasized the potential of the land, he could not say the same of its inhabitants, the Mexican Californians. "The Californians," he decried, "are an idle, thriftless people, and can make nothing for themselves. The country abounds in grapes, yet they buy bad wine made in Boston."[16] The indolent culture that would so attract Melville in the South Seas repelled the commercial-minded Bostonian.

Dana was taken by the physical grace of the Californians, particularly their horsemanship, but he despised their jealousy and found many of their customs dull and cruel. The sensuous dances of local women that would so entice Melville in the Marquesas were not what Dana found in California. After viewing an evening fandango, Dana said of the female dancers, "They looked as grave as though they were going through some religious ceremony, their faces as little excited as their limbs." Dana could not wait to flee

California and soon feared the cultural consequences of lingering too long among either the Californians or the sailors.[17]

His predominantly negative view of the inhabitants of the Pacific was tempered by his affection for the kanakas, or Sandwich Islanders, he met on shore in California. Dana described at length their physical abilities, particularly as swimmers. Although the kanakas did not have the same attitudes toward work and property as Dana, the Bostonian grew extremely fond of them. "Their customs, and manner of treating one another, show a simple, primitive generosity, which is truly delightful." He was deeply distressed by the damaging effects of western civilization on the Polynesians, particularly the consequences of Western introduced diseases. This message would be repeated by many writers who followed him.[18]

Dana's picture of life at sea and on the eastern Pacific coast captured the American consciousness. *Two Years Before the Mast* sold over twenty thousand copies in the first two years. The book's nationalizing consequences were as great as those of *Astoria* in awakening the nation to the potential of the Pacific coast. Within eight years of its publication, California was acquired. Sales of the book then soared, as it became a basic introduction for emigrant goldseekers hastening to the land Dana forsook.

Like Irving, Dana prepared his American audience for a Pacific frontier that extended beyond the eastern shore of the Pacific coast; *Two Years Before the Mast* also had a role in preparing future writers for that frontier. Melville read Dana just as he departed for the Pacific. Upon his return Melville found an audience eager for more novels about the Pacific from the sailor's perspective. Melville and Dana talked about their experiences, and the Bostonian encouraged the New Yorker to give the whaling frontier the literary permanence he had conferred on the hide-and-tallow trade. Dana's influence on Melville became most pronounced after the publication of *Typee* and *Omoo;* Melville's two novels centering on sailor life, *Redburn* (1849) and *White Jacket* (1850), as well as *Moby Dick,* show the strongest influence from Dana. The collaboration between Dana and Melville in the 1840s established a pattern that would be repeated by literary pioneers in the decades to come, as writer after writer departed for the Pacific using the books and novels of their precedessors as guide and inspiration.[19]

By 1860 the Pacific frontier had entered the American literary tradition; one might say it had even helped spawn that tradition. The Pacific provided a literary locale for major American authors matched by few other settings in the first half of the nineteenth century. The works of Washington Irving and Richard Henry Dana first generated a popular appreciation for the eastern Pacific and awakened national interest in acquiring the coast. Herman Melville then drew the national imagination beyond the eastern shore to the South Seas.

The Civil War disrupted the Pacific frontier along with the life of the entire nation. Ships used for whaling and commerce were required for the Union war effort. With the end of the conflict, the commercial and maritime interests of the earlier frontier began to wane. But the literary frontier that Melville had opened would not die, as new writers flocked to the islands he had brought alive. No sooner was the war over than the first new voyager answered the call.

In 1866 Mark Twain, a young reporter for the Sacramento *Union,* took passage from San Francico to Honolulu. Like Dana and Melville, Twain was a participant in the Pacific frontier. But unlike these predecessors, he sailed for Hawai'i specifically as a writer who would compose a series of letters for his paper, proclaiming the future commercial opportunities for California businessmen in Hawai'i. He observed both the whaler-missionary era that Melville had known and the coming sugar-plantation era that would boom in the 1870s.

Twain was very much a part of the San Francisco gold-rush literary frontier of the 1850s and 1860s that spawned the colorful, anecdotal mining-camp stories of Bret Harte and other journalists/ short-story writers who contributed to the *Overland Monthly.* His adventures in Hawai'i were shaped by that literary genre when he concluded *Roughing It* (1872), his account of a sojourn in California and Nevada mining camps, with a condensation of the letters on Hawai'i he had written for the *Union.*[20]

The newspaper letters trumpeted the promise of Hawai'i's land for the sugar industry. Huge profits could be expected for investors, and imported Asian labor would be a potential boon for both

Hawai'i and California. Twain carefully portrayed San Francisco as the Gateway to Hawai'i and the oriental trade.

In *Roughing It* Twain muted the blatant business promotion of the *Union* letters, presenting Hawai'i as a blossoming and intriguing paradise. Like Melville, Twain was taken with the physical beauty of the islands, particularly with the surreal experience of going to the crater floors of both Kilauea and Haleakala volcanoes. When it came to the people of the islands, Twain's approach was more the anecdotal style of the gold-rush tradition than the romantic sensuality of Melville. Twain entered no liaison with a local beauty. Though he was indeed taken by the physical grace of the islanders, particularly their surfing ability, he could not resist joking about their nudity. He delighted in describing a native gentleman who arrived for church wearing nothing but a woman's bonnet and another man who wore a pair of pants tied around his neck.

Like Melville, Twain felt compelled to comment on the effects of western civilization on the Polynesians. On this score he differed dramatically from his whaling predecessor. Twain was ambivalent about what he saw in Hawai'i. As Terry Hammons has noted about Twain's view of Hawai'i in *Roughing It*, "every passage that praised the islands was followed with one damning them." This was particularly true in his handling of the missionaries. He condemned the righteous divines for taking away the islanders' sense of leisure and replacing it with guilt, but in the next breath he praised the missionaries for freeing the Hawaiians from the tyranny of feudalism and the barbaric customs of the old chiefs. In general Twain found westernized Hawai'i to be a step in the right direction. Thus he actually enhanced the lure of Hawai'i for his readers. Those looking for escape would not be unhappy, but those looking for western-style stability and progress would also be drawn to the Pacific.[21]

After four months in Hawai'i, the young reporter sailed back to San Francisco. The Pacific was indelibly etched on his mind, and he always yearned to return to the islands. In 1889 he talked of his love for Hawai'i to a group of traveling baseball players. "No alien land in all the world," he revealed, "has any deep strong charm for me but one, no other land could so longingly and so

beseechingly haunt me, sleeping and waking, through half a lifetime, as that one has done . . . I can hear the splash of its brooks;
in my nostrils still lives the breath of flowers that perished twenty
years ago." Twain's desire to return to the islands was ultimately
thwarted. He hoped to stop in Hawai'i as part of a worldwide
speaking tour in 1895, but a cholera epidemic in Honolulu kept
his ship anchored offshore.[22]

Although Twain never set foot in Hawai'i again after 1866,
he kept the lure of the Pacific literary frontier alive by lecturing
about the islands extensively during the late 1860s and 1870s. In
the 1880s he actually began a novel about Hawai'i, but never
completed it. Some literary scholars believe that Twain transformed the theme for that book into *A Connecticut Yankee in King
Arthur's Court*. The inspiration to write about an industrious
Yankee in a feudal world came from his knowledge of the New
Englanders who confronted Hawaiian feudalism in the early nineteenth century. The Yankee had indeed been in a feudal court, but
it was not King Arthur's; it was King Kamehameha's![23]

Twain's departure from Hawai'i was soon followed by his
continued eastward journey from California to Connecticut. After
1870 the San Francisco literary frontier that had been so vibrant
a decade earlier waned rapidly, as writers such as Bret Harte and
Joaquin Miller joined Twain in moving east. The literary union
of San Francisco, the mining-camp frontier, and the South Seas
that was so natural to Twain in *Roughing It* would not flourish
again. Some publishers even omitted the Hawai'i sections from
later editions of the book. San Francisco drifted into a literary
decline for the remainder of the century, although it continued to
attract a bohemian community of minor writers and painters whose
talent never fully developed. The historian Kevin Starr has noted
that the city's ties to Polynesia and the Orient were overshadowed
by its Mediterranean atmosphere and Latin sympathies. At times
its cultural life was consumed by a quest for a lost Hispanic heritage.[24]

Despite this literary decline, San Francisco still remained the
geographic point of departure for writers who longed for the hedonistic frontier. Charles Warren Stoddard, a kindly, effete San
Francisco poet who worked with Bret Harte on the *Overland
Monthly*, sought escape from the stress of urban California by

journeying to Hawai'i and Tahiti in search of Melville's paradise. Stoddard actually visited Hawai'i before Twain, in 1864, but his literary output on the South Seas did not commence until the late 1860s. After publishing a few articles on Hawai'i in the *Overland Monthly*, Stoddard set out for Tahiti in 1870 and worked for a French merchant. The hedonism of the island soon overcame him, and he abandoned his job to idle through the verdant countryside. In his *South Sea Idylls*, a collection of articles published in 1873, Stoddard recaptured the world of *Omoo* as he described his walks through the island. Tahiti seemed a cure for his urban ills: "Through leagues of verdure I wandered, feasting my five senses and finding life a holiday at last. There were numberless streams to be crossed, where I loafed for hours on the bridges, satisfying myself with sunshine."[25]

Though not remembered in the twentieth century on the same literary level with Twain or Melville, Stoddard was well regarded in his day and kept the gateway to the literary hedonistic frontier open in the first decades after the Civil War. As a leading figure in the San Francisco bohemian community, Stoddard served as a contact for other writers who came to California. In 1879 Robert Louis Stevenson arrived, pursuing a local divorcée he wanted to marry. Stoddard convinced Stevenson to go to the South Seas and reenforced the lure of Melville for the Scot. Seeking to find both paradise and relief from tuberculosis, Stevenson and his California wife set sail for the islands from the Golden Gate a decade later, in 1888, aboard a yacht chartered from an Oakland millionaire.[26]

Following in Melville's path, Stevenson voyaged first to the Marquesas, then to Tahiti, and on to Hawai'i, where he enjoyed the friendship of King Kalakaua. He also became fascinated with Father Damien's leper colony at Molokai. From Hawai'i Stevenson sailed back through the South Seas to Samoa, where he made his home until his death there in 1894. In only six years, Stevenson produced a stream of literature set in the Pacific. His most well-known Pacific works include the epic *In the South Seas* (1890), the short stories "The Beach at Falesa" and "The Bottle Imp," as well as the novella *The Ebb-Tide* (1894).

Like other writers before him, Stevenson was fascinated with the physical and human beauty of the islands, but he chose human degeneration as the main theme of his stories. This is particularly the case in *The Ebb-Tide,* in which the main characters are a set of seedy Caucasians without redeeming features, even in paradise. The debilitating effects on Polynesians stemming from contact with Western civilization that Melville had described in the 1850s had taken on vastly greater proportions by the end of the century. Despite this distressing decline, particularly in the places of greatest Western influence, such as Honolulu, paradise was not completely lost. Stevenson still extolled the warmth of Polynesian affection in the villages; the hedonistic frontier was still evident in Stevenson's work. The author's desire to remain in the South Seas until his death may well have been the greatest testament to this fact.

Stevenson, of course, was not an American. But his journey to the Pacific literary frontier was in many ways an integral part of an American experience. He was lured to the Pacific as an extension of his time in California. He was inspired by American writers, principally Melville and Stoddard, who had gone before him. His works added to the ever-growing Anglo-American literature on the South Seas and would serve as a lure to other writers, both English and American.

By the end of the nineteenth century, the South Seas were becoming a standard stop on the world travels of a growing number of American writers. In the early 1890s Henry Adams, accompanied by the American artist John La Farge, embarked on a world journey to forget the misery he had suffered after the suicide of his wife. Like Stevenson, Adams and La Farge stopped in Hawai'i, Tahiti, and Samoa. Adams's talent as a historian was brought to bear on the South Seas, and in 1893 he published the first history of Tahiti, *Memoirs of Marua Taaroa, Last Queen of Tahiti.*[27]

In the thirty-five years between the end of the Civil War and 1900, the literary frontier sustained American interest in and knowledge of the Pacific beyond the coast of California. It kept the region alive until the imperialistic writings of Captain Alfred Thayer Mahan ignited nationalizing currents once again in the late nineteenth century, launching the last phase of the military frontier. The territorial acquisition of Hawai'i (1898) and American Samoa (1899), along with the Spanish-American War conquest of the Philippines and Guam, were clearly the results of military imperialism. While the military frontier gripped the headlines of the nation's newspapers, it in no way eclipsed the literary frontier. Continental Americans might well have lost interest in the new acquisitions had not the lure of hedonism outlived the journalistic jingoism of 1898. No sooner had Hawai'i been acquired than American writers set sail from San Francisco, following the lead of the literary pioneers who preceded them. They kept the hedonistic frontier as alive and vibrant in the twentieth century as it had ever been in the nineteenth.

If Mark Twain was the tie between the missionary/whaling frontier and the post–Civil War literary frontier, Jack London carried that postwar frontier into the twentieth century and linked San Francisco with both the South Seas and the far northern Pacific. London always considered himself to be a son of the frontier, although the San Francisco into which he was born in 1876 had long since shed its gold-rush luster and was America's undisputed Pacific metropolis. Nonetheless it was still a port where a young man could sign on to a ship in search of escape from urban, industrial America. As the 1890s dawned, London ended his formal education after grammar school and spent several adventuresome, some say rebellious, years on the waterfront of San Francisco and its environs. In 1893 at age seventeen, he signed on as ablebodied seaman, much in the tradition of Melville, on the sealing vessel *Sophia Sutherland,* bound for the seal-hunting grounds of Japan and Siberia. He published a brief account of his adventures in a San Francisco newspaper soon after his return, but in 1893 his writing career was still in its embryonic stages. His full account of the voyage, *The Sea Wolf,* would not appear until 1904.[28]

Over the next few years, London traveled to the East Coast but was back at the Golden Gate by 1895 to continue his education and pursue his literary goals. He first entered high school, but a year later enrolled at the University of California. In early 1897 he left the university and soon prepared to return to sea. The precipitating event for his departure was the July 1897 arrival in San Francisco of the *Excelsior,* a ship bearing news and monetary proof of the discovery of gold in the Canadian Klondike. The last great rush in the Pacific mining frontier immediately ensued.

London responded to the news as quickly as possible. Within

two weeks he sailed north, reaching Dyea, the port for the Chilkoot Pass into the Klondike, by early August. London made it over the Chilkoot that same month and quickly floated through the series of lakes that made up the route to Dawson City. He settled for the winter seventy to eighty miles south of Dawson, at the mouth of the Stewart River, another potential site for gold.

Like thousands of other Klondikers, London found no gold; instead he contracted scurvy by the spring of 1898. To compound his ills, the arrival of the first mail that spring brought the news that his father had died. London was in no condition for further adventure and returned quickly to California. Sick and without treasure, he had nonetheless endured an Arctic winter and gained a set of experiences that would provide a base for his literary career. Like Melville he kept no diary but based his later writings on memory.

The Pacific mining frontier that London followed to the Klondike had been moving steadily northward from San Francisco since the 1850s, with strikes in British Columbia and on the Yukon River in the 1890s. However, in heading north as a potential literary figure, London did not follow in the footsteps of a host of talented predecessors. In fact, other than *Astoria,* there was little sign of a literary frontier north of San Francisco. But the region was by no means unknown. Many of the eighteenth-century explorers who gloried in the South Pacific (such as James Cook, John Ledyard, and George Vancouver) also explored the shores of Russian America. There were sexual liaisons between sailors and native women of the temperate Aleutian Islands. But as the historian William R. Hunt has noted, no picture of a northern Eden emerged in the late-eighteenth- and early-nineteenth-century travel literature. Possibly the romantic landscapes of the Aleutians, depicted occasionally by artists such as Louis Choris in his 1822 *Voyage pittoresque autour de monde,* were too often shrouded in clouds to sustain a hedonistic lure.[29]

The far northern Pacific also failed to inspire an extension of the colorful gold-rush writing of the San Francisco literary frontier; the Klondike rush came too late. Extensive commercial relations had developed between San Francisco and Russian America in the 1850s. In fact fears of a flood of American miners had been one factor in inducing Russia to sell her colony in 1867. But the anticipated boom simply did not come in the 1860s or the 1870s. One can well imagine the works that might have resulted had Bret Harte or Mark Twain gone to Sitka in 1867 to cover the transfer of Alaska from Russia to the United States. Certainly Twain would have found rich ground for a short story among the Russian priests, American soldiers, creoles, and onlooking Tlingits, had he covered that ceremony. But the purchase of Alaska simply did not attract the literary and journalistic talent that was present in the West immediately after the Civil War. By the time the great Klondike strike came, Twain and Harte were far away.

While the gold-rush literary tradition was not drawn north to point the way for London, there was an outpouring of scientific, exploratory literature after the Civil War, largely sponsored by the Smithsonian Institution and other U.S. government agencies, that did at least chronicle the contours of the far North in the late nineteenth century. The Smithsonian promoted the explorations of Robert Kennicott and William Healy Dall, who published *Alaska and Its Resources* in 1870. A decade later the U.S. Army sent Lieutenant Henry T. Allen and Lieutenant Frederick Schwatka to explore the Yukon and Copper rivers; both men produced readable journals of their interior voyages in the 1880s. Henry Wood Elliot, who also went to Alaska under Smithsonian sponsorship, wrote extensively in popular magazines about the fur seals of Alaska. In the 1890s Elliot joined the crusade for the conservation of seals and became famous for his watercolors of these animals. In addition to these government-sponsored publications, the indefatigable Pacific historian Hubert Howe Bancroft published his *History of Alaska* in 1886, a work he produced with the help of Ivan Petroff, a Russian-born immigrant who joined Bancroft's staff as the Alaska expert.[30]

While this late-nineteenth-century scientific and historical literature certainly ranked in quality with the volumes produced by the Wilkes expedition a half-century earlier, it provided little in the way of inspiration for adventurous young authors like London, with one striking exception. The one literary predecessor who might have guided London was his fellow San Franciscan, John Muir. This naturalist made four trips to Alaska in search of glaciers, the first in 1879, when he and an Indian guide discovered the miraculous Glacier Bay. His love affair with icy vistas in the Alaskan summer and fall inspired romantic prose to match that of Bougainville in Tahiti. "The first stages of our journey," he told his readers of his first trip to Glacier Bay, "were mostly enjoyment. The weather was about half bright, and we glided along the green and yellow shores in comfort, the lovely islands passing in harmonious succession, like ideas in a fine poem." Once he saw the sunlit glaciers, his prose hit new peaks, as he rhapsodized:

> The green waters of the fiord were filled with sun-spangles; with the upspringing breeze the fleet of icebergs set forth on their voyages; and on the innumerable mirrors and prisms of these bergs, and on those of the shattered crystal walls of the glaciers, common white light and rainbow light began to glow . . . We turned and sailed away, joining the outgoing bergs, while 'Gloria in excelsis' still seemed to be sounding over all the white landscape, and our burning hearts were ready for any fate, feeling that whatever the future might have in store, the treasures we had gained would enrich our lives forever.[31]

One might well imagine London rushing north to find escape from San Francisco in Muir's romantic bay. But such was not the case. Muir's writings on Alaska did not become extensive until after 1890; those romantic words on Glacier Bay appeared in *Century* magazine in 1895. Although Muir's prose drew tourists to visit Glacier Bay, there is no indication that Muir or any other nature writer inspired London's quest. Instead it was the overwhelming adventure of the mining rush that inspired the young literary explorer. While the beauty of late spring, summer, and early fall attracted Muir, it was the winter of 1897–98, a time known historically for its deprivation because of a lack of supplies, that shaped London and served as the base for his literary work. Before he could experience a summer in the Klondike, he was back in California, never to venture north again.[32]

Upon his return London's literary career began in earnest, as he soon published stories of his northern adventures in magazines and then collected them for his first book, *The Son of Wolf* (1900). In 1903 he published his most famous novel of the North, *The*

Call of the Wild, followed by *White Fang* in 1906. For London the North was an escape from the tensions of modern capitalism and civilization. His release, however, was not to wander idly through a verdant or even an icy valley, but to engage in a dramatic struggle of men and dogs against nature for survival. As the literary historian Franklin Walker has explained, "The 'call' represents the tug on all civilized men to get away from routine tasks, to simplify their lives in somewhat the same way Thoreau wanted them simplified, to find adventure in nature far from cities and family responsibilities."[33]

This kind of escape clearly captivated thousands of readers and placed London in the ranks of the nation's most-read authors. It also appeared that London's call might inspire a new gold-rush literary tradition in the decade immediately after the publication of his northern novels. Rex Beach, a young Chicagoan who set out for the Klondike in 1897 and also ventured to the Nome gold rush in 1900, found upon his return to the Windy City that London's stories had created a substantial literary market. Upon the urging of the magazine publisher S. S. McClure, Beach produced *The Spoilers* in 1906, which portrayed a nationally publicized claim-jumping scandal in Nome known as the McKenzie-Noyes Conspiracy. So successful was this novel that Beach produced four additional books set in Alaska or the Klondike over the next decade: *The Barrier* (1908), *The Silver Horde* (1909), *The Iron Trail* (1913), and *Winds of Chance* (1918). *The Spoilers* was also made into a moving picture in 1914, with a classic barroom brawl scene. The theme of Beach's novels, unlike London's solitary-individual-versus-nature motif, advocated the economic development of the North and usually featured an honest, young developer (miner, fisherman, or railroad builder) battling various corrupt rascals.[34]

Beach's novels, along with the poems of the Canadian Robert Service, who will always be remembered for "The Spell of the Yukon" and "The Shooting of Dan McGrew," seemed to point the way to a northern literary tradition in the first two decades of the twentieth century. The 1901 publication of the first journals of railroad magnate E. A. Harriman's 1899 scientific expedition to Alaska also promised to inspire renewed nature writing about the North. Indeed the narrative of that expedition, written by the eastern naturalist John Burroughs, with chapters by John Muir, still makes good reading today. Despite such promise, however, neither Beach's adventure novels nor Harriman's exploratory ventures gained momentum as the century progressed. Most historians view Harriman's expedition as the end of the great age of northern discovery. And the gold-rush frontier that inspired Beach lost most of its momentum by World War I. The sinking of the passenger liner *Princess Sophia,* which struck a dangerous reef on a journey out of Skagway in the fall of 1918, is seen by some historians as the final blow signaling the decline of the North. Alaska's population, which doubled in the last decade of the nineteenth century, had fallen below its 1900 level by 1920.[35]

By World War I the northern literary tradition had lost most of its initial vigor, but it was not dead. Nature writing continued after 1920, and Rex Beach wrote about Alaska through the 1930s. The motion-picture industry tried to keep the North alive with Charlie Chaplin's classic *The Gold Rush* (1925) as well as *Nanook of the North* (1922) and *Eskimo* (1933), which starred a new Native actor named Mala. Numerous film versions of Beach's novels also appeared in the interwar period. Nonetheless the nascent northern literary tradition that Jack London spawned could not match the South Seas tradition, to which the Californian turned his attention soon after the publication of *White Fang.*[36]

Once established as a successful author with his northern novels, London quickly succumbed to the more alluring Pacific literary frontier. In 1907 he set sail from San Francisco for Hawai'i and the South Seas in the fashion of Robert Louis Stevenson, whom he greatly admired, aboard a yacht named the *Snark,* with his wife, Charmian, and a retinue of followers. London was thus the first major American author to experience Hawai'i as an American territory rather than as a royal kingdom. He and his wife moved in Honolulu society, meeting the revolutionaries of the preceding decade as well as the deposed royals.

Although London enjoyed cosmopolitan Honolulu, city life would not be his primary literary inspiration. He delved into Hawaiian history, customs, and psychology for his short stories. Like Stevenson he was fascinated with leprosy, in particular with the noble battle of Koolau, a native leper who valiantly resisted arrest by white sheriffs. London also explored Hawai'i's racial frontier and the intermarriage between Caucasians, Polynesians, and Asians. His first collection of short stories, *The House of Pride* (1912), stimulated American tourism to Hawai'i and raised popular interest in the islands that were now a part of the nation. London himself was so taken with Hawai'i that he ventured there again in 1915, hoping to find relief from his rapidly deteriorating health. Although he died soon after his return to California in 1916, another series of short stories about Hawai'i dealing with history, legend, and surfing, *On the Makaloa Mat,* was published posthumously in 1919.

For London, Hawai'i was still an exotic escape from mainland America at the turn of the century, but the full literary frontier he sought was not restricted to that island. He looked for something beyond Americanized Hawai'i and sailed onward from Honolulu in 1907, following the muse of Melville and Stevenson to the Marquesas, Tahiti, Samoa, and the Solomon Islands. Beyond Hawai'i London sought a darker side of the Pacific for his short stories. He described the natural violence of typhoons, cannibalism, and the brutality of Caucasians toward natives in the short stories published as *South Sea Tales* in 1911. London's personal travails with disease and climate, which he recounted in *The Cruise of the Snark* (1911), were as violent as any of his fictional accounts.

The themes in London's stories of the South Seas, ranging from reminiscences of paradise to tales of debauchery and decline, portrayed the full spectrum of the Pacific literary tradition that had developed in the nineteenth century. While Melville's world had changed by London's time, the Pacific was still very much a literary frontier. It still lured writers seeking an escape beyond the borders of the western commercial and industrial world; the Pacific was a place to which a person could flee. Even if Western civilization had tainted parts of paradise, there was always an inner valley or an outer island to seek. As one of America's most widely read authors, London pulled that nineteenth-century frontier into the first two decades of the twentieth century.

By 1919 the pioneering work of Herman Melville, Mark Twain, Jack London, and other English-speaking authors, such as Robert Louis Stevenson and Somerset Maugham, had indeed created a literary tradition that would continually lure new writers to the Pacific. Added to the work of these authors was the lure of the French artist Paul Gauguin, whose postimpressionist paintings of Tahiti in the 1890s exuded a sense of both hedonism and melancholy. Gauguin's life formed the basis for Somerset Maugham's novel *The Moon and Sixpence,* published in 1919. World War I seemed to create an even greater need to find relief from the stress and destruction of the modern world. No sooner had the war ended than the lure of this ongoing Pacific frontier drew writer after writer to retrace the steps and rediscover the settings and stories of their literary predecessors.

In 1920 two American flyers who had seen war duty, James Hall and Charles Nordhoff, decided to answer the call of the South Seas and establish themselves as writers in Tahiti. Part of Nordhoff's call was ancestral; his grandfather, the American journalist Charles Nordhoff, had written about Honolulu in the 1870s. Both Hall and Nordhoff decided to take up permanent residence soon after their arrival and eventually married Tahitian women, Nordhoff within the first year and Hall by 1925. The two young men first produced articles for magazines about their life in paradise. As the years progressed, they learned more about the history and romance of the South Seas. By 1929 they had become utterly intrigued with the mutiny at sea described by Captain William Bligh in his 1792 *Voyage to the South Seas* and had decided to write a novel based on the account. In 1932 they published *Mutiny on the Bounty,* followed by *Men Against the Sea* and *Pitcairn's Island* in 1934. These three novels, collectively known as the *Bounty Trilogy,* brought Nordhoff and Hall wide readership and critical acclaim. In the following years, their success continued, again based on themes developed by earlier writers. Using the same setting Jack London had employed for his typhoon short story "The House of Mapuhi," they published *Hurricane* in 1936. Now well established as leading writers of the Pacific, Nordhoff and Hall continued their literary output for the next decade.[37]

The literary frontier of the Pacific that these writers pursued was a profitable one. The two men formed their own firm, Nordhoff and Hall, and earned money from their writing enterprise just as the Boston merchant partners Bryant and Sturgis had done from whaling and furs a century earlier. The literary partners capitalized on the emerging motion-picture industry by selling the film rights to their novels; *Mutiny on the Bounty* was filmed in three different versions with stars including Clark Gable and Charles Laughton. The actress Dorothy Lamour spread the charms of the South Seas in the film version of *Hurricane*. The union of Hollywood and Polynesia assured both the permanence and profitability of this frontier.

Nordhoff and Hall were not alone in writing of the South Seas during the 1920s and 1930s. The New York journalist Frederick O'Brien wrote about Caucasian exploitation of the Marquesas in *White Shadows in the South Seas* (1919). But even after a century of exploitation, O'Brien was still overwhelmed by the hedonistic lure of the South Seas. He radiantly praised the beauty of a Marquesan woman named Hinatini, or "Vanquished Often," whose charms had stood the onslaught of Western civilization; by 1920 paradise had been exploited but not killed. Describing the idyllic village of Vait-hua, O'Brien wrote that "The whites, having desolated and depopulated this once thronged valley, had gone, leaving the remnant of its people to return to their native virtue and quietude. Here, perhaps more than in any other spot in all the isles, the Marquesan lived as his forefathers had before the whites came."[38]

While O'Brien wandered in the Marquesas, Robert Dean Frisbie, an Ohioan who went to school in California, joined Nordhoff and Hall in Tahiti. The influence of earlier prose pioneers enveloped Frisbie; he idolized Robert Louis Stevenson and wanted to write a modern-day version of Melville's *Moby Dick*. Soon after his arrival in 1920, he found a Tahitian mistress, with whom he spent the next few years sailing for more distant islands and writing magazine articles. In 1924 he finally settled on Puka Puka, one of the Cook Islands, where he ran a trading station while continuing his literary endeavors. Beginning with *The Book of Puka Puka* in 1928, followed by *My Tahiti* in 1937, Frisbie launched a series of books published until 1949 on the theme of a young man's life in paradise.[39]

As Frisbie's literary output gained momentum, World War II broke out in the Pacific. After the Japanese bombing of Pearl Harbor, in December 1941, a new Pacific military frontier dawned, and Americans were quickly drawn to the South Seas in numbers never before imagined. As in earlier Pacific Basin frontiers, some participants would become writers. The best-known was James A. Michener, a naval officer who gave his wartime experience in the Pacific a literary life in *Tales of the South Pacific,* published in 1947. During his Pacific travels, Michener encountered Robert Dean Frisbie and modeled one of the stories in his next book, *Return to Paradise* (1951), on the Puka Puka trader's life. One decade's literary pioneer became the next decade's literary hero and model. This frontier seemed to serve as its own self-perpetuating inspiration.[40]

Michener's books about the South Seas reached an ever-widening audience in the late 1940s and early 1950s, with the theatrical and motion-picture productions of the highly popular and acclaimed musical *South Pacific,* an adaptation of *Tales of the South Pacific.* Michener was not alone in telling the American public about the wartime Pacific through literature and film. Mainland audiences responded enthusiastically to the novel and film versions of Thomas Heggen's *Mr. Roberts* (1946) and James Jones's *From Here to Eternity* (1951).

With the rapid dissemination of these books and motion pictures, the nationalizing currents induced by writers in previous generations gained renewed force in the 1950s, as the two Pacific territories of Alaska and Hawai'i sought full incorporation into the American Union as states. Michener was quite conscious of the nationalizing power of literature and of his own part in the process. In 1958 he moved to Honolulu to begin his epic novel *Hawaii,* which encompassed the entire sweep of the islands' history.

As voting on the legislation to bring Hawai'i into the Union reached a congressional climax during the summer of 1958 and the spring of 1959, Michener, as well as Dorothy Lamour, often appeared in newspapers and magazines advocating admission. The literary outpouring of Michener and others kept the Pacific alive in mainland eyes and presented a forceful case against the racial prejudice that had long been a factor in thwarting Hawai'i's entry.

The literary frontier's nationalizing impact had never been more clearly visible than in the years immediately after World War II. Hawai'i joined the Union as the fiftieth state in August 1959, simultaneously with the publication of Michener's *Hawaii*.

While Michener and others contributed to the literary frontier's nationalizing impact in the mid-Pacific, the author Edna Ferber reached out to the far northern Pacific. In 1958 she published *Ice Palace*, proclaiming the glorious prospects and possibilities for life in Alaska. Some observers at the time credited the book with stimulating congressional action for Alaska's admission as the forty-ninth state in January 1959. In this regard *Ice Palace* had greater nationalizing than literary appeal. Neither the book nor the ensuing epic-length movie, starring Richard Burton, are counted among either Ferber's or Burton's best work.[41]

Regardless of the literary acclaim of *Ice Palace*, Ferber's attention to Alaska, as well as the new state's admission to the Union, did stimulate a renewed literary effort in the far North. In the first decades after statehood, nationally recognized writers published volumes that achieved a readership not matched since the works of London and Beach at the turn of the century. John McPhee's *Coming into the Country* (1977) praised the glory of the northern landscape while mocking Caucasian efforts to adapt to it. Joe McInnis carried the mocking theme to the level of the preposterous in *Going to Extremes* (1980), while Barry Lopez revived John Muir's fascination with the natural beauty of icy vistas in *Arctic Dreams* (1986). The tradition of using an older historical account as the source for a modern work also flourished in the North with the 1983 publication of James Houston's *Eagle Song*, a novel based on John Jewitt's 1815 saga of his capture by the Nootka Indians.

This renewed northern literary tradition even attracted James Michener, three decades after he published *Hawaii*. Unfortunately the great writer of the South Seas encountered disappointing results with the publication of *Alaska* in 1988. Some critics claimed that Michener's writing had become stilted by the late 1980s, but it may have been the lack of a northern literary tradition equal to that of the South Pacific that led to such flat and lifeless characters in *Alaska*. There was no counterpart of Robert Dean Frisbie on whom Michener could base a story in the North. Jack London's stories of Hawai'i and the Solomon Islands, where Americans saw military action in World War II, gave Michener more inspiration than London's stories of dogs and northern deprivation in the winter of 1897.[42]

The admission of Alaska and Hawai'i as forty-ninth and fiftieth states provides a convenient point at which to conclude our discussion of the literary frontier and contemplate its impact. It had by no means come to an end in 1959, but its nationalizing currents had reached their limits, as far as anyone could foresee. Stretching from the eighteenth to the twentieth centuries, this frontier stands as one of the most vital and enduring of all the Pacific Basin frontiers. It has fared particularly well in contrast to fiction's cowboy-and-Indian or dime-novel frontier of mainland America, which has come under such attack in recent years. The Pacific literary frontier, with its hedonistic themes, allowed much opportunity for poetic license, but most authors maintained some hold on reality and in fact conveyed what they actually found in the South Seas. Purely from the standpoint of geography and climate, there was a paradise in the Pacific. Writers did not have to create a fictional garden in the desert.

The hedonism in their writing was often balanced with the contrast and reality of native exploitation by Caucasians, although depravity could be as exaggerated as the idyllic life. If there was exploitation in the literature, there was also intermarriage; a theme rarely emphasized in western American fiction. Sex had a humanizing effect on Caucasian men in the Pacific that guns and horses simply could not match in the literary tradition of the mainland West.

The paradise theme that ranged from the travel literature of the eighteenth century to James Michener's *Tales of the South Pacific* had a quality of constant adaptation and change that gave the literary frontier a permanent life. In the eighteenth century, paradise was the untouched world of the Noble Savage, defined as a place where Caucasians had yet to come. By the midtwentieth century, Caucasians had invaded much of the Pacific, but paradise still held on, though often in an altered form. For James Michener the twentieth-century paradise was, in the words of his sometime collaborator A. Grove Day, "not an empty existing spot at which one may arrive, but rather an empty stage to which people of many groups may come, bringing with them their material and cultural assets, by which an Eden may be built."[43]

In the last half of the twentieth century, that Eden, so well portrayed by the pioneers of prose, was still beckoning Americans to the Pacific. There were still special islands and inland valleys luring Americans onward and inward. For two centuries the books, stage plays, and motion pictures of the literary frontier have continually escalated interest in the Pacific Basin as a land of adventure, opportunity, and renewal.

CHAPTER SEVENTEEN

The Frontier Legacy in the Pacific Basin

John S. Whitehead

With the dawn of the twentieth century, Americans had been actively involved in the Pacific Basin for over a hundred years in the capacity of explorers, settlers, traders, missionaries, and writers. Whether one dates American entry into the Pacific to the travels and writings of John Ledyard on Captain Cook's third voyage or to the appearance of the *Empress of China* at Canton in 1784, the Pacific Basin had been one of the new nation's earliest frontiers. Throughout the nineteenth century, the Pacific Basin experience matched and in many ways paralleled continental frontier patterns. As in those frontiers, American presence in the Pacific Basin frequently rivaled and replaced that of other western nations.[1]

Although the United States never gained a monopoly of power in the Pacific, it became the dominant foreign nation there. With the growth of this Pacific power, the nation's territorial boundaries changed. Spanish, later Mexican, and British claims on the eastern shore of the Pacific were acquired by conquest and treaty by 1848. All the lands between San Diego and Puget Sound were incorporated into the Union by the end of the century. In 1867 Russian claims above the fifty-fourth parallel were transferred to the United States in the Alaska Purchase, although the precise status of those lands was still in question at the dawn of the new century. Pushing westward into the island world of the Pacific, the United States annexed Hawai'i in 1898. At the same time, Guam and the Philippines were taken from Spain in the Spanish-American War. By 1900 the arm of national acquisition had also stretched to take in the western part of Samoa as well as smaller islands, including

Wake, Midway, and a set of guano-bearing atolls along the equator. Like Alaska the precise national status of these islands was still a matter for debate. From California to the Philippines and beyond, the influence and imprint of the United States during the nineteenth century was certainly as vast in the Pacific Basin frontier as in any other region of American expansion.

While there were clearly similarities between the pelagic Pacific frontier and the continental frontiers, there were also significant differences that would bequeath a legacy from the nineteenth to the twentieth century. Trade, coupled with natural-resource exploitation, had been the first and primal lure of Americans to the Pacific. By its very definition, trade implies expansion into a region that is already populated. The lure of so-called wilderness or vacant lands of the continental frontiers was not central to Pacific activity. While some of the Pacific lands were less settled than others, trade and the gathering of natural resources presumed partners, whether in sparsely populated California and Russian America or the ancient markets of Japan and China. Like the lure of paradise, which was so important to the writers on the literary frontier, the lure of trade always included the peoples, not just the lands, of the Pacific.

It was not the settling of lands that defined the Pacific Basin frontier; thus that frontier would not be considered closed when a certain number of people per square mile was reached. Using such a measure, the U.S. Census Bureau announced that the continental frontier was closed in 1890. But the Pacific Basin frontier and the lure of trade with Asia were still as open, as enticing, and as alluring as when the *Empress of China* entered Canton over a century earlier. Jack London could set sail for Tahiti with the same excitement that had first drawn Herman Melville there. Some people proclaimed in 1900 that the Pacific was the ocean of the future; but so it had been in the first decade after the American Revolution, when the commerce of the Atlantic was in complete disarray. The Pacific Basin had such a strong allure that after a century of exploration and exploitation, it still seemed newborn.

The legacy of the renewing attraction of trade burst forth in the twentieth century with a series of world's fairs and expositions proclaiming the unlimited riches of the Pacific. Every major Pacific-coast metropolis in the United States except Los Angeles staged such a fair before World War I. Portland, Oregon's, Lewis and Clark Centennial Exposition of 1905 led the way. It was soon followed by Seattle's Alaska-Yukon-Pacific Exposition in 1909 and then in quick succession by San Francisco's Panama-Pacific International Exposition of 1915 and San Diego's Panama-California Exposition of 1915–16. All of these fairs contained elaborate exhibits on the nation's new Pacific possessions, particularly Hawai'i and the Philippines, as well as exhibits from Japan and/or China. The Portland and Seattle fairs proudly proclaimed the future of trans-Pacific trade; the San Francisco and San Diego ventures glorified the newly completed Panama Canal that would make such trade all the more viable.

With the onset of World War I, the nation's attention temporarily turned away from Pacific trade to the affairs of Europe. But it soon returned. During the first half of the century, the fabled "China Market," with its 450 million customers, continually fascinated Americans, even if little trade actually materialized. After World War II, trade with Japan blossomed and boomed, though it seemed to many Americans by the last quarter of the century that the United States was the market for Pacific goods and not vice versa. While certain segments of the business community insisted in the 1980s and 1990s that the Japanese market still had to be "opened," some American companies such as Coca-Cola and IBM had become household words in Japan as well as in China and were garnering substantial portions of their total corporate profits from the western rim of the Pacific. By the last decade of the twentieth century, this remarkable, renewing pull of trade caused some Americans to proclaim that the twenty-first century would be the new "century of the Pacific." The Pacific trade frontier, unlike any of the earlier continental frontiers, remained for century after century the beacon of the future.

There were other differences between the Pacific Basin frontier and its continental counterparts that would bequeath legacies across the centuries. Since the Pacific frontier was populated, Americans would never totally dominate the region as they often did on continental lands. Instead Americans would have to establish influence, both economic and diplomatic, rather than possession in many of the lands they encountered on the Pacific frontier. Certainly the prime example of this role was America's position in Japan. American influence there had first been established in 1854, with Commodore Matthew Perry's opening of that land to the West. For the rest of the nineteenth century, America maintained a sense of proprietorship over Japan's relationship with the West. The United States rushed to retain that influence in the early twentieth century, when Theodore Roosevelt quickly and effectively established himself as the peacemaker of the Pacific by winning the Nobel Prize for his settlement of the Russo-Japanese war in 1905. The level of American influence in Japan reached a historic peak after World War II, when the United States alone occupied and reshaped Japan in its own economic and political image. The nation's presumed success in Japan soon spread to other Pacific countries, with American efforts to influence the development of Korea after World War II. One can even say that the tragedy of Vietnam was the ultimate legacy of the American quest for influence in the Pacific Basin frontier.

The legacy of influence in the twentieth century also carried with it the legacy of missionary effort. The Pacific missionary frontier of the nineteenth century marched headlong into the twentieth century. American missionary effort in Japan and particularly in China hit all-time highs in the first half of the twentieth century and shaped American foreign policy. The pre–World War II view of China as a land of peaceful, earth-tilling peasants fearing the domination of Japanese imperialists was heavily shaped by missionaries and their children. Pearl S. Buck, a popular writer who was the daughter of Presbyterian missionaries to China, popularized this view during the 1920s and 1930s, particularly in her novel *The Good Earth* (1931), which won the Pulitzer Prize and was made into both a stage play and an Academy-Award-winning film. Other children of missionaries to China, such as the journalist Henry R. Luce, became known as the "China lobby" and pressed for American support of China against Japan. After World War II, the missionary frontier in the Pacific found a renewed field of endeavor in South Korea, where some of the largest Protestant congregations in the world have emerged.

The simple mention of World War II obviously suggests the

legacy of the nineteenth-century Pacific military frontier in the twentieth century. The continental western military frontier came to a close with the Battle of Wounded Knee in 1890, virtually coincidental with the Census Bureau's closure of the settlers' frontier. But in the Pacific Basin, the Spanish-American War of 1898 in no way spelled the end of armed action. If anything it augured increased action in the new century.

With the opening of the twentieth century, Americans now held substantial military positions in Hawai'i and the Philippines, as well as on the islands of Samoa, Guam, Wake, and Midway. In the first two decades of the century, new military installations quickly dotted Hawai'i. Schofield Barracks was completed in 1909. The naval base at Pearl Harbor, which had only been contemplated in the nineteenth century, was constructed and opened in 1919. By the 1930s Pearl Harbor stood as a powerful symbol of American military presence in the Pacific, a veritable beacon challenging Japanese ambitions in that same basin; what more striking proof of the legacy of the military frontier in the Pacific can one point to than the bombing of Pearl Harbor in 1941. In the next few years the Japanese seizure, and later American recapture, of the Philippines, as well as the Battles of Wake and Midway, reminded all Americans that the War of 1898 had closed no frontier.

World War II drew thousands of American soldiers and sailors, both men and women, to the Pacific. These new pioneers brought back a knowledge of the Pacific that far surpassed the stories of the returning beachcombers and whalers in the nineteenth century. The drama of World War II in the Pacific assumed a prominent position in American literature, theater, and film by midcentury.

The military pioneers brought home far more than just stories; those thousands of Americans stationed on Pacific islands confronted a racial frontier that would gradually transform the nation. Relations between Caucasians and the peoples of the Pacific had begun with the eighteenth-century arrival of the first American ships into Pacific ports. While there were numerous instances of racial harmony between individuals, the migration of Japanese and Chinese workers to the American continent in the latter half of the nineteenth century bequeathed a legacy of bigotry and exclusion. In the early twentieth century, these tensions strained relations not only between Caucasians and Asians in the United States but also between the United States and the nations from which those immigrants had come.

The onset of World War II initially exacerbated racial hostility toward the Japanese abroad and toward Japanese-Americans at home. As the war became more intense, however, the mixture of the military, racial, and literary frontiers in the crucible of the mid-Pacific elicited a dependency among different races that broke down many preexisting barriers. There is no better description of these emerging racial bonds than in James Michener's *Tales of the South Pacific.* He probed the depths of the relationships between American servicemen and Polynesian women, as well as between Caucasians and African-Americans. The ensuing Broadway musical and motion picture, *South Pacific,* drew the attention of Americans to a reexamination of race relations within the United States. The haunting lines of one of the musical's songs, "You've Got to Be Taught," portrayed racial hatred as an unnatural human emotion that could only be instilled in young children by careful parental indoctrination. The message from this song in turn became the inspiration for sermons in American churches. Racial barriers were also weakened by the military valor and achievements of Japanese-Americans, from both Hawai'i and the mainland, in the all-Nisei 442nd Regimental Combat Team and the 100th Infantry Division. To no small degree, the civil-rights movement of the post–World War II era was ignited by the experience of Caucasians, African-Americans, and Japanese-Americans in the twentieth-century military frontier of the Pacific. Within three years of the war's end, President Harry Truman ordered the integration of the armed forces of the United States.

The conclusion of World War II did not close the Pacific military frontier. In little more than five years, Americans found themselves engaged in the Korean Conflict and later in the quagmire of Vietnam. As the last decade of the twentieth century approached, the perceived need to maintain military security and influence in the Pacific was as open and alive as it had been in the 1890s. In the eighteenth and nineteenth centuries, the American continental and the Pacific Basin frontiers were theaters of international rivalry. Only the Pacific Basin frontier bequeathed this rivalry to the twentieth century and reminded the nation that two oceans did not guarantee free security.

A final legacy from the nineteenth-century Pacific frontier that would haunt Americans in the twentieth century was the status of the newly acquired territories and peoples of the Pacific. How Americanized could the populated Pacific frontier become, and could the different peoples there be incorporated into the American Union? Beginning with the Northwest Ordinance of 1787, new lands on the continental frontiers had been transformed into states. By 1900 only three potential states (New Mexico, Arizona, and Oklahoma) remained outside the Union. By 1912 the continental Union was complete.

Such was not the case with the Pacific Basin frontier. By 1900 only the eastern shore had been transformed into states. In the process it had essentially been subsumed into the continental land-mass, considered more the American West Coast than the Pacific East Coast. Although San Francisco was still a point of departure for Pacific vessels, that metropolis was also a final destination for the transcontinental railroad. A half-century earlier, Americans envisioned a Pacific railroad carrying goods to San Francisco en route to the Orient. But by 1900 most of those goods were destined for the millions of customers in California, not in China. The world's fairs of the early 1900s might proclaim the value of over-seas markets, but they could not alter the reality that the Pacific-coast states now faced east as well as west.

While the eastern shore had been fully Americanized and in-corporated into the Union, the status of the remaining portions of the nineteenth-century Pacific Basin frontier were not at all fixed or clear. Hawai'i had been annexed as an independent republic in 1898 and given territorial status in 1900; the United States had incorporated native Hawaiians natives as American citizens with voting rights. These actions, however, did not imply that all Cau-casians in Honolulu or Washington anticipated statehood for the islands. The full impact of democracy that statehood would entail, including an elected governor and a congressional delegation, as opposed to federal appointees under territorial status, caused con-cern and even alarm to many Americans. Some Caucasians in the islands and the nation's capital envisioned Hawai'i as a federally

417

controlled colony with a limited dose of home rule. In 1900 it was definitely not seen as a tropical twin of California that would quickly write a constitution and enter the Union.

In Alaska the existence of a sparsely settled land with a 50 percent native population in 1900, which increased to 60 percent by 1910, also posed problems of incorporation. Although the Northland had been purchased in 1867, by the turn of the century it existed in the nebulous political form of a district, lacking even an elected legislature. In 1912 Alaska was given territorial status, but with dramatically limited legislative powers; the people's representatives could not regulate the territory's natural resources. In the judicial sector Alaska had only a federal court system; no territorial courts emerged. During the first half of the twentieth century, Alaska was accorded less home rule and more federal control than any other territory in American history.

The Philippines, the least Americanized and most populated of the Pacific Basin acquisitions, posed enormous questions of status as the twentieth century dawned. Had the islands been taken from Spain to be granted independence, to be incorporated into the American Union, or to be retained in some other fashion? While ultimate independence was foreseen by 1900, a commission form of colonial government was installed in the first decade of the twentieth century. The status issue also extended to the other Pacific islands acquired in the last years of the nineteenth century. In Guam and American Samoa, military protectorates were established.

The status of the nation's insular and Pacific possessions became such an issue that the U.S. Supreme Court attempted to divide the new acquisitions into "incorporated" and "unincorporated" categories in a number of cases beginning in 1901 known as the Insular Cases. "Incorporated" Hawai'i and Alaska might one day advance toward statehood, while "unincorporated" Puerto Rico, the Philippines, and other island possessions would not.

Despite the court's ruling, the methods of colonial and military rule established in the Philippines, Samoa, and Guam provided precedents for attempts to further curtail the limited degree of self-government in Alaska and Hawai'i. Alaskans became particularly agitated in 1909, when President William Howard Taft, the first commissioner of the Philippines, appeared at the Alaska-Yukon-

Pacific Exposition in Seattle and recommended a commission form of government for that northern region. A quarter-century later, in 1932, the issue of status resurfaced in Hawai'i. In that year relations between the military and civilian populations of the islands were strained to the breaking point by the *Massie* case, which involved the alleged rape of a Caucasian naval lieutenant's wife by a group of Hawaiian and Asian-American youths. As a result of the crisis, Admiral Yates Stirling, the commander of Pearl Harbor, suggested that home rule be curtailed in the islands in favor of a government by military commission. He was joined in this appeal by several members of Congress and the Hearst newspapers.

Commission government never materialized in either of the incorporated territories. However, the fact that it was so readily suggested highlighted the unending democratic tensions on the twentieth-century Pacific Basin frontier, where the old nineteenth-century continental tradition of statehood for newly acquired lands confronted forces proposing alternative forms of government for American acquisitions. The drama of World War II, which brought so many Americans to the Pacific and which forced Caucasians to look at Asian-Americans in a new light, finally resolved the issue of statehood in Alaska and Hawai'i. Within fifteen years of the war's end, the two territories joined the Union as the forty-ninth and fiftieth states, in 1959.

Statehood for Alaska and Hawai'i changed many Americans' concept of what their country was and could be. With the bonds of contiguity now broken, the American Union was no longer defined solely by land connections. The addition of Asian-American and later Hawaiian representatives and senators in the U.S. Congress expanded the human boundaries of what the nation could be.

Even the placement of two new stars in the flag did not close the Pacific Basin frontier. Just as Alaska and Hawai'i drew closer to the Union, the Philippines gained its independence in 1946, thus causing Americans to think once again about the military and security demands of the Pacific. What would be the American role of influence in those islands now that the role of possession had ceased? Did the United States have special privileges there? The single issue of the Philippines almost defied any writer to bring the Pacific Basin frontier to a close. As the 1990s progressed, the future of American influence there, particularly the status of U.S. air and naval bases, was suddenly thrown into a new perspective by the eruption of Mt. Pinatubo in the summer of 1991, for the first time in six hundred years. With lava ash descending at an unstoppable pace, the fate of Clark Air Force Base was literally sealed. What the volcano began, the Philippine government concluded a few months later, with its decision not to renew the lease on the Subic Bay Naval Station. Where would the American Pacific military frontiersmen go in the 1990s, now that politics and rumblings from the center of the earth had displaced them from the position they had gained in the 1890s? Unexpectedly out of time and space, the rim of fire, that chain of volcanoes that defines the Pacific Rim, burst forth to remind Americans that the Pacific Basin was truly unlike any other frontier Americans had faced.

With the ash still warm from the eruption of Mt. Pinatubo, we may well conclude our assessment of the ultimate legacy of the Pacific Basin frontier. We have observed that patterns similar to those on the continental frontiers emerged in the Pacific Basin in the eighteenth and nineteenth centuries. But peculiarities and differences of trade, war, race, population, climate, and even seismic activity defied the closing of the Pacific frontier. Instead it has continually renewed itself, luring Americans westward throughout the twentieth century. In 1897 a young American historian, a contemporary of Frederick Jackson Turner, made what he thought was a conclusive statement: "There has never yet been a time in our history when we were without an 'East' and a 'West,' but the novel day when we shall be without them is now in sight," announced Princeton University professor Woodrow Wilson. Possibly this was true for a southerner living in New Jersey, who fondly looked across the Atlantic to England. But for anyone like Jack London who sailed the Pacific or marched to the Klondike in 1897, that day was definitely not in sight. The Pacific Basin frontier was still open. In 1900 the Pacific frontier continued to give the nation a chance for new opportunities as it had done in 1800 and as it would continue to do in 1990. It remained the frontier that would not be closed. Possibly the greatest legacy then of the Pacific Basin frontier should be the simple realization that the nation has never truly known just one Pacific century. American life has been and by all evidence will continue to be shaped by the Pacific centuries.

Afterword

A TRIBUTE TO
ARRELL MORGAN GIBSON

Arrell Morgan Gibson (1921–1987) was one of those rare men who are able to contribute very widely to the profession of history. A fifth generation citizen of the greater Southwest, he thought of himself as a southwesterner all of his life. He grew up in the Ozark Mountain country of southwestern Missouri. It was his goal in life to be a professional baseball player, but as with so many people in his generation his hopes were changed by circumstances. Most importantly he aspired to go to college, certainly a hope that had been sponsored by his mother, not in a financial sense but in the sense of a commitment to learning. It is hard to estimate the influence of this highly intellectual woman, even though she was not educated, upon his life. One way to a college education was through athletic ability, and his was used first to get him a scholarship. While his family was not poor, they had financial limitations. He attended college in southwest Missouri where he had grown up; then World War II intervened. He entered the service and when the war was over he decided that his direction would certainly be to study history and to study it under the most interesting historian he had discovered, a man named Edward Everett Dale at the University of Oklahoma. The possibility was doubly attractive to him since the University of Oklahoma was only a short distance from the area where he had grown up—at least short as Americans measure distance.

Gibson plunged into his studies with tremendous gusto. He worked with the historians Gilbert Fite and Gene Hollon, as well as with Edward Everett Dale. He was Dale's last Ph.D. student and thus but barely made the deadline to work with the man that he so admired.

As a historian, Gibson was indeed a man who attracted attention early. His first job was at Phillips University at Enid, Oklahoma, where he was an extremely popular teacher; he later recalled those teaching years as the most satisfying of his professional life. The happy experience at Phillips lasted only eight years, when he was called to the University of Oklahoma.

Always behind his desire to be a professor of history was a more compelling passion to be a writer, and he became a proficient one during the first years working at the University of Oklahoma. There was pressure to publish but that urgency coincided with his desire to write; as a result the long string of books that came from his pen have embellished and enriched the world of western history.

In an interview I conducted with Dr. Gibson in 1985, I asked him to name the best book he had written. He immediately said, "It was *The Kickapoos: Lords of the Middle Border.*" I asked him further in that interview if the writing made it the best book. He replied, "No, it is because I was able to describe the account of these magnificent people and because their saga stands on its own. They were a courageous people who breathed the fire of passion for independence."

Dr. Gibson also had a large number of doctoral students of his own, and there was yet a long list waiting to study with him at his untimely death. There are still more of Gibson's students who are teaching American Indian history than those of any other single scholar in this country. He casts a very long shadow.

In another sense I want to talk about Gibson. I want to speak of him as a man. He was a voracious reader, a dedicated researcher. He was tireless at asking questions, asking "Why?" But another side of him revealed a remarkable gentleman whose manners were polished and even courtly; his was a commanding presence, ruggedly handsome, who spoke very, very well. It is small wonder that the long shadow continues to leave its imprint upon the American West and upon this, his last work, in spite of his passing.

This book is a remarkably appropriate tribute to a man who attempted to push back the frontiers of the history of the American West.

Floyd A. O'Neil, Director
American West Center
University of Utah

Notes

CHAPTER ONE

1. Ernest S. Dodge, "The Pacific: An Expanding Field for Historical Research," in *Geography and Exploration* (Upper Saddle River, N.J., n.d.), 1–3.

CHAPTER TWO

1. See Otis W. Freeman, ed., *Geography of the Pacific* (New York, 1951); and Herman R. Friis, ed., *The Pacific Basin: A History of Its Geographical Exploration* (New York, 1967), for essays discussing environment and reconnaissance of the Pacific Basin.

2. In the days of sailing vessels, the distances in this water hemisphere were mind-boggling. Passage from New York to Honolulu covered eighteen thousand miles and sometimes required up to six months for the voyage.

3. Stuart R. Tompkins, *Alaska: Promyshlennik and Sourdough* (Norman, 1945), 5.

4. Freeman, *Geography of the Pacific*, 3.

5. Ibid., 6–7, 25–31.

6. Donald C. Cutter, *The California Coast: A Bilingual Edition of Documents from the Sutro Collection* (Norman, 1969), 115.

7. William L. Thomas, Jr., "The Pacific Basin," in Friis, *The Pacific Basin*, 3–9, 11–15; Freeman, "Geographical Setting," 6–7, 9–19. Also see Gavan Daws, *Shoal of Time: A History of the Hawaiian Islands* (New York, 1968).

8. In 1946 a tsunami struck the entire Hawaiian Island group, killing two hundred people and destroying thirteen hundred homes; property damage was estimated at $24 million and included the complete destruction of the Hilo waterfront. Fourteen years later a tsunami, precipitated by an earthquake from Chile, swept over Hilo, killing fifty-seven and causing $18 million in damage.

9. Alexander von Humboldt, German naturalist, studied the South American milieu between 1799 and 1804, including the southern equatorial current, and discovered the agricultural value of the guano that abounded on the offshore islands and coast of South America.

10. *Transcript* (Norman, Okla.), 2 June 1975.

11. Richard A. Pierce, *Russia's Hawaiian Adventure, 1815–1817* (Berkeley, 1965), 1.

CHAPTER THREE

1. A. L. Kroeber, *Handbook of the Indians of California,* Bureau of American Ethnology Bulletin 78 (Washington, D.C., 1925), presents a survey of this complex and populous aboriginal community. Also see Frederick W. Hodge, ed., *Handbook of American Indians North of Mexico* (Washington, D.C., 1907–10), reprinted (New York, 1959), 2 vols.

2. Erna Gunther, *Indian Life on the Northwest Coast of North America as Seen by the Early Explorers and Fur Traders during the Last Decades of the Eighteenth Century* (Chicago, 1972), illuminates these themes.

3. See K. Birket-Smith, *The Eskimos* (New York, 1958), and *Alaska Natives and the Land* (Anchorage, 1968).

4. Gavan Daws, *Shoal of Time,* and Edward Joesting, *Hawaii: An Uncommon History* (New York, 1972), provide basic information of the Sandwich Island evolution into the Hawaiian Island kingdom.

CHAPTER FOUR

1. See Ronald Louis Silveira de Braganza and Charlotte Oakes, eds., *The Hill Collection of Pacific Voyages* (San Diego, 1974), for a guide to the copious literature of Pacific exploration.

2. In recent times scurvy has been found to be a disorder resulting from a lack of vitamin C in the diet.

3. William L. Schurz, *The Manila Galleon* (New York, 1939), 63.

4. See Schurz, *Manila Galleon,* for the origins of this mercantilistic trade pattern and an analysis of its function. The last Manila galleon docked at Acapulco in 1815.

5. Spaniards tapped the rich China trade by channels established in the nearby Philippines rather than on the Asian mainland, as did the Portuguese at Macao and the British at Hong Kong.

6. Richard Hawkins, *The Observations of Sir Richard Hawkins . . . in His Voyage into the South Sea in the Year 1593* (London, 1847).

CHAPTER FIVE

1. Allen E. Oliver, *The Pacific Navigators* (Alexandria, Va., 1980), 77.

2. French officials returned the Falkland Islands to Spain in 1767. Shortly thereafter British forces occupied the archipelago, but in 1770 a Spanish expedition in turn forced the Britons to evacuate the islands.

3. Oliver, *Pacific Navigators,* 87.

4. See W. H. Bonner, *Captain William H. Dampier: Buccaneer-Author* (Stanford, Cal., 1934).

5. Selkirk remained on Mas Atierra Island for four years and four months, before his rescue in 1709 by the English privateer. He later became a lieutenant in the Royal British Navy.

6. Vincent T. Harlow, *The Founding of the Second British Empire, 1763–1793* (London, 1952) 1:61.

7. Barry M. Gough, "The Northwest Coast in Late 18th Century British Expansion," in *The Western Shore: Oregon Country Essays Honoring the American Revolution,* ed. by Thomas Vaughan (Portland, n.d.), 47–80.

8. See John Ledyard, *Journal of Captain Cook's Last Voyage to the Pacific Ocean . . .* (Hartford, Conn., 1783).

9. Warren L. Cook, *Flood Tide of Empire, 1543–1819* (New Haven, Conn., 1973), 542.

10. Ibid.

CHAPTER SIX

1. See Josiah Quincy, ed., *The Journals of Major Samuel Shaw . . . with the Life of the Author* (Boston, 1847), for Shaw's report to Congress.

2. Kenneth S. Latourette, "The History of Early Relations between the United States and China, 1784–1844," *Transactions of the Connecticut Academy of Arts and Sciences* 22 (August 1917), 7.

3. William Sturgis, "The Northwest Fur Trade," *Hunt's Merchants' Magazine* 14 (June 1846), 532–39.

CHAPTER SEVEN

1. See John Ledyard, *Journal of Captain Cook's Last Voyage* (Hartford, 1783).

2. Adele Ogden, *The California Sea Otter Trade, 1784–1848* (Berkeley, 1941), 24.

3. William Shaler, *Journal of a Voyage between China and the Northwestern Coast of America Made in 1804* (Claremont, Cal., 1935); and Richard J. Cleveland, *A Narrative of Voyages and Commercial Enterprises* (London, 1842).

4. Hubert H. Bancroft, *History of the Northwest Coast* (San Francisco, 1884) 1:361.

5. Ibid., 369–70.

6. Vincent T. Harlow, *Second British Empire* (London, 1952) 2:174; Bancroft, *Northwest Coast* 1:359.

7. Bancroft, *Northwest Coast* 1:363–64, 367.

8. Alexander Mackenzie, *Voyages from Montreal . . . through the Continent of North America, in the Years 1789 and 1793* (London, 1802) 1:411.

9. See George Vancouver, *A Voyage of Discovery to the North Pacific Ocean . . . in the Years 1790 . . . 1795* (London, 1798), 3 vols., for an account of his role in reducing native threats to Europeans and Americans in the Pacific Basin.

10. Richard A. Pierce, *Russia's Hawaiian Adventure* (Berkeley, 1965), 1.

11. Gabriel Franchère, *Adventure at Astoria, 1810–1814,* trans. and ed. by Hoyt C. Franchère (Norman, 1967), 37.

12. Bancroft, *Northwest Coast* 1:306.

13. Ogden, *Sea Otter Trade*, 45–65.

14. See Kenneth W. Porter, *John Jacob Astor: Business Man* (Cambridge, Mass., 1931), 2 vols.; see also James P. Ronda, *Astoria and Empire* (Lincoln, Neb., 1990).

15. Porter, *Astor* 1:135, 149.

16. James R. Gibson, *Imperial Russia in Frontier America: The Changing Geography of Supply of Russian America, 1784–1867* (New York, 1976), 161.

17. Porter, *Astor* 1:144.

18. See Edgeley W. Todd, ed., *Astoria* (Norman, 1964); and Franchère, *Adventure at Astoria,* for accounts of the founding of this Northwest Coast outpost.

19. See Ross Cox, *Adventures on the Columbia River,* ed. by Edgar I. Stewart and Jane R. Stewart (Norman, 1957); and Franchère, *Adventure at Astoria,* for comparative accounts of the *Tonquin* massacre.

20. See Franchère, *Adventure at Astoria;* and Peter Corney, *Early Voyages in the North Pacific, 1813–1818* (Fairfield, Wash., 1965), 103–11, for accounts of the Northwest Company agents' advent.

21. Barry M. Gough, *The Royal Navy and the Northwest Coast of North America, 1810–1814: A Study of British Maritime Ascendancy* (Vancouver, B.C., 1971), contains an account of the sale of Astoria and its capture by the *Raccoon.*

22. Alexander Ross, *Fur Hunters of the Far West,* ed. by Kenneth W. Spaulding (Norman, 1956), 193–94.

23. The history of the Hudson's Bay Company is related in John S. Galbraith, *The Hudson's Bay Company as an Imperial Factor, 1821–1869* (Berkeley, 1957).

24. For accounts of Russian extension to the California coast, see Gibson, *Imperial Russia,* 113–15; and S. B. Okun, *The Russian-American Company,* ed. with an introduction by B. D. Grekov, trans. from the Russian by Carl Guisburg, preface by Robert J. Kerner (Cambridge, Mass., 1951).

25. Gibson, *Imperial Russia,* 113–15.

26. See Adam J. von Krusenstern, *Voyage Round the World in the Years 1803, 1804, 1805, and 1806,* trans. from the original German by Richard B. Hoppner (London, 1813), 2 vols.; and N. A. Ivashitsov, *Around-the-World Travels from 1803–1849* (St. Petersburg, 1872).

27. Gibson, *Imperial Russia,* 145.

28. Pierce, *Russia's Adventure,* 118.

29. Lawrence H. Battistini, *The Rise of American Influence in Asia and the Pacific* (East Lansing, Mich., 1960), 10–11.

30. Edouard A. Stackpole, *The Sea Hunters* (Philadelphia, 1953), contains accounts of pioneer Yankee seal and whale hunting in the southeastern quadrant of the Pacific Basin.

31. Kenneth J. Bertrand, "Geographical Exploration by the United States," in Friis, *The Pacific Basin,* 261.

32. Ogden, *Sea Otter Trade,* 95–119.

33. Ibid., 109, 113.

34. See Dorothy O. Johansen and Charles M. Gates, *Empire of the Columbia: A History of the Pacific Northwest* (New York, 1967); Oscar O. Winther, *The Great Northwest: A History* (New York, 1947), for details of the early colonizing attempts by Yankees on the Northwest Coast; and Bancroft, *Northwest Coast,* vol. 1.

CHAPTER EIGHT

1. Addison B. Whipple, *The Whalers* (Alexandria, Va., 1979), 53.

2. Ibid., 6.

3. By the 1850s sea hunters were replacing the harpoon with the bomblance gun, a riflelike shoulder weapon that fired a harpoon with a head that exploded after penetrating the whale's body.

4. Stackpole, *The Sea Hunters;* and Alexander Starbuck, *History of the American Whale Fishing from Its Earliest Inception to the Year 1876* (New York, 1964), are basic sources for the sea-mammal hunting industry, including markets and prices.

5. Charles S. Steward, *A Visit to the South Seas in the U.S. Ship "Vincennes"* (New York, 1831) 1:188.

6. R. Gerard Ward, ed., *American Activities in the Central Pacific, 1790–1870* (Ridgewood, N.J., 1966) 2:522.

7. Ernest S. Dodge, *Islands and Empires: Western Impact on the Pacific and East Asia* (Minneapolis, 1976), 71.

8. Ward, *American Activities* 2:470.

9. Ibid. 6:403.

10. Ibid. 2:22–25.

11. Gilbert F. Mathison, *Narrative of a Visit to Brazil, Chile, Peru, and the Sandwich Islands during the Years 1821 and 1822* (London, 1825), 459.

12. Dodge, *Islands and Empires,* 81–83; Ward, *American Activities* 2:470.

13. Foster R. Dulles, *Lowered Boats: A Chronicle of American Whaling* (New York, 1933), 242.

14. A. Grove Day, ed., *Mark Twain's Letters from Hawaii* (New York, 1966), 87.

15. Ralph S. Kuykendall, *The Hawaiian Kingdom, 1778–1854: Foundation and Transformation* (Honolulu, 1947), 311; also see Bernice Judd, *Voyages to Hawaii before 1860* (Honolulu, 1974).

16. Ward, *American Activities* 2:525; and Whipple, *Whalers,* 96.

17. J. Ross Browne, *Etchings of a Whaling Cruise,* ed. by John Seelye (Cambridge, Mass., 1968), 504.

18. Ibid., 505–6.

19. Harry A. Chippendale, *Sails and Whales* (Boston, 1951), 31.

20. Whipple, *Whalers,* 78; James R. Gibson, "Bostonians and Muscovites on the Northwest Coast, 1788–1841," in *The Western Shore: Oregon Country Essays Honoring the American Revolution* (Portland, Ore., n.d.), 95; and Ward, *American Activities* 7:13.

21. Dulles, *Lowered Boats,* 42.

22. See Starbuck, *American Whale Fishing,* for a compendium of whaling-industry statistics.

23. Dulles, *Lowered Boats,* 253–64, relates Confederate operations in the Pacific Basin.

24. See Everett S. Allen, *Children of the Light: The Rise and Fall of New Bedford Whaling and the Death of the Arctic Fleet* (Boston, 1973).

25. See Charles Wilkes, *Narrative of the United States Exploring Expedition, 1838–1842* (Philadelphia, 1845–48), 9 vols., for an exhaustive account of this official United States reconnaissance of the Pacific Basin.

26. Dodge, *Islands and Empires,* 71, 140, 190.

27. Ward, *American Activities,* vols. 1–8, consists largely of extracts from contemporary newspapers, most of them published in New England, relating Yankee maritime experiences in the Pacific Basin.

28. For an illustration of the magnitude of just one class of literature generated by interest in the Pacific Basin, see Ronald Louis Silveiro de Braganza and Charlotte Oaks, eds., *The Hill Collection of Pacific Voyages* (San Diego, 1974); also see Pamela A. Miller, *And the Whale Is Ours: Creative Writing of American Whalemen* (Boston, 1979).

29. Whipple, *Whalers,* 126.

30. Ibid., 19.

CHAPTER NINE

1. For excellent accounts of Yankee gatherer activity in the Pacific Basin see William G. Dix, *Wreck of the Glide, with Recollections of the Fijis and Wallis Island* (New York, 1848); and Edmund Fanning, *Voyages to the South Seas* (New York, 1838).

2. Ward, *American Activities* 2:92.

3. James R. Gibson, "Bostonians and Muscovites on the Northwest Coast, 1788–1841," in *The Western Shore: Oregon Country Essays Honoring the American Revolution,* ed. by Thomas Vaughan (Portland, n.d.), 92.

4. Dodge, *Islands and Empires,* 63.

5. Ibid., 66.

6. Kenneth Scott Latourette, *A History of Early Relations between the United States and China, 1784–1844* (New Haven, 1917), 58.

7. Dodge, *Islands and Empires,* 60.

8. Battistini, *American Influence,* 11–12; and Ward, *American Activities* 2:377.

9. Latourette, *Early Relations,* 44–45.

10. Harold W. Bradley, "The Hawaiian Islands and the Pacific Fur Trade, 1785–1813," *Pacific Northwest Quarterly* 30 (July 1939) 291.

11. Latourette, *Early Relations,* 58; and Gibson, "Bostonians and Muscovites," 91.

12. Judd, *Voyages to Hawaii,* 17.

13. Harold W. Bradley, *The American Frontier in Hawaii: The Pioneers, 1789–1843* (Stanford, Cal., 1942), 60–71.

14. Latourette, *Early Relations,* 58.

15. Richard Henry Dana, Jr., *Two Years Before the Mast* (New York, 1964), is a participant's very readable account of the hide-and-tallow trade.

16. Robert G. Cleland, *A History of California: The American Period* (Westport, Conn., 1975), 43.

17. Ibid., 17.

18. Samuel E. Morison, *The Maritime History of Massachusetts, 1783–1860* (Boston, 1921), 267.

19. Cleland, *History of California,* 38.

20. Chemists rated the composition of Pacific island guano at 6–12 percent phosphorous, 9–16 percent nitrogen, and 2–3 percent potash (potassium).

21. Otis W. Freeman, "Geographic Setting of the Pacific," in *Geography of the Pacific,* ed. by Otis W. Freeman (New York, 1951), 21–22.

22. Ward, *American Activities* 3:369.

23. Ibid. 3:212, 230.

24. *U.S. Statutes at Large* 9:119–20.

25. Ward, *American Activities* 3:427.

26. Ibid. 3:185

27. James A. Michener and A. Grove Day, *Rascals in Paradise* (New York, 1957), 208.

28. Curtis A. Manchester, Jr., "The Exploration and Mapping of the Pacific," in *Geography of the Pacific,* ed. by Otis W. Freeman (New York, 1951), 84, states that blackbirding continued until after World War I; also see Michener and Day, *Rascals in Paradise,* 208.

29. Michener and Day, *Rascals in Paradise,* 209.

CHAPTER TEN

1. William Shaler, *Journal of a Voyage between China and the Northwestern Coast of America Made in 1804* (Claremont, Cal., 1935); and Richard J. Cleveland, *A Narrative of Voyages and Commercial Enterprises* (London, 1842).

2. Morison, *Maritime History,* 267; and Samuel Patterson, *Narrative of the Adventures and Sufferings of Samuel Patterson, Experienced in the Pacific Ocean* (Palmer, Mass., 1817), 138.

3. Battistini, *American Influence,* 26.

4. Morison, *Maritime History,* 328–29.

5. Ward, *American Activities* 2:189, 194. Increasingly after 1800, several newspapers carried accounts derived from ships' logs, letters from ships' officers, and seamen's interviews giving the locations of Pacific shoals, reefs, atolls, rocks, anchorages, discoveries of Pacific islands with locations, accounts of shipwrecks, fates of crews and cargoes, and insurance coverage. The principal maritime journals were the Salem, Mass., *Daily Journal,* Boston *Morning Post,* New Bedford *Daily Evening Standard,* Boston *Missionary Herald,* New Bedford *Daily*

Mercury, New Bedford *Gazette,* Boston *Daily Bee,* Boston *Daily Evening Traveler,* Boston *Post,* New Bedford *Whaleman,* Salem *Gazette,* San Francisco *Alta California,* Honolulu *Polynesian,* Honolulu *Sandwich Island Gazette,* and New York *Observer.* These journals included special maritime columns headed "Whalers," "Pacific Trade," "Notice to Mariners," and "Disasters at Sea."

6. See Tyler Dennett, *Americans in Eastern Asia* (New York, 1941), for an account of the rapid expansion of American trade at Canton.

7. Kenneth S. Latourette, *A History of Early Relations between the United States and China, 1784–1844* (New Haven, 1917), 24; and Cleveland, *Voyages,* 46–47.

8. Cleveland, *Voyages,* vi.

9. Porter, *John Jacob Astor* 2:620.

10. See Arthur Waley, *The Opium War through Chinese Eyes* (London, 1958); and Maurice Collins, *Foreign Mud* (London, 1946).

11. Dodge, *Islands and Empires,* 266; and Morison, *Maritime History,* 278.

12. Latourette, *Early Relations,* 73.

13. Morison, *Maritime History,* 277.

14. Ibid., 277–78.

15. See Edgar Holt, *The Opium Wars in China* (London, 1964), for an analysis of Treaty of Nanking; and Dodge, *Islands and Empires,* 274.

16. Latourette, *Early Relations,* 116–17.

17. Dennett, *Eastern Asia,* 133–34.

18. See C. M. Fuess, *The Life of Caleb Cushing* (New York, 1923), 2 vols.; and Ta-Kong Tang, *U.S. Diplomacy in China, 1844–1860* (Seattle, 1964), for accounts of Cushing's negotiations.

19. See Dennett, *Eastern Asia,* for an analysis of United States commerce with China following the Treaty of Wanghia.

20. See Morison, *Maritime History,* 279; and Battistini, *American Influence,* 27.

21. Ward, *American Activities* 7:393–97.

22. Kuykendall, *Hawaiian Kingdom* 1:299.

23. Ibid. 1:299, 301.

24. Gibson, "Bostonians and Muscovites," 83–91.

25. Morison, *Maritime History,* 269.

26. Principal sources for the so-called "opening of Japan" are Francis L. Hawks, *Narrative of the Expedition of an American Squadron to the China Seas and Japan, Performed in the Years 1852, 1853, and 1854, under the Command of Commodore M. C. Perry, United States Navy* (Washington, D.C., 1856), 3 vols.; Samuel E. Morison, *"Old Bruin": Commodore Matthew C. Perry, 1794–1858* (Boston, 1967); and George Henry Preble, *The Opening of Japan: A Diary of Discovery in the Far East, 1853–1856,* ed. by Boleslaw Szczesniak (Norman, Okla., 1962).

27. See Preble, *Opening of Japan.*

28. M. E. Cosenza, *The Complete Journal of Townsend Harris, First American Consul General and Minister to Japan* (Garden City, N.Y., 1930); and Payson J. Treat, *Diplomatic Relations between the United States and Japan 1835–1895*

(Gloucester, Mass., 1963), 2 vols., give the essentials of these early American negotiations with Japan.

29. Dodge, *Islands and Empires,* 268.

CHAPTER ELEVEN

1. See George F. Parsons, *The Life and Adventures of James W. Marshall, the Discoverer of Gold in California* (Sacramento, Cal., 1870), for an account of the Coloma Placer discovery.

2. John W. Caughey, *The California Gold Rush* (Berkeley, Cal., 1975), 33–34.

3. Candace Floyd, "Chinatown," *History News* 39 (June 1984) 8. This study reports that forty-five vessels left Hong Kong for California in 1850, each with nearly 500 Chinese men "packed into their holds, and by the end of 1851 there were 25,000 Chinese in California."

4. Caughey, *California Gold Rush,* 29.

5. Ibid., 22–23.

6. See Ed Bearss and Arrell Morgan Gibson, *Fort Smith, Little Gibraltar on the Arkansas* (Norman, Okla., 1969), for an account of the alternative routes to the Pacific.

7. Raymond A. Rydell, *Cape Horn to the Pacific: The Rise and Decline of an Ocean Highway* (Berkeley, Cal., 1952), 116–26.

8. See Rodman Paul, *California Gold: The Beginning of Mining in the Far West* (Cambridge, Mass., 1947), for a description of mining technology and methodology.

9. See Charles H. Shinn, *Land Laws of Mining Districts* (Baltimore, 1884), and *Mining Camps: A Study in American Frontier Government* (New York, 1948), for studies in evolution of mining-camp governance.

10. Frederic L. Paxson, *History of the American Frontier, 1763–1893* (New York, 1924), 373.

11. See Robert F. Heizer, ed., *The Destruction of California Indians* (Santa Barbara, Cal., 1974), for information regarding the Native American genocide in California.

12. Caughey, *California Gold Rush,* 230.

13. Quoted in Douglas Branch, *Westward: The Romance of the American Frontier* (New York, 1930), 437–38.

14. Jay Monaghan, *Australians and the Gold Rush: California and Down Under, 1849–1854* (Berkeley, Cal., 1966), 140.

15. E. Daniel Potts and Annette Potts, *Young America and Australian Gold: Americans and the Gold Rush of the 1850s* (St. Lucia, Australia, 1974), 2.

16. Eldon Griffin, *Clippers and Consuls: American Consular and Commercial Relations with Eastern Asia, 1845–1860* (Wilmington, Del., 1972), 18.

17. Seweryn Korzelinski, *Memoirs of Gold-Digging in Australia,* trans. and ed. by Stanley Robe (St. Lucia, Australia, 1979), 196.

18. Monaghan, *Australians,* 196; and Korzelinski, *Memoirs,* 42.

19. Korzelinski, *Memoirs,* 88.

20. Ibid., 148.

21. Potts, *Young America,* 2; Monaghan, *Australians,* 222.

22. Monaghan, *Australians,* 234; also see Jerome O. Steffen, "The Mining Frontiers of California and Australia: A Study in Comparative Political Change and Continuity," *Pacific Historical Review* 52 (November 1983) 428–40.

23. Monaghan, *Australians,* 248.

24. Raffaello Carboni, *Eureka Stockade* (Melbourne, Australia, 1942); Monaghan, *Australians,* 272.

25. See William S. Greever, *The Bonanza West* (Norman, Okla., 1963), 331–83; and William A. Bultmann, "The Canadian Gulf Islands: British Columbia's Marine Paradise," *Journal of the West* 20 (July 1981) 31, for the progression of prospectors up the Pacific Basin's eastern rimland toward the Arctic Circle.

26. David Wharton, *The Alaska Gold Rush* (Bloomington, Ind., 1972), 4–12; also see James Blower, *Gold Rush* (New York, 1971), for an account of the 1898 stampede to the Klondike.

27. Wharton, *Alaska Gold Rush,* 8.

28. Pierre Berton, *The Klondike Quest* (Boston, 1983), 12.

29. Ibid., 41.

30. Chester W. Purington, *Methods and Costs of Gravel and Placer Mining in Alaska* (Washington, D.C., 1905), 88.

31. Berton, *Klondike Quest,* 193.

32. Monaghan, *Australians,* 270.

CHAPTER 12

1. Grenfell Price, *The Western Invasions of the Pacific and Its Continents: A Study of Moving Frontiers and Changing Landscapes 1513–1958* (Oxford, 1963), 3, 56–57.

2. Walter Coote, *The Western Pacific* (New York, 1969), 19.

3. Jean I. Brookes, *International Rivalry in the Pacific Islands, 1800–1875* (New York, 1941), 172.

4. Ward, *American Activities* 2:462.

5. E. Douglas Branch, *Westward: The Romance of the American Frontier* (New York, 1930), 373.

6. Arrell Morgan Gibson, *The West in the Life of the Nation* (Lexington, Mass., 1976), 334.

7. *U.S. Statutes at Large* 9 (1850) 496.

8. Gibson, *West,* 334.

9. Katherine Coman, *Economic Beginnings of the Far West* (New York, 1912) 2:291.

10. Caughey, *California Gold Rush,* 210.

11. See *California Constitution of 1849,* Article I, Section 18 (St. Paul, Minn., n.d.).

12. Hubert H. Bancroft, *History of California* (San Francisco, Cal., 1848–

59), 220–60, 401, 407–8; also see Heizer, *Destruction of California Indians,* for documentary evidence of Indian bondage.

13. *U.S. Statutes at Large 9* (1851); also see Bancroft, *California* 6:529–82.

14. Cecil Moyer, *Historic Ranchos of San Diego* (La Jolla, Cal., 1969), 8–9.

15. Mathison, *Narrative,* 449–51.

16. James Macrae, *With Lord Byron at the Sandwich Islands in 1825, Being Extracts from the Ms. Diary of James Macrae, Scottish Botanist* (Honolulu, 1922), 68; Mathison, *Narrative,* 425–27. Also see Ross H. Gast, *Don Francisco de Paula Marin: A Biography* (Honolulu, 1973).

17. Kuykendall, *Hawaiian Kingdom,* 314–15.

18. See Sarah Joiner Lyman, *Sarah Joiner Lyman: Her Own Story* (Hilo, Hawai'i, 1970), 136; Macrae, *With Lord Byron,* 34; and Dale L. Morgan, ed., *Laura Fish Judd: Honolulu, Sketches in the Hawaiian Islands from 1828 to 1861* (Chicago, 1966), 393.

19. George Washington Bates, *Sandwich Island Notes: By a Haole* (New York, 1854), 318.

20. Ibid., 204.

21. Ibid., 174.

22. Louise E. Levanthes, "Kamehameha," *National Geographic* 154 (November 1983) 589.

23. Ralph S. Kuykendall, *The Hawaiian Kingdom, 1854–1874: Twenty Critical Years* (Honolulu, 1953), 153.

24. Ward, *American Activities* 3:175–76.

25. Neil M. Levy, "Native Hawaiian Land Rights," *California Law Review* 63 (July 1975) 858–59; also see Jon J. Chinen, *The Great Mahele: Hawaii's Land Division of 1848* (Honolulu, 1985).

26. Levanthes, "Kamehameha," 593; Lawrence H. Fuchs, *Hawaii Pono: A Social History* (New York, 1961), 11.

27. Coote, *Western Pacific,* 161.

28. Kuykendall, *Critical Years,* 177.

29. See Edward D. Beechert, *Working in Hawaii, A Labor History* (Honolulu, 1985).

30. See Alan T. Moriyama, *Imingaisha: Japanese Immigration Companies and Hawaii, 1894–1908* (Honolulu, 1985); and Lyman, *Sarah Joiner Lyman,* 145.

31. See Bob Kraus and William P. Alexander, *Grove Farm Plantation: The Biography of a Hawaiian Sugar Plantation* (Palo Alto, Cal., 1965).

32. Kuykendall, *Critical Years,* 142–43.

33. Lyman, *Sarah Joiner Lyman,* 131, 142, 171; and *Honolulu Advertiser,* 3 April 1904.

34. Lawrence H. Battistini, *The Rise of American Influence in Asia and the Pacific* (East Lansing, Mich., 1960), 160.

35. See Earl S. Pomeroy, *Pacific Outpost: American Strategy in Guam and Micronesia* (Stanford, Cal., 1951).

36. See. G. A. Grunder and William E. Livezey, *The Philippines and the United States* (Norman, Okla., 1951).

37. See George H. Ryden, *The Foreign Policy of the United States in Relation to Samoa* (New Haven, Conn., 1933), which traces the diplomacy leading to the partitioning of the Samoan archipelago.

38. See Florence Mann Spoehr, *White Falcon: The House of Godeffroy and Its Commercial and Scientific Role in the Pacific* (Palo Alto, Cal., 1963).

39. See William E. Livezey, *Mahan on Sea Power* (Norman, Okla., 1947).

40. Ward, *American Activities* 7:397–98.

41. Ryden, *Foreign Policy*, 45.

42. See Orlando W. Miller, *The Frontier in Alaska and the Matanuska Colony* (New Haven, Conn., 1975).

CHAPTER THIRTEEN

1. See Dodge, *Islands and Empires*, 207–19.

2. Ibid., 96.

3. William Stanton, *The Great United States Exploring Expedition of 1838–1842* (Berkeley, Cal., 1975), 136.

4. Ward, *American Activities* 5:365.

5. Clifton C. Phillips, *Protestant America and the Pagan World: The First Half Century of the American Board of Commissioners for Foreign Missions, 1810–1860* (Cambridge, Mass., 1969), 91–92.

6. Ibid., 93–94.

7. Bingham to Howell, Honolulu, 27 June 1820; and Bingham to Calvin Bingham, on board the *Thaddeus,* 1 February 1820, Bingham Family Papers, Yale University Library.

8. Hiram Bingham, *A Residence of Twenty-one Years in the Sandwich Islands* (Hartford, 1849), 6; and Stanton, *Exploring Expedition,* 136.

9. Sylvester K. Stevens, *American Expansion in Hawaii, 1842–1898* (Harrisburg, Pa., 1945), 8–9.

10. See Phillips, *Protestant America,* for an extension of this topic.

11. See Lyman, *Sarah Joiner Lyman,* xii; Fuchs, *Hawaii Pono,* 12; and Dodge, *Islands and Empires,* 124.

12. Sheldon Dibble, *History and General View of the Sandwich Islands Mission* (New York, 1839), 42, 58.

13. Lyman, *Sarah Joiner Lyman,* 85.

14. Dibble, *History,* 127.

15. Lyman, *Sarah Joiner Lyman,* 65, 68; and Ralph S. Kuykendall, *Foundation and Transformation,* 312.

16. Bingham, *Twenty-one Years,* 459; and Phillips, *Protestant America,* 114–15.

17. Ward, *American Activities* 4:25.

18. Ibid. 4:22 and 6:202.

19. Bingham to Evarts, Honolulu, 31 December 1831, Bingham Family Papers, Yale University Library; and Dulles, *American in the Pacific,* 141.

20. Judd, *Honolulu,* 167–68; and *Hawaiian Penal Code* 36, Section 2.

21. Dulles, *Lowered Boats,* 243.

22. R. Miller's Memorandum on the Hawaiian Nation, Honolulu, 25 September 1821, Bingham Family Papers, Yale University Library.

23. Frederick J. Teggert, ed., *Around the Horn to the Sandwich Islands and California, 1845–1850, Being a Personal Record Kept by Chester S. Lyman* (Freeport, N.Y., 1971), 69.

24. Stanton, *Exploring Expedition,* 129; and Dulles, *America in the Pacific,* 145.

25. Macrae, *With Lord Byron,* 10–37.

26. Lyman, *Sarah Joiner Lyman,* 113.

27. Dibble, *History,* 97, 100.

28. Evarts to Bingham, Boston, 7 June 1828, Bingham Family Papers, Yale University Library.

29. Kuykendall, *Foundation and Transformation,* 86–87.

30. Ibid., 93.

31. Constance F. Gordon Cumming, *A Lady's Cruise in a French Man-of-War* (New York, 1970) 1:99.

32. Stevens, *American Expansion,* 9.

33. R. A. to Bingham, Boston, 1 June 1828, Bingham Family Papers, Yale University Library.

34. Lyman, *Sarah Joiner Lyman,* 104.

35. Dulles, *America in the Pacific,* 148.

36. For Mormon missionary activity in the Pacific see R. Lanier Britsch, *Unto the Islands of the Sea: A History of the Latter-day Saints in the Pacific* (Salt Lake City, 1986).

37. Branch, *Westward,* 373.

38. Teggert, *Chester S. Lyman,* 206.

39. Ibid., 221.

40. John K. Fairbanks, "Assignment for the 70's," *American Historical Review* 74 (February 1969) 864–65.

41. See Latourette, *United States and China;* and Paul A. Varg, *Missionaries, Chinese, and Diplomats: The American Protestant Missionary Movement in China, 1890–1952* (Princeton, N.J., 1958).

42. Battistini, *American Influence,* 31.

43. See Adrian A. Bennett, *Young J. Allen and His Magazines, 1860–1883* (Athens, Ga., 1983).

44. Henry T. Cheever, *Life in the Sandwich Islands* (New York, 1851), 340.

CHAPTER FOURTEEN

1. Ship of the line: 2200 to 2500 tons, with a crew of 800, sixty-five long- and medium-range 32-pounder guns, and twenty-four 32-pounder carronades (short cannon of large caliber, which gunners mates used in close-range firing). Frigate: 1500 to 1800 tons, with a crew of 500, thirty-three 24-pounder long-range guns and twenty 42-pounder carronades. Sloop of war: 800 tons, with a

crew of 150, four 8-inch shell guns and 18 32-pounder carronades. Schooner: 150 to 200 tons, with a crew of 80, two long-range 18-pounder guns and ten 12-pounder carronades.

2. See David Porter, *Journal of a Cruise Made to the Pacific Ocean* ... (New York, 1822), 2 vols., for the captain's account of his South Seas campaigns.

3. Quoted in Henry E. Gruppe, *The Frigates* (Alexandria, Va., 1979), 118.

4. Porter, *Journal* 2:78–79; the United States Senate failed to ratify Porter's pact of annexation.

5. Bernice Judd, ed., *Voyages to Hawaii before 1860* (Honolulu, 1974), 14.

6. Porter, *Journal* 2:168–73.

7. Quoted in Gruggpe, *The Frigates,* 118.

8. Robert E. Johnson, *Thence Round the Horn: The Story of the United States Navy on Pacific Station, 1818–1923* (Annapolis, Md., 1963), 3–4.

9. Ibid., 11.

10. Completion of the continental telegraph in 1861 substantially expedited the flow of communications to and from this military frontier before wireless transmission, which appeared on the eve of World War I.

11. Foster R. Dulles, *China and America: The Story of Their Relations Since 1784* (Princeton, N.J., 1946), 16–17.

12. Johnson, *Thence Round the Horn,* 37–38.

13. Kuykendall, *Foundation and Transformation,* 99. Also see Charles Oscar Paullin, *Diplomatic Negotiations of American Naval Officers, 1778–1883* (Baltimore, 1912).

14. Ward, *American Activities* 3:132.

15. See Judd, *Honolulu.*

16. See William Walker, *The War in Nicaragua* (Tucson, Ariz., 1985); and Ward, *American Activities* 3:372–73.

17. Judd, *Honolulu,* 77.

18. See Ward, *American Activities* 2:467–68, 471–75; Dodge, *Islands and Empires;* and Johnson, *Thence Round the Horn,* 107.

19. See Judd, *Honolulu;* and Kuykendall, *Foundation and Transformation,* for more commentary on island surveys.

20. Stanton, *Exploring Expedition,* is the definitive study of Wilkes's leadership.

21. Records of the expedition are published in Wilkes, *Narrative,* 9 vols.

22. Ibid. 2:102–4; Ward, *American Activities* 2:455; and William Bixby, *The Forgotten Voyage of Charles Wilkes* (New York, 1966), 50–51.

23. Felix Riesenberg, *The Pacific Ocean* (New York, 1940), 264–65.

24. Donald Dale Jackson, "Around the World in 1,392 Days with the Navy's Wilkes—And His 'Scientifics,'" *Smithsonian* 6 (November 1985) 49; also see Robert Silverberg, *Stormy Voyager: The Story of Charles Wilkes* (Philadelphia, 1968). Herman J. Viola and Carolyn Margolis, eds., *Magnificent Voyagers: The U.S. Exploring Expedition, 1838–1842* (Washington, D.C., 1985). This volume appeared in conjunction with an exhibition by the same name at the Smithsonian's National Museum of Natural History in 1985.

25. Johnson, *Thence Round the Horn,* 54; and Jackson, "Around the World," 62.

26. Ward, *American Activities* 6:383; and Johnson, *Thence Round the Horn,* 106–7.

27. Ward, *American Activities* 3:364–65.

28. Kuykendall, *Twenty Critical Years,* 249.

29. Ward, *American Activities* 2:22.

30. Latourette, *United States and China,* 116–17.

31. Dulles, *China and America,* 27. The Treaty of Wanghia is published in Charles I. Bevans, comp., *Treaties and Other International Agreements of the United States of America, 1776–1949* (Washington, D.C., 1976), 647.

32. Ibid., 47, 60–61.

33. Dodge, *Islands and Empires,* 303–4.

34. See Perry, *Narrative;* Perry, *Japan Expedition;* and William L. Neumann, *American Encounters Japan: From Perry to MacArthur* (Baltimore, 1963).

35. The Treaty of Kanagawa is published in Bevans, *Treaties,* 351.

36. Kuykendall, *Foundation and Transformation,* 144.

37. Ibid., 219.

38. U.S. House of Representatives, *Message from the President . . . Sandwich Islands and China,* 27th Congress, 3rd Sess., 1842, House Executive Document 35, 211.

39. Kuykendall, *Foundation and Transformation,* 389.

40. William Davis, *The Last Conquistadores* (Athens, Ga., 1950), 328.

41. See Ward, *American Activities* 7:336; Ryden, *Foreign Policy;* and Sylvia Masterman, *The Origins of International Rivalry in Samoa, 1845–1884* (London, 1934). The United States–Samoan treaties are published in Bevans, *Treaties,* 116, 437.

42. See Milo Quaife, ed., *The Diary of James K. Polk during His Presidency* (Chicago, 1910), 4 vols.; and Raymond A. Rydell, *Cape Horn to the Pacific: The Rise and Decline of an Ocean Highway* (Berkeley, Cal., 1952), 99–100.

43. See Justin Smith, *The War with Mexico* (New York, 1915), 2 vols.; and Cleland, *History.*

44. Bevans, *Treaties* (Guadalupe Hidalgo). See also Theodore Grivas, *Military Governments in California, 1846–1850* (Glendale, Cal., 1963); and William H. Ellison, *A Self-Governing Dominion: California, 1849–1860* (Berkeley, Cal., 1978).

45. Aurora Hunt, *The Army of the Pacific: Its Operations in California . . . Oregon, Washington, 1860–1866* (Glendale, Cal., 1951), includes an account of naval operations for this period.

46. James D. Horan, ed., *C.S.S., Shenandoah: The Memoirs of Lieutenant Commanding James I. Waddell* (New York, 1960), depicts this raider's Pacific excursion; also see Ward, *American Activities* 6:193–200.

47. Richard S. West, Jr., *Admirals of American Empire: The Combined Story of George Dewey, Alfred Thayer Mahan, Winfield Scott Schley, and William Thomas Sampson* (Indianapolis, Ind., 1948), 116.

48. Ward, *American Activities* 4:549.

49. The Hawaiian–United States treaty of 1887 is published in Bevans, *Treaties,* 878.

50. Frederick C. Drake, *The Empire of the Seas: A Biography of Rear*

Admiral Robert Wilson Shufeldt, U.S.N. (Honolulu, 1984), 116. The Chosen (Korea)–United States treaty is published in Bevans, *Treaties,* 470.

51. See Sanford Ballard Dole, *Memoirs of the Hawaiian Revolution* (Honolulu, 1936).

52. The 1898 United States treaty with Spain is published in Bevans, *Treaties,* 615; and West, *Admirals,* 197–210. Also see Earl S. Pomeroy, *Pacific Outpost: American Strategy in Guam and Micronesia* (Stanford, Cal., 1951); Theodore Friend, *Between Two Empires: The Ordeal of the Philippines, 1929–1946* (New Haven, Conn., 1965); George Taylor, *The Philippines and the United States: Problems of Partnership* (New York, 1964); and Leon Wolff, *Little Brown Brother: How the United States Purchased and Pacified the Philippines at the Century's Turn* (Garden City, N.Y., 1961).

53. See Teggert, ed., *Around the Horn,* 214.

CHAPTER SIXTEEN

1. For a basic interpretative treatment of American novelists in the Pacific see A. Grove Day, *Mad About Islands: Novelists of a Vanished Paradise* (Honolulu, 1987); and Terry Hammons, "Americans and Paradise: The Pacific Basin as a Literary Source," *Journal of the West* 15(2) (April 1976), 102–16. Particularly helpful anthologies include W. Storrs Lee, *Hawaii: A Literary Chronicle* (New York, 1967); A. Grove Day and Carl Stroven, *The Spell of Hawaii* (Honolulu, 1968); A. Grove Day and Carl Stroven, *A Hawaiian Reader* (Honolulu, 1959).

2. For full citation of books listed by title in this chapter, see Bibliography.

3. Louis Antoine de Bougainville, *A Voyage Round the World* (Ridgewood, N.J., 1967), 219.

4. Bougainville, *Voyage,* 227, 228–29.

5. For a discussion of the publishing history of Cook's voyages, see Lynne Withey, *Voyages of Discovery: Captain Cook and the Exploration of the Pacific* (New York, 1987), 175–87, 401–11.

6. John Ledyard, "White Gods with Loose Skins," in Lee, ed., *Hawaii: A Literary Chronicle,* 50–65.

7. Hammons, "Americans and Paradise," 104.

8. Jewitt's *Narrative* was republished in 1851 by Andrus, Gauntlett and Co., New York; in 1896 it was reissued in London by Clement Wilson, with an introduction by Robert Brown, who visited Nootka Sound as commander of the Vancouver Exploring Expedition in the 1860s.

9. For a basic description of Melville see Day, *Mad About Islands,* 58–81.

10. Herman Melville, *Typee* (New York, 1963), 18.

11. Ibid., 168, 200.

12. Ibid., 265, 266.

13. Ibid., 295.

14. For background on Washington Irving and Astoria, see the introduction by Richard Rust in Washington Irving, *Astoria* (Boston, 1976).

15. Ibid., 356.

16. Richard Henry Dana, *Two Years Before the Mast* (New York, 1981), 125.

17. Ibid., 317. Despite Dana's desire to flee California, the Pacific West continued to hold an attraction for him. He returned to California in 1859 and quite enjoyed the reception he received and the prominence his book had achieved. The story of the 1859 trip, "Twenty-Four Years After" appeared in revised editions of *Two Years Before the Mast*, beginning in 1869.

18. Ibid., 207.

19. For the collaboration of Dana and Melville, see the introduction by Thomas Philbrick to the 1981 Penguin Classic edition of *Two Years Before the Mast*. *Redburn* and *White Jacket* indeed increased the American public's desire for novels about sea life. *Redburn* was based on Melville's early seaborne trip to England as a seaman in 1839 and did not touch on the Pacific; *White Jacket* was based on a return trip from Callao, Peru, to New England, and is thus only tangentially one of Melville's Pacific novels.

20. For an introduction to the San Francisco literary tradition that spawned Twain, see Franklin Walker, *San Francisco's Literary Frontier* (New York, 1939); and Kevin Starr, *Americans and the California Dream* (New York, 1973). For Twain's letters to the *Union*, see A. Grove Day, *Mark Twain's Letters from Hawaii* (New York, 1966).

21. Hammons, "Americans and Paradise," 108.

22. Day, *Mad About Islands*, 102.

23. Fred W. Lorch, "Hawaiian Feudalism and Mark Twain's *A Connecticut Yankee in King Arthur's Court*," *American Literature* (March 1958) 50–66; Day, *Mad About Islands*, 97–102.

24. Starr, *California Dream*, 241–45.

25. Charles Warren Stoddard, *South Sea Idylls* (Boston, 1873). For a portrait of Stoddard, see Starr, *California Dream*, 242–45.

26. For a description of Stevenson's life in the Pacific, see Day, *Mad About Islands*, 103–24; Starr, *California Dream*, 241–45; Martha Mary McGaw, *Stevenson in Hawaii* (Honolulu, 1950).

27. Adams's *Memoirs of Marua Taaro* was revised and reprinted in 1901 as *Tahiti: Memoirs of Arii Taimai* (Paris, 1901).

28. For a basic background on London, see Day, *Mad About Islands*, 144–72; see also Joan London, *Jack London and His Times: An Unconventional Biography* (Seattle, 1968); and Franklin Walker, *Jack London and the Klondike* (San Marino, 1972).

29. William R. Hunt, "A Framework for James Cook: The Meaning of Exploration in the 18th Century and Now," *Exploration in Alaska: Captain Cook Commemorative Lectures* (Anchorage, 1980), 89–95. For a portfolio of Choris's landscapes, see Keith Wheeler, *The Alaskans* (Alexandria, Va., 1977), 44–51.

30. For the best description of exploration writing on the North Pacific in the late nineteenth century, see Morgan Sherwood, *The Exploration of Alaska* (New Haven, Conn., 1965). For Smithsonian ventures, see also Herman J. Viola, *Exploring the West* (Washington, D.C., 1987).

31. John Muir, *"The Discovery of Glacier Bay,"* in *Wilderness Essays* (Salt Lake City, 1980), 2, 19.

32. Muir's principal work on the North, *Travels in Alaska,* was not published until 1915, the year after his death and a decade and a half after his last trip to Alaska in 1899. Muir did not begin writing *Travels* until 1914 and died on 24 December 1914.

33. Walker, *Jack London,* 227–28.

34. For Rex Beach's novels, see Frank Buske, "Rex Beach," *Alaska Journal* 10(4) (Autumn 1980) 37–42.

35. For Robert Service's poems, see *The Best of Robert Service* (New York, 1907 and later revisions). For Harriman's expedition, see John Burroughs, John Muir, et al., *Alaska: The Harriman Expedition, 1899* (New York, 1986), first published in two volumes by Doubleday, Page & Co., 1901. For an assessment of the Harriman expedition, see William H. Goetzman and Kay Sloan, *Looking Far North* (New York, 1982). For the decline of the North, see Ken Coates and Bill Morrison, *The Sinking of the Princess Sophia* (Toronto, 1990). Alaska's population in the gold-rush era: 1890, 32,052; 1900, 63,592; 1910, 64,350; 1920, 55,036.

36. For an anthology of nature writing on Alaska, see John A. Murray, *A Republic of Rivers: Three Centuries of Nature Writing from Alaska and the Yukon* (New York, 1990). For films about the North, see Susan Hackley Johnson, "When Moviemakers Look North," *Alaska Journal* 9(1) (Winter 1979) 12–25.

37. For a discussion of Nordhoff and Hall, see Day, *Mad About Islands,* 194–213; and Paul Briand, Jr., *In Search of Paradise: The Nordhoff-Hall Story* (Honolulu, 1987).

38. Frederick O'Brien, *White Shadows in the South Seas* (New York, 1919), 74.

39. For a discussion of Frisbie, see Day, *Mad About Islands,* 214–35.

40. For a discussion of Michener's work in Hawai'i and the South Seas, see Day, *Mad About Islands,* 236–55.

41. For the impact of *Ice Palace,* see Johnson, "Moviemakers Look North," 21–22.

42. For the reaction of Alaskan critics to Michener's work, see Kathleen Lidfors, Stephen Haycox, and Morgan Sherwood, "James Michener's *Alaska,*" *Alaska History* 4(1) (Spring 1989) 45–55.

43. Day, *Mad About Islands,* 249.

CHAPTER SEVENTEEN

1. This summary chapter is based on my own reflections on the twentieth-century Pacific Basin that have come through teaching, reading in both scholarly and popular literature, and personal experience. A number of books have been particularly helpful in shaping my thoughts. The following suggestions for further reading are more an eclectic than a comprehensive selection.

As an overall guide I have particularly enjoyed James C. Thomson, Jr., Peter W. Stanley, and John Curtis Perry, *Sentimental Imperialists: The American Ex-*

perience in East Asia (New York, 1981), along with John Toland, *The Rising Sun* (New York, 1970), and Michael Schaller, *The United States and China in the Twentieth Century* (New York, 1979). Also as a general guide two Public Broadcast System video series are invaluable: *The Pacific Century* (1992), a ten-program series concentrating on history; and *Fire on the Rim*, a four-part series concentrating on geography and culture, particularly on the consequences of earthquakes.

For the series of world's fairs held in the early twentieth century, see Robert W. Rydell, *All the World's a Fair* (Chicago, 1984). For the globalization of American business and its influence in the Pacific Basin, see Kenichi Ohmae, *The Borderless World: Power and Strategy in the Interlinked Economy* (New York, 1990); the Annual Reports of the Coca-Cola Company also drive this point home.

For the impact of Asian migration to the United States, invaluable sources are Roger Daniels, *Asian America: Chinese and Japanese in the United States Since 1850* (Seattle, 1988) and Shih-shan Henry Tsai, *The Chinese Experience in America* (Bloomington, Ind., 1986).

My own special interests have been in Alaska and Hawai'i, particularly the statehood movements. For Hawai'i see Lawrence Fuchs, *Hawaii Pono* (New York, 1961) and Gavan Daws, *Shoal of Time* (New York, 1968), as well as my own article linking Hawai'i to the American West, "Hawai'i: The First and Last Far West?" *Western Historical Quarterly* (May 1992) 153–77. The story of the all-Nisei 442nd Regimental Combat Team and the 100th Infantry Division is told in Masayo Umezawa Duus, *Unlikely Liberators: The Men of the 100th and the 442nd* (Honolulu, 1987). For a comprehensive view of Alaska, see Claus Naske and Herman Slotnick, *Alaska: The 49th State* (Norman, Okla., 1987); and Mary Childers Mangusso and Stephen W. Haycox, *Interpreting Alaska's History: An Anthology* (Anchorage, 1989).

The quotation from Woodrow Wilson comes from, "The Making of the Nation," *Atlantic Monthly* (July 1897) 1–14.

My thoughts on the impact of missionaries in Asia come in large part from personal experience. As a boy in Athens, Georgia, I listened to numerous returning missionaries at the First Methodist Church tell about Japan and Korea, and to a lesser extent China. A local seed merchant brought Korean Presbyterians to town and shaped his country residence to resemble a Korean landscape, complete with stone lanterns and lily ponds. We discussed in church youth groups the fact that Mrs. Sun Yat-sen and other notable Chinese women had been educated at the Methodist Wesleyan College in Macon, Georgia. An English teacher at Athens High School had been the roommate of Pearl Buck in college at Randolph Macon Women's College in Virginia. It was also at the First Methodist Church that I first heard a sermon based on the song from *South Pacific*, "You've Got to Be Taught." As for most Americans in the post–World War II era, the Pacific Basin frontier has been an inescapable personal experience.

Bibliography

Ackerman, Robert, et al. *Ethnohistory in Southwestern Alaska and the Southern Yukon*. Lexington: University Press of Kentucky, 1970.

Adams, Henry Brooks. *Tahiti: Memoirs of Arii Taimai*. Ridgewood, N.J.: The Gregg Press, 1968.

Allen, Everett S. *Children of the Light: The Rise and Fall of New Bedford Whaling and the Death of the Arctic Fleet*. Boston: Little, Brown and Co., 1973.

Allen, Helena G. *The Betrayal of Liliuokalini, Last Queen of Hawaii, 1838–1917*. Glendale, Cal.: Arthur H. Clark Co., 1983.

Allen, Henry T. *Report of an Expedition to the Copper, Tanana, and Koyuk Rivers*. Washington, D.C.: U.S. Government Printing Office, 1887.

Anderson, Bern. *Surveyor of the Sea: The Life and Voyages of Captain George Vancouver*. Seattle: University of Washington Press, 1960.

Anderson, Rufus. *The Hawaiian Islands: Their Progress and Condition under Missionary Labors*. Boston: Gould and Luecoli, 1864.

Ashley, Clifford W. *The Yankee Whaler*. Garden City, N.Y.: Halagon House, 1926.

Bailey, Thomas. *America Faces Russia*. Ithaca, N.Y.: Cornell University Press, 1950.

Bancroft, Hubert Howe. *History of the Northwest Coast*. 2 vols. San Francisco: A. L. Bancroft Co., 1884.

———. *The New Pacific*. New York: The Bancroft Co., 1899.

———. *History of Alaska: 1730–1885*. San Francisco: A. L. Bancroft Co., 1886.

———. *History of California*. 7 vols. San Francisco: History Company, 1886–90.

Bates, George Washington. *Sandwich Island Notes: By a Haole*. New York: Harper and Brothers, 1854.

Bateson, Charles. *Gold Fleet for California: Forty Niners from Australia and New Zealand*. East Lansing: Michigan State University Press, 1963.

Battistini, Lawrence H. *The Rise of American Influence in Asia and the Pacific*. East Lansing: Michigan State University Press, 1960.

Baxley, Henry Willis. *What I Saw on the West Coast of South and North America, and at the Hawaiian Islands*. New York: D. Appleton Co., 1865.

Bayard, Samuel John. *A Sketch of the Life of Commodore Robert F. Stockton.* New York: Derby and Jackson, 1856.

Beach, Rex. *The Barrier.* New York: Harper and Brothers, 1908.

———. *The Iron Trail.* New York: Harper and Brothers, 1913.

———. *The Silver Horde.* New York: Harper and Brothers, 1909.

———. *The Spoilers.* New York: Harper and Brothers, 1906.

———. *The Winds of Chance.* New York: Harper and Brothers, 1918.

Beaglehole, John. *The Exploration of the Pacific.* London: A. and C. Black, 1947.

Beals, Carleton. *Adventure of the Western Sea: The Story of Robert Gray.* New York: Henry Holt, 1956.

Bearss, Ed, and Arrell M. Gibson. *Fort Smith, Little Gibraltar on the Arkansas.* Norman: University of Oklahoma Press, 1969.

Beasley, W. G., ed. *Modern Japan: Aspects of History, Literature and Society.* Berkeley: University of California Press, 1984.

Beechart, Edward D. *Working in Hawaii: A Labor History.* Honolulu: University of Hawaii Press, 1985.

Beechey, Frederick William. *Narrative of a Voyage to the Pacific and Bering's Strait . . . in the Years 1825, 26, 27, 28.* 2 vols. London: Henry Colburn and Richard Bentley, 1831.

Bemis, Samuel Flagg. *John Quincy Adams and the Foundation of American Foreign Policy.* New York: Alfred A. Knopf, 1949.

Bennett, Adrian A. *Missionary Journalist in China: Young J. Allen and His Magazine, 1860–1883.* Athens: University of Georgia Press, 1983.

Bennett, Frederick D. *Narrative of a Whaling Voyage Round the Globe, from the Year 1833 to 1836.* London: Richard Bentley, 1840.

Beresford, William. *A Voyage Round the World, but More Particularly to the Northwest Coast of America.* London: George Goulding, 1789.

Berthold, Victor Maximilian. *The Pioneer Steamer California, 1848–1849.* Boston: Houghton Mifflin Co., 1932.

Berton, Pierre. *The Klondike Quest.* Boston: Atlantic Monthly Press, 1983.

Bevans, Charles I., comp. *Treaties and Other International Agreements of the United States of America, 1776–1949.* Washington, D.C.: U.S. Government Printing Office, 1976.

Bigelow, John. *Memoir of the Life and Public Services of John Charles Frémont.* New York: Derby and Jackson, 1956.

Bingham Family Papers. Sterling Library, Yale University.

Bingham, Hiram. *A Residence of Twenty-one Years in the Sandwich Islands.* Hartford, Conn.: Hezekiah Huntington, 1849.

Birket-Smith, K. *The Eskimos.* London: Methuen, 1959.

Bixby, William. *The Forgotten Voyage of Charles Wilkes.* New York: David McKay Co., 1966.

Bligh, William. *A Voyage to the South Seas.* Dublin, 1792.

Blower, James. *Gold Rush.* New York: American Heritage Press, 1971.

Bonner, W. H. *Captain William Dampier: Buccaneer-Author.* Stanford, Cal.: Stanford University Press, 1934.

Bougainville, Louis de. *A Voyage Round the World.* Ridgewood, N.J.: The Gregg Press, 1967.

Bradley, Harold W. *The American Frontier in Hawaii: The Pioneers, 1789–1843.* Stanford, Cal.: Stanford University Press, 1942.

Braeman, John. *Albert Beveridge: American Nationalist.* Chicago: University of Chicago Press, 1971.

Braisted, William R. *The United States Navy in the Pacific, 1897–1909.* Austin: University of Texas Press, 1958.

Branch, Douglas. *Westward: The Romance of the American Frontier.* New York: D. Appleton and Co., 1930.

Brannon, John, comp. *Official Letters of the Military and Naval Officers of the United States During the War with Great Britain in the Years 1812, 13, 14, and 15.* Washington, D.C.: Way and Gideon, 1823.

Briand, Paul, Jr. *In Search of Paradise: The Nordhoff-Hall Story.* Honolulu: Mutual Publishing Co., 1987.

Britsch, R. Lanier. *Unto the Islands of the Sea: A History of the Latter-day Saints in the Pacific.* Salt Lake City: Deseret Book Co., 1986.

Broek, Jacobus Ten, et al. *Prejudice, War, and the Constitution: Causes and Consequences of the Evacuation of the Japanese-Americans in World War II.* Berkeley: University of California Press, 1954.

Brookes, Jean I. *International Rivalry in the Pacific, 1800–1875.* Berkeley: University of California Press, 1941.

Broughton, William R. *A Voyage of Discovery to the North Pacific Ocean.* London: T. Cadell and Davies, 1804.

Browne, J. Ross. *Etchings of a Whaling Cruise.* Ed. by John Seelye. Cambridge, Mass.: Harvard University Press, 1968.

Buck, Pearl S. *The Good Earth.* New York: John Day Co., 1931.

Burroughs, John, and John Muir, et al. *Alaska: The Harriman Expedition, 1899.* New York: Dover Publications, 1986.

Caldwell, Elsie N. *Last Witness for Robert Louis Stevenson.* Norman: University of Oklahoma Press, 1960.

California Constitution of 1849. Article 1, Section 18 (St. Paul, Minn., n.d.).

Callahan, James M. *American Relations in the Pacific and the Far East.* Baltimore: Johns Hopkins University Press, 1901.

Campa, Miguel de la. *A Journal of Explorations, Northward along the Coast from Monterey in the Year 1775.* Ed. by John Galvin. San Francisco: John Howell, 1964.

Campbell, Archibald. *A Voyage around the World, from 1806 to 1812.* Edinburgh: Archibald Constable, 1816.

Carboni, Raffaello. *The Eureka Stockade.* Melbourne, Australia: Dolphin Publications, 1947.

Carpenter, Edmund. *Eskimo Realities*. New York: Holt, Rinehart and Winston, 1973.

Caughey, John Walton. *The California Gold Rush*. Berkeley: University of California Press, 1974.

———. *Gold Is the Cornerstone*. Berkeley: University of California Press, 1948.

———. *History of the Pacific Coast*. Los Angeles: publ. by author, 1933.

Chapman, Charles Edward. *Catalogue of Materials in the Archivo General de Indias for the History of the Pacific Coast and the American Southwest*. Berkeley: University of California Press, 1949.

———. *The Founding of Spanish California: The Northwestward Expansion of New Spain, 1687–1773*. New York: : Macmillan Co., 1916.

———. *A History of California: The Spanish Period*. New York: Macmillan Co., 1921.

Chase, Owen. *Narrative of the Most Extraordinary and Distressing Shipwreck of the Whale-Ship "Essex," of Nantucket*. New York: W. B. Gilley, 1821.

Cheever, Henry T. *The Island World of the Pacific*. Glasgow: William Colluis, 1850.

———. *Life in the Sandwich Islands*. New York: A. S. Barnes, 1851.

———. *The Whale and His Captors*. New York: Harper and Brothers, 1864.

Chinen, Jon J. *The Great Mahele: Hawaii's Land Division of 1848*. Honolulu: University of Hawaii Press, 1985.

Chippendale, Harry A. *Sails and Whales*. Boston: Houghton Mifflin Co., 1951.

Choris, Louis. *Voyage Pittoresque Autour du Monde*. Paris, Impr. de Firmin Didot, 1822.

Christman, Margaret. *Adventurous Pursuits: Americans and the China Trade, 1784–1844*. Washington, D.C.: U.S. Government Printing Office, 1984.

Christopher, Robert C. *The Japanese Mind: The Goliath Explained*. New York: Simon and Schuster, 1983.

Clark, Joseph G. *Lights and Shadows of Sailor Life*. Boston: J. Putnam, 1847.

Cleland, Robert Glass. *A History of California: The American Period*. Westport, Conn.: Greenwood Press, 1975.

———. *This Reckless Breed of Men*. New York: Alfred A. Knopf, 1950.

Cleveland, Richard J. *In the Forecastle, or the Voyages and Commercial Adventures of the Sons of New England*. New York: Hurst & Co., 1855.

———. *A Narrative of Voyages and Commercial Enterprises*. London: Edward Moxon, 1842.

Clinard, Outten J. *Japan's Influence on American Naval Power, 1897–1917*. Berkeley: University of California Press, 1947.

Coates, Ken, and Bill Morrison. *The Sinking of the Princess Sophia*. Toronto: Oxford University Press, 1990.

Coffin, George. *A Pioneer Voyage to California and Round the World, 1849 to 1852*. Chicago: n.p., 1908.

Collins, Maurice. *Foreign Mud*. London: Faber and Faber, 1946.

Colnett, James A. *Voyage . . . into the Pacific Ocean, for the Purpose of Extending the Spermaceti Whale Fisheries.* London: W. Bennett, 1798.

Coman, Katherine. *Economic Beginnings of the Far West.* New York: Kelley, 1912.

Conroy, H. *The Japanese Frontiers in Hawaii—1868–1898.* Berkeley: University of California Press, 1953.

Cook, James. *A Voyage to the Pacific Ocean Undertaken . . . in the Years 1776, 1777, 1779, 1780.* 3 vols. London: W. and A. Strahan, 1784.

Cook, Warren L. *Flood Tide of Empire, 1543–1819.* New Haven, Conn.: Yale University Press, 1973.

Cooper, James Fenimore. *The History of the Navy of the United States of America.* 2 vols. Philadelphia: Lea and Blanchard, 1839.

Coote, Walter. *The Western Pacific.* New York: Praeger Publishers, 1969.

Corney, Peter. *Early Voyages in the North Pacific, 1813–1818.* Fairfield, Wash.: Ye Galleon Press, 1965.

Cosenza, M. E. *The Complete Journal of Townsend Harris, First American Consul General and Minister to Japan.* Garden City, N.Y.: Macmillan Co., 1930.

Coulter, John W. *The Pacific Dependencies of the United States.* New York: Macmillan Co., 1957.

Cox, Ross. *The Columbia River: Or, Scenes and Adventures during a Residence of Six Years on the Western Side of the Rocky Mountains among Various Tribes of Indians Hitherto Unknown together with a Journey across the . . .* Norman: University of Oklahoma Press, 1957.

Crow, John A. *Spain: The Root and the Flower.* Berkeley: University of California Press, 1984.

Cumming, Constance F. Gordon. *A Lady's Cruise in a French Man-of-War.* 2 vols. New York: Praeger Publishers, 1970.

Cutter, Donald C., ed. *The California Coast: A Bilingual Edition of Documents from the Sutro Collection.* Norman: University of Oklahoma Press, 1969.

———, ed. *Journal of Tomás de Suria of His Voyage with Malaspina to the Northwest Coast of North America in 1791.* Fairfield, Wash.: Ye Galleon Press, 1980.

———. *Malaspina in California.* San Francisco: John Howell, 1960.

Dakin, Susanna B. *A Scotch Paisano in Old Los Angeles.* Berkeley: University of California Press, 1979.

Dall, William H. *Alaska and Its Resources.* Boston: Lee and Shepard, 1870.

Dana, Richard Henry, Jr. *Two Years before the Mast: A Personal Narrative.* New York: New American Library, 1964.

Daniels, Roger. *Asian America: Chinese and Japanese in the United States Since 1850.* Seattle: University of Washington Press, 1988.

Daniels, Roger. *Concentration Camps, North America: Japanese in the United States and Canada During World War II.* Florida: R. E. Krieger Publishing Co., 1981.

Davis, William C. *The Last Conquistadores*. Athens: University of Georgia Press, 1950.

Daws, Gavan. *Shoal of Time*. New York: Macmillan Co., 1968.

Daws, Gavan, and Ed Sheehan. *The Hawaiians*. Norfolk Island, Australia: Island Heritage, 1970.

Day, A. Grove. *Mad About Islands: Novelists of a Vanished Paradise*. Honolulu: Mutual Publishing Co., 1987.

———., ed. *Mark Twain's Letters from Hawaii*. New York: Appleton-Century, 1966.

———. *Pacific Islands Literature: One Hundred Basic Books*. Honolulu: University of Hawaii Press, 1971.

———., ed. *Stories of Hawaii by Jack London*. New York: Appleton-Century, 1965.

Day, A. Grove, and Carl Stroven, eds. *Best South Sea Stories*. New York: Appleton-Century, 1964.

———. *A Hawaiian Reader*. Honolulu: Mutual Publishing Co., 1959.

———. *The Spell of Hawaii*. Honolulu: Mutual Publishing Co., 1968.

Defoe, Daniel. *The Life and Strange Surprizing Adventures of Robinson Crusoe*. Boston: Houghton Mifflin Co., 1908. Originally published 1719.

Dennett, Tyler. *Americans in Eastern Asia*. New York: Barnes and Noble, 1941.

Derrick, R. A. *A History of Fiji*. Suva: Government Press, 1946.

Dibble, Sheldon. *History and General Views of the Sandwich Islands Mission*. New York: Taylor and Dodd, 1839.

Dillon, Richard H. *Embarcadero*. New York: Coward-McCann, 1959.

———. *Shanghaiing Days*. New York: Coward-McCann, 1961.

Dix, William G. *Wreck of the Glide, with Recollections of the Fijiis, and of Wallis Island*. New York: Wiley and Putnam, 1848.

Dmytryshyn, Basil, and E. A. P. Crownhart-Vaughan, eds. and trans. *Colonial Russian America: Kyrill T. Khlebnikov's Reports, 1817–1832*. Seattle: University of Washington Press, 1976.

Dodge, Ernest S. *Islands and Empires: Western Impact on the Pacific and East Asia*. Minneapolis: University of Minnesota Press, 1976.

———. *New England and the South Seas*. Cambridge, Mass.: Harvard University Press, 1965.

Dole, Sanford Ballard. *Memoirs of the Hawaiian Revolution*. Honolulu: Advertiser Publishing Company, 1936.

Drake, Frederick C. *The Empire of the Seas: A Biography of Rear Admiral Robert Wilson Shufeldt, U.S.N.* Honolulu: University of Hawaii Press, 1984.

Duflot de Mofres, Eugène. *Exploration du territoire de l'Oregon, des Californies . . . exécutée pendant les années 1840, 1841 et 1842*. 2 vols. Paris: Arthur Bertrand, 1844.

Dulles, Foster Rhea. *America in the Pacific: A Century of Expansion*. Boston: Houghton Mifflin Co., 1938.

———. *China and America: The Story of Their Relations Since 1784*. Princeton, N.J.: Princeton University Press, 1946.

———. *Lowered Boats: A Chronicle of American Whaling*. New York: Harcourt, Brace and Co., 1933.

Duus, Masaya Umezawa. *Unlikely Liberators: The Men of the 100th and the 442nd*. Honolulu: University of Hawaii Press, 1987.

D'Wolf, John. *A Voyage to the North Pacific*. Cambridge, Mass.: Welch, Bigelow, and Co., 1861.

Dunmore, John. *French Explorers in the Pacific*. Oxford: Clarendon Press, 1965.

Eberhard, Wolfram. *A History of China*. Berkeley: University of California Press, 1984.

Eddy, Daniel C. *Heroines of the Missionary Enterprise*. Boston: Ticknor, Reed and Fields, 1850.

Ellis, William. *Journal of William Ellis: Narrative of a Town of Hawaii*. With an introduction by Thurston Twigg-Smith. Honolulu: Advertiser Publishing Co., 1963.

Ellison, William H. *A Self-Governing Dominion: California, 1849–1860*. Berkeley: University of California Press, 1978.

Fairbanks, John. *Trade and Diplomacy on the China Coast*. Cambridge, Mass.: Harvard University Press, 1953.

Fanning, Edmund. *Voyages round the World*. New York: Collins and Hannay, 1833.

———. *Voyages to the South Seas*. New York, 1838.

Farnham, Thomas Jefferson. *Life, Adventures, and Travels in California*. Nafis and Cornish, 1849.

Farquhar, Francis P., ed. *Up and Down California in 1860–1864: The Journal of William H. Brewer*. Berkeley: University of California Press, 1984.

Fedorovna, Svetlana. *The Russian Population in Alaska and California, Late Eighteenth Century*. Trans. by Richard Pierce and Alton Donnelly. Kingston, Ont.: Limestone Press, 1973.

Ferber, Edna. *Ice Palace*. New York: Doubleday and Co., 1958.

Fisher, Raymond H. *The Russian Fur Trade, 1500–1700*. Berkeley: University of California Press, 1943.

Fiske, John. *American Political Ideas Viewed from the Standpoint of Universal History: Three Lectures Delivered at the Royal Institution of Great Britain in May, 1880*. New York: Harper and Brothers, 1885.

Fletcher, David. *The Diplomacy of Annexation*. Columbia: University of Missouri Press, 1973.

Forbes, Alexander. *California: A History of Upper and Lower California*. San Francisco: Thomas C. Russell, 1919.

Foust, Clifford M. *Muscovite and Mandarin: Russia's Trade with China and Its Setting, 1705–1805*. Chapel Hill: University of North Carolina Press, 1969.

Franchère, Gabriel. *Adventure at Astoria, 1810–1814.* Trans. and ed. by Hoyt C. Franchère. Norman: University of Oklahoma Press, 1967.

———. *Narrative of a Voyage to the Northwest Coast of America in the Years 1811, 1812, 1813, and 1814.* Trans. and ed. by J. V. Huntington. New York: Redfield, 1854.

Freeman, Derek. *Margaret Mead and Samoa: The Making and Unmaking of an Anthropological Myth.* Cambridge, Mass.: Harvard University Press, 1983.

Freeman, Otis W., ed. *Geography of the Pacific.* New York: John Wiley and Sons, 1951.

Friend, Theodore. *Between Two Empires: The Ordeal of the Philippines, 1929–1946.* New Haven, Conn.: Yale University Press, 1965.

Friis, Herman, ed. *The Pacific Basin: A History of Its Geographical Exploration.* New York: American Geographical Society, 1967.

Frisbie, Robert Dean. *My Tahiti.* Boston: Little, Brown and Co., 1937.

———. *The Book of Puka Puka.* New York: Century Co., 1928.

Fuchs, Lawrence H. *Hawaii Pono: A Social History.* New York: Harcourt, Brace and World, 1961.

Fuess, C. M. *The Life of Caleb Cushing.* 2 vols. New York: Harcourt, 1923.

Furber, Holden. *Rival Empires of Trade in the Orient, 1600–1800.* Minneapolis: University of Minnesota Press, 1976.

Galbraith, John S. *The Hudson's Bay Company as an Imperial Factor.* Berkeley: University of California Press, 1957.

Gale, Robert L. *Richard Henry Dana, Jr.* New York: Twayne Publishers, 1969.

Gale, Roger W. *The Americanization of Micronesia: A Story of the Consolidation of U.S. Rule in the Pacific.* Washington, D.C.: University Press of America, 1979.

Gardiner, C. Harvey. *Pawns in the Triangle of Hate: The Peruvian Japanese and the United States.* Seattle: University of Washington Press, 1983.

Gassner, Julius S., trans. *Voyages and Adventures of La Pérouse.* Honolulu: University of Hawaii Press, 1969.

Gast, Ross H. *Don Francisco de Paula Marín: A Biography* and Agnes C. Conrad, ed. *The Letters and Journal of Francisco de Paula Marín.* Honolulu: University of Hawaii Press for the Hawaiian Historical Society, 1973.

Gauguin, Paul. *Paul Gauguin: Letters to His Wife and Friends.* Ed. by Maurice Malingue, trans. by Henry J. Stenning. Cleveland: World Publishing Co., 1949.

———. *Noa Noa: Gauguin's Tahiti.* Ed. with intro. by Nicholas Wadley. Trans. by Jonathan Griffin. London: Phaidon Press, 1985.

Geiger, Maynard S. *The Life and Times of Fray Junípero Serra.* Washington, D.C.: Academy of American Franciscan History, 1959.

Gerhard, Peter. *Pirates on the West Coast of New Spain, 1573–1742.* Glendale, Cal.: Arthur H. Clark Co., 1960.

Gibbs, James A. *Shipwrecks of the Pacific Basin*. Portland, Ore.: Binford and Mort, 1957.

Gibson, Arrell Morgan. *The West in the Life of the Nation*. Lexington, Mass.: Heath, 1976.

Gibson, James R. *Feeding the Russian Fur Trade: Provisionment of the Okhotsk Peninsula, 1639–1856*. Madison: University of Wisconsin Press, 1969.

———. *Imperial Russia in Frontier America: The Changing Geography of Supply of Russian America, 1784–1867*. New York: Oxford University Press, 1976.

Goetzmann, William. *Army Exploration in the American West, 1803–63*. New Haven, Conn.: Yale University Press, 1959.

Goetzmann, William H., and Kay Sloan. *Looking Far North*. New York: Viking Press, 1982.

Golder, Frank A. *Russian Expansion on the Pacific, 1641–1850*. Cleveland: The Arthur C. Clark Co., 1914.

———. *Vitus Bering Voyage*. Vol. 2 of American Geographical Society Research Series, 1 and 2. New York: American Geographical Society, 1922–25.

Goode, George, ed. *The Fisheries and Fishery Industries of the United States*. Washington, D.C.: U.S. Government Printing Office, 1887.

Goodman, Robert B., Gavan Daws, and Ed Sheehan. *The Hawaiians*. New South Wales, Australia: Island Heritage, 1971.

Gough, Barry. *The Royal Navy and the Northwest Coast of North America, 1810–1814*. Vancouver, B.C.: n.p., 1971.

Graebner, Norman. *Empire on the Pacific*. New York: Ronald Press, 1955.

Grattan, C. Hartley. *The Southwest Pacific to 1900 & The Southwest Pacific Since 1900*. Ann Arbor: University of Michigan Press, 1963.

Gray, Captain J. A. G. *Amerika Samoa*. Annapolis, Md.: U.S. Naval Institute, 1960.

Greenbow, Robert. *Memoir, Historical and Political, on the Northwest Coast of North America*. Washington, D.C.: Blair and Reeves, 1840. U.S. Doc. Set, Serial #357, 26 Cong., 1st Sess., Sev. Doc. 174.

Greenwood, Gordon. *Early American-Australian Relations from the Arrival of the Spaniards in America to the Close of 1830*. Melbourne: Melbourne University Press in association with Oxford University Press, 1944.

Greenwood, Gordon, and Norman Harper, eds. *Australia in World Affairs, 1950–55*. Melbourne: F. W. Chashire Co., 1957.

Greever, William S. *The Bonanza West*. Norman: University of Oklahoma Press, 1963.

Griffin, Eldon. *Clippers and Consuls: American Consular and Commercial Relations with Eastern Asia, 1845–1860*. Wilmington, Del.: Scholarly Resources, 1972.

Griswold, A. Whitney. *Far Eastern Policy of the U.S.* New York: Harcourt, Brace and Co., 1938.

Bibliography

Grivas, Theodore. *Military Governments in California, 1846–1850.* Glendale, Cal.: Arthur H. Clark Co., 1963.

Gruening, Ernest. *The State of Alaska.* New York: Random House, 1954.

Grunder, G. A., and William E. Livezey. *The Philippines and the United States.* Norman: University of Oklahoma Press, 1951.

Gruppe, Henry E. *The Frigates.* Alexandria, Va.: Time Life Books, 1979.

Gunther, Erna. *Indian Life on the Northwest Coast of North America as Seen by the Early Explorers and Fur Traders During the Last Decades of the Eighteenth Century.* Chicago: University of Chicago Press, 1972.

Hammond, L. Davis, ed. *News from New Cytherea: A Report of Bougainville's Voyage, 1766–1769.* Minneapolis: University of Minnesota Press, 1970.

Hanna, Warren L. *Lost Harbor: The Controversy over Drake's California Anchorage.* Berkeley: University of California Press, 1979.

Hall, Basil. *Account of a Voyage of Discovery to the West Coast of Corea and the Great Loo-Choo Islands.* London: John Murray, 1818.

Harlow, Neal. *California Conquered: War and Peace on the Pacific 1846–1850.* Berkeley: University of California Press, 1982.

Harlow, Vincent T. *The Founding of the Second British Empire, 1763–1793.* 2 vols. London: Longman Group, 1952, 1964.

Hawkins, Richard. *The Observations of Sir Richard Hawkins . . . in His Voyage into the South Sea in the Year 1593.* London: Hakuyt Society, 1847.

Hawks, Francis L. *Narrative of the Expedition of an American Squadron to the China Seas and Japan, Performed in the Years 1852, 1853, and 1854, under the Command of Commodore M. C. Perry.* 3 vols. Washington, D.C.: A. O. P. Nicholson, 1856.

Heggen, Thomas. *Mr. Roberts.* Boston: Houghton Mifflin Co., 1946.

Heizer, Robert F., ed. *The Destruction of California Indians.* Santa Barbara, Cal.: Peregrine Smith, 1974.

Heizer, Robert F., and Albert B. Elsasser. *The Natural World of the California Indians.* Berkeley: University of California Press, 1980.

Heyerdahl, Thor. *Kon-Tiki.* Trans. by F. H. Lyon. Chicago: Rand McNally, 1950.

Hinckley, Theodore C. *The Americanization of Alaska, 1867–1897.* Palo Alto, Cal.: Pacific Books, 1972.

———, ed. *The Westward Movement and Historical Involvement of the Americas in the Pacific Basin.* San Jose, Cal.: Journal of the West Press, 1966.

Hodge, Fredrick W. *Handbook of American Indians North of Mexico.* 2 vols. Washington, D.C.: U.S. Government Printing Office, 1907–1910. Reprinted New York: Pageant Books, 1959.

Hogbin, H. Ian. *Law and Order in Polynesia.* New York: Harcourt, Brace and Co., 1934.

Holmes, Maurice G. *From New Spain by Sea to the Californias, 1519–1668.* Glendale, Cal.: Arthur H. Clark Co., 1963.

Holt, Edgar. *The Opium Wars in China.* London: Putnam, 1964.

Horan, James D., ed. *C.S.S. "Shenandoah": The Memoirs of Lieutenant Commanding James I. Waddell*. New York: Crown Publishers, 1960.

Hort, Dora. *Tahiti: The Garden of the Pacific*. London: T. Fisher, 1891.

Houston, James A. *Eagle Song: An Indian Saga Based on True Events*. San Diego, Cal.: Harcourt, Brace and Jovanovich, 1983.

Howard, Leon. *Herman Melville: A Biography*. Berkeley: University of California Press, 1951.

Howay, Frederic W. *Voyages of the "Columbia" to the Northwest Coast, 1787–1790 and 1790–1793*. Boston: Massachusetts Historical Society, 1941.

Humboldt, Alexander freiherr von, and Aime Bonoland. *Personal Narrative of Travels to the Equinoctial Regions of the New Continent During the Years 1799–1804*. 7 vols. London: Longman . . . Brown, 1818–29.

Humboldt, Alexander freiherr von. *Political Essay on the Kingdom of New Spain*. London: Longman . . . Brown, 1811.

Hunt, Aurora. *The Army of the Pacific*. Glendale, Cal.: Arthur H. Clark Co., 1951.

Hunt, William. *Arctic Passage*. New York: Scribners, 1975.

Irving, Washington. *Astoria*. New York: Putnam, c. 1895. Reprinted Portland, Ore.: Binford and Mort, 1951.

Ivashitsov, N. A. *Around-the-World Travels from 1803–1849*. St. Petersburg, 1872.

Jacobs, Melvin. *Winning Oregon: A Study of an Expanionist Movement*. Caldwell, Idaho: The Caxton Printers, Ltd., 1938.

Jensen, Ronald J. *The Alaska Purchase and Russian-American Relations*. Seattle: University of Washington Press, 1975.

Jewitt, John R. *Narrative of the Adventures and Sufferings of John R. Jewitt Only Survivor of the Ship Boston*. 1815.

Jockelson, Waldemar. *History, Ethnology, and Anthropology of the Aleut*. Washington, D.C.: Carnegie Institution of Washington, 1933.

Joesting, Edward. *Hawaii: An Uncommon History*. New York: Norton, 1972.

Johansen, Dorothy O., and Charles M. Gates. *Empire of the Columbia: A History of the Pacific Northwest*. New York: Harper and Brothers, 1967.

Johnson, Robert E. *Thence Round Cape Horn: The Story of the United States Naval Forces on Pacific Station, 1818–1923*. Annapolis, Md.: U.S. Naval Institute, 1963.

Johnson, Theodore Tayler. *Sights in the Gold Region and Scenes by the Way*. New York: Bauer and Scribner, 1849.

Johnstone, Arthur. *Recollections of Robert Louis Stevenson in the Pacific*. London: Chatto and Waus, 1905.

Jones, James. *From Here to Eternity*. New York: Charles Scribner's Sons, 1951.

Jones, John D. *Life and Adventure in the South Pacific*. New York: Harper and Brothers, 1861.

Bibliography

Judd, Bernice. *Voyages to Hawaii before 1860*. Honolulu: University of Hawaii Press, 1974.

Judd, Laura Fish. *Honolulu: Sketches of Life in the Hawaiian Islands from 1828 to 1861*. Ed. by Dale L. Morgan. Chicago: R. R. Donnelley and Sons Co., 1966.

Kelley, Hall J. *A Geographical Sketch of That Part of North America Called Oregon*. J. Howe, 1831.

Khlebnikov, K. T. *Baranov: Chief Manager of the Russian Colonies in America*. Kingston, Ont.: Limestone Press, 1973.

Korzelinski, Seweryn. *Memoirs of Gold-Digging in Australia*. Trans. and ed. by Stanley Robe. St. Lucia, Australia: University of Queensland Press, 1979.

Koskinen, Aarne. *Missionary Influence as a Political Factor in the Pacific Islands*. Helsinki: Dissertation, 1953.

Kotzebue, Otto von. *A New Voyage Round the World, in the Years 1823, 24, 25, and 26*. London: Colburn and Blutley, 1830.

————. *A Voyage of Discovery, into the South Sea and Bering's Straits . . . in the Years 1815–1818*. 3 vols. London: Longman . . . Brown, 1821.

Kraus, Bob, and William P. Alexander. *Grove Farm Plantation: The Biography of a Hawaiian Sugar Plantation*. Palo Alto, Cal.: Pacific Books, 1965.

Kroeber, A. L. *Handbook of the Indians of California*. Washington, D.C.: Bureau of American Ethnology Bulletin 78, 1925.

Krusenstern, Adam J. von. *Voyage Round the World in the Years 1803, 1804, 1805, and 1806*. Trans. by Richard B. Hoppner. London: John Murray, 1813.

Kuykendall, Ralph S. *The Hawaiian Kingdom, 1778–1854: Foundation and Transformation*. Honolulu: University of Hawaii Press, 1947.

————. *The Hawaiian Kingdom, 1854–1874: Twenty Critical Years*. Honolulu: University of Hawaii Press, 1953.

Laperouse, Jean Francois Galup. *The First French Expedition to California*. Los Angeles: Glen Dawson, 1959.

Latourette, Kenneth S. *The Chinese, Their History and Culture*. New York: Macmillan Co., 1946.

————. *A History of Early Relations between the United States and China, 1784–1844*. New Haven, Conn.: Yale University Press, 1917.

Ledyard, John. *A Journal of Captain Cook's Last Voyage to the Pacific Ocean, and in Quest of a Northwest Passage, between Asia and America: Performed in the Years 1776, 1777, 1778, and 1779*. Hartford, Conn.: Nathaniel Patten, 1783.

Lee, W. Storrs. *Hawaii: A Literary Chronicle*. New York: Funk and Wagnalls, 1967.

Leff, David. *Uncle Sam's Pacific Islets*. Stanford, Cal.: Stanford University Press, 1940.

Lennon, Nigey. *Mark Twain in California: The Turbulent California Years of Samuel Clemens.* San Francisco: Chronicle Books, 1982.

Lensen, George A. *Russia's Japan Expedition of 1852 to 1855.* Gainesville: University of Florida Press, 1955.

Lewis and Dryden. *Marine History of the Pacific Northwest.* Portland, Ore.: Lewis and Dryden, 1895.

Lewis, Oscar, ed. *California in 1846, Described in Letters from Thomas O. Larkin.* San Francisco: Grabhorn Press, 1934.

Lind, Andrew W. *Hawaii—The Last of the Magic Isles.* London, New York: Oxford University Press, 1969.

———. *An Island Community: Ecological Succession in Hawaii.* Chicago: University of Chicago Press, 1938.

Livezey, William E. *Mahan on Sea Power.* Norman: University of Oklahoma Press, 1947.

London, Jack. *Cruise of the Snark.* New York: Macmillan Co., 1911.

———. *On the Makaloa Mat.* New York: Macmillan Co., 1919.

———. *South Sea Tales.* New York: Macmillan Co., 1911.

———. *The Call of the Wild.* New York: Macmillan Co., 1903.

———. *The House of Pride.* New York: Macmillan Co., 1912.

———. *The Son of Wolf: Tales of the Far North.* New York: Grosset and Dunlap, 1900.

———. *White Fang.* Chatham River Press, 1906.

London, Joan. *Jack London and His Times: An Unconventional Biography.* Seattle: University of Washington Press, 1974.

Lopez, Barry. *Arctic Dreams: Imagination and Desire in a Northern Landscape.* New York: Scribners, 1986.

Lott, Arnold S. *A Long Line of Ships: Mare Island's Century of Naval Activity in California.* Annapolis, Md.: U.S. Naval Institute, 1954.

Lovett, Richard. *The History of the London Missionary Society, 1795–1895.* 2 vols. London: H. Fronde, 1899.

Lyman, Sarah Joiner. *Sarah Joiner Lyman: Her Own Story.* Comp. and ed. by Margaret Green Martin. Hilo, Hawaii: Lyman House Memorial Museum, 1970.

Mackenzie, Alexander. *Voyages from Montreal, on the River St. Lawrence, through the Continent of North America, to the Frozen and Pacific Oceans: In the Years 1789 and 1793.* 2 vols. London: printed for T. Cadell, jun. and W. Davies [etc.] Edinburgh, W. Creech, 1802.

Macrae, James. *With Lord Byron at the Sandwich Islands in 1825, Being Extracts from the Ms. Diary of James Macrae, Scottish Botanist.* Honolulu: University of Hawaii Press, 1922.

Mahan, Alfred Thayer. *The Interest of America in Sea Power, Present and Future.* Boston: Little, Brown and Co., 1897.

Malo, David. *Hawaiian Antiquities.* Bernice Bishop Museum Special Publication 2. Trans. from the Hawaiian by Nathaniel B. Emerson. Honolulu: Bishop Museum Press, 1898.

Mangusso, Mary Childers, and Stephen W. Haycox. *Interpreting Alaska's History: An Anthology.* Anchorage: Alaska Pacific University Press, 1989.

Masterman, Sylvia. *The Origins of International Rivalry in Samoa, 1845–1884.* Stanford, Cal.: Stanford University Press, 1934.

Mathison, Gilbert F. *Narrative of a Visit to Brazil, Chile, Peru, and the Sandwich Islands during the Years 1821 and 1822.* London: Charles Knight, 1825.

Matloff, Maurice, ed. *American Military History.* Washington, D.C.: Office of the Chief of Military History, 1969.

Maugham, W. Somerset. *The Moon and Sixpence.* New York: Doubleday and Co., 1919.

Maury, Matthew Fontaine. *The Physical Geography of the Sea.* New York: Harper and Brothers, 1885.

May, Ernest, and James Thomson. *American East Asian Relations: A Survey.* Cambridge, Mass.: Harvard University Press, 1972.

McCracken, Harold. *Hunters of the Stormy Sea.* New York: Doubleday and Co., 1957.

McFeat, Tom. *Indians of the North Pacific Coast.* Seattle: University of Washington Press, 1966.

McGaw, Martha Mary. *Stevenson in Hawaii.* Honolulu: University of Hawaii Press, 1950.

McGinnis, Joe. *Going to Extremes.* New York: Alfred A. Knopf, 1980.

McPhee, John. *Coming into the Country.* New York: Farrar, Straus and Giroux, 1977.

Mead, Margaret. *Coming of Age in Samoa.* New York: W. Morrow and Co., 1928.

Meares, John. *Voyages Made in the Years 1788 and 1789 from China to the North West Coast of America.* New York: DeCapo Press, 1967.

Mechling, Jay. *The Pacific Basin: An Annotated Bibliography.* New York: Garland Publishing Co., 1985.

Melville, Herman. *Mardi, and a Voyage Thither.* Boston: The St. Botolph Society, 1923.

———. *Moby Dick, or, The Whale.* New York: Dodd, Mead and Co., 1923.

———. *Omoo: A Narrative of Adventures in the South Seas.* Ed. by Harrison Hayford and Walter Blair. New York: Hendricks House Inc., 1969.

———. *Redburn, His First Voyage, . . .* New York: Doubleday, 1957.

———. *Typee, A Real Romance of the South Seas.* New York: Russell and Russell, 1963.

———. *White Jacket, or, The World on a Man-of-War.* New York: Harper and Brothers, 1850.

Merk, Frederick. *Manifest Destiny and Mission in American History.* New York: Alfred A. Knopf, 1963.

———. *The Oregon Question.* Cambridge, Mass.: Harvard University Press, 1967.

Meyers, William H. *Journal of a Cruise to California and the Sandwich Islands in the United States Sloop-of-War Cyane, 1841–1844.* Ed. by John Haskell Kemble. San Francisco: Book Club of California, 1955.

Michener, James A. *Alaska.* New York: Random House, 1988.

———. *Hawaii.* New York: Random House, 1959.

———. *Return to Paradise.* New York: Random House, 1951.

———. *Tales of the South Pacific.* New York: Macmillan Co., 1947.

Michener, James A., and A. Grove Day. *Rascals in Paradise.* New York: Random House, 1957.

Miller, Orlando W. *The Frontier in Alaska and the Matanuska Colony.* New Haven, Conn.: Yale University Press, 1975.

Miller, Pamela A. *And the Whale Is Ours: Creative Writing of American Whalemen.* Boston: David R. Godine, 1979.

Miyamoto, Kazuo. *Hawaii: End of the Rainbow.* Rutland, Vt.: Charles E. Tuttle Co., 1964.

Monaghan, Jay. *Australians and the Gold Rush: California and Down Under, 1849–1854.* Berkeley: University of California Press, 1966.

Morgan, Dale. *Jedediah Smith and the Opening of the West.* Indianapolis: Bobbs-Merrill, 1953.

Morgan, Neil. *Westward Tilt: The American West Today.* New York: Random House, 1963.

Morison, Samuel E. *The Maritime History of Massachusetts, 1783–1860.* Boston: Houghton Mifflin Co., 1921.

———. *"Old Bruin": Commodore Matthew C. Perry.* Boston: Little, Brown and Co., 1967.

Morrell, Benjamin. *A Narrative of Four Voyages to the South Sea, North and South Pacific Ocean, Chinese Sea, Ethiopic and Southern Atlantic Ocean, Indian and Antarctic Ocean from the Year 1822–1831.* New York: J. & J. Harper, 1832.

Morrell, W. P. *Britain in the Pacific Islands.* Oxford: Clarendon Press, 1960.

———. *The Gold Rushes.* New York: Macmillan Co., 1941.

Moriyama, Alan T. *Imingaisha: Japanese Emigration Companies and Hawaii, 1894–1908.* Honolulu: University of Hawaii Press, 1985.

Moyer, Cecil. *Historic Ranchos of San Diego.* La Jolla, Cal.: Union-Tribune Publishing Co., 1969.

Mrantz, Maxine. *R. L. Stevenson: Poet in Paradise.* Honolulu: Alotta Graphics, 1977.

Munford, James Kenneth, ed. *John Ledyard's Journal of Captain Cook's Last*

Voyage. Intro. by Sinclair H. Hitchings. Corvallis: Oregon State University Press, 1963.

Murray, John A. *A Republic of Rivers: Three Centuries of Nature Writing from Alaska and the Yukon.* New York: Oxford University Press, 1990.

Nash, Roderick. *Wilderness and the American Mind.* New Haven, Conn.: Yale University Press, 1967.

Naske, Claus, and Herman Slotnick. *Alaska: A History of the 49th State.* Norman: University of Oklahoma Press, 1987.

Nelson, Edna. *The California Dons.* New York: Appleton-Century-Crofts, Inc., 1962.

Nelson, Edward W. *The Eskimo about Bering Strait.* Washington, D.C.: Smithsonian Institution Press, 1983.

Neuman, William L. *America Encounters Japan: From Perry to MacArthur.* Baltimore: Johns Hopkins University Press, 1963.

Nichols, Jeannette P. *Alaska: A History of Its Administration, Exploitation, and Industrial Development During Its First Half Century under the Rule of the United States.* Cleveland: The Arthur C. Clark Co., 1924.

Nichols, Roy Franklin. *Advance Agents of American Destiny.* Philadelphia: University of Pennsylvania Press, 1956.

Nickerson, Roy. *Robert Louis Stevenson in California.* San Francisco: Chronicle Books, 1982.

Nordhoff, Charles, and James Hall. *Hurricane.* Boston: Atlantic Monthly Press, 1936.

———. *Men Against the Sea.* Boston: Little, Brown and Co., 1934.

———. *Mutiny on the Bounty.* Boston: Little, Brown and Co., 1932.

———. *Pitcairn's Island.* Boston: Little, Brown and Co., 1934.

O'Brien, Frederick. *White Shadows in the South Seas.* New York: Century Co., 1919.

Ogden, Adele. *The California Sea Otter Trade.* Berkeley: University of California Press, 1941.

Ohmae, Kenichi. *The Borderless World: Power and Strategy in the Interlinked Economy.* New York: Harper and Brothers, 1990.

Okubo, Mine. *Citizen 13660.* Seattle: University of Washington Press, 1946. (Reprinted 1983.)

Okun, S. B. *The Russian-American Company.* Ed. with intro. by B. D. Grelsov; trans. from the Russian by Carl Guisburg; preface by Robert J. Kerner. Cambridge, Mass.: Harvard University Press, 1951.

Oliver, Allen E. *The Pacific Navigators.* Alexandria, Va.: Time Life Books, 1980.

Oliver, Douglas L. *The Pacific Islands.* Cambridge, Mass.: Harvard University Press, 1951.

Olmstead, Francis A. *Incidents of a Whaling Voyage.* Rutland, Vt.: Charles E. Tuttle, Co., 1970.

Paolino, Ernest N. *The Foundations of the American Empire*. Ithaca, N.Y.: Cornell University Press, 1973.

Parry, John. *The Age of the Reconnaissance*. London: Weidenfeld and Nicolson, 1963.

Parsons, George F. *The Life and Adventures of James W. Marshall, the Discoverer of Gold in California*. Sacramento: James W. Marshall and W. Burke, 1870.

Patterson, Samuel. *Narrative of the Adventures and Sufferings of Samuel Patterson, Experienced in the Pacific Ocean*. Palmer, Mass.: n.p., 1817.

Paul, Rodman W. *California Gold: The Beginning of Mining in the Far West*. Cambridge, Mass.: Harvard University Press, 1947.

———. *Mining Frontiers of the Far West, 1848–1880*. New York: Holt, Rinehart and Winston, 1963.

Paullin, Charles. *Diplomatic Negotiations of American Naval Officers, 1778–1883*. Baltimore: Johns Hopkins University Press, 1912.

Paxson, Frederic L. *History of the American Frontier 1763–1893*. Boston: Houghton Mifflin Co., 1924.

Perry, Matthew C. *The Japan Expedition, 1852–1854: The Personal Journal of Commodore Matthew C. Perry*. Ed. by Roger Pineau. Washington, D.C.: Smithsonian Institution Press, 1968.

———. *Narrative of the Expedition of an American Squadron to the China Seas and Japan, Performed in the Years 1852, 1853, and 1854*. Washington, D.C.: A. O. P. Nicholson, 1856.

Pethick, Derek. *The Nootka Connection: Europe and the Northwest Coast, 1790–1795*. Seattle: University of Washington Press, 1980.

Phillips, Clifton C. *Protestant America and the Pagan World: The First Half Century of the American Board of Commissioners for Foreign Missions, 1810–1860*. Cambridge, Mass.: Harvard University Press, 1969.

Phillips, Paul C. *The Fur Trade*. 2 vols. Norman: University of Oklahoma Press, 1961.

Pierce, Richard A., comp. *H.M.S. Sulphur at California, 1837 and 1839*. San Francisco: Book Club of California, 1969.

———, ed. and comp. *Rezanov Reconnoiters California, 1806: A New Translation of Rezanov's Letter, Parts of Lieutenant Khvostov's Log of the Ship Juno, and Dr. Georg von Langsdorff Observations*. San Francisco: Book Club of California, 1972.

———. *Russia's Hawaiian Adventure, 1815–1817*. Berkeley: University of California Press, 1965.

Pomeroy, Earl. *In Search of the Golden West: The Tourist in Western America*. New York: Alfred A. Knopf, 1957.

———. *Pacific Outpost: American Strategy in Guam and Micronesia*. Stanford, Cal.: Stanford University Press, 1951.

———. *The Territories of the United States 1861–1890: Studies in Colonial Administration*. Seattle: University of Washington Press, 1969.

Porter, David. *Journal of a Cruise Made to the Pacific Ocean . . . in the U.S. Frigate "Essex," in the Years 1812, 1813, and 1814.* New York: Wiley and Halsted, 1822.

Porter, Kenneth W. *John Jacob Astor: Business Man.* 2 vols. Cambridge, Mass.: Harvard University Press, 1931.

Potts, E. Daniel, and Annette Potts. *Young America and Australian Gold: Americans and the Gold Rush of the 1850s.* St. Lucia, Australia: University of Queensland Press, 1974.

Prange, Gordon W., Donald M. Goldstein, and Katherine V. Dillon. *Miracle at Midway.* New York: McGraw-Hill Book Co., 1982.

Pratt, Julius W. *America's Colonial Experiment: How the United States Gained, Governed, and in Part Gave Away a Colonial Empire.* New York: Prentice-Hall, 1950.

———. *Expansionists of 1898: The Acquisition of Hawaii and the Spanish Islands.* Baltimore: Johns Hopkins University Press, 1936.

Preble, George H. *A Chronological History of the Origin and Development of Steam Navigation.*

———. *The Opening of Japan: A Diary of Discovery in the Far East, 1853–1856.* Ed. by Boleslaw Szczesniak. Norman: University of Oklahoma Press, 1962.

Price, Grenfell. *The Western Invasions of the Pacific and Its Continents: A Study of Moving Frontiers and Changing Landscapes, 1513–1958.* Oxford: Clarendon Press, 1963.

Purington, Chester W. *Methods and Costs of Gravel and Placer Mining in Alaska.* Washington, D.C.: U.S. Government Printing Office, 1905.

Quincy, Josiah, ed. *The Journals of Major Samuel Shaw, the First American Consul at Canton, with a Life of the Author.* Boston: W. Crosby and H. P. Nichols, 1847.

Richardson, James D. *A Compilation of the Messages and Papers of the Presidents, 1789–1897.* Washington, D.C.: U.S. Government Printing Office, 1896.

Rickard, Thomas A. *The Romance of Mining.* Toronto: Macmillan Co., 1944.

Riesenberg, Felix. *The Pacific Ocean.* New York: McGraw-Hill Co., 1940.

Robinson, Alfred. *Life in California.* New York: Wiley and Putnam, 1846.

Robinson, W. W. *Land in California.* Berkeley: University of California Press, 1979.

Rose, Roger G. *Hawaii: The Royal Isles.* Seattle: University of Washington Press, 1983.

Rudkin, Charles N., trans. *The First French Expedition to California: Laperouse in 1786.* Los Angeles: Glen Dawson, 1959.

Russ, William A. *The Hawaiian Revolution, 1893–94.* Sellensgrove, Pa.: Susquehanna University Press, 1959.

Rust, Richard. *Astoria.* Boston: Twayne Publishing, 1978.

Rydell, Raymond A. *Cape Horn to the Pacific: The Rise and Decline of an Ocean Highway.* Berkeley: University of California Press, 1952.

Rydell, Robert W. *All the World's a Fair.* Chicago: University of Chicago Press, 1984.

Ryden, George Herbert. *The Foreign Policy of the United States in Relation to Samoa.* New Haven, Conn.: Yale University Press, 1933.

Schaller, Michael. *The United States and China in the Twentieth Century.* New York: Oxford University Press, 1979.

Schroeder, Seaton. *A Half Century of Naval Service.* New York: D. Appleton and Co., 1922.

Schurz, William L. *The Manila Galleon.* New York: E. P. Dutton and Co., 1939.

Schwatka, Frederick. *Along Alaska's Great River.* New York: Cassell, 1885.

Service, Robert. *The Best of Robert Service.* New York: Dodd Mead, 1907.

Shaler, William. *Journal of a Voyage from China to the Northwestern Coast of America Made in 1804.* Claremont, Cal.: Saunders Studio Press, 1935.

Shaw, Samuel. *The Journal of Major Samuel Shaw.* W. Crosby and H. P. Nichols, 1847.

Sherwood, Morgan. *The Exploration of Alaska.* New Haven, Conn.: Yale University Press, 1965.

Shinn, Charles H. *Land Laws of Mining Districts.* Baltimore: Johns Hopkins University Press, 1884.

———. *Mining Camps: A Study of American Frontier Government.* New York: Charles Scribner's Sons, 1888.

Silveira de Braganza, Ronald. Ed. by Louis Oakes and Charlotte Oakes. *The Hill Collection of Pacific Voyages.* San Diego: University of California Library, 1974.

Silverberg, Robert. *Stormy Voyager: The Story of Charles Wilkes.* Philadelphia: J. B. Lippincott Co., 1968.

Smith, Bradford. *Yankees in Paradise: The New England Impact on Hawaii.* Philadelphia: J. B. Lippincott Co., 1956.

Spate, O. H. K. *The Pacific Since Magellan: Monopolists and Freebooters.* Minneapolis: University of Minnesota Press, 1983.

———. *The Pacific Since Magellan: The Spanish Lake.* Minneapolis: University of Minnesota Press, 1979.

Spaulding, Kenneth A., ed. *Alexander Ross: The Fur Hunter of the Far West.* Norman: University of Oklahoma Press, 1956.

Spears, John. *The Story of the New England Whalers.* New York: Macmillan Co., 1908.

Sperry, Armstrong. *Pacific Islands Speaking.* New York: Macmillan Co., 1955.

Spoehr, Florence Mann. *White Falcon: The House of Godeffroy and Its Commercial and Scientific Role in the Pacific.* Palo Alto, Cal.: Pacific Books, 1963.

461

Stackpole, Edouard. *The Sea Hunters: The New England Whalemen During Two Centuries, 1635–1835*. Philadelphia: J. B. Lippincott Co., 1953.

Stanton, William. *The Great United States Exploring Expedition of 1838–1842*. Berkeley: University of California Press, 1975.

Starbuck, Alexander. *History of the American Whale Fishery from Its Earliest Inception to the Year 1876*. New York: Argosy-Antiquarian, 1964.

Starr, Kevin. *Americans and the California Dream*. New York: Oxford University Press, 1973.

Stephens, Henry Morse, and Herbert Eugene Bolton. *The Pacific Ocean in History*. New York: Macmillan Co., 1917.

Stevens, Sylvester K. *American Expansion in Hawaii 1842–1898*. Harrisburg: Archives Publishing Company of Pennsylvania, 1945.

Stevenson, Fanny, and Robert Louis Stevenson. *Our Samoan Adventure*. Ed. and intro. by Charles Neider. New York: Harper and Brothers, 1955.

Stevenson, Robert Louis. *In the South Seas*. New York: Charles Scribner's Sons, 1923.

―――. *R.L.S.: Stevenson's Letters to Charles Baxter*. Ed. and intro. by De Lancey Ferguson and Marshall Waingrow. New Haven, Conn.: Yale University Press, 1966.

―――. *The Ebb-Tide*. New York: W. Heinemann, 1894.

―――. *Travels in Hawaii*. Ed. with an intro. by A. Grove Day. Honolulu: University of Hawaii Press, 1973.

Steward, C. S. *A Residence in the Sandwich Islands*. Boston: Jordan and Co., 1839.

―――. *A Visit to the South Seas in the U.S. Ship Vincennes 1829–1830*. 2 vols. New York: John P. Haven, 1833.

Stoddard, Charles Warren. *South Sea Idylls*. Boston: J. R. Osgood, 1873.

Strauss, Wallace P. *Americans in Polynesia, 1783–1842*. East Lansing: Michigan State University Press, 1963.

―――. *Early American Interest and Activity in Polynesia: 1783–1842*. Ann Arbor: University of Michigan Press, 1959.

Strong, Josiah. *Our Country*. Baker and Taylor, 1885.

Stroven, Carl, and A. Grove Day, eds. *The Spell of the Pacific: An Anthology of Its Literature*. New York: Macmillan Co., 1949.

Tang, Ta-Kong. *U.S. Diplomacy in China, 1844–1860*. Seattle: University of Washington Press, 1964.

Tate, Merze. *The United States and the Hawaiian Kingdom*. New Haven, Conn.: Yale University Press, 1965.

Taylor, George E. *The Philippines and the United States: Problems of Partnership*. New York: Published for the Council on Foreign Relation by Praeger, 1964.

Teggart, Frederick J., ed. *Around the Horn to the Sandwich Islands and California, 1845–1850, Being a Personal Record Kept by Chester S. Lyman*. Freeport, N.Y.: Books for Libraries Press, 1971.

Teilhet-Fish, Johanne. *Paradise Reviewed: An Interpretation of Gauguin's Polynesian Symbolism.* Ann Arbor, Mich.: NMI Research Press, 1975.

Thacker, Christopher. *The Wildness Pleases: The Origins of Romanticism.* New York: St. Martin's Press, 1983.

Thomas, Benjamin Platt. *Russo-American Relations, 1815–1867.* Baltimore: Johns Hopkins University Press, 1930.

Thomas, John N. *The Institute of Pacific Relations: Asian Scholars and American Politics.* Seattle: University of Washington Press, 1973.

Thomson, James C., Jr., Peter W. Stanley, and John Curtis Perry. *Sentimental Imperialists: The American Experience in East Asia.* New York: Harper and Row, 1981.

Tikhmenev, P. A., Richard A. Pierce, and Alton S. Donnelly, eds. and trans. *A History of the Russian-American Company.* Seattle: University of Washington Press, 1978.

Todd, Edgeley W. *Astoria.* Norman: University of Oklahoma Press, 1964.

Toland, John. *The Rising Sun.* New York: Random House, 1970.

Tompkins, E. Berkeley. *Anti-Imperialism in the United States: The Great Debate, 1890–1920.* Philadelphia: University of Pennsylvanian Press, 1970.

Tompkins, Stuart R. *Alaska: Promyshlennik and Sourdough.* Norman: University of Oklahoma Press, 1945.

Tonnessen, Johan Nicolay, and Arne Odd Johnsen. *The History of Modern Whaling.* Berkeley: University of California Press, 1981.

Totman, Conrad. *Japan before Perry: A Short History.* Berkeley: University of California Press, 1981.

Treat, Payson J. *Diplomatic Relations between the United States and Japan, 1853–1895.* Gloucester, Mass.: Peter Smith Co., 1963.

Trumbull, Robert. *Paradise in Trust.* New York: William Sloane Associates, 1959.

———. *Tin Roofs and Palm Trees: A Report on the New South Seas.* Seattle: University of Washington Press, 1977.

Tsai, Shih-shan Henry. *The Chinese Experience in America.* Bloomington: Indiana University Press, 1986.

Twain, Mark. *A Connecticut Yankee in King Arthur's Court.* New York: Harper, 1906.

———. *Letters from the Sandwich Islands: Written for the Sacramento Union.* Stanford, Cal.: Stanford University Press, 1938.

———. *Roughing It.* Hartford, Conn.: American Publishing Company, 1899.

Tyler, Lyon G. *The Letters and Times of the Tylers.* 3 vols. New York: DeCapo Press, 1970.

U.S. House of Representatives. Message from the President . . . Sandwich Islands and China, 27th Cong., 3rd Sess., 1842, House Exec. Doc. 35.

Valentin, F., ed., and Julius S. Gassver, trans. *Voyages and Adventures of La Pérouse.* Honolulu: University of Hawaii Press, 1969.

Vancouver, George. *A Voyage of Discovery to the North Pacific Ocean, and* round the World; in which the Coast of North-west America Has Been Carefully Examined and Accurately Surveyed. London: Printed for G. G. and J. Robinson [etc.], 1798.

Van Deusen, G. G. *William Henry Seward.* New York: Oxford University Press, 1967.

Varg, Paul A. *Missionaries, Chinese, and Diplomats: The American Protestant Missionary Movement in China, 1890–1952.* Princeton, N.J.: Princeton University Press, 1958.

Viola, Herman J. *Exploring the West.* Washington, D.C.: Smithsonian Institution Press, 1987.

———. *Magnificent Voyagers: The U.S. Exploring Expedition, 1838–42.* Washington, D.C.: Smithsonian Institution Press, 1985.

Wagner, Henry R. *Spanish Voyages to the Northwest Coast of America.* San Francisco: California Historical Society, 1929.

Waley, Arthur. *The Opium War through Chinese Eyes.* London: George Allen and Unwin, c. 1958.

Walker, Ernest P. *Alaska: America's Continental Frontier Outpost.* Washington, D.C.: Smithsonian Institution, 1943.

Walker, Franklin. *Jack London and the Klondike.* San Marino, Cal.: Huntington Library, 1972.

———. *San Francisco's Literary Frontier.* New York: Alfred A. Knopf, 1939.

Walworth, Arthur. *Black Ships Off Japan.* New York: Alfred A. Knopf, 1946.

Ward, R. Gerard, ed. *American Activities in the Central Pacific, 1790–1870.* With an introduction by Ernest S. Dodge. 8 vols. Ridgewood, N.J.: The Gregg Press, 1966–67.

Warner, Denise, et al. *The Sacred Warriors: Japan's Suicide Legions.* New York: Van Nostrand Reinhold Co., 1982.

Webb, Nancy and Jean. *Kaiulani: Crown Princess of Hawaii.* New York: Viking Press, 1962.

Weinberg, Albert. *Manifest Destiny.* Baltimore: Johns Hopkins University Press, 1953.

West, Richard S., Jr. *Admirals of American Empire: The Combined Story of George Dewey, Alfred Thayer Mahan, Winfield Scott Schley, and William Thomas Sampson.* Indianapolis: Bobbs-Merrill, 1948.

Wharton, David. *The Alaska Gold Rush.* Bloomington: University of Indiana Press, 1972.

Wheeler, Gerald. *Prelude to Pearl Harbor: The United States Navy and the Far East, 1921–1931.* Columbia: University of Missouri Press, 1963.

Wheeler, Keith. *The Alaskans.* Alexandria, Va.: Time Life Books, 1977.

Whipple, Addison B. C. *Vintage Nantucket.* New York: Dodd, Mead and Co., 1978.

———. *The Whalers.* Alexandria, Va.: Time Life Books, 1979.

————. *Yankee Whalers in the South Seas*. Garden City, N.Y.: Doubleday and Co., 1954.

Wienpahl, Robert W. *A Gold Rush Voyage on the Bark "Orion" from Boston around Cape Horn to San Francisco, 1849–1850*. Glendale, Cal.: Arthur H. Clark Co., 1978.

Wiens, Herold J. *Pacific Island Bastions of the United States*. Princeton, N.J.: Van Nostrand, 1962.

Wilkes, Charles. *Narrative of the United States Exploring Expedition, 1838–1842*. 9 vols. Philadelphia: Lea and Blanchard, 1845–48.

Winther, Oscar. *The Great Northwest: A History*. New York: Alfred A. Knopf, 1947.

Withey, Lynne. *Voyages of Discovery: Captain Cook and the Exploration of the Pacific*. New York: William Morrow, 1987.

Wolff, Leon. *Little Brown Brother: How the United States Purchased and Pacified the Philippine Islands at the Century's Turn*. Garden City, N.Y.: Doubleday and Co., 1961.

Wright, Julia McNair. *Among the Alaskans*. Philadelphia: Presbyterian Board of Publications, 1883.

Wright, Louis B., and Mary Isabel Fry. *Puritans in the South Seas*. New York: H. Holt and Company, 1936.

Yamamura, Kozo, ed. *Policy and Trade Issues of the Japanese Economy: American and Japanese Perspectives*. Seattle: University of Washington Press, 1983.

Young, Lucien. *The Real Hawaii: Its History and Present Conditions*. New York: Arno Press, 1970.

Anderson, Bern. "The Career of George Vancouver." *U.S. Naval Institute Proceedings* 64 (September 1938) 1304–11.

Bailey, Thomas. "Why the U.S. Purchased Alaska." *Pacific Historical Review* 3 (1934) 39–49.

Barrett, Glynn. "The Russian Interest in Arctic North America: The Kruzenstern-Romanov Projects, 1819–32." *Slavonic and East European Review* 53 (January 1975) 27–43.

Bertrand, Kenneth J. "Geographical Exploration by the United States." In *The Pacific Basin: A History of Its Geographical Exploration*, ed. Herman R. Friis, 256–91. New York: American Geographical Society, 1967.

Blue, George. "French Interests in Pacific America in the Eighteenth Century." *Pacific Historical Review* 4 (1935) 246–66.

Bradley, H. W. "Hawaii and the American Penetration of the Northern Pacific, 1800–1845." *Pacific Historical Review* 12 (September 1943) 277–86.

———. "The Hawaiian Islands and the Pacific Fur Trade, 1785–1813." *Pacific Northwest Quarterly* 30 (July 1939) 275–99.

Brand, Donald D. "Geographical Explorations by the Spaniards." In the *Pacific Basin: A History of Geographical Exploration*, ed. Herman R. Friis, 109–44. New York: American Geographical Society, 1967.

Buck, Peter. "Cook's Discovery of the Hawaiian Islands." *Bernice P. Bishop's Museum Report for 1944* Bulletin 186 (1946) 26–44.

Buske, Frank. "Rex Beach." *Alaska Journal* 10(4) (Autumn 1980) 37–42.

Clark, William. "Journal of the Ship *Empress of China*." *American Neptune* 11 (1950) 59–71.

Coughlin, Magdalen. "California Ports: A Key to Diplomacy for the West Coast, 1820–1845." *Journal of the West* 5 (April 1966) 153–72.

Couper, Alastair. "Islands at Sea: Change, and the Maritime Economies of the Pacific" In *The Pacific in Transition: Geographic Perspectives on Adaptation and Change*, ed. Harold Brookfield. New York: St. Martin's Press, 1973.

Cutter, Donald C. "Plans for the Occupation of Upper California: A New Look at the 'Dark Age' from 1602 to 1769." *Journal of San Diego History* 24 (Winter 1978) 78–90.

———. "Spain and the Oregon Coast." In *The Western Shore: Oregon Country Essays Honoring the American Revolution*, ed. Thomas Vaughan, 31–46. Portland: Oregon Historical Society, n.d.

Dahlby, Tracy. "Micronesia: Fragmented on American Support." *Far Eastern Economic Review* (3 October 1975).

Davidson, Donald Curtis. "The Alaskan-Canadian Boundary." In *Greater America: Essays in Honor of Herbert Eugene Bolton*, 455–73. Berkeley: University of California Press, 1945.

Day, Arthur. "The Earliest Explorers-Traders of the Northwest Coast." *U.S. Naval Institute Proceedings* 57 (December 1941) 1677–83.

Essig, E. O. "The Russian Settlement at Ross." *California Historical Society Quarterly* 12 (September 1933) 191–209.

Fairbanks, John K. "Assignment for the 70's." *American Historical Review* 74 (February 1969) 861–79.

———. "China Missions in History: Some Introductory Remarks." *Journal of Presbyterian History* 49 (Winter 1971) 283–86.

Floyd, Candace. "Chinatown." *History News* 39 (June 1984) 6–11.

Freeman, Otis W. "Geographic Setting of the Pacific." In *Geography of the Pacific*, ed. Otis W. Freeman. New York: John Wiley and Sons, 1951.

Gerus, Oleks. "The Russian Withdrawal from Alaska: The Decision to Sell." *Institute of Panamerican Geographical History* 75 (1973) 157–78.

Gibson, James R. "Bostonians and Muscovites on the Northwest Coast, 1788–1841." In *The Western Shore: Oregon Country Essays Honoring the American Revolution*, ed. Thomas Vaughan, 81–119. Portland: Oregon Historical Society, n.d.

Gilbert, Benjamin F. "Spain's Port of San Francisco, 1755–1822." *Journal of the West* 20 (July 1981) 21–30.

Golder, Frank. "The Purchase of Alaska." *American Historical Review* 25 (April 1920) 411–25.

Gough, Barry M. "The Northwest Coast in Late 18th Century British Expansion." In *The Western Shore: Oregon Country Essays Honoring the American Revolution,* ed. Thomas Vaughan, 47–80. Portland: Oregon Historical Society, n.d.

Hammons, Terry. "Americans and Paradise: The Pacific Basin as a Literary Source." *Journal of the West* 15(2) (April 1976) 102–16.

Hautcilly, Auguste Bernard du. "A Visit to the Russians in 1828." *California Historical Society Quarterly* 8 (December 1929).

Hopson, Janet L. "Miners Are Reaching for Metal Riches on the Ocean's Floor." *Smithsonian* 12 (April 1981) 51–58.

Howay, Frederic W. "Captain Simon Metcalfe and the Brig *Eleanora.*" *Pacific Northwest Quarterly* 16 (1925) 114–21.

———. "An Outline Sketch of the Maritime Fur Trade." *Canadian Historical Association Annual Report* (1932) 5–14.

———., ed. "Voyages of the *Columbia* to the Northwest Coast, 1787–1790 and 1790–1793." Boston: Massachusetts Historical Society, 1941.

Hunt, William R. "A Framework for James Cook: The Meaning of Exploration in the 18th Century and Now." In *Exploration in Alaska: Captain Cook Commemorative Lectures.* Anchorage: Cook Inlet Historical Society, 1980.

Jackson, Donald Dale. "Around the World in 1,392 Days with the Navy's Wilkes—And His 'Scientifics.'" *Smithsonian* 6 (November 1985).

Johnson, Susan Hackley. "When Moviemakers Look North." *Alaska Journal* 9(1) (Winter 1979) 12–25.

Kemble, John Haskell. "Mail Steamers Link the Americas, 1840–1890." In *Greater America: Essays in Honor of Herbert Eugene Bolton,* 475–97. Berkeley: University of California Press, 1945.

Kushner, Howard I. "Seward's Folly? American Commerce in Russian America and the Alaska Purchase." *California Historical Society Quarterly* 54 (Spring 1975) 4–26.

Latourette, Kenneth Scott. "The History of Early Relations between the United States and China, 1784–1844." *Transactions of the Connecticut Academy of Arts and Sciences* 22 (August 1917) 1–209.

———. "Voyages of American Ships to China, 1784–1844." *Transactions of the Connecticut Academy of Arts and Sciences* 28 (April 1927) 237–71.

Ledyard, John. "White Gods with Loose Skins." In Lee, *Hawaii: A Literary Chronicle.* New York: Funk and Wagnalls, 1967.

Levanthes, Louise E. "Kamehameha." *National Geographic* 154 (November 1983) 589.

Levy, Neil M. "Native Hawaiian Land Rights." *California Law Review* 63 (July 1975) 848–85.

Lidfors, Kathleen, Stephen Haycox, and Morgan Sherwood. "James Michener's *Alaska.*" *Alaska History* 4(1) (Spring 1989) 45–55.

Lorch, Fred W. "Hawaiian Feudalism and Mark Twain's *A Connecticut Yankee in King Arthur's Court.*" *American Literature* (March 1958) 50–66.

Luthern, Reinhard A. "The Sale of Alaska." *Slavonic and Eastern European Review* 16 (1937) 168–82.

Macboy, David. "British Interests in the Southern Oceans, 1782–1794." *New Zealand Journal of History* 3 (October 1969) 124–42.

Manchester, Curtis A., Jr. "The Exploration and Mapping of the Pacific." In *Geography of the Pacific,* ed. Otis W. Freeman. New York: John Wiley and Sons, 1951.

Manley, Thomas. "Vancouver's Brig *Chatham* in the Columbia." *Oregon Historical Quarterly* 43 (December 1942) 318–27.

Manning, W. R. "The Nootka Sound Controversy." In *American Historical Annual Report for the Year 1904,* 279–478. Washington, D.C.: American Historical Assn., 1905.

Morison, Samuel E. "Boston Traders in the Hawaiian Islands, 1789–1823." *Washington Historical Quarterly* 12 (April 1921) 116–201.

Muir, John. "The Discovery of Glacier Bay." In *Wilderness Essays.* Salt Lake City: Peregrine Smith Books, 1980.

Nichols, Irby. "The Russian Ukaze and the Monroe Doctrine: A Reevaluation." *Pacific Historical Review* 36 (February 1967) 13–26.

Ogden, Adele. "New England Traders in Spanish and Mexican California." In *Greater America: Essays in Honor of Herbert Eugene Bolton,* 395–413. Berkeley: University of California Press, 1945.

———. "Russian Sea-Otter Hunting on the California Coast, 1803–41." *California Historical Review* 12 (September 1933) 217–39.

Parker, Robert J. "Larkin, Anglo-American Businessman in Mexican California." In *Greater America: Essays in Honor of Herbert Eugene Bolton,* 415–29. Berkeley: University of California Press, 1945.

Paullin, Charles O. "Early Voyages of American Naval Vessels to the Orient." *U.S. Naval Institute Proceedings* 36 (September 1910) 707–16.

———. "Early Voyages of American Naval Vessels to the Orient: Explorations, Surveys, and Missions, 1838–57.' *U.S. Naval Institute Proceedings* 37 (June 1911) 407–17.

Rose, Holland. "Captain Cook and the Founding of British Power in the Pacific." *Geographical Review* 73 (February 1929) 102–10.

Rudenko, Oleks. "Russia in the Pacific Basin." *Journal of the West* 15 (April 1976) 49–64.

Steffen, Jerome O. "The Mining Frontiers of California and Australia: A Study in Comparative Political Change and Continuity." *Pacific Historical Review* 52 (November 1983) 428–40.

Stirling, Matthew W. "Indians of Our North Pacific Basin." *National Geographic* 87 (January 1945) 25–52.

———. "Nomads of the Far North." *National Geographic* 96 (October 1949) 471–504.

Sturgis, William. "The Northwest Fur Trade." *Hunt's Merchants' Magazine* 14 (June 1846) 532–39.

Thomas, William L. "The Pacific Basin: An Introduction." In *The Pacific Basin: A History of Its Geographical Exploration,* ed. Herman R. Friis, 1–17. New York: American Geographic Society, 1967.

Tower, Walter. "A History of the American Whale Fishery." *University of Pennsylvania Publications in Political, Economic, and Public Law* 20 (1907) 1–145.

Vaughan, Thomas. "Introduction." In *The Western Shore: Oregon Country Essays Honoring the American Revolution,* ed. Thomas Vaughan. Portland: Oregon Historical Society, n.d.

Ver Steeg, Clarence. "Financing and Outfitting the First U.S. Ship to China." *Pacific Historical Review* 22 (February 1953) 1–12.

Welch, Richard E., Jr. "American Public Opinion and the Purchase of Russian America." *Slavic and East European Review* 37 (1958).

Wheeler, Mary E. "Empires in Conflict and Cooperation: The 'Bostonians' and the Russian-American Company." *Pacific Historical Review* 40 (November 1971) 419–41.

Whitehead, John. *"Hawai'i: The First and Last Far West." Western Historical Quarterly* 23(2) (May 1992) 153–77.

Wilson, Woodrow. "The Making of the Nation." *Atlantic Monthly* 80 (July 1897) 1–14.

Woodhouse, Samuel. "The Voyage of the Empress of China." *Pennsylvania Magazine of History* 43 (January 1939) 24–36.

Wright, Ione Stressy. "Early Spanish Voyages from America to the Far East, 1527–1567." In *Greater America: Essays in Honor of Herbert Eugene Bolton,* 59–78. Berkeley: University of California Press, 1945.

Index

Index

480

Index

Index

San Diego, 15, 46, 59, 117, 164, 339, 413

San Francisco, 15, 59, 122, 413; harbor, 362; hide trade, 164; investment from, 257; mining and, 211, 218, 226; missions and, 291; naval port, 166; steamer service, 177; sugar refinery in, 258; trade port, 188, 190; writers and, 393, 394, 397; Yankee military at, 340, 342, and Wilkes expedition, 328

San José, 59, 209

Sandwich Islands: British interest in, 113, 283; fur trade, 113; geography, 18; missionaries, 269–70, 283, 285; name, 64; natives, 35–37; Russian interest in, 124; Spanish interest in, 72; writers and, 382; Yankee interest in, 104, 269, 270, 316. *See also* Hawaiian archipelago/Islands

Sandwich Island Notes: By a Haole, 353

Santa Barbara Channel, 46

Santa Cruz Island, 44, 57, 74, 329

Santalum album 159

Saranac, the, 340

Schäffer, Georg, 124

Schofield, John M., 330

schools, missionary, 266, 267, 273, 274, 281, 287

schooner, 156, 175–76, 189, 267, 277, 314, 319, 320

Schouten, William, 47

Schwatka, Frederick, 399

science, 373, 399, 401–2

scrimshaw, 153

scurvy (scorbutus), 41, 58, 230, 398

sea cucumber ("fish"), 157, 158

Sea Gull, the, 327

sea otter, 23, 103, 125; pelt processing, 110; trade in, 58, 68, 70, 99, 105, 106, 109, 127

Sea Otter, the, 67

Sea Wolf, The, 397

Seamen's Bethel (seamen's chapel), 276

seasons, 19

Seattle, 15, 325, 413

Second World War, 380; as World War II, 406, 413

Selkirk, Alexander, 61

sericulture, 251

Serra, Junípero, 59, 264

Service, Robert, 401

settlement: Alaskan, 226, 228, 261; Aleutian relocation, 58; a settler class, 236; Astoria, 318; Australian, 184; British/English, 49, 71, 72, 122; Californian, 164, 215–16, 243; Chinese treaty ports, 183; church stations, 277, 294; consular, 153, 364; Dutch, 47; French, 54, 68; guano island, 167; Hawaiian, 143, 144, 249, 254, 256, 270, 273, 295; leper colony, 395, 402; mining camps, 208, 211, 215–16, 218, 222, 226, 228, 231; missions, 236, 239, 240, 243, 249, 254, 256, 270, 273, 277, 286–88, 290, 294, 295; Northwest Coast, 239, 240, 290, 352; penal colony, 184; pirate sanctuary, 324; Samoan, 186; scavenger, 159; Spanish, 46, 59, 71; Yankee, 117, 119–20, 127, 128, 140, 141, 148, 259, 314, military stations, 319, 320, 321, 323, 329, 330, 331, 335, 342–43, 357, 362, 368, 415

Seward, William H., 360, 369

Seward's folly, 366

Shaler, William, 108, 171, 187, 351, 352, 383

shallops, 109

Shanghai, 183, 294

Shaw, Samuel, 95–98, 351, 383

Shelikhov, Grigorii, 68, 105

Shenandoah, the, 150, 340

Shields, James, 136

Shimoda, 335